"A wonderful, thoughtful, a~~n~~ covenant at Sinai to the gospel, a topic that has been at the center of controversy in the guild and in the pews. Estelle, Fesko, and VanDrunen have laid out a coherent argument in this collection that the original covenant with Adam in the garden has been 'republished' in the covenant with Moses at Sinai. Future discussions of 'faith and obedience' controversies will be indebted to the argument here laid out. This is a highly competent and pastorally rich collection by some of the finest minds in the Reformed community today."

—Richard Lints, Andrew Mutch Distinguished Professor of Theology,
Gordon-Conwell Theological Seminary

"*The Law Is Not of Faith* is not an easy book to read for the busy pastor. Every page evidences careful, methodical exploration into one of the thorniest brambles of biblical-theological discussion—the relationship between the old and new covenants. Yet, like a great detective story, the authors of these essays, through diligent spadework—biblical, theological, and historical—uncover and expose to the light of day a great lost truth of the Reformed faith: the doctrine of the republication of the covenant of works in the Mosaic covenant. The effort expended will yield rich reward in the end. You will learn not only how to preach Christ from Scripture, but to preach Christ better."

—Alfred Poirier, Pastor,
Rocky Mountain Community Church (PCA), Billings, Montana

"This anthology argues that the Mosaic covenant in some sense replicates the original covenant with Adam in the garden, and that this notion is neither novel to nor optional for Reformed theology. The authors locate it within the fabric of federal theology in its Reformation and post-Reformation development, and more importantly, they demonstrate how it is firmly embedded in the flow of redemptive history. Finally, they explain why a thin and merely soteric Calvinism, without the support of federal theology, cannot withstand the challenges to Reformed orthodoxy today. While varying among themselves in their expression of this 'republication thesis,' these authors together make a compelling and coherent argument with rich historical, exegetical, and theological insights."

—John Muether,
Library Director and Associate Professor of Theological Bibliography
and Research, Reformed Theological Seminary, Orlando

"I am delighted with this book. I plan to require it in my hermeneutics class."

—Robert J. Cara, Professor of New Testament,
Reformed Theological Seminary, Charlotte

THE LAW
IS NOT OF
FAITH

Essays on Works and Grace in the Mosaic Covenant

EDITED BY

Bryan D. Estelle,

J. V. Fesko,

and David VanDrunen

PUBLISHING
P.O. BOX 817 • PHILLIPSBURG • NEW JERSEY 08865-0817

Unless otherwise indicated, Scripture quotations are from The Holy Bible, English Standard Version, copyright © 2001 by Crossway Bibles, a division of Good News Publishers. Used by permission. All rights reserved.

Italics within Scripture quotations indicate emphasis added.

Page design and typesetting by Lakeside Design Plus

Printed in the United States of America

Library of Congress Cataloging-in-Publication Data
 The law is not of faith : essays on works and grace in the mosaic covenant / edited by Bryan D. Estelle, J. V. Fesko, and David VanDrunen.
  p. cm.
  Includes bibliographical references and indexes.
  ISBN 978-1-59638-100-1
  1. Law (Theology)—Biblical teaching. 2. Grace (Theology)—Biblical teaching. 3. Bible. O. T.—Theology. I. Estelle, Bryan D., 1959– II. Fesko, J. V., 1970– III. VanDrunen, David, 1971–
 BS1199.L3L39 2009
 241'.2—dc22

                                                                2008042774

Now it is evident that
no one is justified before God by the law, for
"The righteous shall live by faith."
But the law is not of faith, rather
"The one who does them shall live by them."
(Gal. 3:11–12)

CONTENTS

Part Three: Theological Studies

Acknowledgments

The editors of this volume are aware of their debt during the process of bringing this book to fruition. First we wish to thank the contributors, who agreed to participate in this project from an early stage and who submitted their essays in a timely way. We are grateful for their efforts and appreciative of their many theological insights into the Mosaic covenant.

We also thank Marvin Padgett, Thom Notaro, and their fine colleagues at P&R for agreeing to publish this volume and for guiding it through the process of publication.

Our own families have also been supportive through this endeavor. We are grateful to them for putting up with our dreams for producing this book.

We are also thankful for the institutional support we received from Westminster Seminary California and Geneva Orthodox Presbyterian Church and pray that this volume will be of great benefit to both the academy and the church.

INTRODUCTION

BRYAN D. ESTELLE, J. V. FESKO, AND DAVID VANDRUNEN

O*n a sultry September afternoon, the Presbytery of Springfield recon-vened after a short break over donuts and overripe bananas. As the presbyters shuffled back to their seats, a candidate for the gospel ministry came forward to be examined for ordination. The candidate, wear-ing a slightly ill-fitted suit, took his place behind a microphone and wiped his sweaty hands down the front of his pants. The examination began.*

For nearly an hour the examiner asked the usual range of questions, which the candidate answered with methodical orthodoxy while the occasional presbyter's head nodded under the temptation of daytime sleep. After ask-ing a couple of questions about eschatology and receiving assurance that the thousand years of Revelation 20 are by no means literal, the examiner relinquished the floor to the moderator in order to solicit questions from the body. A few brief questions probed the candidate's commitment to pre-suppositional apologetics and his attitude toward remarriage after divorce, and then a minister rose from the back and asked: "Could you tell us more about your views on the Mosaic covenant?"

The candidate's brows furrowed for a moment, and then he began: "Well . . . that's a big question, but I'll do my best. It was a covenant that God made with Moses—with all of Israel—after he brought them out of Egypt, on Mount Sinai. It had lots of stipulations, and rewards and curses depend-ing upon the people's obedience. So the works principle was operative in it—a republication of the covenant of works. It was filled with typology. The land, the priests, the sacrifices, the temple—lots of things—pointed ahead to

1

the coming of Christ and redemption and attaining the heavenly kingdom. All of this was to lead them to Christ. The people were usually disobedient and were often punished by God because of this, but God kept his promises and sent Christ. Now that Christ has come and fulfilled all of the types and shadows, the church is no longer under the Mosaic covenant."

The candidate paused, uncertain whether this general question required a longer response, and immediately the minister stood again and asked to follow up. *"A republication of the covenant of works, did you say? Claiming that Israel had to be right with God by their works sounds like dispensationalism to me. How could there be any way of salvation for sinners except through Christ? But maybe I missed something."*

"No, sir, I did say 'republication of the covenant of works,'" the candidate answered, *"but I definitely didn't mean to say anything supporting dispensationalism. I'm very sorry if I gave that impression. I think a minute ago I was just trying to elaborate on what I said earlier in my exam. The Old Testament saints were clearly saved only by faith and by looking to the Messiah who was to come. I believe I mentioned earlier that Paul pointed to David and Abraham in Romans and Galatians as models of faith in Christ. And of course Hebrews 11. There was never any other way of salvation. When I said something about a republication of the covenant of works, I wasn't suggesting a different way of getting to heaven, just the historic Reformed view that the Mosaic law had this typological function. It demanded strict obedience, and God said that he would give them blessings or curses in the land depending on whether they obeyed. So their receiving blessings and curses on the basis of their own obedience—or usually disobedience, actually—was not about gaining salvation or heaven, but was typological. You know, it reminded them of God's demand for perfect obedience and of Adam's disobedience to the original covenant of works . . . and it showed them the impossibility of keeping the law perfectly. And so it pointed them to Christ. Galatians 3 speaks about the law being a pedagogue unto Christ. And Galatians 4 speaks of Christ being born 'under the law.' So Christ came under the Mosaic law and fulfilled its demands perfectly for our salvation. That's all I was getting at."*

Immediately another minister down the aisle jumped to his feet and demanded the moderator's attention. *"Mr. Moderator, I'd like to pursue this last issue a little more."* He turned to the candidate. *"You've told us that you're not a dispensationalist. I'm sure you meant that sincerely. But I want to make this more concrete. I heard you refer to historic Reformed views, but our confessional standards speak in a very different way from the way in which you're speaking. You talk of the Mosaic covenant as a covenant of works, yet the Westminster Confession of Faith calls it an administration of the covenant of grace. But I didn't hear you take an exception to the Confession at this point. Do you wish to state one now?"*

The candidate adjusted his glasses, wiped his forehead with his palms, and cleared his throat. "No, I don't wish to take an exception, not at all. I'm happy with what the Confession says about the Mosaic covenant. It's Chapter 7, I believe, that says that there are not two covenants of grace, but one—they are the same in substance. But Chapter 7 also speaks about this covenant being administered differently under the law and under the gospel. The things that seem to make the Mosaic era distinct is that it was administered through promises and types and ordinances that signified the Christ who was to come. So that's exactly what I was trying to express before. The works principle under Moses—the connection of their obedience and disobedience with blessing and curse in the land—was typological, showing the people their sinfulness while pointing them to Christ who would fulfil the law. I hope that you didn't understand me to say that the Mosaic covenant is a covenant of works; I believe that it is an administration of the covenant of grace, but that there is this principle of works operative at a typological level as part of this administration. I believe that even the republication of the covenant of works in the Mosaic covenant is meant ultimately to lead to Christ."

The candidate cleared his throat again and reached for the Styrofoam cup of water that had been sitting untouched on the communion table next to him. The same minister's hand and body shot up again as he sought the floor a second time. "Mr. Moderator, I'd like to follow up. This strikes me as a very novel interpretation of the Confession. Perhaps the candidate could enlighten us as to why he thinks this body should take this new view of our confessional standards."

The candidate looked over to the moderator, who prompted him to answer. He said: "Well, I didn't think—with all due respect, sir—I didn't think that I was saying anything novel. And I wasn't implying that everyone here has to agree with my particular view. I admit, I'm certainly not an expert on the historical interpretation of the Confession on this issue, but as far as I can tell there have been some differences among Reformed people on this point and no single view was required of everyone. But I think my view was pretty common historically. I know that Charles Hodge, for example, held a position basically like mine, so it's been an accepted reading of the Confession in American Presbyterianism. I've also noticed some of the proof-texts that Presbyterian churches have commonly used to support the Confession's statements about the covenant of works at creation. Romans 10:5 and

Galatians 3:12 are cited—more than once, I think. Both of these verses cite Leviticus 18:5: the one who does these things will live by them. If the church has thought that Leviticus 18:5 teaches the covenant of works, then it must be reading the Old Testament law in a way similar to my understanding. So those are some reasons why I feel very comfortable about affirming what the Confession says about the covenant theology."

"Just one more question, Mr. Moderator," said the minister. "You mention Romans 10 and Galatians 3. Isn't Paul addressing a Jewish misunderstanding of the law? The Judaizer problem? Do you agree with the Judaizer view of the law—and are you saying that the Confession and the church support this view?"

The candidate shifted his feet and folded his hands in front of his chest while he paused for a moment's thought. "I'm sorry that I'm taking a moment here. Of course I don't agree with the Judaizers; I'm just thinking about how to answer this as best I can. I understand the Judaizer problem to be teaching that obedience to the law contributes in some way to our justification, failing to see that the law was never designed to overturn the promise to Abraham and failing to see that the law was meant to point to Christ. I don't have a Bible open in front of me, but isn't it in Romans 10:5 that Paul makes a point of saying that Moses describes the righteousness of the law in this way—and then quotes Leviticus 18:5? And then in Galatians 3 doesn't he say that the law is not of faith, and then quotes Leviticus 18:5 to prove it? So Paul seems to make a special point of saying that the law, that Moses himself, taught a works principle—the one who does these things shall live—that in and of itself is very different from the principle of faith—the righteous will live by faith. So I think the issue for Paul was not whether the law teaches that blessing and curse are tied to obedience and disobedience—he clearly seems to affirm this—but whether the Mosaic law's ultimate purpose was to lead people to trust in Christ rather than in their own works. And I guess I don't see how the church could cite these verses as proof-texts for the covenant of works if it didn't see a strong works principle taught here. But clearly our churches haven't held Judaizing views. In fact, it's interesting how Paul quotes Leviticus 18:5 in discussions of justification. It seems from Paul that understanding the works principle in the Mosaic law enables one to understand the doctrine of justification better. The law requires perfect obedience; no one can meet that requirement. But Christ has met this requirement for us, and by faith in him his obedience to the law is imputed to his people. So seeing a works principle in the Mosaic law, which Christ took upon himself and perfectly fulfilled, helps us to have a strong view of Christ's active obedience."

A momentary lull settled upon the presbytery. The moderator opened his mouth, about to ask if there were any more questions, when an aged presbyter, an elder in one of the local congregations for many years, slowly rose to his feet and motioned for the floor. The moderator called his name.

"Young man," the elder began, "I'm not a trained theologian, and I'm not sure that I follow all of these theological debates. But that's my problem with what you're saying. It's so complicated. The ordinary people in the pews, like me, can't understand this sort of thing. What's important to me is whether you can preach what you believe. Do you really think that you can preach this? Will the children in your congregation be able to understand this? I have serious doubts, but perhaps you'd care to comment on that."

The candidate responded: "I'm glad that you ask me that; that's very important. I haven't meant to get into a technical theological debate. And I agree, these debates aren't to take place from the pulpit. But I'm convinced that it is possible to preach this view of the Mosaic covenant, and that it's actually very helpful for explaining many parts of Scripture—and I think that it can be presented in simple ways for all people in the church to understand, though I probably have a lot to learn about how to do this effectively.

"Just take the passages in Galatians and Romans that we were discussing earlier. Every Reformed minister loves preaching from Romans and Galatians. Presenting the Mosaic law as teaching a works principle really helps in explaining Paul's doctrine of justification: what sin is all about, why people can't rely on their own law-keeping, how faith is radically different from works, how Christ fulfilled the terms of the law so that we may be justified. That's just the gospel as I see it, but you can't explain the gospel without understanding the law. Or take all of those Old Testament passages that call for Israel's obedience and promise blessing and threaten curse in the land depending on their response. For example, the beginning of Deuteronomy 4, which tells Israel to follow the law so that they may live and take possession of the land. Or Deuteronomy 28, which recounts all sorts of earthly blessings in the land if the Israelites are careful to obey and all sorts of earthly curses if they aren't. I don't want a congregation to think that God was holding out a works-based way of salvation here, and I also can't tell the congregation that this is the same way that God deals with the New Testament church when he calls her to obedience, for there's nothing equivalent in the New Testament, no promise of earthly blessing for the church today if we meet a standard of obedience. Saying either of those things might be simple, but of course they'd be misleading, and damaging for the church to hear.

"So how do we preach these kinds of texts? We can begin by showing how Israel illustrates the basic problem of the whole human race: obligated

to obey God's law yet unable to do so. If we then explain how Israel's dis-
obedience brought curse, we can show humanity's sinful condition. If we
explain that obedience really does bring blessing from a just God, then we
can show them their need for a Savior and proclaim how Christ has provided
this obedience. If we explain how the Promised Land of the Old Testament
was a type of the heavenly kingdom, as the New Testament teaches, then we
can teach them to see how the earthly blessings given to Israel are a shadow
of the much greater things that we will experience on the last day. This is
not simplistic, but I think it's actually fairly simple. At least as simple as the
gospel message itself. We have to teach our children the Old Testament one
way or another, and I believe that this is a theologically accurate way to do
so, and one that shows them the gospel even from parts of Scripture that
may not seem very much related to it."

The candidate again reached for his water, took a sip, and took a step back
from the microphone. After a few moments of silence, a presbyter moved that
the exam be arrested. The motion passed. Then the presbyter moved that the
exam be sustained and so the moderator opened the floor for debate.

What Is the Doctrine of Republication?

The preceding fictional narrative introduces the real issue with which this
book deals, namely, the doctrine of republication, which holds that the
covenant of works is in some sense republished in the Mosaic covenant at
Sinai. When people first hear of the doctrine of republication, one reaction
is that it is a theological novelty, yet it might surprise some to discover that
far from a novelty, it is part of the warp and woof of Scripture and sound
doctrine. We can briefly survey Scripture from the biblical-theological and
systematic-theological perspectives to substantiate this claim. It will also
prove helpful to note a few historical expressions of the doctrine and to
dismiss common misconceptions of it.

In Biblical Theology

Adam's Probation in the Garden-Temple
There are many narrative threads that begin in the Old Testament and run
throughout the whole of the Scriptures, such as redemption as new creation,
exodus/second exodus, and the flood judgment.[1] Another prominent theme

---

1. See, e.g., G. K. Beale, "The New Testament and New Creation," in *Biblical Theology: Retro-*
spect & Prospect, ed. Scott J. Hafemann (Downers Grove, IL: InterVarsity, 2002), 159–73; Rikki E.
Watts, *Isaiah's New Exodus in Mark* (Grand Rapids: Baker, 1997); Meredith G. Kline, *Kingdom*

is that of the probation of God's sons. Genesis 1 begins with the creation of the heavens and earth and culminates with the creation of man (Gen. 1:28). The Genesis account tells us that man was created in the image and likeness of God. Shortly thereafter, we see hints that image- and likeness-bearing are bound together with the idea of sonship when we read that Adam had a son who bore his image and likeness (Gen. 5:3). Because of what is said of Adam and his image-bearer Seth, we can in some sense say that Adam was God's son, as he bore God's image. This is the import of Luke's statement in his Gospel that Adam was God's son (Luke 3:38).[2] We see, then, that not only did God create his son Adam, but he placed him in a garden environment and gave him a twofold command with appended blessings and curses. Adam was told not to eat of the fruit of the tree of knowledge upon the penalty of death. He was also told to be fruitful, multiply, and fill the earth with offspring who also would bear the image of God. Were Adam to be obedient to these commands, he would secure his place eternally and indefectibly in God's presence. Adam, however, disobeyed.

Often people look at the Genesis account too literally and scratch their heads wondering why Adam did not immediately die, when God explicitly told him that in the day that he ate from the tree he would surely die (Gen. 2:17). The Genesis narrative clearly tells us that Adam lived for another 930 years (Gen. 5:5). Theologians at times have explained this by saying that while Adam could have legitimately been immediately stricken dead, God relented and gave him a stay of execution of sorts.[3] Yet what many often miss is the significance of being cast out of the garden-temple of Eden.[4] To be exiled from the presence of God was akin to death itself.[5] In this sense, Adam surely did die on the day that he was exiled from the benevolent presence of the Lord. This story of the probation and exile of God's son is one that is repeated beyond the pages of the Genesis narrative. It is repeated in the rest of the Old Testament, especially in the books of Exodus and Deuteronomy, and in the prophets, especially Ezekiel.

Prologue: Genesis Foundations for a Covenantal Worldview (Overland Park, KS: Two Age Press, 2000), 212–41; Geerhardus Vos, *The Eschatology of the Old Testament*, ed. James T. Dennison Jr. (Phillipsburg, NJ: P&R, 2001), 81–84.

2. See E. Earle Ellis, *The Gospel of Luke*, New Century Bible (1966; Grand Rapids: Eerdmans, 1996), 93.

3. E.g., Gleason L. Archer, *Encyclopedia of Bible Difficulties* (Grand Rapids: Zondervan, 1982), 72.

4. On the garden as the archetypal earthly temple, see G. K. Beale, *The Temple and the Church's Mission: A Biblical Theology of the Dwelling Place of God*, New Studies in Biblical Theology (Downers Grove, IL: InterVarsity, 2004), 66–122; Gordon J. Wenham, "Sanctuary Symbolism in the Garden of Eden Story," in *I Studied Inscriptions from Before the Flood: Ancient Near Eastern, Literary, and Linguistic Approaches to Genesis 1–11*, ed. Richard S. Hess and David Toshio Tsumura (Winona Lake, IN: Eisenbrauns, 1994), 399–404.

5. So Wenham, "Sanctuary Symbolism," 404.

Israel's Probation in the Garden-like Land

When we look at later portions of the Pentateuch, we find that the story of the probation and exile of God's son resurfaces once again. We see hints of this in the opening chapters of Exodus when God tells Moses to inform Pharaoh to release Israel, his firstborn son (Ex. 4:22). We see further clues on a grand scale that just as Adam bore the image and likeness of his heavenly Father, so too Israel was supposed to bear the characteristics of his Father. Israel was to be holy as God was holy (Lev. 19:2). God's son was redeemed from Egypt so that he could dwell in the presence of his heavenly Father (cf. Hos. 11:1). Yet there was still the matter of the probation of God's son.

On the eve of entering the Promised Land, a land flowing with milk and honey, a description evocative of the garden-temple of Eden (Gen. 13:10; Isa. 51:3; Ezek. 36:35; 47:12; Joel 2:3), Moses told God's firstborn son that he was to receive the land as his inheritance, but that his ability to dwell in the land and before the presence of God was conditioned upon his obedience: "And if you faithfully obey the voice of the LORD your God, being careful to do all his commandments that I command you today, the LORD your God will set you high above all the nations of the earth" (Deut. 28:1; cf. Lev. 26:3–6).[6] If Israel was obedient to the stipulations of the covenant, then God's son would receive blessings, the land would yield its fruit, Israel would multiply, and he would live long in the land (Deut. 7:12–13). If Israel was disobedient, on the other hand, he would be, like his predecessor Adam, exiled from the presence of God (Deut. 8:19). Israel the disobedient son would be taken outside the camp, outside the dwelling place of the Lord, and put to death—Israel would suffer exile-death (Deut. 21:18–21; cf. Jer. 5:23; Isa. 1:2–4). While Israel's probation ended in exile, Ezekiel prophesied of a time when God would resurrect his son from the exilic graveyard in which he was buried and return him to dwell once again in his presence (Ezek. 37:1–14).[7] At this point, neither Adam nor the people of Israel as God's sons were able successfully to pass their probation and offer unto their heavenly Father the obedience he required. This did not mean, however, that no one would ever pass the test.

The Successful Probation of God's Only Son

When we come to the pages of the New Testament, Jesus does not emerge on stage divorced from antecedent redemptive history. In fact, it is against

---

6. See G. K. Beale, "Garden Temple," *Kerux* 18.2 (2003): 44; also Stephen G. Dempster, *Dominion and Dynasty: A Theology of the Hebrew Bible*, New Studies in Biblical Theology (Downers Grove, IL: InterVarsity, 2003), 115–18.

7. Dempster, *Dominion*, 126, 172–73.

the backdrop of the theme of the probation and exile of God's son that so many of the seemingly disparate statements about Jesus cohere and make sense. At the beginning of Jesus' ministry at his baptism, in actions evocative of the creation, flood, and Red Sea crossing, God's only begotten Son emerged from the waters of baptism as the Holy Spirit descended upon him in the form of a dove and God the Father declared, "This is my beloved Son, with whom I am well pleased" (Matt. 3:17).[8] Then, Jesus, like God's son of old, Israel, was led into the wilderness for forty days, echoing Israel's wilderness wanderings for forty years.[9]

Unlike God's disobedient son, Jesus was perfectly obedient to the will of his Father. In fact, one of the exegetical flags that alerts the reader that Jesus is retracing Israel's steps, especially as it relates to the Mosaic covenant, is that, in his temptation, Jesus responds with three quotations from Deuteronomy (6:13, 16; 8:3). Jesus' obedience, however, was not merely in his wilderness temptation, but was throughout his life and culminated in his crucifixion. It was because of this obedience unto death that Jesus' heavenly Father gave him the name that is above every name (Phil. 2:5–11). In terms of the antecedent preredemptive and redemptive history, or Adam's and Israel's failure, Jesus the faithful Son successfully passed the probation, yet though he was faithful and obedient, he nevertheless suffered exile on behalf of his bride, the covenant people of God (Heb. 13:11–12).

From the biblical-theological perspective, we can see that the doctrine of republication is not in any way imposed upon the Scriptures but rather grows organically from it. Recognizing that Adam's probation in and exile from the garden-temple was repeated on the grand scale in terms of Israel's probation in and exile from God's presence in the land in no way undermines the grand narrative of redemptive history. Instead, both Adam and Israel point forward to the person and work of Christ. Paul makes this very point in the fifth chapter of Romans. Paul explains that death entered the world through one man, Adam (Rom. 5:12). We should not miss the implied comparison between Adam and Israel, in that both transgressed expressly revealed commands, whether Adam's transgression of the prohibition to eat from the tree of knowledge or Israel's transgression of the Torah, the stipulations of the Mosaic covenant. Succinctly stated, both of God's sons, Adam and Israel, lived under *nomos*-governed circumstances.[10] Adam's circumstances in the

8. Geerhardus Vos, *Biblical Theology* (1948; Edinburgh: Banner of Truth, 1996), 322.
9. D. A. Carson, *Matthew 1–12*, Expositor's Bible Commentary (Grand Rapids: Zondervan, 1995), 112–15.
10. See C. E. B. Cranfield, *Romans*, International Critical Commentary (1975; Edinburgh: T&T Clark, 2001), 1:283; John Murray, *Romans*, New International Commentary on the New Testament (Grand Rapids: Eerdmans, 1968), 189–90; James D. G. Dunn, *Romans 1–8*, Word Biblical

garden-temple were repeated in Israel's circumstances in the land of promise, though we should note that Israel was not a federal head as Adam was and as Jesus would be. And Jesus also lived under *nomos*-governed circumstances, as he was born under the law, yet he completely fulfilled its requirements unlike Adam and Israel (Gal. 4:4; Matt. 5:17).

In Systematic Theology

When we turn to the discipline of systematic theology, we can see that these biblical-theological patterns have been recognized under the theological rubrics of the covenants of works and grace, which cover the works of the first and last Adams respectively (Westminster Confession of Faith 7.2–3). Though fallen man is unable to fulfil the broken covenant of works, nevertheless God sends Jesus to take up and complete that broken covenant. Since the fall, then, man has been saved by grace alone through faith alone in Christ alone—this is how God's people become partakers of the covenant of grace.[11] The covenant of grace began immediately upon the heels of the fall. However, this does not mean that the covenant of grace has always been administered in the same manner. The Westminster divines explain that the covenant of grace "was differently administered in the time of the law, and in the time of the gospel: under the law, it was administered by promises, prophecies, sacrifices, circumcision, and paschal lamb, and other types and ordinances delivered to the people of the Jews, all foresignifying Christ to come" (7.5). Because the covenant of grace was administered in terms of "sacrifices . . . and ordinances delivered" to Israel, which were given through the Mosaic covenant, we can see that the Mosaic covenant looked forward to the work of Christ.

The Westminster divines also believed that the Mosaic covenant looked back to Adam's state in the garden. The divines explain, "God gave to Adam a law, as a covenant of works, by which he bound him and all his posterity to personal, entire, exact, and perpetual obedience" (19.1). They go on to say in the next paragraph, "This law," referring to the law given to Adam, "after his fall, continued to be a perfect rule of righteousness; and, as such, was delivered by God upon Mount Sinai, in ten commandments, and writ-

Commentary (Dallas: Word, 1988), 290–91; Charles Hodge, *Romans* (1835; Edinburgh: Banner of Truth, 1989), 160–61; Thomas R. Schreiner, *Romans*, Baker Exegetical Commentary on the New Testament (Grand Rapids: Baker, 1998), 279; Douglas J. Moo, *Romans*, New International Commentary on the New Testament (Grand Rapids: Eerdmans, 1996), 331–33.

11. For standard explanations of the covenants see Louis Berkhof, *Systematic Theology* (1932–38; Grand Rapids: Eerdmans, 1996), 211–18, 272–83; Herman Bavinck, *Reformed Dogmatics*, ed. John Bolt, trans. John Vriend, 4 vols. (Grand Rapids: Baker, 2003–8), 2:563–80; 3:193–232.

ten in two tables" (19.2).[12] In this regard, the divines saw that the law given to Adam was of a piece with that given to Israel at Sinai. In other words, in some sense, the covenant of works was republished at Sinai. It was not republished, however, as the covenant of works per se, but as part of the covenant of grace, which pointed to the person and work of Christ. In terms of the classic threefold distinction on the uses of the law, the republication of the covenant of works falls under the pedagogical use of the law, that which drives the sinner to Christ by bringing the requirement for perfect obedience before the fallen creature, forcing him to turn to the only one who has been obedient. These biblical-theological and systematic-theological observations have long been part and parcel of Reformed theology.

Various Expressions of the Doctrine of Republication

Historic Reformed theology has acknowledged the doctrine of republication, but this is not to say that it has always been expressed in the same way. As chapter 3 in this present volume shows, there are a number of different formulations, some unorthodox, that have been offered over the years. In the period of early orthodoxy (1565–1630), Amandus Polanus (1561–1610), professor of Old Testament at the University of Basel in 1596 and dean of the theological faculty from 1598 to 1609, expresses the doctrine of republication by writing: "The repetition of the covenant of works is made by God" (Ex. 19:5; Deut. 5:2; 1 Kings 8:21; Heb. 8:9).[13] He then cites four reasons for this repetition of the covenant of works in the Mosaic covenant:

1. That God by all means might stir up men to perform obedience.
2. That every mouth might be stopped, and all the world might be made subject to the condemnation of God for not performing perfect obedience (Rom. 3:19).
3. That he might manifest man's sin, and naughtiness (Rom. 3:19–20; 7:7–11).
4. That he might thrust us forward to seek to be restored in the covenant of grace (Gal. 3:22; 5:23).[14]

---

12. Contra D. Patrick Ramsey, "In Defense of Moses: A Confessional Critique of Kline and Karlberg," *Westminster Theological Journal* 66 (2004): 394–96; cf. Rowland S. Ward, *The Westminster Confession of Faith: A Study Guide* (Wantirna: New Melbourne Press, 1996), 115–16; Robert Shaw, *An Exposition of the Westminster Confession of Faith* (1845; Fearn, Ross-shire: Christian Focus, 1998), 240–41.

13. Richard A. Muller, *Post-Reformation Reformed Dogmatics*, 4 vols. (Grand Rapids: Baker, 2003), 1:44.

14. Amandus Polanus, *The Substance of the Christian Religion* (London, 1585), 88. For a

Another Reformed continental theologian, Francis Turretin (1623–87), John Calvin's (1509–64) successor at the Academy of Geneva after the tenure of Theodore Beza (1519–1605) and his father Benedict Turretin (1588–1631), expressed his understanding of republication in a slightly different manner. Turretin writes, "It pleased God to administer the covenant of grace in this period under a rigid legal economy." He goes on to state that the covenant of grace had a twofold relation (*duplex*, σχέσις), one legal and the other evangelical. Under the legal aspect, he argues that the Mosaic covenant was "a new promulgation of the law and of the covenant of works" (*nova legis et foederis operum promulgatione*). The evangelical aspect of the Mosaic economy was that the law was a schoolmaster unto Christ and contained a shadow of things to come (Gal. 3:24; Heb. 10:1). While Turretin does not explicitly state it in these terms, when he discusses the "external economy" (*externam oeconomiam*) of the Mosaic covenant being legal in nature, he relies upon an old medieval distinction between substance and accidents, or substance and form.[15] Succinctly stated, the form of the Mosaic covenant was the covenant of works, but its substance was the covenant of grace.

One can find other variations of the doctrine of republication in the theology of Charles Hodge (1797–1878). In Hodge's commentary on 1–2 Corinthians the Princetonian theologian explains: "Every reader of the New Testament must be struck with the fact that the apostle often speaks of the Mosaic law as he does of the moral law considered as a covenant of works; that is, presenting the promise of life on the condition of perfect obedience." He goes on to write that this apparently contradicts the gospel, in that men are saved by faith in Christ, not their works. He explains, however, that Paul's characterization of the moral law as the covenant of works does not contradict the gospel. Hodge writes:

1. The law of Moses was, in the first place, a re-enactment of the covenant of works. A covenant is simply a promise suspended upon a condition. The covenant of works, therefore, is nothing more than the promise of life suspended on the condition of perfect obedience.

---

brief but helpful survey that covers Polanus see Robert Letham, "Amandus Polanus: A Neglected Theologian?" *Sixteenth Century Journal* 21.3 (1990): 463–76.

15. Francis Turretin, *Institutes of Elenctic Theology*, trans. George Musgrave Giger, ed. James T. Dennison Jr. (Phillipsburg, NJ: P&R, 1992–97), 12.7.31–32: "Interim, quia Foedus gratiae in hac aetate sub rigida oeconomia legali administrare Deo placuit" (idem, *Institutio Theologiae Elencticae*, 3 vols. [Edinburgh: John D. Lowe, 1847]). Cf. Richard A. Muller, *Dictionary of Latin and Greek Theological Terms: Drawn Principally from Protestant Scholastic Theology* (Grand Rapids: Baker, 1985), 123–24, 290, q.v. *forma, substantia*.

2. The Mosaic economy was also a national covenant; that is, it presented national promises on the condition of national obedience. Under this aspect also it was purely legal.

3. As the gospel contains a renewed revelation of the law, so the law of Moses contained a revelation of the gospel. It presented in its priesthood and sacrifices, as types of the office and work of Christ, the gratuitous method of salvation through a Redeemer. This necessarily supposes that faith and not works was the condition of salvation.[16]

In distinction to Turretin, Hodge raises the idea of a national covenant of works, which substantively raises the issue of the grand narrative of redemptive history, namely, the idea of Israel as God's son who prefigures God's only begotten Son. Moreover, Hodge's view is somewhat different from Polanus's expression, as Polanus seems to be interested in exploring the doctrine of republication only vis-à-vis the *ordo salutis*.

In these three examples, we can easily see that the doctrine of republication was not a novelty but was a regular staple in Reformed dogmatics. In this regard, though disagreeing with the doctrine of republication, Professor John Murray (1898–1975) recognized the commonplace nature of the doctrine when he once wrote: "The view that in the Mosaic covenant there was a repetition of the so-called covenant of works, current among covenant theologians, is a grave misconception."[17] Murray also admitted that the doctrine of republication "has exercised a profound influence upon the history of interpretation and it has cast its shadow over the exegesis of particular passages."[18] Murray certainly did not agree with the doctrine, but the point still stands that he recognized that the doctrine was common and widespread in Reformed theology. We will explore more on Murray's views vis-à-vis the Mosaic covenant below. In classic historic Reformed theology, despite the variegated expression, the same thread runs throughout, namely, the idea that in some sense the covenant of works was repeated or republished in the Mosaic covenant.

Common Misconceptions

Several things should be clear for a proper comprehension of the doctrine of republication, since the contemporary reception of the doctrine is often

16. Charles Hodge, *1 & 2 Corinthians* (1857; Edinburgh: Banner of Truth, 1994), 432–34.
17. John Murray, *Collected Writings*, 4 vols. (Edinburgh: Banner of Truth, 1977), 2:50.
18. John Murray, *Principles of Conduct: Aspects of Biblical Ethics* (1957; Grand Rapids: Eerdmans, 2001), 196.

met with criticism rather than careful attention to both Scripture and historic Reformed theology. First, to affirm that in some sense the covenant of works is republished at Sinai is not to say that there is a different way of salvation in the Old Testament from the New. The doctrine of republication is not in any way dispensationalism.[19] Advocates of republication universally affirm that salvation is by grace alone through faith alone in Christ alone, and that the gospel was in operation from the instant of man's fall.

Second, to affirm the doctrine of republication does not entail the view that the Mosaic covenant is not part of the covenant of grace. While there are perhaps those in the past who separated the Mosaic covenant and argued that there are two separate covenants of grace, the vast majority of those who hold to the doctrine of republication affirm that the Mosaic covenant is a part of or connected to the covenant of grace (Westminster Confession of Faith 7.6).[20]

Third, and finally, to affirm the doctrine of republication is in no way to deny the third use of the law; it is not antinomianism. To hold that the Mosaic covenant republishes the covenant of works does not therefore mean that because Christ fulfilled the obligations of the moral law the believer therefore has no use for the law post-conversion. Rather, in concert with historic Reformed theology, the doctrine of republication merely points the redeemed sinner to Christ as the one who has fulfilled the broken covenant of works and has redeemed him from the curse of the law. Moreover, because the believer is no longer under the curse of the law, and because Christ has written the law of God upon his heart, the believer is thereby enabled to walk in the statutes of the Lord by the power of the Holy Spirit (Westminster Confession of Faith 19.1–2, 5–7). So, then, while these criticisms are perhaps common objections, one should note that they are unfounded when one carefully examines the Scriptures and historic Reformed theology.

What Happened to the Doctrine of Republication?

During the early years of the development of Reformed orthodoxy there was significant discussion about the nature of the Mosaic covenant and its

19. Dispensationalists have historically rejected classic Reformed covenant theology. See Charles Caldwell Ryrie, *Dispensationalism Today* (1965; Chicago: Moody, 1970), 110–31, esp. 123.

20. See chapter 2 in this present volume. Also, for information surrounding the views extant during the Westminster Assembly see Samuel Bolton, *The True Bounds of Christian Freedom* (1645; Edinburgh: Banner of Truth, 2001), 99; Anthony Burgess, *Vindiciae Legis* (London, 1647), 229.

relationship to the covenant of works in Eden, or as it is sometimes called, the covenant of creation. With the dawn of clarity on the doctrine of justification that the Protestant Reformation brought, there also seems to have been some weighty deliberations within the church regarding the principle of continuity and discontinuity of the Sinaitic covenant and its teaching on the law and freedom from the curse of that law in the new covenant.

As previously mentioned, chapter 3, concerned with historical description, takes pains to develop a taxonomy of various views held on these subjects by Reformed ministers and theologians after the Reformation. After reading that chapter, one has to ask some of the following questions. What happened? How is it that such a dominant concern with so many Reformed luminaries in the past slipped off the table of discussion and was no longer, generally speaking, a matter that exercised the best minds among theologians, ministers, ruling elders, and educated laypersons? Extended questions immediately arise as well. What were the consequences following on the heels of this silence? Moreover, were they negative or positive in nature? In other words, did such silence issue in some kind of injury to the theological acuity of deliberations inside and outside the church, especially within church courts, and most importantly, among the understanding of all those filling the pew? Did such silence, dare we say historical ignorance, lead to a kind of unwitting torpor in the thinking of ministers, exegetes, and theologians in areas of theological inquiry such as the nature of the law, grace, typology, and merit?

There is no doubt that Professor John Murray, who held a position as instructor at Princeton Theological Seminary before following J. Gresham Machen and others to Westminster Theological Seminary, exercised a profound influence on generations of pastors and teachers through the numerous students that sat under him. One can be thankful for many areas in Professor Murray's life and teaching that exercised a strong influence on future ministers. Nevertheless, with sadness it must be said that the extant evidence is irrefutable concerning his views of the doctrines of the covenant of works and the Mosaic covenant. Not only did he see the need for "recasting" covenant theology and especially the confessional and classical doctrine of the covenant of works,[21] but he also eschewed the notion that the Sinaitic covenant was in some sense a "repetition of the so-called cov-

---

21. John Murray, "The Theology of the Westminster Confession of Faith," in *Scripture and Confession: A Book about Confessions Old and New*, ed. J. H. Skilton (Nutley, NJ: Presbyterian and Reformed, 1973), 146; idem, "Covenant Theology," in *The Encyclopedia of Christianity* (Marshallton, DE: National Foundation for Christian Education, 1972), 199–216; idem, "The Adamic Administration," in *Collected Writings*, 2:47–59; idem, "Covenant Theology," in *Collected Writings*, 4:216–40; and esp. idem, *The Covenant of Grace: A Biblio-Theological Study* (1953; Phillipsburg, NJ: Presbyterian and Reformed, 1988).

enant of works," and he employed unfortunate diction in describing such
views as a "grave misconception" involving "an erroneous construction
of the Mosaic covenant, as well as fail[ure] to assess the uniqueness of the
Adamic administration."[22]

It has been argued that Murray was not only willing to stand against many
of his Reformed predecessors from a perspective beginning with the Mosaic
covenant looking backward to Eden, but was also willing, from a perspective
starting with Moses and looking forward to the new covenant, to break with
many in the Reformed tradition in his arguments for a radical continuity
between the testaments in regard to the nature of obedience. It is true that
that tradition had maintained that individual election to eschatological life
was only by grace through faith throughout both testaments in the postlapsarian period; however, with respect to the national election of Israel, a great
many in that same Reformed tradition had taught that a principle of works
did exist and was operative in the covenant of Sinai. Israel was like another
Adam in some sense. Canaan was another Eden, and sincere, real obedience
to the stipulations set out by God was the condition of either tenure in or
extirpation from the land of promise.

Contrary to this, Murray's view, which has been called "monocovenantal," teaches that the demand for obedience in the Sinaitic covenant was
principally the same in the new covenant of the gospel age. Additionally,
Murray was at least monocovenantal in the sense that he affirmed no other
kind of covenant than a covenant of redemptive grace and, in doing so, he
ironically blurred distinctions between the covenant of works and grace. In
fairness to Murray, however, monocovenantalism is a slippery term that is used
in many different ways.[23] Nevertheless, what can be said is the following.

Murray saw continuity between the Sinaitic and new covenants with
respect to the demands of each. Some of Murray's construals may have been
consistent outworkings of terminological distinctions and methodological
commitments he had from the beginning. However, it has been argued, and
is argued below in the following pages, that the most important impetus for
"recasting" was motivated in response to the errors of classical dispensa-

---

22. Murray, *Collected Writings*, 2:50.

23. Some, for example, describe it as a view that blurs the distinctions between law and gospel
because many monocovenantalists suggest that the law-gospel distinction is a Lutheran notion not
shared by Calvin. Others use the label to describe those who emphasize the gracious nature of the
covenants to the exclusion of any meritorious conditions placed upon human parties of the covenant
and with no sensitivities to the changing nature of God's work in each succeeding covenant context.
Still others have described as monocovenantal those who reject or deemphasize classical construals of the order of salvation (*ordo salutis*) and emphasize union with Christ (*unio cum Christo*).
Whether Professor Murray was a monocovenantalist in some or all these respects is beyond the
purview of this brief introduction.

tionalist hermeneutics of the Mosaic covenant. In the classical expression of this theology, law was identified as the means of salvation in the Mosaic covenant. Classic dispensationalism, that of C. I. Scofield (1843–1921) and J. N. Darby (1800–1882) for example, viewed the means of obtaining righteousness in the Sinaitic covenant as law and the means of obtaining righteousness in the new covenant as grace. Professor Murray thought this construal was fundamentally contrary to the teaching of the continuity of the covenant of grace: there are not "two covenants of grace differing in substance, but one and the same under various dispensations" (Westminster Confession of Faith 7.6). Centuries of discussion about republication in the Mosaic covenant, even as recent as Charles Hodge (only one generation removed), could be dismissed if they were perceived to be a look-alike to the dispensational scheme.

With such rhetoric, Murray released the clutch, and those who had studied under him or were influenced by his writings without appropriate reflection and criticism in these areas set in motion a chain of events that would produce deleterious injuries for confessional Reformed theology and beyond. Norman Shepherd, professor of systematic theology at Westminster Theological Seminary from 1963 to 1982, is a case in point. In his recent book, he too showed great antipathy to any construal of republication in the Mosaic covenant and a works principle represented in such an important passage as Leviticus 18:5, for example.[24]

Recent evidence of this agitation in the church and elsewhere can be seen in the fact that the notion that Sinai republished a works principle has received much hostility in books, peer-reviewed journals, and trials in the courts of the church. Some are even calling for formal judicial discipline of ministers who hold to any view of the Sinaitic covenant that smacks of works being in place for pedagogical and typological purposes. Therefore, the essays in this book have profound contemporary relevance for the church and her theology.

There are other reasons why this book should receive a wide reading: it is impossible to write about Paul and his theology as presented in the New Testament without commenting on the Mosaic covenant. Paul was a Yeshiva boy, raised in the womb of the Hebrews and therefore profoundly familiar with the Hebrew Bible and early Judaism. He was probably on a trajectory to become one of the leading rabbis in Jerusalem prior to his conversion. Therefore, to plumb the depths of Paul's thought necessarily means under-standing the Mosaic covenant.

24. Norman Shepherd, *The Call of Grace: How the Covenant Illuminates Salvation and Evange-lism* (Phillipsburg, NJ: P&R, 2000), 35–38.

Beyond Reformed confessional circles, the subject of these essays also has significant relevance. The so-called New Perspective(s) on Paul, a primarily academic movement which began with E. P. Sanders's important writings on Second Temple Judaism and has been carried forward especially by the teachings of James D. G. Dunn and N. T. Wright, shows great interest in Israel and her covenants. Likewise, the so-called Federal Vision movement, which has been associated with the Auburn Avenue Presbyterian Church in Monroe, Louisiana, and Steve Schlissel, Douglas Wilson, James Jordan, and some ministers of the Presbyterian Church of America (e.g., Peter Leithart, Steve Wilkins, Joel Garver), has demonstrated significant interest in both the theology of the covenants and sacraments, which are integrally related to the subject of republication. Beyond the provincial conservative Reformed world, the seismic influence of Karl Barth's (1886–1968) teaching has been felt through his writing that suggests a basic unity between gospel and law.[25] The Dutch theologian G. C. Berkouwer (1904–96), formerly professor of systematic theology at the Free University of Amsterdam, was affected by this shift. Additionally, the Swiss Roman Catholic theologian Hans Küng (1928–) and others who have had a great concern for ecumenism have tried to bring together Protestant and Roman Catholic perspectives on the doctrine of justification which have consequently affected people's understanding of the Mosaic covenant.[26] Other examples could be mentioned as well.

Additionally, Reformed theology has taught the planned obsolescence of the Sinaitic covenant and its promised rest in the land: the old covenant was doomed to failure. Indeed, the Abrahamic covenant with its associated promises to usher in a new age with Gentiles as well as Jews entailed the eventual collapse of the Sinaitic arrangement. In the old covenant, what was passing, prototypical, symbolic, and provisional had to give way to what was perfective, permanent, and antitypical: the new covenant. Many of the essays in this book address this point.

But what does the doctrine of republication do for us today? Is this not an arcane preoccupation with precision and theological minutiae on the part of Reformed scholastics and others with too much time on their hands? Are not these finer nuances of the Mosaic covenant too, too difficult for the ordinary person in the pew, let alone his children? The answer to these questions is an unequivocal no! We offer at least two reasons why. First, if ministers let the doctrine of republication die out and do not teach it faithfully, then they

25. Karl Barth, "Gospel and Law," in *Community, State, and Church: Three Essays* (Eugene, OR: Wipf and Stock, 2004), 71–100.
26. Hans Küng, *Justification: The Doctrine of Karl Barth and a Catholic Reflection* (1957; Philadelphia: Westminster, 1981).

destroy a part of Old Testament typology that God gave for the edification of the church. Secondly, if there really is some principle of works operative in the Mosaic economy, and it is not just hypothetical but it is put there by God's design, then we dare not do injury to our own selves by ignoring what God has placed in his holy Word for our instruction.

In short, the doctrine of republication is integrally connected to the doctrine of justification. The Mosaic law was necessary to make manifest a works principle that Christ the Messiah would have to fulfil. Jesus Christ stands in the stead of his people to take the curses of the law. But this is only half of the equation. There must be positive righteousness to merit the Father's approbation and meet the just demands of the law. Christ fulfilled that as well. Since the doctrine of republication highlights the need for a true son of Israel to accomplish this righteousness, and ultimately does make manifest the obedience of Christ as the fulfilment of that demand, a misunderstanding of the Mosaic economy and silence on the works principle embedded there will only leave us necessarily impoverished in our faith. We will see in only a thin manner the work of our Savior. God desires that we have the whole richness of his Word displayed before our eyes and ears so that we might respond to his immeasurable grace with grateful hearts filled with joy.

The Plan of This Book

Before offering an overview of the chapters of this volume, we present a few considerations for readers to keep in mind. First, readers should remember that the doctrine of republication, though in basic respects simple enough for a child to understand, is in other respects a *difficult* and *complex* matter. The idea that a typological principle of works is operative in the Mosaic covenant is not obscure—many Old Testament passages, after all, clearly connect Israel's obligation of obedience with their tenure in the land. Yet some of the most theologically rich texts in which this doctrine is at least arguably taught—such as Leviticus 18:5, Hosea 6:7, Galatians 3:10–12, and Romans 9:30–10:8—are exegetically challenging passages that have been subject to long debates. One goal of this volume is to encourage the church and academy to avoid simplistic solutions to harmonizing the array of biblical teaching on the Mosaic covenant and its significance for the church today. But this is hard work, and we ask our readers to engage with us in this hard work by reading these chapters with care.

Second, we also wish readers to recognize that this volume does not intend to thrust a single, monolithic view of the Mosaic covenant upon Reformed churches. The Reformed tradition has always acknowledged and tolerated a variety of positions on the Mosaic covenant. This volume, therefore, does not wish to squelch debate but instead to encourage and catalyze discussion about what we believe are important issues for the doctrine and life of the church. Careful readers will even perceive subtle differences among the contributors to this book. No particular view expressed by one contributor should be automatically imputed to any other contributor. Though all of the contributors share a general sympathy with the republication idea and a general desire to recover serious theological reflection on issues related to it, not all share exactly the same sentiments on how best to express the relation of works and grace under Moses or the relation of the Mosaic covenant to the Adamic and new covenants. We hope that the various essays in this volume will serve to renew significant conversations that have not been taking place in recent years, toward the goal of seeing Reformed churches come mutually to a richer understanding of the Old Testament in God's larger redemptive plan.

Third, we encourage readers to take up these essays in the order in which they are presented. Though there may be temptation to skip to one's favorite author or topic, we believe that readers will profit most by studying these chapters consecutively. The historical essays in Part One lay important groundwork for the constructive essays that follow in Parts Two and Three by illuminating some of the relevant discussions that have gone on through much of the Reformed tradition. In Part Two itself, the Old Testament essays discuss important themes that are picked up in the New Testament essays. In fact, some of the New Testament essays contain discussion of Paul's exegesis of some of the Old Testament verses which the Old Testament essays consider. Likewise, the systematic and moral themes addressed in the theological essays in Part Three will themselves be better appreciated against the exegetical foundations laid in Part Two.

Part One presents three historical studies. In chapter 1, J. V. Fesko examines two undoubtedly significant figures of the early Reformed tradition, the sixteenth-century Genevan Reformer John Calvin and the seventeenth-century writer Herman Witsius, one of the preeminent covenant theologians in the history of Reformed thought. Fesko brings to light these theologians' nuanced and balanced understandings of the Mosaic covenant as well as some of the developments in Reformed covenant theology in its first couple of centuries. In chapter 2, D. G. Hart takes up various issues pertaining to the view of the Mosaic law among some significant theologians of old Princeton Seminary. Hart connects the Princeton appreciation for the republication idea with their engagement with the intellectual climate of their day and with their broader Reformed convictions about sin, natural law, and the atonement. Brenton C. Ferry presents a taxonomy of Reformed views of Moses in chapter 3. This essay, which considers theologians primarily of the sixteenth and seventeenth centuries, but also several of more recent times, displays the variety of ways in which Reformed theologians have spoken about the Mosaic covenant, yet also reveals a widespread appreciation among these theologians for a distinctive works principle under Moses.

Part Two consists of six exegetical essays. The first of three Old Testament studies is Bryan D. Estelle's examination of Leviticus 18:5 and Deuteronomy 30:1–14. Estelle first considers these crucial passages in their original Mosaic context and then examines the interpretation of these verses in later biblical revelation, culminating in Paul. He finds that these passages, which Paul places in antithesis, point ultimately to the fact that obedience to the law results in the right to eschatological life, an obedience that Christ alone satisfied. Richard P. Belcher's study of the kingship and Torah Psalms in chapter 5 is the second Old Testament essay. Belcher concludes that these psalms, juxtaposed in significant ways in the Psalter, display the close relationship between the law and the Davidic king, thereby pointing to the fulfilment of the original kingly role of mankind in the garden through the active obedience of Christ. In chapter 6, Byron G. Curtis considers the republication idea in the Old Testament prophetical books through a thorough study of Hosea 6:7. Curtis presents a new interpretation of the reference to "Adam" in this verse that seeks to account for the strengths and weaknesses of past proposals, and he argues that Hosea not only makes reference to a prelapsarian covenant of works with Adam, whose violation is analogized to Israel's violation of the Mosaic covenant, but also to the place-name, a double entendre.

Three New Testament essays follow in the remainder of Part Two. In chapter 7, Guy P. Waters considers Romans 10:5 in context and argues that Paul indeed sets two statements by Moses (from Leviticus 5 and Deuteronomy 30) in contrast to each other. Waters concludes from this passage that though the Mosaic law was promulgated within the context of a gracious covenant, the moral demands of this law set forth the standard of righteousness that the covenant of works required. T. David Gordon follows with a study of Galatians 3:6–14 in chapter 8. Though Paul did not build a comprehensive covenant theology in these verses, Gordon argues that he did make an important contribution to our overall understanding of the biblical covenants by contrasting the Abrahamic and Sinaitic covenants in regard to faith and works and by explaining the new covenant in terms of its similarity to the Abrahamic and dissimilarity to the Sinaitic. The final

New Testament essay is S. M. Baugh's study of Galatians 5:1–6 in chapter 9. Baugh argues that while the Mosaic covenant is an administration of the covenant of grace, these verses teach that the Mosaic law more narrowly considered embodies a works principle, namely, an obligation to personal and perfect obedience. Attaining eschatological righteousness through this works principle and attaining it through faith in Christ the covenant mediator are, he claims, mutually exclusive options in Paul's mind.

Part Three presents two essays on theological topics. In chapter 10, David VanDrunen claims that the natural law proclaims the works principle revealed in Scripture, with both its requirements and sanctions. He argues from this idea that the revelation of the works principle in the Mosaic covenant serves to make Israel a microcosm of the whole human race, displaying in clear terms both the predicament of every human being under the curse of sin and the need for a Savior to satisfy the works principle. Finally, Michael S. Horton reflects upon the republication idea in the light of the doctrine of the active obedience of Christ. Through examination of the common Old Testament declaration that God considers obedience better than sacrifice and of New Testament interpretation of this declaration, Horton sets forth Christ as the Last Adam and True Israel who fulfils God's desire, personal as well as legal, for an image-bearer who responds to his Creator with perfect love and who establishes a people who themselves are being conformed unto true obedience.

PART ONE
HISTORICAL STUDIES

1

———⌇⌇⌇———

CALVIN AND WITSIUS
ON THE MOSAIC COVENANT

J. V. FESKO

hen it comes to the Mosaic covenant, an ocean of ink has been spilled by theologians in their efforts to relate it both to Israel's immediate historical context and to the church's existence in the wake of the advent of Christ. Anthony Burgess (d. 1664), one of the Westminster divines, writes: "I do not find in any point of divinity, learned men so confused and perplexed (being like Abraham's ram, hung in a bush of briars and brambles by the head) as here."[1] Among the Westminster divines there were a number of views represented in the assembly: the Mosaic covenant was a covenant of works, a mixed covenant of works and grace, a subservient covenant to the covenant of grace, or simply the covenant of grace.[2] One can find a similar range of views represented in more recent literature in our own day.[3] In the limited amount of space

---

1. Anthony Burgess, *Vindicae Legis* (London, 1647), 229.
2. Samuel Bolton, *The True Bounds of Christian Freedom* (1645; Edinburgh: Banner of Truth, 2001), 92–94.
3. See, e.g., Mark W. Karlberg, "Reformed Interpretation of the Mosaic Covenant," *Westminster Theological Journal* 43.1 (1981): 1–57; idem, *Covenant Theology in Reformed Perspective* (Eugene, OR: Wipf and Stock, 2000), 17–58; D. Patrick Ramsey, "In Defense of Moses: A Confessional Critique of Kline and Karlberg," *Westminster Theological Journal* 66.2 (2004): 373–400;

here, it is not possible to set forth a complete case for the proper place of the Mosaic covenant. Nevertheless, it is certainly worthwhile to take a comparative historical-theological snapshot of two continental Reformed theologians on this challenging issue.

John Calvin (1509–64) is certainly a theologian who needs no introduction, as he is one who is familiar to most if not all serious students of the sixteenth-century Reformation. While Calvin's views were certainly not prescriptive for the Reformed tradition in his day, they were nevertheless influential both in continental and British Reformed theology. One particular continental Reformed theologian in whom Calvin's influence is found, especially on the nature and role of the Mosaic covenant, is Herman Witsius (1636–1708). Witsius is perhaps best known for his *Economy of the Covenants between God and Man* (1677), as well as his exposition of the Apostles' Creed (1681), though perhaps little else is known about the man. Witsius studied at the universities of Utrecht and Groningen. He served as a pastor for nearly twenty years before he was appointed as a professor of theology at the University of Franecker. He subsequently served as a professor at the University of Utrecht before finishing out his career at the University of Leiden, being forced out of teaching because of poor health before his death in 1708.[4] What makes a comparison of Calvin and Witsius worthwhile is not only that the former influenced the latter on his explanation of the Mosaic covenant, but also for other factors, particularly the later developments in early (ca. 1565–1640) and late orthodoxy (ca. 1640–1700) in the Reformed tradition.

Since the decades of dominance of Barthian theology in the twentieth century not only in international systematic theology but also in historical theology, a new wave of scholarship has reversed the common portrait of the relationship between Calvin and the subsequent Reformed tradition. The typical line of argumentation was that Calvin was a biblical humanist pastor-theologian whose scriptural insights were hijacked by a horde of scholastic academics interested in Aristotle more than the Bible and in presenting the teachings of Scripture in a rationalistic and logical rather than in a biblical manner. Recent scholarship, however, has demonstrated that the historical analysis coming out of the Barthian-influenced school was more interested in vindicating their monocov-

---

Daniel P. Fuller, *Gospel and Law: Contrast or Continuum? The Hermeneutics of Dispensationalism and Covenant Theology* (Grand Rapids: Eerdmans, 1980); Wayne G. Strickland, ed., *Five Views on Law and Gospel* (1993; Grand Rapids: Zondervan, 1996); Ernest F. Kevan, *The Grace of Law* (1976; Morgan: Soli Deo Gloria, 1999).

4. Richard A. Muller, *Post-Reformation Reformed Dogmatics*, vol. 1, *Prolegomena to Theology* (Grand Rapids: Baker, 1987), 49.

enantal understanding of Scripture rather than doing accurate contextualized historical theology.[5]

In a comparative exploration of Calvin and Witsius on the Mosaic covenant, then, one will be able to see the continuity that exists between these two Reformed theologians despite coming from different periods. One will be able to see the influence Calvin yielded upon Witsius's understanding of the Mosaic covenant. At the same time, one will be able to see some differences between the two theologians. The differences do not amount to a distortion of Calvin's theology, never mind the fact that such a notion seems inherently fraught with unchecked assumptions. That is, at no time did any early or late orthodox Reformed theologian understand himself to be a Calvin clone restricted to reproducing Calvin's theology in his own. Rather, the differences lay in the emphasis that Witsius places upon the use and role of typology in his explanation of the Mosaic covenant.

There is a case to be made that, due to the greater attention to biblical theology in the late orthodox period, explanations of the Mosaic covenant were expressed less in the Aristotelian heuristic use of the terms "accidents" and "substance" and more in terms of the *historia salutis*, or redemptive history.[6] The bottom line, at least in terms of the previous Barthian character-

---

5. For analysis and bibliography see Richard A. Muller, *The Unaccommodated Calvin: Studies in the Foundation of a Theological Tradition* (Oxford: Oxford University Press, 2000); idem, *After Calvin: Studies in the Development of a Theological Tradition* (Oxford: Oxford University Press, 2003).

6. First, one should note that by the use of the term "biblical theology" the specific discipline as defined by the historical-critical school is not intended (see Johann P. Gabler, "An Oration of the Proper Distinction between Biblical and Dogmatic Theology and the Specific Origins of Each," in *The Flowering of Old Testament Theology*, ed. Ben C. Ollenburger, Elmer A. Martens, and Gerhard F. Hasel [Winona Lake, IN: Eisenbrauns, 1992], 489–502; Geerhardus Vos, "The Idea of Biblical Theology as a Science and as a Theological Discipline," in *Redemptive History and Biblical Interpretation: The Shorter Writings of Geerhardus Vos*, ed. Richard B. Gaffin Jr. [Phillipsburg, NJ: Presbyterian and Reformed, 1980], 3–24, esp. 15). Rather, as Geerhardus Vos (1862–1949) has defined it, the term is here intended in its broader usage denoting the unfolding of special revelation (*Biblical Theology: Old and New Testaments* [1948; Edinburgh: Banner of Truth, 1996], v). The biblical-theological hermeneutic versus the distinct discipline as it was defined by Gabler has a long pedigree in the history of interpretation and is not bound to the idea of severing biblical from dogmatic, or systematic, theology, but largely to one's commitment to understanding the Scriptures and its teachings in terms of the revelatory whole, both Old and New Testaments. Such a hermeneutic can be found in the church fathers and in the Reformers (see Craig G. Bartholomew and Michael W. Goheen, "Story and Biblical Theology," in *Out of Egypt: Biblical Theology and Biblical Interpretation*, ed. Craig Bartholomew et al. [Grand Rapids: Zondervan, 2004], 153; cf. James Barr, *The Concept of Biblical Theology* [Minneapolis: Fortress, 1999], 351). Second, the use of the term *historia salutis* is not intended to imply that Reformed theologians of the sixteenth through eighteenth centuries employed it, as it is of recent origins (see Herman Ridderbos, *Paul: An Outline of His Theology*, trans. John Richard de Witt [Grand Rapids: Eerdmans, 1975], 14; cf. Richard B. Gaffin, *Resurrection and Redemption: A Study in Paul's Soteriology* [1978; Phillipsburg, NJ: Presbyterian and Reformed, 1987], 14). Rather, it is being used to describe the unfolding of redemptive history, something the Reformers materially acknowledge, though they formally do not use the term.

ization of the relationship between Calvin and the Calvinists, is that Witsius's theology is "more biblical" than Calvin's. It is preferable to say, however, that Calvin and Witsius have similar formulations but with different emphases in the ways in which they express their formulations. Therefore, one should first explore Calvin's understanding of the nature and place of the Mosaic covenant, and then move to the views of Witsius, so that one may compare and contrast the two continental Reformed theologians' views.

Calvin on the Mosaic Covenant

This section will survey Calvin's understanding of the Mosaic covenant by first exploring his understanding of Old Testament (OT) soteriology and then the place and function of the Mosaic covenant.

Soteriology in the OT

In any survey of Calvin's understanding of the law, it is important that one delineate his different uses of the term. In Calvin's *Institutes*, the term "law" can mean the "form of religion handed down by God through Moses" (2.7.1), which means the Mosaic covenant in its entirety as one finds it in the Pentateuch. For Calvin the term "law" can also refer to the moral law, that is, the Decalogue and Christ's summary of it (2.8). Lastly, the term can also refer to various civil, judicial, and ceremonial statutes (4.20.14–16).[7] When one explores Calvin's understanding of the function of the law, he must therefore carefully distinguish whether he has the moral law or the law as the Mosaic covenant in view.

Keeping these definitions in mind, then, we find that, for Calvin, salvation has always been the same in every age, by grace through faith in Christ, even for OT saints. Calvin writes, "The covenant made with all the patriarchs is so much like ours in substance and reality that the two are actually one and the same. Yet they differ in the mode of dispensation" (2.10.2).[8] Here is a programmatic, if not formulaic, construction for Calvin's understanding of soteriology in both the OT and New Testament (NT). Notice that the Abrahamic *foedus* is so much like ours in *substantia et re*, yet he states that the covenant differs only in the *administratio*. Elsewhere Calvin applies the term *spirituale foedus* (2.10.7) to the one single covenant that unites both OT and

---

7. See John Calvin, *Institutes of the Christian Religion*, ed. John T. McNeill, trans. Ford Lewis Battles, 2 vols., Library of Christian Classics 21–22 (Philadelphia: Westminster, 1960), 348 n. 1.

8. "Patrum omnium foedus adeo substantia et re ipsa nihil a nostro differet, ut unum prorsus atque idem sit: administratio tamen variat" (John Calvin, *Opera Selecta*, ed. Peter Barth and Wilhelm Niesel, 5 vols. [Munich, 1926–52]).

NT saints in salvation. What changes, therefore, in the transition from the OT to the NT is not the covenant, but rather the form or administration of the covenant (2.11.13).[9] Here then is what one may describe as Aristotelian language in the use of the distinction between substance and form, which was commonplace in the theology of Calvin's day.[10] One should ask, then, Why does Calvin employ these distinctions of form and substance, and what role do they play in his understanding of the function of the law and more specifically the function of the Mosaic covenant?

Calvin explains that the form of the *spirituale foedus* in the OT was necessarily wrapped in shadows and ceremonies which pointed to Christ, who is the foundation of salvation in every age, because the OT saints were the underage church requiring simple instruction (2.6.2; 2.11.4–5). Calvin states,

> The same church existed among them, but as yet in its childhood. Therefore, keeping them under this tutelage, the Lord gave, not spiritual promises un-adorned and open, but ones foreshadowed, in a measure, by earthly prom-ises. When, therefore, he adopted Abraham, Isaac, Jacob, and their descen-dants into the hope of immortality, he promised them the Land of Canaan as an inheritance. It was not to be the final goal of their hopes, but was to exercise and confirm them, as they contemplated it, in hope of their true in-heritance not yet manifested to them. And that they might not be deceived, a higher promise was given, attesting that the land was not God's supreme benefit. Thus Abraham is not allowed to sit by idly when he receives the promise of the land, but his mind is elevated to the Lord by a greater promise. (2.11.2)[11]

The spiritual promises, or the gospel of Christ, therefore were pres-ent in substance in the initial covenant made with the patriarchs, but the mode of administration was earthly and temporal. The earthly possession, however, was a mirror in which the patriarchs were able to see the future inheritance prepared for them in heaven (2.11.1). Seeing the nature of

9. "Quod externam formam et modum mutavit."

10. See Richard A. Muller, *Dictionary of Latin and Greek Theological Terms: Drawn Princi-pally from Protestant Scholastic Theology* (Grand Rapids: Baker, 1985), q.v. *substantia* and *forma*, 290–91, 123–24.

11. "Eadem inter illos ecclesia: sed cuius aetas adhuc puerilis erat. Sub hac ergo paedagogia illos continuit Dominus, ut spiritualis promissiones non ita nudas et apertas illis daret, sed terrenis quodammodo adumbrates. Abraham ergo, Isaac et Iacob, eorumque posteritatem quum in spem immortalitatis cooparet, terram Chanaan in haereditatem illis promisit: non in qua spes suas ter-minarent, sed cuius aspectu in spem verae illius, quae nondum apparebat, haereditatis se exercer-ent ac confirmarent. Ac ne hallucinari possent, dabatur superior promissio quae terram illam non supremum esse Dei beneficium testaretur. Sic Abraham in accepta terrae promissione torpere non sinitur: sed maiori promissione erigitur illius mens in Dominum."

God's administration of the gospel in the OT, specifically to the patriarchs, one can begin to understand how the Mosaic covenant will function in the *historia salutis*.

The Place and Function of the Mosaic Covenant

Given Calvin's explanation of soteriology in the OT, one has a framework in which to understand the place and function of the Mosaic covenant in his theology. Calvin explains that with the dispensation of the Mosaic covenant there are two separate covenants, the *foedus legale* and *foedus evangelicum*, the ministries of Moses and Christ (2.11.4). There is a sense in which Calvin sees these two covenants in an antithetical relationship to one another, as the law functions within the *foedus legale* only "to enjoin what is right, to forbid what is wicked; to promise a reward to the keepers of righteousness, and threaten transgressors with punishment" (2.11.7).[12] In other words, Calvin is not afraid to say that the Mosaic administration of the law sets forth a covenant governed by a works principle, namely, eternal life through obedience: "We cannot gainsay that the reward of eternal salvation awaits complete obedience to the law, as the Lord has promised" (2.7.3).[13] The problem, however, with this covenant of obedience is, because of man's sinfulness, "righteousness is taught in vain by the commandments until Christ confers it by free imputation and by the Spirit of regeneration" (2.7.2).[14] Calvin, therefore, sees the Mosaic covenant characterized by the promise of eternal life which can be obtained by Israel's obedience, yet because of her sin, Israel is unable to fulfil the requirements of the covenant—only Christ was able to do this.

In this sense, then, the *foedus legale* and *foedus evangelicum* are antithetical, in that they both extend the promise of salvation, the former through obedience and the latter through faith in Christ. This is not to say, though, that the Mosaic covenant as a *foedus legale* is totally absent of grace, mercy, or any reference to the gospel. Recall that Calvin believed that the *spirituale foedus* had a changing form or *administratio* as one crosses over from the OT to the NT. This is especially true as it pertains to the Mosaic covenant for three reasons. First, Calvin clearly states that OT Israel participated in the *spirituale foedus* (2.10.15). Second, because Israel was still the underage church, God dealt with them as children:

12. "Ut praecipiat quae recta sunt, scelera prohibeat, praemium edicat cultoribus iustitae, poenam transgressoribus minetur."
13. "Nec refragari licet quin iustam Legis obedientiam maneat aeternae salutis remunerat, quemadmodum a domino promissa est."
14. "Nampriore quidem significat frustra doceri iustitiam praeceptis, donec eam Christus et gratuita imputatione et spiritu regenerationis conferat."

[Paul] also confesses that they were sons and heirs of God, but because of their youth they had to be under the charge of a tutor. It was fitting that, before the sun of righteousness had arisen, there should be no great and shining revelation, no clear understanding. The Lord, therefore, so meted out the light of his Word to them that they still saw it afar off and darkly. Hence Paul expresses this slenderness of understanding by the word "childhood." It was the Lord's will that this childhood be trained in the elements of this Word and in little external observances, as rules for children's instruction, until Christ should shine forth, through whom the knowledge of believers was to mature. (2.11.5)[15]

Third, given Israel's underage status and the need to deal with them in simple terms, the ceremonies of the law were "accidental properties of the covenant, or additions and appendages, and in common parlance, accessories of it" (2.11.4).[16] Once again we see Calvin explain the relationship between the Abrahamic and Mosaic covenants in terms of form and substance.

Calvin uses the distinction between form and substance to explain that the Mosaic covenant, as to its substance, is part of the *spirituale foedus*, but as to its form, its *administratio* is a *foedus legale*. Calvin states, for example, that God "willed that, for the time during which he gave his covenant to the people of Israel in a veiled form, the grace of future and eternal happiness be signified and figured under earthly benefits, the gravity of spiritual death under physical punishment" (2.11.3). Where Calvin is quite pronounced in his usage of the form-substance distinction regarding the Mosaic covenant is in his commentary on Galatians. Calvin states concerning the nature of gospel in both testaments: "All this leads to the conclusion that the difference between us and the ancient fathers lies not in the substance but in accidents."[17] Calvin can speak of the OT saints partaking of the *spirituale foedus* but also says that "their freedom was not yet revealed, but was hid-

15. "Illos quoque filios et haeredes Dei fuisse fatetur: sed qui propter pueritiam sub paedagogi custodia habeni essent. Conveniebat enim, sole iustitiae nondum exorto, nec tantum esse revelationis fulgorem, nec tantam intelligendi perspicaciam. Sic ergo verbi sui lucem illis Dominus dispensavit, ut eam eminus adhuc et obscure cernerent. Ideo hanc intelligentiae tenuitatem pueritiae vocabulo Paulus notat, quam elementis huius mundi et externis observatiunculis, tanquam regulis puerilis disciplinae, voluit Dominus exerceri, donec effulgeret Christus: per quem fidelis populi cognitionem adolescere oportebat."

16. "Hae vero tametsi foederis duntaxat accidentia erant, vel certe accessiones ac annexa, et (ut vulgus loquitur) accessoria."

17. John Calvin, *Galatians, Ephesians, Philippians, and Colossians*, trans. T. H. L. Parker, ed. David W. Torrance and Thomas F. Torrance, Calvin's New Testament Commentaries II (1965; Grand Rapids: Eerdmans, 1996), 71; *Ioannis Calvini Opera Quae Supersunt Omnia*, ed. G. Baum, E. Cunitz, E. Reuss (Brunswick: Schwetschke, 1892), 50:224: "His omnibus consentaneum est, discrimen inter nos et veteres patres non in substantia esse, sed in accidentibus." *Calvini Opera* hereafter abbreviated as CO.

den under the coverings and the yoke of the law."[18] Where one finds some of Calvin's most crystalized statements on the function and place of the Mosaic covenant is in his sermons on Galatians.

In Calvin's sermons on Galatians one finds the same characteristics as were set forth in the *Institutes* and his commentary on Galatians concerning the nature and function of the Mosaic covenant. Calvin emphasizes that the OT saints were saved by grace, not by works.[19] He also explains that what differentiates the OT from the NT saint is not the promise of the gospel, but "the diversity in the outward government," or the outward administration of the gospel.[20] Calvin explains, "The law reigned and had its full scope as in respect of outward order before the coming of our Lord Jesus Christ."[21] The outward order, of course, was marked by typology that found its telos in Christ: "It is said that the salvation is manifested unto us by the Gospel, yet was it also already before: and although there was a veil in the Temple, and other shadows, yet nevertheless the fathers had always an eye unto Jesus Christ, unto whom we be led at this day."[22] So, Calvin once again delineates between the substance of the OT administration, which was the gospel of Christ, and the form, which was legal in nature.

When Calvin explains to his congregants the nature of the Mosaic covenant, he does not withdraw or modify the conceptual framework that he has established in his theological writings. Calvin explains, for example, that the Mosaic covenant is characterized by a works principle, that is, redemption by obedience, but at the same time because of man's sinfulness it only shows man's inability to merit eternal life by his obedience and therefore drives the sinner to Christ:

> The law then is not transitory in respect of showing us what is good, for it must continue to the world's end. But we must mark Saint Paul's discourse: for he takes the law, as containing the promises and threatenings, and also the ceremonies. Then on the one side there is [this promise,] he that does these things shall live in them, as we have seen heretofore. And on the other side there is this threat, cursed is he that does not fulfil all that is contained

18. Calvin, *Galatians*, 76: "Quia scilicet libertas eorum nondum erat revelata, sed inclusa sub legis involucris et iugo" (CO 50:229).
19. John Calvin, *Sermons on Galatians* (1574; Audubon: Old Paths, 1995), 500; CO 50:569–70.
20. Calvin, *Sermons on Galatians*, 501: "Diversité au regime exterieur" (CO 50:571).
21. Calvin, *Sermons on Galatians*, 448: "La response à cela est que la Loy a bien eu son regne et sa vogue devant la venue de nostre Seigneur Iesus Christ quant à l'ordre exterieur" (CO 50:539).
22. Calvin, *Sermons on Galatians*, 516: "Mais quand il est dit que le salut qui nous est manifesté par l'Evangile estoit desia auparavant, combine qu'il y eust des ombrages, combine qu'il y eust le voile du temple: neantmoins que les Peres ont tousiours regardé à Iesus Christ, au quell nous sommes auiourd'huy conduits" (CO 50:580).

herein. Now the law (as we see) promises salvation to none but such as live purely and incorruptly: but all of us come short of that, and therefore the promise of the law is to no purpose.[23]

Here Calvin emphasizes a works principle in the Mosaic covenant, but he is clear regarding the role of this principle—it drives the sinner to Christ by showing him his inability to render perfect obedience to the law.[24]

Summary

Calvin's understanding of the place and function of the Mosaic covenant can be summarized in the following manner: (1) salvation has always been by grace through faith in Christ; (2) all of God's people, whether in the OT or NT, participate in the same *spirituale foedus* which was begun with the patriarchs; (3) in the OT the *spirituale foedus* had a different outward administration than in the NT, which Calvin uses the form-substance distinction to explain; (4) the outward OT administration of the *spirituale foedus* is marked by shadows and types of Christ; (5) the Mosaic administration of the law is specifically a *foedus legale* in contrast to the *foedus evangelicum*, the respective ministries of Moses and Christ; and (6) the *foedus legale* is based upon a works principle but no one is able to fulfil its obligations except Christ. One finds these characteristics in Calvin's *Institutes* and in his commentary and sermons on Galatians. Keeping these summary points in mind, the investigation can now proceed to examine Witsius's understanding of the Mosaic covenant and then compare and contrast the views of the two continental theologians.

Witsius on the Mosaic Covenant

In the theology of Witsius, there are many of the same themes and emphases that exist in Calvin's theology. These parallels exist, of course, given that both Calvin and Witsius are continental Reformed theologians. While such a broad comparison is accurate, the more that one delves into the details, he finds nuances or emphases that exist in the formulations of Witsius but to a lesser degree in Calvin. These differences can be attributed to

---

23. Calvin, *Sermons on Galatians*, p. 445: "La Loy donc entant qu'elle nous monstre ce qui est bon, n'a pas esté temporelle: car elle doit durer iusques à la fin du monde. Mais il nous faut noter la dispute de sainct Paul: car il prend la Loy d'autant qu'elle contient les promesses et les menaces, et puis les ceremonies. Il y a donc d'un costé, Qui fera as choses, il vivra en icelles: comme desia nous avons veu. Il y a la menance: Maudit sera celuy qui n'accomplira tout ce qui est ici contenu. Or la Loy (comme nous voyons) ne promet salut sinon à ceux qui aurons vescu purement et en toute integrité: mous defaillons tous, la promesse donc de la Loy est inutile" (CO 50:538).

24. See Calvin, *Sermons on Galatians*, 459–60; CO 50:546.

the progression and development of Reformed theology—the move from early formulation of the Reformation (1509–65) to that of codification and defense of those formulations in the period of high orthodoxy (ca. 1640–1700). Witsius uses Calvin's formulations in his own understanding of the Mosaic covenant, but at the same time employs developments that occurred well after Calvin's death. The similarity that exists between the two theologians is the insistence that salvation is and always has been by grace through faith in Christ. Like Calvin, Witsius maintains that since the fall God's redemptive intentions have always been by grace.[25] Where the differences lie, however, are in Witsius' employment of the theological construct of the covenant of works and the greater use of typology in explaining the nature of the Mosaic covenant.

The Refinement of Covenant Theology

In the days following Calvin, Reformed theologians continued to refine the categories under which they placed various scriptural data. Calvin, for example, placed God's gracious postfall dealings with man reaching back to the garden and extending to the eschaton under the theological rubric of a *spirituale foedus*, or spiritual covenant. Yet around the same time theologians such as Zacharias Ursinus (1534–83) employed a twofold bifurcation to describe the pre- and postfall relationship between God and his people. In Ursinus's Larger Catechism (1561–62) he writes:

> The law contains the natural covenant, established by God with humanity in creation, that is, it is known by humanity by nature, it requires our perfect obedience to God, and it promises eternal life to those who keep it and threatens eternal punishment to those who do not. The gospel, however, contains the covenant of grace, that is, although it exists, it is not known at all by nature; it shows us the fulfilment in Christ of the righteousness that the law requires and the restoration in us of that righteousness by Christ's Spirit; and it promises eternal life freely because of Christ to those who believe him.[26]

Here the prefall relationship between God and man is placed under the theological rubric of a *natural covenant* and the postfall under the *covenant of grace*. While the precise date and source of the term "covenant of works"

25. Herman Witsius, *The Economy of the Covenants between God and Man: Comprehending a Complete Body of Divinity*, trans. William Crookshank, 2 vols. (1822; Phillipsburg, NJ: Presbyterian and Reformed, 1990), 4.1–2; 2:108–40. In all subsequent references, the first set of numbers indicates book, chapter, and paragraph numbers, the second set the page numbers to this English translation.

26. Zacharias Ursinus, "The Larger Catechism," q. 36, in Lyle D. Bierma et al., eds., *An Introduction to the Heidelberg Catechism* (Grand Rapids: Baker, 2005), 168–69.

are debated, nevertheless by the late sixteenth century theologians were using the covenants of works and grace to describe the pre- and postfall relationship between God and man.[27] It is the development of this covenantal framework, a development of nomenclature rather than theological substance, that one finds in Witsius's explanation of the Mosaic covenant.

Witsius on the Relationship between the Two Covenants

Witsius's understanding of the relationship between the covenant of works and grace is substantively similar to that of Ursinus.[28] At the same time, however, Witsius also explains that the covenant of grace may be further subdivided into two distinct economies, which he defines as the old and new testaments.[29] The two economies are similar in some respects, but in others they are quite different. In language quite similar to that of Calvin, Witsius explains that the substance of the covenant of grace in both the old and new economies is the same. What differs, however, is the *circumstantials* of each economy:

> It is a matter of the greatest moment, that we learn distinctly to consider the covenant of grace, either as it is in its *substance* or essence, as they call it, or as it is in divers ways proposed by God, with respect to *circumstantials*, under different economies. If we view *the substance* of the covenant, it is but only *one*, nor is it possible it should be otherwise.[30]

27. One of the earliest uses of the terms "covenants of works and grace" comes from Amandus Polanus (1561–1610): "The eternal covenant is a covenant in which God promises men eternal life. And that is two fold, the covenant of works and the covenant of grace. The covenant of works is a bargain of God made with men concerning eternal life, to which is both a condition of perfect obedience adjoined, to be performed by man, and also a threatening of eternal death if he shall not perform perfect obedience (Gen. 2:17)." It is also of interest to note that Polanus believed that the covenant of works was repeated in the Mosaic covenant (*The Substance of Christian Religion Soundly Set Forth in Two Books* [London, 1595], 88). For the relevant literature regarding Ursinus and the development of the term "covenant of works" see Robert Letham, "The *Foedus Operum*: Some Factors Accounting for Its Development," *Sixteenth Century Journal* 14 (1983): 457–67; Peter A. Lillback, "Ursinus' Development of the Covenant of Creation: A Debt to Melanchthon or Calvin?" *Westminster Theological Journal* 43 (1981): 247; cf. Dirk Visser, "The Covenant in Zacharias Ursinus," *Sixteenth Century Journal* 18 (1987): 531–44.

28. Witsius, *Economy*, 3.1.7; 1:284. For a full exposition of Witsius's understanding of the covenant of works, see Richard A. Muller, *After Calvin: Studies in the Development of a Theological Tradition* (Oxford: Oxford University Press, 2003), 175–89; idem, "The Covenant of Works and the Stability of Divine Law in the Seventeenth-Century Reformed Orthodoxy," *Calvin Theological Journal* 22 (1994): 75–101.

29. Herman Witsius, *Sacred Dissertations on the Lord's Prayer*, trans. William Pringle (1839; Phillipsburg, NJ: P&R, 1990), diss. 9, 212: "Regnum Gratiae rursus considerari potest, vel uti olim fuit sub Oeconomia Testamenti Veteris; vel uti nunc est sub Testamento Novo" (Herman Witsius, *Exercitationes Sacrae in Symbolum quod Apostolorum Dicitur et in Orationem Dominicam* [Basel, 1739], 9.5).

30. Witsius, *Economy*, 3.2.1; 1:291: "Maximi res momenti est, ut Foedus Gratiae, vel ut est in *substantia* & essential, quam voccant, sua vel ut quoad *circumstantialia*, sub diversis Oeconomiis,

Keeping this distinction between the substance and circumstances in mind, one finds Witsius emphasizing the legal nature of the Mosaic covenant as he explains its role in redemptive history.

While the covenant of grace is of the same substance throughout both the old and new economies, Witsius is nevertheless prepared to say that the Mosaic covenant is legal in nature because the Mosaic covenant was primarily an administration of the law with three aspects: the Decalogue was given to Israel, and as to its substance was one and the same with the law of nature; Israel received the law as the church, and as such, they received the ceremonial law, which pointed to the person and work of Christ; and Israel received the law as a peculiar people, as a theocracy, and therefore they received the political laws.[31] In this threefold understanding of the law one finds the historic division of the law: the moral, ceremonial, and civil. It is important to note, however, that the telic goal of the threefold law finds its fulfilment in the person and work of Christ. In other words, the law, especially the ceremonial and civil, finds its significance in typology. It is typology that plays a major part in Witsius's understanding of the Mosaic covenant.

The Mosaic Covenant and Typology

Recall that Witsius believes that the covenant of grace is the same in substance in both the old and new economies. At the same time, however, Witsius can also argue that the Mosaic covenant is a repetition of the covenant of works.[32] This is not to say that Witsius believed that the covenant of works was republished so that Israel might attain their salvation by their obedience to the law.[33] On the contrary, Witsius believed that the Mosaic covenant was connected to both the *ordo* and *historia salutis* in different ways. Witsius argued along the same lines as Calvin that the Mosaic covenant vis-à-vis the *ordo salutis* functioned in such a way as to reveal sin and drive Israel to Christ: "And so their being thus brought to a remembrance of the covenant of works tended to promote the covenant of grace."[34] In other words, the republication of the covenant of works served the pedagogical function of the law—that which drives the sinner

---

diversimode a Deo proponitur. Si ipsam Foederis *substantiam* spectemus non nisi unum illud unicumque est, neque vero, ut aliud sit, fieri ullo modo potest" (Herman Witsius, *De Oeconomia Foederum Dei cum Hominibus. Libri Quatuor* [Basel, 1739]).

31. Witsius, *Economy*, 4.4.1–2; 2:162–63.

32. Ibid., 4.4.48; 2:183.

33. Ibid., 4.4.49; 2:183.

34. Ibid., 4.4.49; 2:183–84: "Atque ita ea ipsa commemoratio foederis operum inserviit promotioni foederis gratiae."

to Christ. To support his understanding of this function of the Mosaic covenant as the republished covenant of works, Witsius sought the support and argumentation of Calvin from his commentary on Romans 10:4.[35] Citing Calvin, Witsius argued that it was only "crass Israelites" who misunderstood the purpose of the Sinai covenant, thinking that they could secure their salvation by their obedience rather than through the work of Christ.[36]

The Mosaic covenant vis-à-vis the *historia salutis*, on the other hand, had a different aim. Witsius argued that the Mosaic covenant was a national covenant between God and Israel. The Mosaic covenant was an agreement whereby Israel promised to God a sincere obedience to all of the commands of the covenant, especially the Decalogue, and God in return would bless Israel with reward, both temporal and eternal.[37] Given that Witsius argued that there were eternal rewards annexed to the Mosaic covenant, we see that, like Calvin before him, Witsius believed that God set forth a legal covenant before the nation of Israel, one by which they could earn their salvation through their obedience. Given man's sinfulness, however, the Mosaic covenant as the republished covenant of works only revealed Israel's sinfulness. At the same time the Mosaic covenant had temporal rewards annexed, namely, the hope of securing Israel's presence in the Promised Land through their obedience.

In terms of Witsius's understanding of typology, this means that he understood Israel's existence in the Promised Land as harkening back to Adam's probation in the garden, but also looking forward to the person and work of Christ, the Last Adam. OT people, places, and events such as the land of Canaan, the exodus from Egypt, the Red Sea crossing, the manna from heaven, water from the rock, the fall of Jericho, the conquest of Canaan, the exile and exodus from Babylon all pointed to greater NT people, events, and places, especially to the person and work of Christ:

> But these very things certainly cease not, according to the sentiments of very learned men, to be all of them types of the greatest things to the Christian church. The city of Jerusalem itself, the very temple with its whole pomp of ceremonies, though no longer in being, any more than Adam and the deluge, yet ought also to be considered by us Christians as types of the heavenly city

---

35. Cf. John Calvin, *Romans and Thessalonians*, trans. Ross Mackenzie, ed. David Torrance and T. F. Torrance, Calvin's New Testament Commentaries (Grand Rapids: Eerdmans, 1960), 221–22; CO 49:196.

36. Witsius, *Economy*, 4.4.52; 2:184–85: "Crassos Israëlitas mentem Dei perperam intellexisse, foedere Dei turpiter abusos esse."

37. Ibid., 4.4.54; 2:186.

and temple not made with hands. In a word, the whole of the Mosaic law, though abrogated as to any obligation of observance, ceases not to exhibit to us, for our instruction, a type of spiritual things.[38]

Given this typological thrust of the Mosaic covenant, Witsius is prepared to say that the Sinai covenant is therefore neither exclusively of the covenant of works nor of grace. Rather, it is a national covenant of "sincere piety" that presupposes both covenants.[39] This covenant of sincere piety in terms of the land inheritance did not require perfect obedience, but sincere obedience, which for the godly Israelite was the fruit of his faith.[40] The purpose of this national covenant was not so that Israel would earn the land through their obedience, but rather so that as a nation they would foreshadow the person and work of Christ.

Summary

The Mosaic covenant is unique in redemptive history, as it combines elements of the covenants of both works and grace. The republication of the covenant of works drives the sinner to Christ in its connection with the *ordo salutis,* and in terms of the *historia salutis* it is a typological sketch that has Israel foreshadowing the person and work of Christ. With this understanding, Witsius calls the Decalogue an "instrument of the covenant." Witsius writes:

As an *instrument of the covenant* they point out the way to eternal salvation; or contain the condition of enjoying that salvation: and that both under the covenant of grace and works. But with this difference; that under the covenant of works, this condition is required to be performed by man himself; under the covenant of grace it is proposed, as already performed, or to be performed by a mediator.[41]

38. Ibid., 3.3.4–5; 1:307–8: "At eadem omnia, certe ex Doctissimorum Virorum hypothesibus, non desinunt Ecclesiae Christianae rerum maximarum typi esse. Ipsa civitas Hierosolymitana, ipsum templum cum omni cerimoniarum choragio, licet in rerum natura amplius non exstent, aeque ac Adamus ac Diluvium, a nobis tamen Christianis quoque uti typi civitatis coelestis, & templi sine manibus facti, considerari debent. Tota denique Lex Mosaica, quamvis quoad observationis obligationem abrogate sit, non desinit quoad doctrinam nobis exhibere typum rerum spiritualium."
39. Ibid., 4.4.54; 2:186: "foedus sincerae pietatis."
40. Ibid., 4.4.45–46; 2:182.
41. Ibid., 4.4.57; 2:187: "Qua *instrumentum foederis* viam monstrant ad aeternam salutem; sive continent conditionem potiundae beatitudinis. Idque tam sub foedere gratiae, quam sub foedere operum. Verum hoc discrimine: quod sub foedere operum exigatur haec conditio praestanda ab ipso homine: sub foedere gratiae proponatur, ut praestanda vel praestita per Mediatorem."

Given these data, we can move forward and summarize the similarities and differences that exist between Witsius's and Calvin's understanding of the Mosaic covenant.

Calvin and Witsius Compared

Thus far the investigation has explored Calvin's and Witsius's understanding of the Mosaic covenant and has revealed some parallels in their understandings, particularly in the areas of soteriology in the OT and NT, the employment of the substance-accident distinction, and the legal nature of the Mosaic covenant, that is, it embodies a works principle. The distinct differences between Calvin and Witsius are primarily in their nomenclature and the emphasis given to typology. The different emphases seem to emerge in terms of Calvin's and Witsius's respective understandings of the works principle.

For Calvin, the works principle is primarily aimed at the individual and the *ordo salutis*. The promise of eternal life for perfect obedience offered by the law is merely hypothetical.[42] In other words, it seems a fair conclusion to say that Israel's possession of the land was by grace through faith, the same manner by which they obtained eternal life. For Witsius, however, while the Mosaic covenant carries the same function that Calvin sees in terms of the pedagogical use of the law, at the same time there is also an added dimension brought about by typology. It is for this reason that Witsius calls the Mosaic covenant a *national* covenant, one that requires sincere, not perfect, obedience. In contrast to Calvin, Witsius therefore relates the Mosaic covenant to both the *ordo* and *historia salutis*. Calvin's use of typology sees the Promised Land merely as a foreshadow of heaven, whereas Witsius sees the Promised Land both in terms of the Promised Land and also in terms of the foreshadow of Christ's obedience, that which secures eternal life. It is particularly this difference in the use of typology between the two theologians that is of interest and deserves attention.

First, as observed above, with the march of time the Reformed tradition saw the refinement of its covenant theology, particularly in the development of the terms of the covenants of works and grace. Despite the attempts of those who see a substantive difference between Reformation and post-Reformation theology on this point, there is no difference.[43] This is a difference in nomenclature, not theological substance.

42. See, e.g., John Calvin, *Calvin's Commentaries on the Four Last Books of Moses*, Calvin Translation Society 3 (1854; Grand Rapids: Baker, n.d.), 202–5; CO 25:7.
43. See, e.g., Muller, *After Calvin*, 63–104, and relevant bibliography refuting the Calvin vs. the Calvinists thesis. Muller explains that Calvin virtually identified natural law with Mosaic law and

Second, concerning typology, there are some differences between Calvin and Witsius, though, again, this difference is not substantive but instead one of emphasis. It is without question that there is a greater use and employment of typology in the theology of Witsius. In fact, Witsius devotes an entire chapter to the subject of OT types, something that is unparalleled in Calvin.[44] Moreover, one sees Witsius's greater emphasis upon the *historia salutis* in the title of his work, "The Economy of the Covenants between God and Man." This is not to say, however, that Calvin did not use and employ typology in his explanation of his understanding of the Mosaic covenant. In fact, Witsius saw his own understanding and explication of the nature and place of typology as grounded in the theology of Calvin. Witsius writes:

> According to us and Paul, the Old Testament denotes the testament [or covenant] of grace, under that dispensation, which subsisted before the coming of Christ in the flesh, and was proposed formerly to the fathers under the veil of certain types, pointing out some imperfections of that state, and consequently that they were to be abolished in their appointed time; or as Calvin has very well expressed it (*Institutes* 2.11.4): "the Old Testament was a doctrine involved in a shadowy and ineffectual observation of ceremonies, and was therefore temporary, because a thing in suspense, till established on a firm and substantial bottom."[45]

Here in this statement we see that both Calvin and Witsius recognize the role and place of typology in explaining the function of the Mosaic covenant. It is fair to say, however, that Witsius places greater emphasis upon typology, at least in terms of the amount of space he gives the subject, than does Calvin.

It seems that both Calvin and Witsius are comfortable using the Aristotelian substance-accident distinction to explain the relationship of the

---

that he also recognized that the Mosaic law was covenantally administered. Given these two points, though Calvin did not speak of the creation in terms of a *foedus naturale* or a *foedus operum*, he certainly assumed that Adam's state in the garden was governed by law (see Muller, *After Calvin*, 182; cf. Calvin, *Institutes*, 2.8.1; 4.20.16; idem, *Commentary on Genesis*, Calvin Translation Society [Grand Rapids: Baker, n.d.], Gen. 2:16, 125–26; Susan E. Schreiner, *The Theater of His Glory: Nature and the Natural Order in the Thought of John Calvin* [1991; Grand Rapids: Baker, 1995], 22–28, 77–79, 87–90).

44. Witsius, *Economy*, 4.6; 2:188–230.

45. Ibid., 3.3.2; 1:307: "Sed Vetus Testamentum nobis, & Paulo, notat Testamentum Gratiae sub illa dispensatione, quae ante Christi in carnem adventum obtinuit, quaeque sub typorum quorundam, imperfectionem aliquam illius status connotantium, & consequenter suo tempore abolendorum, involucris, Patribus quondam proponebatur, vel, uti *Calvinus* noster id optime expresiit. *Instit. Lib.* II Cap. 11 Sect. IV. *Vetus Testamentum fuit, quod umbratili et inefficaci ceremoniarum observatione involutum tradebatur: ideoque temporarium fuit, quia in suspenso erat, donec firma et substantiali confirmatione subniteretur.*"

Mosaic covenant to the rest of God's redemptive purposes, whether in the *spirituale foedus* for Calvin or the covenant of grace for Witsius. When it comes, however, to explaining the function of the Mosaic covenant, Witsius seems to place greater emphasis upon the role of the Mosaic covenant vis-à-vis the *historia salutis*, especially as it relates to the work of Christ. Calvin, on the other hand, has a greater interest in the function of the Mosaic covenant vis-à-vis the *ordo salutis*. What accounts for this greater emphasis?

There are no airtight solutions to the question of why Witsius places a greater emphasis upon typology in his explication of the Mosaic covenant, but there are some general indicators that surrender some clues. First, Richard Muller notes that there were different exegetical tendencies during the Reformation. He explains that Calvin had a tendency to deemphasize christological readings of the OT, whereas by contrast, other Reformers such as Peter Martyr Vermigli (1499–1562) employed a more typological approach to the OT, which was carried forward by post-Reformation exegetes such as Johannes Cocceius (1603–69). Muller notes that exegetes such as Cocceius employed a highly typological and prophetic reading of the OT.[46] It is especially the theology of Cocceius that is of interest for this study.

Cocceius was highly influential during the period of high orthodoxy, and at times his influence is noticeable upon Witsius's thought.[47] For example, in Witsius's chapter dedicated to typology he explains the typological connection between the goats of expiation (Lev. 16) and the sacrifice of Christ. In the points of similarity between type and antitype, Witsius acknowledges that he learned of these connections from both Francis Turretin (1623–87) and Cocceius. Witsius quotes Cocceius's commentary on Hebrews at length to explain how the protoevangelium says that Christ was to be delivered into the hands of the devil (Gen. 3:15), and that the slaying of the first sacrificial goat was a type of Christ's death, whereas the sending of the second goat into the wilderness was a type of handing Christ over to the devil. Witsius cites Cocceius to prove that the two goats are types of "the twofold delivering up of Christ."[48] Given Cocceius's influence, though Turretin also influenced Witsius on these points, one may say that Witsius had a greater interest in typology, which impacted his theological understanding of the

46. Richard A. Muller, *Post-Reformation Reformed Dogmatics*, vol. 2, *Holy Scripture: The Cognitive Foundation of Theology* (Grand Rapids: Baker, 2003), 449, 470–71.
47. See, e.g., Frederic W. Farrar, *History of Interpretation* (1961; Grand Rapids: Baker, 1979), 385.
48. Witsius, *Economy*, 4.6.73; 2:228–29: "Habemus itaque figuram duplicis traditionis, qua Christus traditus est."

nature, role, and place of the Mosaic covenant.[49] In other words, it is fair to say that Witsius used a redemptive-historical hermeneutic, whereas Calvin used a hermeneutic that placed more emphasis upon grammatical-historical interpretation. Despite these differences, if one may borrow some of Calvin and Witsius's terminology, there are no substantive differences between the two theologians' understanding of the Mosaic covenant, rather only different accidental emphases.

Conclusion

In this comparative analysis of Calvin and Witsius there are great similarities between the two continental Reformed theologians, both of whom agreed that salvation has always been by grace through faith in Christ. They both acknowledge that God made a covenant with his people, and this covenant was marked by grace and not a works principle. The Mosaic covenant occupies a unique place for both theologians. Both agree that the Mosaic covenant brings forward legal demands and truly offers eternal life, but because of man's sinfulness the legal demands drive the sinner to Christ. The manner in which Calvin and Witsius express the legal demands of the Mosaic covenant is the same; however, the latter gives greater attention and emphasis to typology than does the former. These conclusions, however, are in no way unique, even as they are variously expressed by Calvin and Witsius.

In Reformed confessions such as the Westminster Confession of Faith (1646), one finds these same substantive points in the explication of the func-

49. It should be noted that Cocceius and another scholastic theologian of the period, Gisbert Voetius (1589–1676), were engaged in a significant debate that has been often characterized as the biblical-theological Cocceian school against the systematic-theological Voetian school. According to some, the former was more interested in biblical categories whereas the latter in speculative and arcane scholastic theology (see J. I. Packer, "Introduction," § 5, in Witsius, *Economy*, vol. 1; Farrar, *History*, 385; Charles McCoy, "Johannes Cocceius: Federal Theologian," *Scottish Journal of Theology* 16 [1963]: 352–70). Two things should be noted regarding this debate. First, it has been demonstrated that Cocceius was a scholastic theologian (see Willem van Asselt, "Cocceius Anti-Scholasticus?" in *Reformation and Scholasticism: An Ecumenical Enterprise*, ed. Willem van Asselt and Eef Dekker [Grand Rapids: Baker, 2001], 227–52; cf. idem, *The Federal Theology of Johannes Cocceius (1603–69)*, trans. Raymond A. Blacketer [Leiden: Brill, 2001], 139–92). Second, there were significant doctrinal issues that divided Cocceius and Voetius and their respective followers, such as Cocceius's at times fanciful interpretation of Scripture, his rejection of the abiding nature of the fourth commandment, his peculiar understanding of the abrogations of the covenants, and that many of his followers embraced a Cartesian epistemology (see Farrar, *History*, 385, nn. 1, 8; Willem van Asselt, "The Doctrine of the Abrogations in the Federal Theology of Johannes Cocceius (1603–69)," *Calvin Theological Journal* 29 [1994]: 101–16; idem, *Federal Theology*, 81–94; Ernst Bizer, "Reformed Orthodoxy of Cartesianism," *Journal for Theology and Church* 2 [1965]: 20–82). The debate, therefore, cannot be reduced to biblical versus systematic theology, but revolved around these many issues. Those involved on both sides employed the scholastic method as well as both biblical and systematic theology in their theological formulations.

tion and place of the Mosaic covenant. The divines, for example, employ the covenants of works and grace to define man's pre- and postfall relationship to God (7.2).[50] The covenant of grace, however, "was differently administered in the time of the law, and in the time of the gospel" (7.5). "Under the law," the divines explain, the covenant "was administered by promises, prophecies, sacrifices, circumcision, the paschal lamb, and other types and ordinances delivered to the people of the Jews, all foresignifying Christ to come" (7.5). So here, as in Calvin and Witsius, there is an emphasis upon typology, as well as an implicit biblical-theological hermeneutic concerning the interpretation of and relationship between the OT and NT. At the same time, however, the divines employ the Aristotelian substance-accident distinction. Under the gospel, when Christ, the substance of the OT, was exhibited, it was done with greater fullness, simplicity, and outward glory. The divines write: "There are not therefore two covenants of grace, differing in substance, but one and the same, under various dispensations" (7.6).

One also finds the same legal characterization of the Mosaic covenant even in terms of the republication of the covenant of works, with the Westminster Confession bearing similarities to both Calvin and Witsius.[51] The divines write that "God gave to Adam a law, as a covenant of works" (19.1) and that "this law, after his fall, continued to be a perfect rule of righteousness, and, as such, was delivered by God upon Mount Sinai" (19.2). While space does not permit a full-blown exposition of these points, it is nevertheless useful to see that Calvin's and even Witsius's formulations were certainly in the mainstream of Reformation and post-Reformation thought. So, then, whether in Calvin's more grammatical-historical or Witsius's more redemptive-historical hermeneutic, one finds that both were making essentially the same point with different emphases: the Mosaic covenant is unique in that it is legal in nature, demonstrating vis-à-vis the *ordo salutis* man's inability to fulfil the demands of the law, which drives man to Christ, and in terms of the *historia salutis*, painting a typological portrait of Christ's person and work.

50. *Westminster Confession of Faith* (1646; Glasgow: Presbyterian Publications, 1995).
51. Contra Ramsey, "In Defense of Moses," 394–96.

2

---–〜〜–---

PRINCETON AND THE LAW
Enlightened and Reformed

D. G. HART

The theologians at Princeton Seminary between 1812 and 1929 were a confident lot. In their polemics with American and European theologians, they employed arguments that often revealed a measure of amusement over the follies of erroneous systems of thought. The Princeton sense of humor owed not simply to the difficulties of theologians who attempted to square incompatible ideas, whether philosophical or theological, but also to the relative ease Princetonians had in maintaining and defending Reformed orthodoxy. For instance, Charles Hodge asserted in 1870 that Princeton's theological journal of record had never expressed "an original idea." For Hodge this was a virtue because it meant that the phrase "Princeton Theology" was without "distinctive meaning." Princeton simply repeated the truths American Presbyterians had received from the Reformed creeds and theologians of the sixteenth and seventeenth centuries. In 1912, at the centennial celebration of Princeton Seminary's founding, Francis Landey Patton gave further testimony to the school's confident conventionality. Princeton, he said, "had no oddities of manner, no shibboleths, no pet phrases, no theological labels, no trademark. She simply taught the old Calvinistic theology without modification. . . . There has been a New Haven Theology and an Andover Theology; but there never was a distinctly Princeton Theology." "Princeton's boast," he concluded, "if she have reason to boast at all, is her unswerving fidelity to the theology of the Reformation."[1]

Within the last twenty-five years, studies of the Princeton Theology have shown that Princeton's self-confidence may have involved a measure of self-deceit, and that the seminary's confidence was also the reason for its blindness to intellectual unresolved tensions in its theological system. Many historians and theologians have determined that Hodge and company's use of Enlightenment philosophy and the tradition of natural law that accompanied appeals to human reason was out of step with Princeton's courageous and usually thoughtful defense of Reformed orthodoxy. On the one hand, the seminary's professors worked within the milieu of Enlightenment moral philosophy and apparently endorsed ideas about human capacities for virtue that were at odds with Calvinist teaching on the deep-rooted nature of human sinfulness. On the other hand, in their exegesis of Scripture and noble defense of Reformed views of sin, guilt, imputation, and the atonement, the Princeton divines stood courageously and almost alone for an account of salvation that ran directly counter to the optimism and innocence of the new nation's cultural ideals.

This interpretation of old Princeton as a curious mélange of modern philosophy and premodern theology looks less plausible when considered in the context of Reformed orthodoxy's teaching about man's moral duties and the penalties that follow from failure to keep the law. Instead of being at odds with Calvinist teaching, Princeton's appeal to the Enlightenment, especially its adaptation of Scottish moral philosophy, was actually consistent with older Reformed appeals to natural law and civic or external virtue. What makes Princeton's mix of the Enlightenment and Reformed teaching particularly plausible is the way Reformed federal theology interpreted the Decalogue and the Mosaic covenant as both a republication of a works principle originally articulated in the covenant of works and a reminder of man's need for a redeemer who would fulfil the law's demands and remove its curse through a vicarious sacrifice. Instead of contradicting Calvinism, Princeton's moral philosophy may have actually fit quite comfortably with the contours of Reformed federal theology and its seemingly paradoxical pairing of strict justice and merit on the one side with divine mercy and mediation on the other. In fact, when understood from the perspective of

---

1. *The Princeton Theology, 1812–1921: Scripture, Science, and Theological Method from Archibald Alexander to Benjamin Breckinridge Warfield*, ed. Mark A. Noll (Grand Rapids: Baker, 1983), 38–39.

the Reformed tradition's reliance upon natural law and man's knowledge of the good even after the fall, Princeton's Calvinism may look even less inconsistent than it did to some of Hodge's contemporaries.

Of course, this reading of old Princeton stands in pronounced contrast to the consensus that has emerged among both religious historians and Reformed theologians in North America. To take one example, Mark A. Noll has been the most persistent and perceptive interpreter of Princeton's distinct brand of Calvinism and its intellectual context. At the beginning of his investigation of old Princeton, Noll used an anthology of various writings by Archibald Alexander, Charles Hodge, and Benjamin B. Warfield to sketch the contours of Princeton's mix of Reformed orthodoxy and Enlightenment philosophy. The compound of this curious mixture was in Noll's early estimate far from stable. While giving the Princetonians high marks for their allegiance to strict Calvinism, Noll detected that their high view of reason and epistemological objectivity may have been a fatal flaw in their attempt to defend and maintain Calvinism. Critics of Princeton, Noll explained, "acknowledge the continuing value of the Princeton Theology, especially its biblical Calvinism and warm piety," but they "demur at the Princeton convictions concerning the natural apologetical powers of even Christians."[2]

Noll followed up with a study of the College of New Jersey that explored the intellectual matrix that guided the Presbyterians who founded Princeton Seminary across town from the college. In the teaching of John Witherspoon, Noll detected not simply an Enlightenment epistemology but also a new system of ethics that compromised important features of Calvinism. "Witherspoon set aside the Augustinian distrust of human nature," according to Noll.

> In practice, [Witherspoon] denied that original sin harmed the ability to understand and cultivate natural virtue; he regarded the achievements of science as triumphs of empirical inquiry more than as insights into the effulgence of God's glory; and he pictured God more as the originator of material and moral order than as the constantly active creator of the world.[3]

Noll concludes that a study of the Christian Enlightenment propounded by the likes of Witherspoon and his successor at the College of New Jersey, Samuel Stanhope Smith, raises fundamental questions about whether

---

2. Ibid., 42.
3. Mark A. Noll, *Princeton and the Republic, 1768–1822: The Search for a Christian Enlightenment in the Era of Samuel Stanhope Smith* (Princeton: Princeton University Press, 1989), 43.

"the science of the Enlightenment, with its large claims for human autonomy of perception and action, could ever rest comfortably with Reformed Protestantism."[4]

Most recently, in *America's God: From Jonathan Edwards to Abraham Lincoln* (2002), Noll expanded what had been an institutional portrait of Princeton to the broad landscape of American Protestantism in the first half of the nineteenth century. The effort to harmonize historic Christianity with revolutionary American politics resulted in a peculiar national theology that departed significantly from earlier versions of Protestant orthodoxy. The four principal convictions of this American theology were: (1) American Protestants granted much more agency to the human will in the reception of grace than did earlier theologians; (2) they affirmed the infallibility of Scripture but also insisted that "personally appropriated understanding" of the Bible, as opposed to tradition, was "the only reliable means of interpretation"; (3) American theologians continued to affirm providence but were more confident of their abilities to "know and adapt" to the ways of God than were earlier Protestants; and (4) these Protestants regarded the church as "constructed by those who constituted it rather than as an inheritance from saints of former generations."[5]

When Noll turned to Charles Hodge, who made a cameo appearance in *America's God*, he detected exactly the defects that afflicted Protestant theologians of the era. In defense of Reformed teaching on the authority of the Bible, the imputation of Adam's sin, and limited atonement, Hodge invariably resorted to "uncritical Baconianism" and "the deliverances of consciousness."[6] The result of this Americanization of Protestantism, in which the Princetonians participated, according to Noll, was to damage the Christian faith. "If in a great surge of evangelization and moral reform, American Protestants almost converted the nation, so too did the nation mold the Christian gospel in the contours of its own shape."[7]

The Princeton theologians' teaching on the law, then, is a case in point of the failure of American theology that Noll describes, or so it would seem. What follows is an all too brief survey of the writings of Archibald Alexander and Charles Hodge on the law and the related topics of the covenant of works, the covenant of grace, and the atonement. The Princetonians did argue exactly in the manner that Noll finds; they freely invoked Enlighten-

---

4. Ibid., 295.
5. Mark A. Noll, *America's God: From Jonathan Edwards to Abraham Lincoln* (New York: Oxford University Press, 2002), 231.
6. Ibid., 317.
7. Ibid., 443.

ment methods and arguments in the hopes of defending the plausibility of the Reformed faith. But instead of causing the Princetonians to compromise their stalwart allegiance to the Reformed faith, their appropriation of Scottish moral philosophy actually reinforced important elements in Princeton's explanation of federal theology. In sum, Princeton's moral philosophy reaffirmed the works principle universally required by God's demand for righteousness. At the same time, the universal standards of the law and its demand for justice established the framework for Princeton's teaching on the doctrines of grace and the work of Christ. Only a redeemer who could both meet the demands of the law and pay its penalty provided any hope for sinners. Seen in the light of the interconnectedness of justice and mercy, Princeton's appeals to human virtue were not necessarily a contradiction of the doctrines of grace. Instead, their teaching on virtue simply underscored the criteria for righteousness, man's inability to meet those criteria, and his need for a redeemer.

If this is a responsible way of reading the Princeton Theology, then the apparent tension between Alexander's moral philosophy and Hodge's federal theology is not so much the fault of the Princetonians' mix of Calvinism and the Enlightenment as it is the historians' failure to recognize the ongoing vitality of natural law in nineteenth-century Reformed thought. This interpretation of old Princeton looks particularly plausible from the perspective of Presbyterian debates with the New England Theology over the atonement during the decade running up to the split between the Old and New School churches. In countering New England's moral government view of the atonement, Princeton not only defended the notion of a vicarious sacrifice.[8] Hodge in particular also grounded his defense of Reformed orthodoxy on an understanding of the law, justice, and merit that assumed the continuing and universal demands for holiness revealed in man's conscience and the created order (i.e., natural law). In which case, in the context of antebellum America, Princeton may have been more creative and less predictable than its own self-understanding allowed. By appropriating the new moral philosophy, Princeton was not undermining its Calvinist teaching but actually reinforcing it.

8. According to Louis Berkhof, the governmental theory of the atonement "denies that the justice of God necessarily demands that all the requirements of the law be met. The law is merely the product of God's will, and He can alter or even abrogate it, just as He pleases." Christ's death did render "a certain satisfaction, but this was only a nominal equivalent of the penalty due to man; something which God was pleased to accept as such. If the question is asked, why God did not remit the penalty outright . . . the answer is that He had to reveal in some way the inviolable nature of the law and His holy displeasure against sin, in order that He, the moral Ruler of the universe, might be able to maintain His moral government" (Berkhof, *Systematic Theology* [Grand Rapids: Eerdmans, 1939], 388).

The Science of Morals

"Ethical philosophy" was the last subject on which Archibald Alexander wrote, according to his son, James W. Alexander, who penned the preface for *Outlines of Moral Science*, published in 1852. That a work of moral philosophy concluded Alexander's important career is at least unusual since it was the sort of project that presidents of denominational colleges usually produced in connection with their responsibility for the senior year course that gave integrity to the curriculum by proving the existence of God and the necessity of virtue. Alexander had served as president of Hampden-Sydney College early in his career after pastoring small Presbyterian congregations in his native Virginia. In 1807 he moved to Philadelphia to minister at Pine Street Church. Five years later he completed his northern migration when the General Assembly appointed him the founding professor of Princeton Theological Seminary. From 1812 until his death in 1851, Alexander taught at Princeton and was responsible for the entire theological curriculum during his first three years until Samuel Miller joined the faculty.[9] During his tenure at Princeton, Alexander informally taught moral philosophy to recent college graduates about to embark on seminary studies. The print version of Alexander's instruction, according to his son, was "dedicated to Him, without whose blessing, no human effort, even in the best cause, is other than worthless."[10]

Dedicating the lectures to God, however, was not the same as starting a system of ethical reflection with appeals to the maker of heaven and earth. As Allen C. Guelzo has helpfully explained, the science of duty arose in the United States as a field approaching an academic discipline for eminently practical and public reasons. Protestant leaders sensed that public morality and Christian influence were under siege in the young republic. European skeptics could be read with ease; the dangers of revolution, as the French case had shown, were pressing; and with the divisions among the churches, in the words of Ashbel Green, "open and avowed infidelity" went unchecked in the young nation. The solution that many Ivy League presidents hit upon, and that their imitators at denominational colleges across the land followed, was a science of morals that would fill the vacuum left by religious disestablishment. Revivalism was another solution. If the nation's citizens would get religion, chances were that good behavior would follow. But revivals

9. On Alexander's life, see Lefferts A. Loetscher, *Facing the Enlightenment and Pietism: Archibald Alexander and the Founding of Princeton Theological Seminary* (Westport, CT: Greenwood, 1983).

10. From James W. Alexander's preface to Archibald Alexander, *Outlines of Moral Science* (New York: Charles Scribner, 1852), 18.

were unpredictable and sporadic. What was needed, according to Guelzo, "was to find a way of reshaping Christian moralism so as to put forward a Christian public voice" while also "accommodating Christian theism to the secular voice of the Enlightenment."[11] All the way down to the Civil War and beyond, college and seminary faculty like Alexander kept trying to reinforce the barricades of public order against the assault of infidelity and moral license by investing in the project of moral philosophy.

The public nature of Alexander's treatment was obvious from the outset. "As all men," he began, "when reason is developed, have a faculty by which they can discern difference between objects of sight which are beautiful and those which are deformed, so all men possess the power of discerning a difference between actions, as to their moral quality."[12] This was clearly a book that addressed the moral capacities of all people, and so assumed from the start that questions of grace, operations of the Spirit, or the nature of regeneration were not fair game for moral science. Alexander simply proceeded to discuss conscience, the uniformity of moral judgments, moral obligation, free will, and virtue seemingly independent of Reformed anthropology or the revealed sources of morality. Consequently, his very first point concerned the moral faculty, namely, the conscience, by which "it is universally admitted that men, in all ages and countries, have judged some actions to be good and deserving of approbation, while they have judged others to be bad, and of ill desert."[13] Alexander insisted that all people, with full rational capacities, have such a moral faculty, and so are capable of knowing right from wrong. The conscience was even prior to moral education. Without conscience "the idea of virtue or vice could never have entered the human mind."[14]

The universality of conscience led Alexander to assert next that certain self-evident truths "are intuitively perceived by everyone who has the exercise of reason, as soon as they are presented to the mind."[15] Here the Princeton theologian was eager to counter the notion that people from different backgrounds and environments possessed different notions of virtue and vice. This was patently untrue. As Alexander explained, "All intuitively discern that for a ruler to punish the innocent and spare the guilty, is morally wrong."[16] This was a principle that he conceded might look different when

11. Allen C. Guelzo, "'The Science of Duty': Moral Philosophy and the Epistemology of Science in Nineteenth-Century America," in David N. Livingstone, D. G. Hart, and Mark A. Noll, eds., *Evangelicals and Science in Historical Perspective* (New York: Oxford University Press, 1999), 270.
12. Alexander, *Outlines*, 19.
13. Ibid., 18–19.
14. Ibid., 28.
15. Ibid., 35.
16. Ibid., 36.

applied in different circumstances. In fact, sometimes virtuous action would require reasoning from "sound principles" to correct applications. But even if applied poorly, such moral incompetence did not disprove the existence of self-evident moral truths.

On the question of moral obligation, Alexander engaged in the sort of discourse that could make moral philosophy not only seem dull but obviously so. Still, the self-evident character of the argument was precisely the point. Certain aspects of moral duties were plain. "A moral act is one which ought to be performed," Alexander reasoned; "an immoral act is one which ought not to be performed." In other words, it would be morally nonsensical to say that a certain act was moral and yet that human beings had no duty to perform it. If this logic followed, then, figuring out one's duty was not overly complicated. Because of a common and universal sense of moral truth, all that was necessary to convince moral agents of duty was to "bring it distinctly before our minds."[17] Contrary to some ethicists who argued that moral duty was best understood in relation to self-interest or social well-being, a sense of right and wrong existed "independent of all considerations of personal happiness."[18]

As obvious and coherent as this science of morals was, Alexander did concede that an occasional riddle plagued his scheme. One case was that of the relationship between conscience and the good. Did the idea of virtue depend simply on the conscience of a moral agent, or did the good exist independently of a person's conscience so that one could engage in vice even when acting in accordance with his conscience? Contrary to the view that a man has "no law but his own opinion," Alexander insisted that the knowledge "necessary to duty is within the reach of every man, were he disposed sincerely to seek after it."[19] The problem was human depravity, a subject that did not come up until almost fifty pages into this Calvinist's book on ethics. Sin, he explained, "produces blindness of mind, in regard to the beauty and excellency of moral objects." But everyone should be free, Alexander argued, from erroneous opinions about the principles of right conduct. Even so, his larger point was that an action is morally right if two criteria are met: the first is a right and reasonable state of mind, and the second is "conformity with the law under which we are placed."[20]

Another difficulty for this orderly science was the case of the atheist and whether someone who does not fear God is "completely divested of the

17. Ibid., 49.
18. Ibid., 59.
19. Ibid., 66–67.
20. Ibid., 71.

feeling of moral obligation."[21] This question only gave Alexander another chance to insist on the immediacy of the sense of moral duty for all people, no matter whether they acknowledge a "law-giver" or not. "We have a law written within us, and from the sense of obligation to obey this law, we cannot escape." A person might suppress the knowledge of God that follows from this moral sense, but he "cannot obliterate the law written on his heart; he cannot divest himself of the conviction that certain actions are morally wrong; nor can he prevent the stings of remorse, when he commits sins of an enormous kind."[22] Alexander admitted that belief in God led to "distinct and forcible" dictates of conscience. But the moral faculty of atheists was no more deformed than that of a God-fearer.[23]

To the topic of moral agency (read: free will) Alexander devoted ten chapters. But the substance of his approach was to affirm both divine sovereignty and human responsibility, a theme that revealed Alexander's Calvinism more than did other sections of the book. He was particularly eager not to be misunderstood on the relationship between necessity and liberty. "An event may be absolutely certain without being necessary," Alexander asserted. God's acting wisely was a matter of both certainty and liberty, as was the case of angels whose love of God was necessary but also free.[24] Accordingly, no good reason existed for considering uncertainty essential to freedom. Free agency was essential to moral actions. At the same time, such freedom did not compromise God's providential control of all things. Neither did free agency imply that a person could choose or determine the nature of his will. Man had "the liberty, within the limits of his power, to act as he pleases." But to suppose that he could act "independently of all reasons and motives, would be to confer on him a power for the exercise of which he could never be accountable."[25]

The last significant topic that Alexander addressed was virtue. His definition of this much contested subject was almost as blithely indifferent to the debates surrounding virtue as it was simple. It was "that quality in certain actions which is perceived by a rational mind to be good." In contrast, vice was "that which a well-constituted and well-informed mind sees to be evil."[26] Such a basic definition, though consistent with Alexander's commonsense approach, was not innocent of debates among moral philosophers. His philosophical enemies included Thomas Hobbes, who denied a natural

21. Ibid., 84.
22. Ibid., 86.
23. Ibid., 88.
24. Ibid., 104–5.
25. Ibid., 127.
26. Ibid., 185.

distinction between virtue and vice, Bernard Mandeville, who regarded the pursuit of virtue as basically hypocritical, and Archbishop William Paley, who rooted virtue in the pursuit of happiness.[27] Alexander also entertained reservations about Jonathan Edwards's and Samuel Hopkins's efforts to ground virtue in the New Divinity notion of disinterested benevolence or "being in general," as Edwards put it.[28] In addition, the Princetonian quibbled with the Scottish moral philosopher Adam Smith over the idea that moral sentiments stemmed from sympathy because it was an "irregular and capricious" theory.[29] Alexander even objected to a definition of virtue that equated it with conformity to God's will. He was still holding out for the atheist who because of conscience could know right from wrong even if denying God's existence.[30]

Whether or not rational human beings have such a reliable moral faculty, historians of moral philosophy have not seemed to need a theological sense of Calvinism to detect a variety of intellectual difficulties in Alexander's construction of ethical science. In his study of nineteenth-century American moral philosophy, D. H. Meyer spots something seriously wrong with Alexander's contribution to the development of Protestant ethical reflection. Aside from the intellectual weaknesses of Enlightenment moral philosophy in general, Meyer stresses that the very construction of a science of morals runs contrary to Calvinism.

Further, for many intellectual historians, Jonathan Edwards is the standard from which American Calvinists departed. Even while engaging the demands of Reformed piety and the new philosophy, according to Meyer, Edwards "regarded man as primarily a sinner in the hands of an angry God." But the later moral philosophers regarded humans "primarily as responsible moral agents performing the duties of a citizen in a vast moral government." And where Edwards approached the soul with a sense of "profound awe," American moral philosophers, "for all their pious rhetoric, usually thought of the soul (the mind) as the object of empirical inquiry, subject to precise analysis."[31] Meyer adds that Alexander is particularly guilty of philosophical depravity because a faithful Calvinist would recognize that "the human soul has been damaged beyond recognition." The Princeton theologian failed

27. See ibid., 159–62.
28. See Jonathan Edwards, *The Nature of True Virtue* in *The Works of Jonathan Edwards*, vol. 8, *Ethical Writings*, ed. Paul Ramsey (New Haven: Yale University Press, 1989), 539ff.
29. Alexander, *Outlines*, 175–77.
30. Alexander's *Outlines* concludes with three chapters on the being and attributes of God. These were added to the printed version of his lectures and not part of his regular instruction, as his son James W. indicated in his preface, 12.
31. D. H. Meyer, *The Instructed Conscience: The Shaping of the American National Ethic* (Philadelphia: University of Pennsylvania Press, 1972), 53–54.

at his "difficult feat" by trying to combine the Reformed "assessment of man's depravity with his own moral theory."[32]

Alexander's chief weakness in Meyer's view is the link he assumed between moral responsibility and moral agency. Alexander was on firm ground when he followed Edwards and asserted that actions depend on volitions or desires. But his footing became less sure when Alexander distinguished between rational desires and appetites or passions. Meyer assumed that Alexander's conception of the hidden disposition that forms the basis for moral judgment should have led a good Calvinist to understand that man's fundamental moral faculty is good. Meyer put the problem this way:

> Either man lacks the ability to alter his disposition—in which case Alexander would be implying that there can be moral responsibility without moral agency, thus contradicting himself—or man has the ability (along with the duty) to alter his hidden disposition, in which case Alexander would be, theologically, moving in the direction of Pelagianism and even perfectionism.[33]

Meyer concedes that Alexander was not alone in failing to see this difficulty. The appeal to a universal and rational moral consciousness "threatened orthodoxies of every kind." By means of "intuitive first principles," according to Meyer, "American thought was moving inexorably toward free human agency, unshackling the will at whatever cost to theological doctrines."[34] But because Alexander was the lone Calvinist among the most prominent American moral philosophers, Meyer argues that Alexander should have known better. So, "attention was no longer centered on the logical connection of cause and effect, with which Edwards had riveted the sinner to his own depravity, nor on the troublesome relation between human nature and grace." Instead, moral philosophers looked to man's moral constitution, "with all its intellectual, affective, and active powers—as something in need of proper training and instruction."[35]

Princeton's appeal to a general or common moral sense, as exemplified in Alexander's *Outlines of Moral Science*, revealed an apparently serious weakness in the seminary's theological position. On the one hand, it compromised its stand for historic Calvinism by jeopardizing Reformed teaching on original sin and total depravity. On the other hand, it reflected Princeton's capitulation to the secular moralizing that steadily flowed from America's debt to Enlightenment philosophy. Even Guelzo, who is sympathetic to the tradition

32. Ibid., 55.
33. Ibid., 56.
34. Ibid., 57.
35. Ibid., 59.

of moral philosophy, could not resist mentioning the difficulty for a Calvinist moral philosophy. "No one less than the twin doyens of Princeton Calvinism, Archibald Alexander and James McCosh, decided that, for the purposes of moral philosophy, it was enough to believe in a self-evident, intuited freedom that, when they were speaking theologically, they did *not* believe in."[36] The ineluctable verdict is that the Princeton Theology unwittingly contributed to that development in American Protestantism that Joseph Haroutunian aptly used for the title of his powerful book, *Piety versus Moralism*.[37]

Princeton's Paradox

At the same time that Alexander was developing his own strand of moral philosophy, his colleague and, at one time, spiritual apprentice, Charles Hodge, was defending Reformed orthodoxy against all comers. A native of Philadelphia, Hodge at a young age accompanied his widowed mother to Princeton where he attended the College of New Jersey and underwent a conversion experience as an undergraduate during a campus revival led by Alexander. True to the other side of revivalistic Presbyterianism, Alexander also instructed Hodge in the verities of the Shorter Catechism. The seminary professor would remain a mentor to Hodge throughout the rest of his studies as both an undergraduate and a seminary student. Hodge acknowledged his debt to Alexander when he named his first son after his father in the faith. When Hodge took over responsibility for teaching theology at Princeton after Alexander's death, he assumed as well the duty of passing on what he had learned from his former professor and spiritual father. In 1851, just prior to Alexander's death, Hodge confided to his brother in a letter, "It is forty years next spring since I first, as a boy, attracted his notice. He has ever since acted to me as a father, and God has given me grace to love and revere him as a child would such a father."[38]

Yet when Hodge discussed the theological aspects of moral science in his three-volume *Systematic Theology*, he sounded distinctly different from Alexander. With Alexander, Hodge continued to rely on the intuitive epistemology of Scottish philosophy in frequent appeals to the common sense and general consciousness of humankind to prove the plausibility of seemingly contested points. But unlike Alexander, Hodge's theological instruc-

36. Guelzo, "'Science of Duty,'" 279, emphasis his.
37. Joseph Haroutunian, *Piety versus Moralism: The Passing of the New England Theology* (New York: H. Holt, 1932).
38. Hodge to H. L. Hodge, quoted in A. A. Hodge, *The Life of Charles Hodge D.D., LL.D.* (New York: Charles Scribner's Sons, 1880), 383.

tion on moral duties was clearly Calvinistic. For instance, in the anthropological portion of his systematics, Hodge had no hesitation affirming moral depravity and original sin. "The Augustinian or Protestant doctrine," he explained, "teaches that such is the nature of inherent, hereditary depravity that men since the fall are utterly unable to turn themselves unto God, or to do anything truly good in his sight."[39] That assertion would appear to have provided little support for the sort of appeals that Alexander made to man's moral sense.

Behind Hodge's understanding of human depravity was the covenant theology that he had learned from Alexander who had had the theological insight to assign a version of Francis Turretin's *Institutes* as the text for seminarians. Hodge referred to Turretin as "one of the most perspicuous books ever written."[40] (It continued to be used as the required text until 1871 when Hodge's own lectures replaced Turretin.) Before Hodge ever turned to the question of sin, moral capability, and virtue, he grounded his considerations in the doctrine of the covenant that he learned from Turretin and Alexander. Succinctly put, "God entered into a covenant with Adam," "the promise annexed to that covenant was life," "the condition was perfect obedience," and the penalty of this covenant was "death."[41] The covenant of works, predicated on the command "This do and thou shalt live," required perfect obedience by Adam and established the principle of strict justice or merit. It was called the covenant of works because "works was the condition on which that promise was suspended."[42] The requirement of perfect obedience, Hodge also explained, was not a peculiarity of the "Mosaic economy" but "a declaration of a principle which applies to all divine laws." The entire argument of Paul in Romans and Galatians was "founded" on this assumption. If it were not true, his entire teaching "falls to the ground."[43] Even more, the context of the covenant of works still applied to all mankind:

> Hence the Apostle in the second chapter of his Epistle to the Romans, says that God will reward every man according to his works. To those who are good, He will give eternal life; to those who are evil, indignation and wrath. This is only saying that the eternal principles of justice are still in force. If any man can present himself before the bar of God and prove that he is free from sin, either imputed or personal, either original or actual, he will not be

---

39. Charles Hodge, *Systematic Theology*, 3 vols. (1871–73; Grand Rapids: Eerdmans, 1979), 2:259.

40. Charles Hodge, "Historical Sermon," reprinted in Hodge, *Life of Charles Hodge*, 553.

41. Hodge, *Systematic Theology*, 2:117.

42. Ibid., 2:118.

43. Ibid., 2:119.

condemned. But the fact is that the whole world lies in wickedness. Man is an apostate race. Men are all involved in the penal and natural consequences of Adam's transgression. They stood their probation in him, and do not stand each man for himself.[44]

The covenant of grace, according to Hodge, stood in direct contrast with that of works. Having fulfilled the covenant of redemption with God the Father, Christ became the mediator of the covenant of grace. "By fulfilling the conditions on which the promises of the covenant of redemption were suspended, the veracity and justice of God are pledged to secure the salvation of his people." Thus the condition of the covenant of grace is faith in Christ. In one sense, Hodge explained, this condition is meritorious since it rests on Christ's performing the perfect obedience that Adam failed to render.[45] But in another sense the covenant of grace involves no merit because "there is no merit in believing." "Without the work of Christ there would be no salvation; and without faith there is no salvation."[46]

Also crucial to Hodge's explanation of the covenant of grace was the idea that its conditions were the same under the patriarchal, Mosaic, and Christian dispensations of its application. The gracious aspect of this covenant may have been hardest to perceive in the period from Moses to Christ when God enjoined upon his people "a multitude of new ordinances of polity, worship, and religion." Even so, the promises set forth more clearly "by the instructions of the prophets the person and work of the coming Redeemer as the prophet, priest, and king of his people." "The nature of the redemption He was to effect," Hodge wrote, "and the nature of the kingdom He was to establish were thus more and more clearly revealed."[47]

And yet the Mosaic covenant also contained two other important aspects that for some may have rendered it less plausible as part of a gracious promise. First, it contained a national covenant in which Moses was mediator. "The promise was national security and prosperity," and the condition "was the obedience of the people as a nation to the Mosaic law." In this respect the Mosaic arrangement was a "legal covenant" which commanded "Do this and live." Second, it was a "renewed proclamation of the original covenant of works." "It is as true now," Hodge elaborated, "as in the days of Adam . . . that rational creatures who perfectly obey the law of God are blessed in the enjoyment of his favour; and that those who sin are subject to his wrath

44. Ibid., 2:122.
45. Ibid., 2:364.
46. Ibid., 2:365.
47. Ibid., 2:374–75.

and curse."[48] These two aspects of the Mosaic covenant helped to unravel the New Testament's apparent inconsistency regarding the law under Moses. In regard to the people of God before Christ's advent, it was "obligatory." For the church after the advent it was "obsolete." As part of the preparation for the promised mediator, "it is spoken of as that which the Apostles themselves preached." When regarded in relation to those who rejected the gospel, it was a "ministration of death and condemnation." And in contrast to the new covenant, it is "spoken of as a state of tutelage and bondage, far different from the freedom and filial spirit of the dispensation under which we now live."[49] For this reason Hodge could speak of the gospel dispensation as "more purely evangelical" than the Mosaic covenant. Although the New Testament contained a legal element by revealing "the law as still binding on those who reject the gospel," in the New Testament "the gospel greatly predominates over the law"; in the Old Testament, by contrast, the "law predominated over the gospel."[50]

When Hodge turned to the Decalogue in the third volume of his systematics, he continued to work with the covenantal categories he had established earlier in his instruction. Abstractly considered, law was that which "binds the conscience." It imposed an "obligation of conformity to its demands upon all rational creatures."[51] A further preliminary consideration was that law implies a lawgiver. As such, moral duty "is the obligation to conform our character and conduct to the will of an infinitely perfect Being." The moral law, accordingly, was the revelation of "the will of God."[52] In contrast to moral philosophers, then, especially those like Grotius, religion and morality could never be separated or considered independently. For "moral excellence is the very essence of God."[53] Hodge ratcheted up the contrast with moral philosophy, and seemingly with his own theological and academic mentor, when he asserted that "the Bible contains the whole rule of duty for men in their present state of existence." "Nothing can legitimately bind the conscience that is not commanded or forbidden by the Word of God."[54] Perhaps Hodge was thinking of Alexander when he backed down and conceded that "the law is revealed in the constitution of our nature, and more fully and clearly in the written Word of God."[55] But Hodge's ethical reflection was

48. Ibid., 2:375.
49. Ibid., 2:376.
50. Ibid.
51. Ibid., 3:259.
52. Ibid., 3:260.
53. Ibid., 3:261.
54. Ibid., 3:262.
55. Ibid., 3:266.

following more directly on Reformed theological lines than those of Scottish philosophy. From these introductory remarks he moved into a specific discussion of the Decalogue, underscoring again the legal nature of the Mosaic economy in contrast to the gospel as fully revealed in Christ.

Instruction such as this all too hasty overview of the law in its relation to Reformed covenant theology earned Hodge the reputation as the most prominent defender of Calvinism in nineteenth-century America. In 1967, Sydney E. Ahlstrom remarked that "nonrecognition of Hodge's continuing role in American Protestantism betokens a serious misunderstanding of the contemporary science."[56] More recently, James Turner wrote that "the Old School ship of traditional Presbyterianism could not have enlisted an abler captain in his time and place."[57]

These encomiums stand in marked contrast to the tradition of moral philosophy in which Alexander participated. Hodge continues to be assigned to seminarians. Alexander's moral science sets restfully on library shelves. But aside from the contrast of influence stands an even more glaring discrepancy between Hodge's Calvinism and Alexander's scientific account of ethics. To be sure, each man was gifted intellectually and had no problem spotting difficulties that nonorthodox philosophers were posing for the Reformed faith. Even so, the Enlightenment along with the progressive views of history that the *philosophes* encouraged, even among Protestants like Princeton's theologians, had a way of obscuring tensions within systems of thought. Perhaps the failure to acknowledge this inconsistency stemmed from ignorance of its existence.

Princeton Resolved?

Few theologians or historians have attempted to resolve the apparent tension within the Princeton Theology. Liberal theologians have not had any stake in Princeton's Calvinism, while historians look at Hodge's defense of Reformed orthodoxy as admirable but comparable to Sisyphus's encounter with a rock and a steep hill.[58] Reformed theologians have certainly admired old Princeton's Calvinism but have scratched their heads trying to reckon

56. Sydney E. Ahlstrom, *Theology in America: The Major Protestant Voices from Puritanism to Neo-Orthodoxy* (Indianapolis: Bobbs-Merrill, 1967), 252.

57. James Turner, "Charles Hodge in the Intellectual Weather of the Nineteenth Century," in John W. Stewart and James H. Moorhead, eds., *Charles Hodge Revisited: A Critical Appraisal of His Life and Work* (Grand Rapids: Eerdmans, 2002), 61.

58. See, for instance, the recent effort of historians and theologians to assess Hodge in Stewart and Moorhead, eds., *Charles Hodge Revisited*.

with the seminary's theologians' reliance on Enlightenment philosophy.[59] Furthermore, some evangelical theologians have taken sustenance from Princeton's high estimate of man's rational capacity but have not been particularly interested in the fine points of Princeton's Calvinism.[60] To harmonize Princeton's reliance upon covenant theology and moral philosophy, then, is a feat that looks foolhardy.

What follows is a modest attempt to do so, though. And the means for accomplishing this undertaking is the works principle in both the covenant of works and the Mosaic economy. The basic hunch is this: because the Princetonians understood the Decalogue as a republication of the covenant of works and as a pedagogue unto Christ who fulfilled all the requirements of God's covenant with Adam, they could explain the law both as obligatory on all people (e.g., Alexander's moral science) and as having a specific function in God's redemption of his people (e.g., Hodge's systematics). The further implication is that because theologians and historians have generally abandoned or ignored Protestantism's continued use of natural law, that is, a range of moral truths known even by unregenerate persons, scholars have been able to see only inconsistency or contradiction in Princeton's theological and ethical outlook. In other words, Alexander's moral science was a nineteenth-century version of Protestant reflection on natural law that was no more at odds with his junior colleague's covenant theology than was Calvin's, Turretin's, or Owen's combination of natural law and Reformed theology.[61]

The resolution attempted here must be tentative if only because of the constraints of space. Limited knowledge is another factor since the history of nineteenth-century American Calvinism has yet to receive the sort of attention that looks at it not from the perspective of intellectual history (an approach that stresses philosophical categories such as epistemology and ethics) but as historical theology (a path that looks at the unfolding of Reformed orthodoxy as articulated by the scholastics and subsequent school or seminary men). As such, two examples will have to suffice for outlining

59. Compare, for example, the perspectives represented in David F. Wells, ed., *The Princeton Theology* (Grand Rapids: Baker, 1989), and John C. Vander Stelt, *Philosophy and Scripture: A Study in Old Princeton and Westminster Theology* (Marlton, NJ: Mack, 1978).

60. See, for instance, Millard J. Erickson, Paul Kjoss Helseth, and Justin Taylor, eds., *Reclaiming the Center: Confronting Evangelical Accommodation in Postmodern Time* (Wheaton, IL: Crossway, 2004); and D. A. Carson and John D. Woodbridge, eds., *Scripture and Truth* (Grand Rapids: Baker, 1992).

61. For valuable recent efforts to recover natural law for Reformed Christians, see Stephen J. Grabill, *Rediscovering the Natural Law in Reformed Theological Ethics* (Grand Rapids: Eerdmans, 2006); and David VanDrunen, *A Biblical Case for Natural Law* (Grand Rapids: Acton Institute, 2006).

how such a harmonization of Alexander and Hodge might work. The first concerns Hodge's own appeal to the categories of moral science within his explanation of Reformed theology, particularly in his discussion of original sin. The second involves Princeton's critique of a Calvinist rival, namely, the New England Theology, specifically on the doctrine of the atonement. As it happened, without seeing the direct links between the Decalogue and the covenant of works, and the demand for perfect satisfaction of the law and its remedy through the vicarious atonement, some so-called Calvinists wound up treating Christ's sacrificial death as a pedagogue, not unto grace, but unto God's law.

In his discussion of original sin, Hodge attempted to hold two important truths together. On the one hand, he resolutely defended the idea that all mankind fell in Adam's first sin. This meant that all people descending from Adam by "ordinary generation" were born "destitute of original righteousness," that this corruption affects the whole person—not simply the body or the lower faculties, and that without regeneration fallen men are "utterly disposed, disabled, and opposed to all good."[62] That position would seem to fly in the face of appeals to a universal moral conscience as moral philosophy did. On the other hand, Hodge also affirmed that total depravity did not leave man "destitute of all moral virtues." He explained:

> The Scriptures recognize the fact, which experience abundantly confirms, that men, to a greater or less degree, are honest in dealings, kind in their feelings, and beneficent in their conduct. Even the heathen, the Apostle teaches us, do by nature the things of the law. They are more or less under the dominion of conscience, which approves or disapproves their moral conduct. All this is perfectly consistent with the Scriptural doctrine of total depravity, which included the entire absence of holiness; the want of the apprehensions of the divine perfections, and of our relation to God as our Creator, Preserver, Benefactor, Governor, and Redeemer. . . . All men worship and serve the creature rather than, and more than the Creator.[63]

Instead of regarding the moral consciousness of fallen human nature as at odds with original sin or as teaching the opposite of what Calvinism affirms about the enmity between sinners and their creator, Hodge turned the relative goodness of man into a proof of Reformed teaching about the fall. "Men are not so besotted even by the fall as to lose their moral nature," Hodge wrote.

62. Hodge, *Systematic Theology*, 2:231.
63. Ibid., 2:233–34.

They know that sin is an evil, and that it exposes them to the righteous judgment of God. From the beginning of the world, therefore, they have tried not
only to expiate, but also to destroy it. They have resorted to all means possible to them for this purpose. They have tried the resources of philosophy
and of moral culture. They have withdrawn from the contaminating society
of their fellow-men. They have summoned all the energies of their nature,
and all the powers of their will.[64]

All of this moral effort testified to how morally destitute mankind is.
Throughout all of this moral strenuousness, Hodge concluded, "men have
been slow to learn what our Lord teaches, that it is impossible to make the
fruit good until the tree is good."[65]

Hodge did not think he was going out on a limb in asserting the moral
nature of man but believed he had Reformed orthodoxy on his side. "It is
admitted in all the Confessions above quoted," he insisted, "that man since
the fall has not only the liberty of choice or power of self-determination, but
also is able to perform moral acts, good as well as evil. He can be kind and
just, and fulfil his social duties in a manner to secure the approbation of his
fellow-men." Hodge did not want to be misunderstood. These good works
were not ultimately good. "It is not meant that the state of mind in which
these acts are performed, or the motives by which they are determined, are
such as to meet the approbation of an infinitely holy God; but simply that
these acts, as to the matter of them, are prescribed by the moral law."

Historically theologians called these works "civil" or "external" justice or
goodness. It was a category of virtue quite distinct from "things concerned
with salvation." The difference revolved around the distinction between
"those religious affections of reverence and gratitude which all men more or
less experience, and true piety." It was the difference between "holiness" and
"mere natural feeling." The Bible and the Reformed confessions were clear
that man "cannot, in short, put forth any exercise or perform any act in such
a way as to merit the approbation of God."[66] But neither did this distinction
and the truths behind it bar appeals to the residue of moral consciousness
remaining in man after the fall. The existence of God, man's forfeited relationship with him, and the reality of the moral law all cultivated appeals to
man's ethical disposition. The claims of God's law, Hodge wrote, declared
"what is obligatory upon those to whom it is addressed." It did not imply an
ability to perform all of the duties required by God. "We are required to be
perfect as our Father is perfect. The obligation is imperative and constant."

64. Ibid., 2:235.
65. Ibid., 2:235–36.
66. Ibid., 2:263–64.

Yet "no sane man," even readers of Alexander's moral philosophy, "can assert his own ability to make himself thus perfect."[67]

As already implied, Hodge's construction of the moral law in the context of federal theology left room for the sort of moral instruction that Alexander provided to young men about to start seminary. The covenant of works, republished in the Decalogue and also expressed in natural law, was still binding in the sense of showing men and women their sin and need for a savior, not to mention the benefits of living in accord with the created order. Here Hodge appealed to Christ's and the apostle Paul's own examples: "Our Lord assured the young man who came to Him for instruction that if he kept the commandments he should live. And Paul says (Rom. ii. 6) that God will render to every man according to his deeds; tribulation and anguish upon every soul of man that doeth evil; but glory, honour, and peace to every man who worketh good."[68] This was simply the way God had created man and constituted the world in which man as a moral creature lived. Obedience to the law and the abiding obligation to do so "arises from the relation of intelligent creatures to God. It is in fact nothing but a declaration of the eternal and immutable principles of justice."[69] To regard Princeton's participation in the project of nineteenth-century moral philosophy as nothing else but reiterating "the eternal and immutable principles of justice" may be a stretch. But it is one that few of Princeton's interpreters have tried and is certainly one for which Hodge's own teaching calls since his consideration of the moral stood upon the base of covenant theology.

The second example where the dual function of the law, both as judge and as pedagogue, makes better sense of Princeton's teaching comes from nineteenth-century debates over the atonement. Hodge's statement of the doctrine, like most of his explanations, was pithy and direct. "The work of Christ," he wrote, "is a real satisfaction, of infinite merit, to the vindicatory justice of God; so that He saves his people by doing for them, and in their stead, what they were unable to do for themselves, satisfying the demands of the law in their behalf, and bearing its penalty in their stead."[70] The brevity of Hodge's statement misses the lengthy explication of the covenant of works, the law, and its requirements and penalties that he rendered in the chapter that preceded his explanation of the atonement. Therefore, several phrases in his succinct articulation of the atonement are crucial for recognizing Hodge's dependence on the works principle first expressed in

67. Ibid., 2:267.
68. Ibid., 2:375.
69. Ibid.
70. Ibid., 2:563.

the covenant of works and later republished in the Decalogue. The phrases bearing closer scrutiny are "vindicatory justice of God" and "demands of the law."

When treating the topic of the satisfaction of Christ, Hodge insisted that the Savior's work satisfied the justice of God. This justice was not vindictive but "vindicatory." "If justice is that perfection of the divine nature which renders it necessary that the righteous be rewarded and the wicked punished, then the work of Christ must be a satisfaction of justice in that sense of the term." God's justice, according to Hodge, was clearly revealed both by "the constitution of our nature" and "all the divinely ordained institutions of religion, whether Patriarchal, Mosaic, or Christian." These revelations "take for granted that men are sinners; and that, being sinners, they need expiation for their guilt as well as moral purification, in order to salvation."[71] The Mosaic administration established that without the shedding of blood "(i.e., without vicarious punishment) there is no remission," but this point held as well "under all dispensations."

About the justice of God Hodge was adamant:

> This is the corner-stone, and the whole fabric falls into ruin if that stone be removed. That God cannot pardon sin without a satisfaction to justice, and that He cannot have fellowship with the unholy, are the two great truths which are revealed in the constitution of our nature as well as in the Scriptures, and which are recognized in all forms of religion, human or divine. It is because the demands of justice are met by the work of Christ, that his gospel is the power of God unto salvation, and that it is so unspeakably precious to those whom the Spirit of God have convinced of sin.[72]

Just as the Decalogue recapitulated the demands of the covenant of works and pointed to the need for a redeemer, so the atonement reasserted the claims of God's justice while also revealing the satisfaction of divine law. Because of man's guilt, no one can be "justified by works." The Bible was clear in assuming that "if a man sins he must die." Accordingly, the chief design of Christ's satisfaction "is neither to make a moral impression upon the offenders themselves, nor to operate didactically on other intelligent creatures, but to satisfy the demands of justice; so that God can be just in justifying the ungodly."[73]

Hodge further elaborated that satisfaction of divine justice was not the same as satisfying the "demands of the law." The law demanded far more

71. Ibid., 2:490–91.
72. Ibid., 2:492.
73. Ibid., 2:492–93.

than punishment of sin. It also required God's creatures to be holy. It could never cease to be obligatory for man "to love and obey God." And thus humanity's relationship to the law was both "federal and moral." It was as if God had stamped the created order with the promise of life for all those who kept his law, and the threat of death for everyone who sinned. But the gospel delivered man from his "federal relation" to the law. "We are no longer bound to be free from all sin. . . . We are not under law but under grace."[74] But this deliverance did not stem from the abrogation of the law or "by lowering its demands." Freedom from the law came by the work of Christ. "He was made under the law that He might redeem those who were under the law." Through his passive and active obedience, "he endured all that the law demands." Hodge established the principle that a proper understanding of grace depended on comprehending the law, and conversely, that the law and its demands set the very terms for grace.

Hodge's defense of the Reformed doctrine of the atonement was something of an anomaly among American theologians north of the Mason-Dixon Line. The New England Theology in general, and the New Haven Theology in particular, was deviating significantly from Reformed teaching. These departures were of special concern to the Presbyterians at Princeton because of the agreement by Congregationalists and Presbyterians in the 1801 Plan of Union to plant churches in the Northwest Territory in a way that suggested the closest of fraternal relations. Since the late eighteenth century, New England had generally adopted the governmental theory of the atonement, partly because of theological developments among Edwardsians or the New Divinity and partly to counter charges against Calvinism for rendering God vindictive and arbitrary.[75]

Jonathan Edwards Jr. in 1785 articulated the governmental theory of the atonement in a series of sermons. To maintain the authority of divine law, he argued, atonement was necessary. Without the atonement, the law and the lawgiver would have fallen into contempt. "It is no impeachment of the divine power and wisdom to say that it is impossible for God himself to uphold his moral government over intelligent creatures once his law hath fallen into contempt." He could, Edwards explained, govern simply

74. Ibid., 2:493.
75. For an overview of these developments, see Mark A. Noll, "Jonathan Edwards and Nineteenth-Century Theology," in Nathan O. Hatch and Harry S. Stout, eds., *Jonathan Edwards and the American Experience* (New York: Oxford University Press, 1988), 260–87; and D. G. Hart and John R. Muether, *Seeking a Better Country: 300 Years of American Presbyterianism* (Phillipsburg, NJ: P&R, 2007), 91–146.

by "irresistible force."[76] But this would be a different kind of government from a moral one of "rewards and punishments." And thus the atonement was "designed to answer the same ends of supporting the authority of the law, the dignity of the divine moral government, and the consistency of the divine conduct in legislation and execution."[77]

Edwards was unable to see something like the law in the Mosaic economy as both part of the older covenant of works and a stage in the covenant of grace as Princeton did. The antithetical character of grace and justice was clearly evident when Edwards asserted, "His atonement is not a payment of our debt. If it had been, our discharge would have been an act of mere justice, and not of grace."[78] The reason was that "grace is ever so opposed to justice that they mutually limit each other. Wherever grace begins, justice ends; and wherever justice begins, grace ends." Did this view of grace and justice render the atonement graceless? Edwards's answer was to appeal to general or public justice. "In this sense, whatever is right is said to be just, or an act of justice; and whatever is wrong or improper to be done, is said to be unjust, or an act of injustice." Justice of a general or public kind was in accord then with the Edwardsian notion of virtue, or disinterested benevolence. To act in conformity to the "dictates of general benevolence, or to see the glory of God and the good of the universe" was to practice general justice.[79]

After Edwards the younger the governmental theory of the atonement became the reigning view among New England theologians. Nathaniel Emmons, who helped to elaborate Edwardsian theology while pastoring in Massachusetts, explained the doctrine of God on which the governmental theory was based: "the goodness, justice, and the mercy of God are founded in the nature of things. That is, so long as God remains the Creator, and men remain his creatures, he is morally obliged to exercise these different and distinct feelings towards them." With the introduction of sin into the relationship between God and man, the situation altered. To maintain the original moral government that God had instituted at creation, he needed to display his hatred of sin, which he did in the atonement. By so doing, God restored his moral government which relied on "laws, rewards, and punishments."[80] According to Edward D. Griffin, who taught at Andover Seminary before presiding over Williams College, a moral government was fundamentally a

76. Jonathan Edwards Jr., quoted in Frank Hugh Foster, *A Genetic History of the New England Theology* (Chicago: University of Chicago Press, 1907), 201.

77. Ibid., 202.

78. Ibid., 203.

79. Ibid., 202.

80. Emmons in Foster, *Genetic History*, 211.

rule of "motives" because "these are the instruments by which it works." This moral government was the order that undergirded the entirety of God's revelation and dealings with man. "It comprehends the atonement, and all the covenants made with man, and all the institutions of religion, with the whole train of means and privileges." In other words, for Griffin, the moral government and its vindication in the atonement turned men from "passive receivers of sovereign impressions" into responsible active moral agents.[81]

Nathaniel W. Taylor, who taught at Yale Divinity School and whose views were directly infiltrating the Presbyterian church, underscored the necessity of a moral government as the fundamental aspect of God's rule and its influence on the cultivation of genuine human virtue. A moral governor who is "truly and perfectly benevolent, must feel the highest approbation of right moral action and the highest disapprobation of wrong moral action on the part of his subjects." And in order for God to secure as far as he was able the right moral actions of his subjects, to re-establish the original pattern of laws, rewards, and punishments, he needed an atonement for sin.[82] In other words, the atonement was not an instance of divine mercy in accordance with the demands of the law, but it was for New England theologians an expression and vindication of the universal standard of benevolence. As Frank Hugh Foster explained it, "The New England writers emphasized the divine government as the sphere within which the atonement was wrought." In so doing, they "all with increasing clearness founded that government upon an ethical idea, a conception of the character of God as love, which redeems the theory from the charge of artificiality and superficiality."[83]

The Princeton theologians rejected outright the governmental view, arguably the tipping point in demonstrating the profound problems that were influencing the Presbyterian church thanks to the Plan of Union.[84] In his *Systematic Theology*, Hodge dissected this view along with other erroneous departures from the vicarious atonement. But one of his most sustained critiques of the governmental theory came in his 1845 review of "Christ, the Only Sacrifice," a pamphlet by the New School Presbyterian minister Nathan S. Beman. This essay, published in the *Biblical Repertory and Princeton Review*, was again a model of Hodge's own indebtedness to Reformed

81. Griffin in Foster, *Genetic History*, 212.

82. Taylor, quoted in Foster, *Genetic History*, 214. For Taylor's lengthier treatment of the moral government and its implications for justification and the atonement, see his discussion of justification in Nathaniel W. Taylor, *Essays, Lectures, etc., upon Selected Topics in Revealed Theology* (New York: Clark, Austin and Smith, 1859), 310–72.

83. Foster, *Genetic History*, 215–16.

84. Earl A. Pope, "The New England Theology and the Disruption of the Presbyterian Church," Ph.D. diss. Brown University, 1962, remains one of the most theologically astute readings of the controversy between Princeton and New England.

scholasticism and the Westminster Standards; throughout the piece he cited Turretin and quoted the Confession and Shorter Catechism. Yet the important aspect of this review for the argument here is the degree to which Hodge both faulted Beman for neglecting the covenantal context of the atonement and explained the Reformed view by relying on the notions of law, justice, penalty, and merit involved in God's original relationship with man.

In faulting Beman, Hodge went right after his denial of the covenant. Beman's theory yielded "the general offer of the gospel" but overlooked "the fact that Christ came into the world and accomplished the work of redemption, in execution of the covenant of grace."[85] In contrast, Beman assumed that Christ's death, his entire saving work even, "had no reference to one class of men more than to another. . . . It simply made the pardon of all men possible."[86]

Hodge also objected to the governmental theory's conception of the atonement's effect as merely bringing "the sinner within the reach of mercy," or making "pardon possible." This notion, according to Hodge, clearly contradicted Scripture's teaching on the covenant. "If Christ suffered by covenant," he explained, "if that covenant promised to him his people as his reward and inheritance, on condition of his obedience and death, then assuredly, when he performed that condition, the salvation of all whom the Father had given to him was rendered absolutely certain."[87] Even the gift of the Spirit to the church was part of the covenantal arrangement. Because the covenant promised that the Holy Spirit would be given to the redeemed on the basis of Christ's fulfilment of the law, Hodge argued, Christ "is, therefore, said to have redeemed us from the curse of the law, that we might receive the promise of the Spirit, Gal. iii.13, 14." Yet Beman denied this truth by teaching that "Christ's death had as much reference to one man as to another, or that it merely renders mercy possible." "If Christ suffered by covenant, and if that covenant include the promise of the Holy Spirit, to teach, renew, and sanctify his people, then it cannot be denied that those thus taught, renewed, and sanctified, are those for whom he died."[88]

At the same time that Hodge faulted Beman and others under the influence of New England's governmental theory for missing the Bible's teaching on the covenant, the Princeton divine could not explain the orthodox view of the atonement without relying on categories supplied by the law and its

85. Hodge, "Beman on the Atonement," reprinted in Charles Hodge, *Essays and Reviews Selected from the Princeton Review* (New York: Robert Carter & Bros., 1879), 175.

86. Hodge, "Beman on the Atonement," 176.

87. Ibid., 179.

88. Ibid., 180–81.

covenantal dimension. While the New Englanders vitiated "the essential nature of the atonement," made it "a mere governmental display, a symbolical method of instruction, in order to do what was better done without any such corruption," the Reformed taught not of possibility but of certainty. That Reformed doctrine ran as follows: "That Christ, by really obeying the law, and really bearing its penalty in the place of his people, and according to the stipulations of the covenant of grace, secured the salvation of all whom the Father had given him, and at the same time throws open the door of mercy to all who choose to enter it."[89] Hodge knew that many in New England believed that the orthodox view restricted the love and mercy of God in a way that might bring disfavor on the gospel. But he countered that the real restriction came from a view of the atonement that only made mercy possible. New England taught a "possible salvation," while leaving "out the very soul of the doctrine."[90]

These two examples, first, the Alexander-like categories of moral philosophy in Princeton's understanding of original sin, and second, Princeton's critique of the New England Theology's doctrine of the atonement, do not produce an airtight case for resolving the apparent tensions between nineteenth-century moral philosophy and Calvinist orthodoxy. But they do suggest that the contradictions often leveled against Princeton overlook a body of theological reflection that relied upon natural law and did so in a way that made possible affirmations of both fallen man's knowledge of and duty to keep the law of God, and man's total depravity and need for a mediator. Furthermore, the habit of regarding the Mosaic administration and the Decalogue as both a republication of the covenant of works and a dispensation of the covenant of grace facilitated the sort of duality in Princeton's teaching that historians and theologians have concluded is mere inconsistency, the function of combining such inhospitable elements as Enlightenment moral philosophy and Reformed theology. Instead of representing a contradiction between naturalistic accounts of virtue and Calvinistic notions of sin, the Princeton Theology may have actually articulated in a nineteenth-century idiom the older Reformed scholastic teaching that drew freely on the ancient philosophers, Christian theologians, and the authors of Scripture to unfold and elaborate a created order that everywhere testified to man's moral duty to divine will, his guilt in not meeting his obligations, and his need for deliverance from his guilt. Rather than the gullible Calvinists who played with the strange fire of Scottish philosophy, the Princetonians may have very well been the level-headed Presbyterians who were shrewd enough to

89. Ibid., 183.
90. Ibid.

know the needs of their times and grounded enough not to let those needs distract from enduring theological truths.

To make that case, the argument here has leaned greatly on Hodge. But Alexander was no intellectual slouch even if he did not produce a systematic theology. One place where Alexander displayed his intellectual savvy was in a review of the most popular moral philosophy textbook of his day, Francis Wayland's *The Elements of Moral Science* (1835). Aside from its merits, the review is important for showing that Alexander's theological convictions were never far from his philosophizing about morals. Alexander used Wayland to critique the New England version of moral theory that stressed disinterested benevolence as the highest ethical ideal. Wayland had been critical of utilitarian theories of morality taught by the likes of Paley and Mandeville. Alexander argued that Jonathan Edwards and his followers in the New Divinity were not essentially different from this school which made "happiness the highest and ultimate good."[91] "The advocates of disinterested benevolence, as the essence of virtue or holiness," he explained, "are explicit in asserting and maintaining, that the only reason why holiness is preferable to sin, is because of its tendency to promote the greatest possible degree of happiness." Alexander went on to lament that this theory had "entered our schools of theology, and has given a complexion to our theological systems."[92] The correct moral theory was that "the morality of actions is only known by the perception of a moral faculty, commonly called conscience, without which faculty we should have no more idea of a moral quality than the brutes have." A sense of right and wrong was not the product of a moral calculus of reason but a judgment of "the moral faculty" independent of the act's consequences either individually or collectively, or either temporally or eternally.[93]

By recognizing that a certain theory of morality was responsible for defective theological systems, Alexander saw that specific systems of moral philosophy were more compatible with Reformed orthodoxy than others. His comments also suggest that he himself had been careful to elaborate a science of morals that reflected his own Reformed convictions. In which case, Alexander and the Princeton Theology stood in contrast to New England not only on the substance of both ethical theories and Calvinist theology but also formally with regard to the relationship between ethics and theology. As Alexander suggested in his review of Wayland, the New England Theol-

91. Archibald Alexander, "Review of Francis Wayland's *Elements of Moral Science*," *Biblical Repertory and Princeton Review* 7 (1835): 389.
92. Ibid., 383.
93. Ibid., 389–90.

ogy let Jonathan Edwards's treatment of virtue color both its theology and its moral philosophy. In contrast, Princeton followed a different course, one where its theological system shaped its moral science so that ethics would fit what was true about the moral order of creation and the redemption revealed in Scripture. The resolution of Princeton's contradictory theology and ethics, then, may owe less to gaps in the school's scope of instruction and more to the way that modern interpreters of American Calvinism have misunderstood the relationship between law and grace in Reformed views of human depravity.

Princeton and the Road Not Taken

As tentative as conclusions must be about the links between old Princeton's Calvinism, its use of moral philosophy, and the place of biblical conceptions of the law in Princeton's teaching, one point is worth developing. It is that instead of resulting in a watered-down Protestantism that left Calvinist notions of the covenant of works, original sin, imputation, and the atonement on the sand of autonomous reason, Princeton's theologians did just the opposite. They continued to defend not simply the basic features of Reformed orthodoxy but received and handed on a wide range of the considerations that had informed the development of Reformed scholasticism during the convening of the Westminster Assembly and beyond. At a time when most American Protestants—except for Presbyterians in the South— were switching allegiance from Calvinist austerity to American optimism, Princeton held out unapologetically for the Reformed faith expressed in the confessional standards of the Presbyterian Church.[94] In fact, if the danger of letting moral philosophy set the course for theology became clear anywhere, it was in New England where the followers of Jonathan Edwards, the standard by which Princeton is so often judged to be inferior, abandoned Calvinism for the sake of categories that Edwards himself had introduced when he used late-seventeenth- and early-eighteenth-century moral philosophy to defend original sin, true virtue, the freedom of the will, and religious affections.[95] The Princeton theologians may not have been as philosophically inclined as the New Englanders. But theologically the New

94. On Princeton's remarkable allegiance to strict Calvinism when Arminianism was winning the U.S., see Noll, *America's God*; and E. Brooks Holifield, *Theology in America: Christian Thought from the Age of the Puritans to the Civil War* (New Haven: Yale University Press, 2003).
95. On the mixed legacy of Edwards, see Allen C. Guelzo, *Edwards on the Will: A Century of Theological Debate* (Middletown, CT: Wesleyan University Press, 1989); and Douglas A. Sweeney, *Nathaniel Taylor, New Haven Theology, and the Legacy of Jonathan Edwards* (New York: Oxford University Press, 2003).

Englanders were no match for Princeton, a point seldom acknowledged by historians and theologians who continue to squint in the aura of Edwards's genius and bow to the school of divinity he inaugurated.

The different outcomes of the Princeton and New England theologies are worth noting in conclusion if only because at the time of the 1758 reunion of the Old and New Side Presbyterians the leadership of the colonial church was oriented clearly toward New England. The College of New Jersey, a New Side and pro-revival institution founded in 1747, had emerged as the Presbyterians' school for training clergy. It was located in the Presbytery of New Brunswick, a district in northern New Jersey originally created for the most vociferous Presbyterian advocates of revival and cordial to Presbyterians in New York and Congregationalists in New England. When the trustees of the college in 1756 appointed Jonathan Edwards to be its president, the intellectual momentum of colonial Presbyterianism lurched even more decidedly toward New England and the particular brand of Calvinism that Edwards taught.[96]

But within seventy-five years of Edwards's appointment at Princeton, the intellectual fortunes of American Presbyterians changed dramatically. First came the selection in 1768 of John Witherspoon to preside over the College of New Jersey. Witherspoon quickly replaced the idealist philosophy on which Edwards had relied with Scottish Common Sense Realism.[97] This philosophical tradition not only made a difference for theories of virtue, but was also responsible for an antispeculative streak among the Princetonians that regarded the New England Theology as inherently abstract and overly metaphysical. Indeed, one of the greatest stylistic differences between Princeton and New England during the debates over Calvinism in the nineteenth century was the former's reliance on exegetical theology in conjunction with its use of Reformed dogmatics in contrast to New England's almost exclusively philosophical and speculative approach.

Then in 1812 when the Presbyterian church decided to found its own institution, dedicated exclusively to training ministers, Princeton Theological Seminary, it took another step away from the trajectory of New England Theology, especially in its subscription requirements for professors.[98] While conservative New Englanders debated conceptions of psychology and virtue elaborated by Edwards without trying to offend Unitarians who were still part of their communion thanks to the state-church system in Massachusetts and Connecticut, Princeton assumed responsibility for instructing ministe-

96. On the College of New Jersey's origins, see Noll, *Princeton and the Republic*, ch. 3.
97. See ibid., ch. 4.
98. See Hart and Muether, *Seeking a Better Country*, 91–146.

rial candidates in the features of the Westminster Assembly's Calvinism. The addition of Turretin as a textbook in theology added another layer of theological ballast that prevented Princeton from tipping in New England's doctrinal sea change.

Finally, by 1831 Princeton's faculty, especially Alexander, who had supported revivals throughout most of his ministry and was partial to the older synthesis of Presbyterianism and Puritanism at the original College of New Jersey,[99] saw where the Edwardsians had taken New England Calvinism and had had enough. When Princeton finally repudiated New England, Old School Presbyterians had a sufficient majority to revoke the 1801 Plan of Union and to exscind that region of the church (e.g., the New School) where New England's influence was ferocious.

One of the greatest consequences of the different courses of the Princeton and New England theologies was a significant divergence on the federal theology of the Reformed tradition. Peter Y. De Jong made this the subject of his doctoral dissertation at Hartford Seminary, eventually published as *The Covenant Idea in New England Theology* (1945). Although De Jong wrote with only New England in view, his conclusions find support in the study of Princeton above. "The theological modifications" introduced by the New Divinity, according to De Jong, "did much to overthrow the covenant idea." "What Edwards rather innocently had maintained concerning human responsibility on the basis of the distinction between natural and moral ability and inability had disastrous consequences." Edwardsians developed these distinctions in such a way that "sin and holiness were thought of only in terms of individual acts" and that children, especially infants, "could not be regarded as guilty and depraved before God." De Jong adds that one of the most glaring changes in New England involved the doctrine of the atonement. For Calvinists, the vicarious atonement was bound up with "the ideas of imputation, representation, substitution," with "legal satisfaction" being the basis "for the theological superstructure."[100] But after Edwards, "the emphasis fell on man's moral relation to God" and paved the way for the governmental theory of the atonement. De Jong concludes, "Since the covenant idea . . . sustains such an intimate relation to the forensic pattern in theology, it was inevitable that a change would obliterate the traditional

99. For Alexander's positive estimate of the experimental Calvinism that informed originally the College of New Jersey, see Archibald Alexander, *The Log College: Biographical Sketches of William Tennent and His Students; Together with an Account of the Revivals under Their Ministries* (London: Banner of Truth, 1851).

100. Peter De Jong, *The Covenant Idea in New England Theology* (Grand Rapids: Eerdmans, 1945), 176–77.

theory of the covenant." Indeed, the strict logic of the Edwardsians ousted "the whole structure of Covenant theology."[101]

Another dissertation written for a New England academic institution supports De Jong's conclusion. Earl A. Pope's "The New England Theology and the Disruption of the Presbyterian Church," completed in 1962 at Brown University, not only shows how the influence of New England precipitated the 1837 break between the New and Old School Presbyterians. He also provides a careful reading of Edwards and his theological descendants that shows the effects of trying to maintain Calvinism without the support of federal theology. For instance, Pope asserts that Edwards set aside the idea that "Adam was the legal representative of man." "Edwards helped bring about its downfall in New England by treating it as irrelevant."[102] Pope also finds that Edwards subverted federal theology by maintaining that "the imputation of sin was impossible without the prior existence of personal innate depravity."[103] Another example with important repercussions for federal theology, according to Pope, was Edwards's notion of the mystical unity of the race. For Edwards, "man was not condemned for the sinful act of another but for his own personal act." As such, the "principle of sin rising in each man was identical to that which afflicted Adam." Pope again regards this formulation as having "disastrous consequences" for federal theology.[104] His conclusion is that the Old School–New School controversy originated in the revisions of the doctrines of imputation, total inability, and the atonement conducted first by Edwards and subsequently modified by Hopkins, Bellamy, Dwight, and Taylor. In other words, while Princeton continued to work within the categories of Reformed federal theology, the New Divinity changed course to develop a system that was perhaps more creative but had disastrous effects for Calvinism.

The contrast between Princeton and New England puts into perspective Hodge's remark that began this essay on his school of theology's lack of originality. The Princeton Theology was not as original as New England, and that may explain why Princeton has not fascinated historians and theologians in the way that Edwards and his followers have.[105] If Hodge and

---

101. Ibid. 179.
102. Pope, "New England Theology," 15.
103. Ibid., 12.
104. Ibid., 18.
105. Bruce Kuklick neatly summarizes, using the example of Hodge, why New England Theology has fared better in American intellectual history than Princeton. "What makes a Christian thinker worth reading in an age when many intellectuals have rejected Christianity? The thinker must give due regard both to the texts *and* to experience and knowledge. It is the synthesis that vivifies the writing. If that synthesis is absent, the writing remains dead. In Edwards this synthesis exists. Indeed, some commentators might claim that he sacrifices sacred doctrine to the demands of his

company were simply repeating the views of seventeenth-century theologians, what possible intellectual fun could there be in arguing that Hodge was a footnote to Turretin? But even if the Princeton Theology lacks the scholarly curves that excite academics, the intellectual feat of planting one foot in Reformed scholasticism and the other in Scottish moral philosophy has its own marvelous quality. The reason has less to do with the apparent inconsistency or naiveté of the Princeton theologians than with their ability to hold together notions about law and grace that apart from covenant theology look antithetical. But when viewed aright those seeming disparate elements of the Princeton Theology emerge as part of a complexly coherent system of theological reflection. One instance of these doctrinal subtleties is the relationship of the Mosaic economy to the covenant of works and the covenant of grace. Princeton perpetuated the long-standing Reformed habit of seeing the Decalogue as a republication of the covenant of works and as a pedagogue unto the covenant of grace's promise of a redeemer. This way of understanding the law suggests that Princeton may have had more intellectual flexibility in combining Reformed orthodoxy and Scottish moral philosophy than what they are usually given credit for. If Princeton was as theologically nimble as suggested here, then historians and theologians may find that connecting the dots between seventeenth-century Reformed scholastics and nineteenth-century Presbyterians, a topic that has yet to receive adequate scrutiny, yields as much academic pleasure as following the trail blazed by the Calvinist modifier, Jonathan Edwards.

---

own experience and his culture's knowledge. In Hodge, there is no such synthesis. He subordinates his own experience and the knowledge of his culture to the inspired book over whose interpretation he presided. That is why Hodge has been called a Biblicist and a dogmatist." See Kuklick, "The Place of Charles Hodge in the History of Ideas in America," in Stewart and Moorhead, eds., *Charles Hodge Revisited*, 76. As telling as Kuklick's conclusion may be for the history of ideas, it may be equally revealing of Princeton Theology's place in historical theology and especially the history of Calvinism.

3

———— ∿ ————

WORKS IN THE MOSAIC COVENANT
A Reformed Taxonomy

BRENTON C. FERRY

I do not find in any point of Divinity, learned men so confused and perplexed (being like Abraham's Ram, hung in a bush of briars and brambles by the head) as here.[1] —Anthony Burgess (d. 1664)

The New Testament confronts a frequent question: How does Christianity relate to the Old Testament? Jesus was crucified by zealous followers of Moses, and Paul was hounded by them for the entire course of his ministry. Rodney Peterson writes, "The first question in the interpretation of Scripture for the Christian after acknowledging the Lordship of Jesus Christ is how to relate the Hebrew Scriptures to the New Testament."[2] Answering this question was part of Christ's agenda between his resurrection and ascension (Luke 24:44–47). It was an evangelistic necessity (Acts 8:30),

1. Anthony Burgess, *A Vindication of the Morall Law and the Covenants* (London, 1647), 229. In my quotes and citations I replicate all unconventional spelling from old English publications.
2. Rodney Peterson, "Continuity and Discontinuity: The Debate throughout Church History," in *Continuity and Discontinuity: Perspectives on the Relationship between the Old and New Testaments*, ed. John S. Feinberg (Wheaton, IL: Crossway, 1988), 18.

76

an apologetic point of contact (Rom. 3:9), a pastoral warning (Rom. 9:6), and of paradigmatic importance for the Christian life (Rom. 4; 1 Cor. 10; Heb. 11). The importance of this topic for the church fathers followed the need to defend Christianity against people who rejected the New Testament because it is not the Old (Justin Martyr vs. Trypho), or rejected the Old Testament because it is not the New (Augustine vs. Faustus).[3]

During the seventeenth century in England there was no shortage of debate about the Mosaic covenant. Leading the far left, the antinomians opposed the need to confess sin, while on the far right Saturday-sabbatarians argued for the necessity of circumcision, the observation of the whole Mosaic law, including sacrifices, the rebuilding of the stone temple at Jerusalem, and the possession of the land of Canaan.[4] Some even rejected the New Testament and Christ as the Messiah.[5] In the middle of these poles, the orthodox divines were at least concerned to maintain the perpetuity of the moral law and the abiding nature of the gospel throughout redemptive history, notwithstanding differences and disagreements in the particulars. These particulars are our present concern.

Specifically, the purpose of this chapter is to profile Reformed thought on the unique function of works in the Mosaic covenant by creating a taxonomy of views. My approach follows three questions. First, how does the Mosaic covenant relate forward to the new covenant? In this section my focus is on the aspect of discontinuity I call the problem of antithesis. Second, how does the Mosaic covenant relate backward to the covenant of works? My focus here is on an aspect of continuity designated the principle of republication.

3. Justin Martyr, *Dialogue of Justin Martyr, Philosopher and Martyr, with Trypho, a Jew*, Ante-Nicene Fathers 1:199–208; Martyr explains repeatedly that the Jews' hard hearts necessitated the temporary, now discontinued Old Testament laws; see also Tertullian, *An Answer to the Jews*, Ante-Nicene Fathers 3:151–57. Tertullian interprets the change of law through a carnal-spiritual paradigm, writing, "Therefore, as we have shown above that the coming cessation of the old law and of the carnal circumcision was declared, so, too, the observance of the new law and the spiritual circumcision has shown out into the voluntary obedience of peace" (3:154). See also Novatian, *On Jewish Meats*, Ante-Nicene Fathers 5:645–50. Novatian explains that the legal restrictions, which are now discontinued, were designed to teach man about his fallen nature through symbolism. Also Augustine, *Reply to Faustus the Manichaean*, Nicene and Post-Nicene Fathers 4:161–75.

4. Chad B. Van Dixhoorn, "Reforming the Reformation: Theological Debate at the Westminster Assembly" (Ph.D. diss., Cambridge University, 2004), 3.1:90r; Edmund Calamay, *Two Solemne Covenants between God and Man* (London, 1646); Thomas Gataker, *Gods Eye on His Israel* (London, 1644); Thomas Gataker, *Antinomianism Discovered and Confuted: and Free-Grace as It Is Held Forth in God's Word* (London, 1652); John Cowell, *The Snare Broken* (London, 1677), 2–6; George Abbot, *Vindiciae Sabbathi* (London, 1641), ii. Abbot says that such sectarians writing upon the subject "are too many to name except with an &c." See also John Owen, *Exertations concerning the Name, Original, Nature, Use, and Continuance of a Day of Sacred Rest* (London, 1671), 6–13.

5. Cowell, *Snare Broken*, 12.

Third, how does the Mosaic covenant relate to the covenant of grace? This question concerns the organic relationship between them. I hope to provide the reader with a tool to assess modern developments and trends within the Reformed community regarding the Mosaic covenant. An appendix is also provided charting this subject as it relates to the broader order of the covenants.[6]

This taxonomy is needed because nothing like it exists to my knowledge.[7] As a result, very basic errors of representative positions continue to multiply themselves. For example, Mark Karlberg misrepresents the views of John Calvin (1509–64), Tobias Crisp (1600–1643), Samuel Bolton (1606–54), and David Dickson (1583–1662).[8] Jeong Koo Jeon misreads John Owen

---

6. A fourth question about works in the Mosaic covenant, yet which is beyond the scope of this study, needs to be addressed in a taxonomic manner. Namely, in what sense is the covenant of grace conditional? See Charles Hodge, *Systematic Theology*, 3 vols. (Grand Rapids: Eerdmans, 1997), 2:364–65; Robert Rollock, *A Treatise of God's Effectual Calling*, trans. Henry Holland (London, 1603), 13–14; William G. T. Shedd, *Dogmatic Theology*, ed. Alan W. Gomes (Phillipsburg, NJ: P&R, 2000), 13–20; Louis Berkhof, *Systematic Theology* (Grand Rapids: Eerdmans, 1994), 280; Herman Witsius, *The Economy of the Covenants*, 2 vols. (1822; Phillipsburg, NJ: Presbyterian and Reformed, 1990), 2:284–85; Norman Shepherd, *The Call of Grace* (Phillipsburg, NJ: P&R, 2000), 13–20; John Murray, *The Covenant of Grace* (Phillipsburg, NJ: Presbyterian and Reformed, 1988), 18–19; John Ball, *A Treatise of the Covenant of Grace* (London, 1645), 10, 132–33, 142; Thomas Blake, *A Treatise of the Covenant of God Entered with Man-kinde* (London, 1658), 99–148; Obadiah Sedgwick, *The Bowels of Tender Mercy Sealed in the Everlasting Covenant* (London, 1661), 181–221.

7. Other taxonomies include Calamay, *Two Solemne Covenants*; Rowland Ward, *God and Adam: Reformed Theology and the Covenant of Creation* (Wantirna: New Melbourne Press, 2003), 126–39; Samuel Bolton, *The True Bounds of Christian Freedome . . . Whereunto Is Annexed a Discourse of the Learned John Camerons, Touching the Threefold Covenant of God with Man*, trans. Samuel Bolton (London, 1645), 22, 122–30 (pages 21–25 of Bolton's book, and the taxonomy within those pages, are omitted without notation in The Banner of Truth reprint [1994]); Samuel Rutherford, *The Covenant of Life Opened* (London, 1655), 57–65; Blake, *The Covenant of God*, 220–95; John Owen, *An Exposition of the Epistle to the Hebrews*, vol. 6 (1855; Carlisle: Banner of Truth, 1991), 71–98; Peter Golding, *Covenant Theology: The Key of Theology in Reformed Thought and Tradition* (Fearn, Ross-shire: Christian Focus Publications, 2004), 164–70.

8. Mark Karlberg, "Legitimate Discontinuities between the Testaments," *Journal of the Evangelical Theological Society* 28.1 (1985): 12, infers that Calvin understands Israel's land of Canaan as inherited by works, not faith. Calvin, however, calls such a view "mistaken" and in "error." See John Calvin, *Calvin's Commentaries of the Four Last Books of Moses Arranged in the Form of a Harmony*, vol. 3 (Grand Rapids: Baker, 1999), 204. Golding replicates Karlberg's incorrect assessment of Calvin (see Golding, *Covenant Theology*, 164).

Karlberg says, "Tobias Crisp (1600–1643), more than most in his time, strove to develop in greater fullness and clarity the precise sense in which the Mosaic covenant had to be considered as a Covenant of Works." He says that for Crisp "the two covenants [Mosaic and New] are not . . . two essentially different covenants." He goes on to describe Crisp as concerned to protect the symbolic, typological works aspect of the Mosaic covenant (Mark Karlberg, *Covenant Theology in Reformed Perspective: Collected Essays and Book Reviews in Historical, Biblical, and Systematic Theology* [Eugene, OR: Wipf and Stock, 2000], 31). Karlberg is mistaken. Crisp's thesis is that the Mosaic covenant is a distinct, second covenant of grace, inferior to the New Testament covenant of grace, in that the Mosaic covenant operates in a sacerdotal manner within the Old Testament *ordo salutis*. Amazingly, Crisp emphatically and repeatedly and systemically denies everything Karlberg says Crisp affirms. For Crisp the order of salvation is different in the Old Testament (see Tobias

(1616–83) in a most unfortunate manner.[9] Furthermore, existing taxonomies are either organizationally confused or too brief to represent the field. For instance, Rowland Ward discusses the Mosaic covenant in a chapter titled "The Relationship of the Covenant of Works to the Sinai Covenant" in which he lists five "representative statements of the relation of the covenant of works with Adam and the covenant with Moses."[10] Yet the views he presents pertain, more specifically, to the organic relation of the Mosaic covenant to the covenant of grace. Ward's information is generally correct, but being organized under the wrong chapter heading, the direction of his discussion is, for the most part, beside the point of the chapter. As a result, the most important issues pertaining to the relationship between Adam and Moses are never properly identified. What is worse, if one attempts to organize the field under Ward's categories, one ends up with people in the same category who actually have different views on the Mosaic covenant's relation to the covenant of works, and people in competing categories with the same view of this relationship.[11] Perhaps the most confusing taxonomy is

---

Crisp, *Christ Alone Exalted; in Seventeen Sermons*, vol. 2 [London, 1643], 44–68). This formulation is presumably why the Westminster Confession of Faith specifically denies the presence of two distinct covenants of grace between the Old and New Testaments (7.6). It affirms, against Crisp, a single order of salvation before and after the coming of Christ. Golding replicates Karlberg's wrong assessment of Crisp (Golding, *Covenant Theology*, 165). Ward says, "It is not really obvious that this [Crisp's] position differs in substance from the classic view" (*God and Adam*, 132). Crisp's views do not match the various offered explanations.

In describing Bolton's view, Karlberg writes, "Bolton contends that there are only two distinct covenants in scripture, not three. He expresses dissatisfaction with the idea of a third, subservient covenant" (*Covenant Theology*, 34). Bear in mind, Bolton argues at length in favor of a third, subservient covenant (Bolton, *The True Bounds*, 145–46). He even translates and publishes John Cameron's *Three-Fold Covenant of God with Man* as an appendix to *The True Bounds*, saying in the preface to the reader, "It [the three-fold covenant] is the key to the gospel, and the best resolver that I have met with of all those intricate controversies, and disputes concerning the law." This is on an unnumbered page titled "A Preface to the Ensuing Discourse of the Learned John Cameron" between pages 352 and 353.

Dickson's view, according to Karlberg, was that "as a punishment, God promulgated the law on Mount Sinai as a repetition of the original Covenant of Works, though hypothetical in nature" (*Covenant Theology*, 33, 157). Yet Dickson never explains the giving of the Ten Commandments as a punishment by God. Instead, Dickson says the Israelites perverted the covenant, themselves turning it into a covenant of works. Dickson calls the product a bastard covenant "of man's own devising" (David Dickson, *Therapeutica Sacra* [London, 1664], 83). See also Ward, *God and Adam*, 139 n. 20.

9. Jeon misrepresents Owen's position on the Mosaic covenant, describing, via quotation, Owen's position: "The Old and New Covenants . . . were 'not indeed two distinct covenants, as unto their essence and substance, but only different administrations of the same covenant'" (Jeong Koo Jeon, *Covenant Theology: John Murray's and Meredith Kline's Response to the Historical Development of Federal Theology in Reformed Thought* [Lanham, MD: University Press of America, 1999], 50). In the portion of Owen quoted by Jeon, however, Owen is describing the view with which he disagrees (Owen, *Hebrews*, 70–100).

10. Ward, *God and Adam*, 126–39.

11. For example, Samuel Rutherford, William Bridge, and Meredith Kline all fit into Ward's first category, that the Mosaic covenant is an administration of the covenant of grace. Yet Rutherford,

that of Peter Golding.[12] The present essay at least replaces such confusion with some proper categories of organization.

The Problem of Antithesis

> There is perhaps no part of divinity attended with so much intricacy, and wherein orthodox divines do so much differ as stating the precise agreement and difference between the two dispensations of Moses and Christ.[13] —Jonathan Edwards (1703–58)

How does the Mosaic covenant relate to the new covenant? This question involves two seemingly competing principles: those of discontinuity and continuity.[14] While the Reformed tradition since the time of Ulrich Zwingli's (1484–1531) battle with the Anabaptists has placed sufficient stress on the unity of the Old and New Testaments, it has not been without significant intramural dialogue about the positive character of the

---

on the one hand, denies that the Mosaic covenant is a covenant of works (Rutherford, *The Covenant of Life*, 60). On the other hand, he does say, "relative to that [unregenerate] people . . . it is a covenant of works." (63). Below I identify Rutherford's view as relative, formal republication. Bridge explains that the covenant of works was "declared" on Sinai, but only the covenant of grace was "made" (William Bridge, *Christ and the Covenant . . . The New Covenant Opened. Sermon III* [London, 1667], 64). Below I identify Bridge's view as pedagogical, formal republication. Meredith Kline believes the Mosaic covenant is organically part of the covenant of grace, yet at the administrative level it is a typological covenant of works (Meredith Kline, *Glory in Our Midst: A Biblical-Theological Reading of Zechariah's Night Visions* [Eugene, OR: Wipf and Stock, 2001], 105). Below I identify Kline's view as typological, formal republication.

Ward has Samuel Bolton and Tobias Crisp in different categories, because Bolton believes the Mosaic covenant is a distinct subservient covenant, and Crisp believes the Mosaic covenant is a distinct covenant of grace. Yet they both deny the formal republication of the covenant of works, so they actually belong in the same category with respect to Moses and the covenant of works.

12. Golding, *Covenant Theology*, 164–75.

13. Jonathan Edwards, *The Works of President Edwards*, vol. 1 (New York: Leavitt & Allen, 1858), 160.

14. Meredith Kline, *By Oath Consigned* (Eugene, OR: Wipf and Stock, 1998). I say "*seemingly* competing principles" because as they apply to the relationship between Moses and Christ they work in harmony to establish covenantal continuity in strongest terms. Kline explains, "For all its difference, the New Covenant of Jeremiah 31 is still patterned after the Sinaitic Covenant. In fact, Jeremiah's concept of the New Covenant was a development of that already presented by Moses in the sanctions section of the Deuteronomic renewal for the Sinaitic Covenant (Deut. 30:1–10). According to Jeremiah, the New Covenant is a writing of the law on the heart rather than on tables of stone (v. 33; cf. 2 Cor. 3:3), but it is another writing of the law. It is a new law covenant. Hence, for Jeremiah, the New Covenant, though it could be sharply contrasted with the Old Covenant (v. 32), was nevertheless a renewal of the Mosaic covenant. It belonged to the familiar administrative pattern of periodic covenant renewal (of which the cycle of sabbatical years was an expression), and renewal is the exponent of continuity" (75). Further along Kline says, "But if the distinctiveness of the New Covenant is that of consummation, if when it abrogates it consummates, then its very discontinuity is expressive of its profound, organic unity with the Old Covenant" (76).

discontinuity existing between the time of Moses and the time of Christ.[15] Why?

Sometimes the New Testament employs a law-gospel contrast to describe the transition from the old covenant to the new covenant. For example, John 1:17 reads, "the law was given through Moses; grace and truth came through Jesus Christ," as if to say, in some respect the redemptive-historical transition from Moses to Christ was not unlike the systematic-theological contrast between law and gospel.[16] The transition from the old covenant to the new covenant was in some way like the transition from the covenant of works to the covenant of grace. William Bridge (d. 1670) of the Westminster Assembly writes, "you have the difference between the law and the gospel; the excellency of the state of the church under the new testament above the state of the church under the old testament."[17]

On the other hand, Moses and all the saints of old knew the gospel, and Christ was no antinomian. Salvation has always been a matter of grace received through faith. How, then, can the old and new covenants be different in terms of a law-gospel contrast, while at the same time coordinate parts of the covenant of grace? This is what I am calling the problem of antithesis. Samuel Rutherford (d. 1661) says, "And it is true, Gal. 4.22, 23, 24, &c. they seeme to be made contrare Covenants."[18]

This "problem" is succinctly illustrated by a sentence in the Westminster Confession (7.5) which reads, "This Covenant [of Grace] was differently administered in the time of the Law, and the time of the Gospel."[19] Here the Mosaic administration is termed "the time of the *law*," against the New Testament's "time of the *gospel.*" Nevertheless, both eras are recognized as administrations of the continuous covenant of grace. Like the Bible, the

15. For example, see Heinrich Bullinger, *The Old Faith or an Evident Probation out of the Holie Scriptures, That the Christian Faith (Which Is the Right, True, Olde, and Undoubted Faith) Hath Endured since the Beginning of the World* (London, 1581).

16. For an exposition of this passage contra antinomianism, see John Arrowsmith, *Theanthropos, or God-Man: Being an Exposition upon the First Eighteen Verses of the First Chapter of the Gospel according to St. John* (London, 1659), 286–91. See also Gal. 4:21–31. The critical issue surrounding this "problem of antithesis" involves Paul's interpretation of Lev. 18:5 in Rom. 10:5 and Gal. 3:12. If Leviticus is part of the covenant of grace, then why does Paul treat Lev. 18:5 as if it expresses the covenant of works with its principle of obedience? John Murray explains that Paul skewed the words of Lev. 18:5 out of context because they were best "suited to express the principle of law-righteousness" (John Murray, *The Epistle to the Romans*, vol. 2 [Grand Rapids: Eerdmans, 1965], 51). For a taxonomy of interpretations of Lev. 18:5 in relation to this subject see Bolton, *True Bounds*, 153–57.

17. Bridge, *Christ and the Covenant*, 54.

18. Rutherford, *Covenant of Life*, 63.

19. *Articles of the Christian Religion, Approved and Passed by Both Houses of Parliament, after Advice Had with the Assembly of Divines by Authority of Parliament Sitting at Westminster* (London, 1648), 15.

Confession describes the transition from the old covenant to the new covenant in terms of a law-gospel contrast, while maintaining the foundational continuity of the covenant of grace. What accounts for this? The Reformed tradition suggests a number of interpretive approaches to this, which are listed below. Most of these approaches complement one another.

Substance and Accidents

First, the Mosaic covenant is described as having two levels: an administrative level of accessories that are changeable, and an essential level that is unchangeable. Whatever discontinuity (antithesis or otherwise) exists between the Mosaic and new covenants is commonly relegated to the administrative level of the covenant, while the continuity is located with the essential, substantive level. For instance, David Dickson (1754–1820) explains this by using a common analogy:

> We see here indeed a diverse manner of dispensing, and outward managing the making of the covenant with men, but the covenant was still the same, clothed and set forth in a diverse manner, and did no other wayes differ then and now, but as one and the self same man differeth from himself, cloathed sutably one way in his minority, and another way in his riper age.[20]

In other words, just as the same man dresses one way when he is young and another way when he is old, the same covenant is clothed in one way when it is young and another when mature.[21]

This distinction is an issue of disagreement below, where the organic relationship between the Mosaic covenant and covenant of grace is in question. According to some people, the discontinuities are so antithetical as to require extracting the Mosaic covenant from the stream of the covenant of grace, recognizing an organically independent covenant rather than a distinct covenant administration.[22]

Ceremonial-Civil-Moral Distinctions

The Mosaic covenant is also described as having three aspects: the ceremonial, civil, and moral. The ceremonial portions govern old covenant worship, the civil portions apply to the old covenant national government, and the moral law pertains to absolute principles of morality summarized

20. Dickson, *Therapeutica Sacra*, 98.
21. For a few descriptions of accidental differences see John Calvin, *Institutes of the Christian Religion*, ed. John T. McNeill, trans. Ford Lewis Battles, 2 vols., Library of Christian Classics 21–22 (Philadelphia: Westminster, 1960), 2.11.1–12; Bridge, *Christ and the Covenant*, 65–67.
22. Owen, *Hebrews*, 76.

in the Ten Commandments. The abrogation of the civil and ceremonial aspects of the old covenant law accounts for the discontinuity between the old and new covenants, while the continuation of the moral law accounts for their continuity. Samuel Bolton, for example, describes the ceremonial law as "an appendix to the first table of the moral law," and the judicial law as "an appendix to the second table,"[23] by which he means they are part of the discontinuous, accidental make-up of the old covenant from which the New Testament saints are freed. The ceremonial part of the Old Testament, Dickson explains, was "super-added" as an "external yoke . . . which neither they nor their posterity were able to bear."[24]

Law Emphasis—Gospel Emphasis

These legal, discontinuous accidentals add up, casting a law emphasis upon the old covenant in contrast to the new covenant's gospel emphasis. For example, Louis Berkhof (1873–1957) says the "free and gracious character" of the Mosaic covenant (in distinction from the Abrahamic and new covenant eras) "is somewhat eclipsed by all kinds of external ceremonies and forms which, in connection with the theocratic life of Israel, placed the demands of the law prominently in the foreground, cf. Gal 3."[25] John Ball (1585–1640) observes this understanding among a majority of the Reformed divines of his day, writing, "Most Divines hold the old and new Covenants to be one in substance and kind, to differ only in degrees."[26]

The emphatic legality of life under the old covenant, which grew out of the civil and ceremonial laws, is highlighted at different points by various writers. John Lightfoot (1602–75) describes the gospel's revelation in the old covenant as dark, obscure, "veiled in types and shadows," and "groped after," in contrast to its clear and evident representation in the new covenant.[27] Francis Turretin (1623–87) says, "it pleased God to administer the Covenant of Grace in this period under a rigid legal economy," which he further describes as "legal" and "more severe."[28]

Others mention the limited distribution of spiritual benefits and the restrained activity of the Holy Spirit in the Old Testament as accounting for

23. Bolton, *True Bounds*, 71–72. See also Arrowsmith, *Theanthropos*, 289.

24. Dickson, *Therapeutica Sacra*, 85. See also Ball, *The Covenant of Grace*, 140–41. Especially see Francis Roberts, *The Mystery and Marrow of the Bible* (London, 1657), 661–77; *Articles* (19.3–4), 15–16.

25. Berkhof, *Systematic Theology*, 296–97.

26. Ball, *Covenant of Grace*, 95; see also Bolton, *True Bounds*, 146.

27. John Lightfoot, *The Whole Works of the Rev. John Lightfoot*, vol. 4 (London, 1822), 395.

28. Francis Turretin, *Institutes of Elenctic Theology*, 3 vols. (Phillipsburg, NJ: P&R, 1994), 2:227.

the legal tone of the old covenant. For example, the Westminster Confession (20.1) reads, "Under the New Testament, the Liberty of Christians is further enlarged in their freedom from the yoke of the Ceremonial Law, to which the Jewish Church was subjected; and in greater boldness of access to the Throne of Grace; and in fuller communications of the Free Spirit of God, than Believers, under the Law, did ordinarily partake of."[29]

Herman Witsius (1636–1708) mentions four things that contribute to the old covenant's legal emphasis. First, there is a more "rigid" requirement of obedience under Moses. Second, "the promises of spiritual and saving grace were more rare and obscure" under the ministry of Moses. Third, the Holy Spirit is given to the Israelites in "scanty and short" measure. Fourth, "the denunciation of the curse" is expressed frequently. All this accounts for why Paul calls the ministry of Moses "the ministration of death and condemnation" in 2 Corinthians 3.[30]

John Calvin (1509–64) explains that among five administrative differences between the old and new covenants, three portray a law-gospel contrast between the Testaments. First, the gospel is obscure and the law is clear under Moses, because the gospel is taught through earthly legal-ritual shadows under Moses. Second, the Mosaic covenant prominently exemplifies the failure of the dead letter to change the heart, whereas the new covenant prominently exemplifies the effectual penetration of the Holy Spirit. Third, the Mosaic covenant produces fear and bondage among God's people, but the New Testament era is one of greater assurance of spiritual freedom.[31] Elsewhere Calvin says the "evangelical promises" in the writings of Moses are "scattered . . . and also somewhat obscure," while "the precepts and rewards, allotted to the observers of the law, frequently occur" in order to teach "the real righteousness of works." He explains that this is why Moses is contrasted with Christ in John 1:17.[32]

---

29. *Articles*, 33. See also B. B. Warfield, *The Person and Work of the Holy Spirit* (Amityville, NY: Calvary Press, 1997), 23–29.

30. Witsius, *Economy*, 2:183; see also ch. 1 in the present volume.

31. Calvin, *Institutes*, 2.11.4–10.

32. John Calvin, *Romans* (Grand Rapids: Baker, 1999), 386–87. See also Marshall, *The Baptizing of Infants* (London, 1644): "Theirs was dispenced in darker prophecies, and obscurer sacrifices, types, and sacraments, ours more gloriously and clearly" (12). Robert Harris, *A Treatise of the New Covenant: Delivered Sermon-wise upon Ezechiel 11. Verse. 19, 20* (London, 1632), says God's covenant with the people of Israel "was a covenant of grace too, as well as with us, and the very same in substance with ours, but yet we have very great advantages, that they wanted." Harris identifies three of them. First, they looked forward to Christ, "but now we look upon all as done, dispatcht, and finished." Second, "their seals were more painfull and chargeable than ours, which in comparison of theirs, are cheape and easie." Third, "our writings are far more cleare, and fairelier written then theirs was; theirs was done more darkly, ours is apparent and conspicuous." He explains that this takes us "beyond, not heathens onely who were without God . . . but even beyond Adam in his innocency, beyond God's ancient people of Israel" (164–65). Oddly, out of 196

John Ball comments that "most Divines" who hold that the old and new covenants differ only in degree explain the differences "so obscurely, that it is hard to find how they [the old and new covenants] consent with themselves" in substance. Regarding explanations like Calvin's, Ball says, "many things herein are spoken truly, but how all these differences should stand, if they be not covenants opposite in kind, it is not easy to understand."[33]

National Principle of Works Inheritance

For some writers, the contrast is also accounted for by the presence of a national principle of works inheritance under Moses (absent in the New Testament), such that the works principle of inheritance applied to the corporate nation generally, with a view to the earthly inheritance of Canaan. For instance, Berkhof explains, "It was not the salvation of the Israelite, but his theocratic standing in the nation, and the enjoyment of external blessings that was made dependent on the keeping of the law."[34] While the faith principle applied to the individual Israelite's inheritance of heaven, a corporate works principle governed the nation's inheritance in the land in some measure.

It is helpful to consider this national perspective on a scale from moderate to extreme expressions. The most conservative expression says that the carnal covenant of temporal blessing was promised to the likes of Ishmael, but the spiritual covenant of soteric, heavenly blessing is promised to Abraham and his spiritual descendants. The note to Genesis 17:19 in the 1599 Geneva Bible says, "The everlasting covenant is made with the children of the Spirit; and with the children of the flesh is made the temporal promise, as was promised to Ishmael."[35] Here a distinct difference is made between the Abrahamic heavenly promise and the Ishmaelian temporal promise. This view of the national-temporal principle effectively removes the temporal feature from the old covenant, and involves no works principle to speak of.

Second on the scale are those who stress that the covenant was made with the whole nation of Israel, in distinction from the new covenant, which

---

pages devoted to the topic of the new covenant Harris addresses the differences between the Old and New in the space of only two pages. The rest of the treatise is a discussion on regeneration. As for the order of the covenants, Harris believes in the covenant of works in Adam and the covenant of grace in Christ (167–68). The covenant of grace was made with Christ, "and next, in Christ it is made with all Christian men and women" (160).

33. Ball, *Covenant of Grace*, 95–96.

34. Berkhof, *Systematic Theology*, 298. See also Hodge, *Systematic Theology*, 2:375; Bolton, *True Bounds*, 156; Thomas Boston, *Complete Works of Thomas Boston*, vol. 7 (Stoke-on-Trent: Tentmaker, 2002), 215–16; A. A. Hodge, *Outlines of Theology* (Carlisle: Banner of Truth, 1999), 376–77.

35. *1599 Geneva Bible* (White Hall: Tolle Lege Press, 2006), 19.

incorporates people among all the nations of the world. William Bridge says, "Then also the covenant was made with that nation of the Jews only, but now it takes in all the world, Jew and Gentile."[36] Whereas the previous view restricts the old covenant order to the spiritual nation, giving little place to carnal participants, this second position opens the covenant order to the earthly nation in a certain sense. Neither of these positions, however, necessarily embraces a principle of *works* inheritance.

Third on the scale, a national works principle is expressed by some writers as an actual aspect of the covenant of grace in the Old Testament. For example, though Berkhof disagrees with those who perceive a separate, national covenant established on Sinai, as quoted above, he does, nevertheless, accept the presence of a national works principle within the Sinai administration of the covenant of grace.[37] The same position is taken by Charles Hodge (1797–1878), who understands organic continuity between the Mosaic covenant and the covenant of grace. While at the same time, the Mosaic covenant "was a national covenant with the Hebrew people . . . the condition was the obedience of the people as a nation to the Mosaic law."[38] Similarly, John Ball, though specifically talking about the Davidic administration of the old covenant of grace, distinguishes between the external and internal administrations of the old covenant. The external administration offered temporal promises to the general populace upon condition of obedience: "If they consent and obey, they shall inherit the good things of the land." The internal administration, however, offered unconditional spiritual blessings by effectual calling. Ball continues, "To the other being effectually called, all other promises are made absolutely, or at least shall absolutely be made good, because God will give them to do what he requireth."[39]

Fourth on the continuum, Witsius calls the Mosaic covenant a national covenant, which is neither the covenant of grace nor the covenant of works. The national covenant is conditioned upon a measure of imperfect obedience. Its focus is on the land of Canaan, but spiritual blessings also attend the national covenant.[40] This view differs from the previous in that the national works aspect is separated from the covenant of grace, composing a distinct covenant.

The fifth point on our continuum is the view of Samuel Bolton, John Owen, and others who believe that the Mosaic covenant is national and

36. Bridge, *Christ and the Covenant*, 66.
37. Berkhof, *Systematic Theology*, 297–99.
38. Hodge, *Systematic Theology*, 375. See also A. A. Hodge, *Outlines of Theology*, 376–77.
39. Ball, *Covenant of Grace*, 154.
40. Witsius, *Economy*, 2:186.

distinct from the covenants of works and grace (like Witsius), but *spiritually ineffectual* (to be distinguished from Witsius).[41] I will speak more about the views of Witsius and Bolton below, pertaining to the relationship between the Mosaic covenant and the covenant of grace.

Sixth, Peter Bulkeley (1583–1659) describes "the Swinish opinion of some Anabaptists, who make the fathers before Christ, to have lived only under a temporall covenant, promoting to them temporall good things . . . without promise or hope of eternall life."[42] Socinians and others might be classified under this heading as well, who admit no presence of the covenant of grace in the Old Testament.[43]

The Redemptive-Historical Perspective

Geerhardus Vos (1862–1949) and Charles Hodge explain the problem of antithesis by appealing to the perspective in redemptive history from which one considers the Mosaic covenant. "It is evident," writes Vos, "that there are two points of view from which the contents of the old dispensation can be regarded." If the Old Testament is viewed relative to what is fulfilled in the New, then "negative judgments are in place" about the Old Testament.[44] For example, Paul speaks about the New Testament era as one of faith in contrast to the Old in Galatians 3:23, 25. It would be a mistake to take Paul as meaning that the old dispensation was a works-based, faithless, nonredemptive era, as some have. Rather, Paul is making a historically relative contrast in absolute terms. In other words, Paul overstates the negative, legal aspect of the old covenant only when considering it from the perspective of the New Testament's fulfilment. Charles Hodge says the same thing: "When viewed in relation to the state of the Church after the advent, it [the Mosaic covenant] is declared to be obsolete. It is represented as a lifeless husk from which the living kernel and germ have been extracted, a body from which the soul has departed."[45] It is worth noting that this same perspective appears in Vos's *Biblical Theology* and in Hodge's *Systematic Theology*.

The Principle of Abstraction

When the New Testament contrasts itself to the Old in terms of a law-gospel antithesis, it is speaking about the law from an absolute perspective, apart

41. Bolton, *True Bounds*, 145.

42. Peter Bulkeley, *The Gospel Covenant* (London, 1651), 141. See also Owen's criticism of the Socinians' view of the Mosaic covenant (*Hebrews*, 98).

43. Blake, *The Covenant of God*, 220. Blake describes this view as "carnal, typical." He says of it that "Papists have led the way, and Socinians and Anabaptists follow."

44. Geerhardus Vos, *Biblical Theology: Old and New Testaments* (1949; Carlisle: Banner of Truth, 1992), 128.

45. Hodge, *Systematic Theology*, 2:376.

from its redemptive context and function in the covenant of grace. The
law is abstracted and compared to the new covenant. For example, Francis
Turretin (1623–87) writes of the Old Testament that it can be viewed from
two perspectives. "Broadly, . . . it contained the doctrine of grace delivered
to the ancients." Of the second perspective he says, "Strictly, however, it
denotes the covenant of works or the moral law given to Moses—the un-
bearable burden . . . of legal ceremonies being added, absolutely and apart
from the promise of grace."[46] Thomas Blake (d. 1657) states this principle
in these words:

> Though the whole law that Moses delivered from God on Mount Sinai to the
> people . . . do containe a covenant of grace, yet the law is taken sometime in
> that strict sense, as containing a covenant of works, holding forth life upon
> condition of perfect obedience. So the apostle, Rom. 10:5, 6. puts an opposi-
> tion between the righteousnesse of the law, and the righteousnesse of faith; so
> also Gal. 3:18 . . . so that, there is a necessity of distinguishing, between the
> law, abstracted from the promise, the promise of Christ. . . .[47]

Rutherford says, "He [Paul] speaks of the law absolutely, as contradistinguished from the gospel, Gal. 4.21. so it is a covenant of works begetting
children to bondage."[48] By "absolutely," Rutherford means abstracted from
the covenant of grace.

John Murray (1898–1975) employs the principle of abstraction, though
roughly stated. Concerning Paul's use of Leviticus 18:5 in Romans 10, Murray writes, "In the original setting it does not appear to have any reference
to legal righteousness as opposed to that of grace. Suffice it to say now that
the formal statement Paul appropriates as one suited to express the principle
of law righteousness."[49] In other words, Paul abstracted the statement from
its original, gracious context.

A Softer Contrast

All are not happy using the law-gospel contrast as a rubric for describing
the relationship between the old and new covenants and have proposed a
softer contrast of promise-fulfilment. To be sure, the previous approaches
do not deny a promise-fulfilment relationship between Moses and Christ.
But writers like Robert Dabney (1820–98) and John Murray propose the

---

46. Turretin, *Institutes*, 2:233–34.
47. Blake, *Covenant of God*, 218.
48. Rutherford, *Covenant of Life*, 63. See also William Strong, *A Discourse of the Two Covenants* (London, 1678), 88.
49. Murray, *Romans*, 51.

promise-fulfilment paradigm in place of the law-gospel paradigm. Dabney boasts he "overthrows Calvin's idea of the [old covenant] dispensation as a less liberal one," contending for a typical-commemorative (i.e., promise-fulfilment) contrast instead.[50] Likewise, Murray says the new covenant "is not contrasted with the old because the old has law and the new has not. The superiority of the new does not consist in the abrogation of that law but in its being brought into . . . more effective fulfillment in us." Further along he refers to the new covenant as the "richest and fullest expression" of the covenant of grace.[51] Murray supports this softer contrast by appealing to the principle of abstraction, mentioned above, and the misinterpretation theory mentioned below.

A seventeenth-century example of this soft contrast is found in Tobias Crisp. Crisp believes in Adam's covenant of works and Christ's covenant of grace. He also holds "that the articles of the covenant of works are drawn up in the Decalogue of the moral law" (material republication). But he maintains that the difference between the old covenant and new covenant is not of law and grace. In particular, regarding Hebrews 7–10, Crisp explains: "The apostle doth not so much as take notice of the moral law, nor hath he to do one jot with any clause of the same. But all the opposition here is not between Christ and Moses; but between priest and priest, office and office."[52] Crisp further describes the testamental transition as from one kind of covenant of grace to another.

The Misinterpretation Theory

In building a case for a softer contrast, Dabney and others interpret passages that would otherwise favor a testamental law-gospel contrast through the lens of the misinterpretation theory.[53] This theory maintains that Paul contrasts the new covenant against a legalistic misinterpretation of the old covenant (i.e., legalism). The antithesis is between Paul and the Pharisees rather than the actual old and new covenants themselves. For example, Norman Shepherd says, "Paul uses an *ad hominem* argument by quoting Scriptures according to the sense in which his opponents understood it."[54] Granted, writers who believe in a real testamental law-gospel contrast also give expression to the misinterpretation theory *periodically*, as they do the

---

50. Robert L. Dabney, *Systematic Theology* (Carlisle: Banner of Truth, 1996), 457–58, 461–62.
51. Murray, *Covenant of Grace*, 29.
52. Crisp, *Christ Alone*, 39–40.
53. Dabney, *Systematic Theology*, 458.
54. Shepherd, *Call of Grace*, 37.

promise-fulfilment paradigm.[55] However, those in favor of a softer contrast attempt to use the misinterpretation theory *systemically* to eliminate any real antithesis from the old and new covenants.[56]

Conclusion

Is the Mosaic covenant antithetical to the new covenant? My purpose is not to answer the question but to survey the Reformed tradition's field of discussion. Most of the writers surveyed say yes and no at the same time. In one or more senses there is antithesis, but at the same time there is a sense of strong continuity. Whatever a particular writer says, he draws from the principles above to explain his view, such that there is no single Reformed answer to the question, only a list of applied principles.

The Principle of Republication

> This is (I confess) somewhat a knotty question, and therefore I would speak warily unto it.[57] —Obadiah Sedgwick (1600–1658)

Having discussed the relation of the Mosaic covenant to the new covenant, I turn to a second question: How does the Mosaic covenant relate to the covenant of works? The issue surrounding the Mosaic covenant's relationship to the new covenant centers on the concept of discontinuity, but questions of continuity surface when the Mosaic covenant is related to the covenant of works.

The Use of Leviticus 18:5 in Romans 10:5 and Galatians 3:12

The Reformed tradition recognizes a principle of republication operating between the covenant of works and the Mosaic covenant, as if to say one is somehow like the other, or one explains the other. For example, William Perkins (1558–1602) calls the Ten Commandments "an abridgment of the whole law, and the covenant of workes."[58] Thomas Goodwin (1600–1679) calls the Mosaic law a "renewing" of the "first covenant," which "was truly the promulgation of the covenant of nature made with Adam in paradise."[59] Examples of various expressions are vast.

---

55. Berkhof, *Systematic Theology*, 297, 300; Calvin, *Institutes*, 1.13.14; Turretin, *Institutes*, 2:234, 267–68; Witsius, *Economy*, 2:184–85.

56. Bulkeley, *Gospel Covenant*, 65, 70, 71, 72.

57. Sedgwick, *Bowels of Tender Mercy*, 172.

58. William Perkins, *The Works of That Famous and Worthie Minister of Christ, A Golden Chaine* (Cambridge, 1603), 26.

59. Thomas Goodwin, *The Works of Thomas Goodwin*, vol. 5, *The Work of the Holy Ghost in Our Salvation* (Eureka: Tanski, 1996), 353–54. See also Boston, *Works*, 195–98; Owen, *Hebrews*, 76; Rollock, *God's Effectual Calling*, 7; Geerhardus Vos, *Redemptive History and Biblical*

It is not uncommon for writers to quote Leviticus 18:5 of the Mosaic covenant, "Do this and live," when describing the principle on which the covenant of works is governed. Paul set this precedent in Galatians 3:12 and Romans 10:5. Therefore, many Reformed explanations of the covenant of works follow Paul's example. For instance, Robert Harris (d. 1660) says, "The covenant of workes stands upon personall obedience to all Gods commandments, the sanction of this covenant is, Do this and live, faile in doing of it and dye."[60] Obadiah Sedgwick says, "In the covenant of works, it is, Do this and Live."[61] In other words, Reformed writers describe the covenant of works and support what they say about it by citing Leviticus 18:5 where Moses is talking about the Mosaic covenant. Thus Karlberg writes, "The Mosaic Covenant is to be viewed *in some sense* as a covenant of works."[62] In what sense?

For the sake of avoiding verbal arguments, it is important to define the sense in which the Mosaic covenant republishes the covenant of works, since some writers emphatically oppose relating the Mosaic covenant with the covenant of works. John Ball says, "Herein there appears no intexture of the covenant of workes with the covenant of grace."[63] Samuel Rutherford echoes Ball: "But the truth is, the law as pressed upon Israel was not a covenant of works."[64] But even blunt statements like these are not without nuance and qualification elsewhere, so as to grant a measure of continuity between the covenant of works and the Mosaic covenant. Therefore, to avoid a verbal argument it is necessary to define the sense in which the covenant of works might be republished in the Mosaic covenant.

Material Republication (the Moral Law)

The Mosaic covenant is referred to loosely or generally as a republication of the covenant of works, but this is understood in a variety of ways. The principle of republication is expressed, first, in terms of moral law. Dabney says "the transactions at Sinai," among other things, include a "republica-

---

Interpretation: The Shorter Writings of Geerhardus Vos, ed. Richard B. Gaffin Jr. (Phillipsburg, NJ: P&R, 2001), 254–55; Witsius, *Economy*, 2:182–83; Marshall, *The Baptizing of Infants*, 10.

60. Harris, *New Covenant*, 169. See also William Perkins, *A Commentarie . . . upon the First Five Chapters of the Epistle to the Galatians* (Cambridge, 1604), 182.

61. Sedgwick, *Bowels of Tender Mercy*, 8. See also Strong, *Two Covenants*, 88. He explains that this principle describes the covenant made with Christ. Rutherford, *Covenant of Life*, 349, explains that this principle was required of Adam and fulfilled by Christ.

62. Karlberg, *Covenant Theology*, 18. Also cf. Henry Ainsworth, *Annotations upon the Five Bookes of Moses* (London, 1627); Ball, *The Covenant of Grace*. Ainsworth maintains that Leviticus 18:5 promises "eternal life for doing them" (103), but Ball says, "These words, Doe this and live, must not be interpreted, as if they did promise life upon condition of perfect obedience" (136–37).

63. Ball, *Covenant of Grace*, 142.

64. Rutherford, *Covenant of Life*, 60.

tion of the moral law."[65] This means the precepts, as a rule of life, are continuous and consistent with the prelapsarian era. When Edmund Calamay (1600–1666) calls the Mosaic covenant "a perfect copy of the covenant of works, yet being given to another end," he means the Ten Commandments are a copy of the covenant of works in a very restricted way; namely to function only as a rule of life, not as a covenant. Calamay repeatedly calls the Ten Commandments a "copy" or a "perfect copy" of the covenant of works. But he heavily qualifies this at the same time, saying the Ten Commandments are neither the covenant of works nor of grace, but "a rule of life for those already in covenant." Further along he calls it "the moral law."[66]

Perhaps with more precision, Obadiah Sedgwick distinguishes between the *matter* and *form* of the Ten Commandments, the former referring to the *precepts* of the law, the latter referring to the precepts *functioning as a covenant*. "Though materially it [the Decalogue] respected works, yet formally and intentionally, it was not then given and established as a covenant of works, by which we should be justified and live."[67] This is soft republication, or material republication, because it extracts any sense of a covenantal function or intent from the likeness between Adam and Moses, admitting only a moral continuity, which can be said about every historical dispensation of time from the probation to the eschaton.

Formal Republication (the Covenant of Works)

While some employ the matter and form designation to soften the nature of this republication, others employ it to strengthen the republication, as if to say that the Mosaic covenant republished the covenant of works as a rule *and a covenant*. This is hard republication, or formal republication. William Strong (d. 1654) follows this track, though with the important qualification that the Lord never intended the Mosaic law to be used as a mechanism for actually earning eternal life. For Strong, the Decalogue

---

65. Dabney, *Systematic Theology*, 453.

66. Calamay, *Two Solemne Covenants*, 10–11.

67. Sedgwick, *Bowels of Tender Mercy*, 10: "Which [the law given to Moses] may be considered two wayes, viz. 1. As to the matter of it, as to which I grant that therein is the covenant of works to be found. 2ly As to the form or sanction of it, as given (at this time) to the people of Israel, thus I deny it to be the covenant of works" (173). See also Ball, *Covenant of Grace*: "The law hath a double respect: one as the unchangeable rule of life and manners, according to which persons in covenant ought to walke before and with the Lord, and in this sense it belongs to the covenant of grace. The other, as it is propounded in forme of a covenant, as if he must necessarily perish, who doth neglect or break it in the least jot or tittle, and in this sense the covenant of grace and works are opposite. The matter of evangelicall precepts and of the morall law is the same, but the forme of promulgation is not the same: the rule is one, but the covenants differ" (15). See also Boston, *Works*, 171–72.

was more than a republication of the moral law (the matter), but also the covenant of works properly speaking (the form). He says, "It was not only delivered as a rule of righteousness, but in the form and terms of a covenant." Further along he writes, "It was delivered after a sort in the form of the covenant of works."[68] The exact nature of this hard, formal republication varies from writer to writer. The following views are versions of formal republication.

Relative, Formal Covenant of Works

One of the most notable among such expressions is that the Mosaic covenant is relatively the covenant of works. This means that to some people it is the covenant of works, but to others it is the covenant of grace. The difference depends upon whether or not one is in the state of nature or grace. For example, William Strong writes,

> The Lord's intention in giving the Law was double, unto the carnal Jews to set forth to them the old covenant which they had broken; and yet unto the believing Jews it did darkly shadow and set forth unto them the Covenant of Grace made with Christ, and therefore it was not only delivered as a rule of righteousness, but in the form and terms of a covenant, *this do and thou shalt live.*[69]

In other words, if a person was a believer, then the Ten Commandments represented the precepts that Christ perfectly performed in the believer's stead (below referred to as typological, formal republication) and a rule of righteousness governing the believer's behavior (above referred to as material republication). But if a person is not a believer, then the Ten Commandments represent the broken covenant of works (relative, formal republication).

This principle of relativity is found also in the Westminster Larger Catechism (q. 93), in which the moral law functions as a covenant of works "to unregenerate men . . . to leave them inexcusable, and under the curse thereof." Whereas "they that are regenerate" are "delivered from the Morall Law as a Covenant of works, so as thereby they are neither justified nor condemned." Further along the Ten Commandments are described "as the rule of their obedience."[70] Rutherford, while denying that the Mosaic covenant is truly a covenant of works, does say, "But Paul speaks, Gal. 3, of the law as relative to that people.

---

68. Strong, *Two Covenants*, 88.
69. Ibid., 88.
70. *The Humble Advice of the Assembly of Divines, Now by Authority of Parliament Sitting at Westminster, Concerning a Larger Catechism: Presented to Both Houses of Parliament* (London, 1647), 25.

. . . He speaks of the Law absolutely as contradistinguished from the gospel, Gal. 4.21. So it is a covenant of works begetting children to bondage."[71] Ball speaks of the Mosaic law as having a "two-fold servitude," one to damnation in relation to those who seek to establish their own righteousness, and another as a tutor to Christ and a rule for godly living in relation to the regenerate.[72]

Thomas Blake, on the other hand, opposes the relativity principle, saying it "is a mistake in some that say, that the law is, doubtless a pure covenant of works to some men, but not to all." Blake contends, "What this covenant is to any, it is to all, whether it be of works or of grace." His argument is that "no occasion or accident can change the nature of a thing."[73]

Pedagogical, Formal Republication

The next expression of the formal principle may be called pedagogical republication, which means the Mosaic covenant was given to the Israelites on Sinai in such a way as to teach them about the covenant of works, but no further. The pedagogical principle is taken from Galatians 3:24 where Paul says, "The Law has become our tutor to lead us to Christ" (NASB).

William Bridge, citing Galatians 3 and 4, says the Mosaic covenant "declared and promulgated" the covenant of works to Israel, but did not "make" the covenant of works. Rather, the covenant of grace was "made." Formal republication functioned pedagogically, "to be a school master to bring to Christ. It was there in subserviency, and upon a gospel design."[74]

Peter Bulkeley grants that at Mount Sinai "the Covenant of workes was then revealed and made known to the children of Israel, as being before almost obliterated and blotted out of man's heart, and therefore God renewed the knowledge of the Covenant of workes to them." He further explains that the law "contained the sum of the Covenant of workes" but it did not function as a covenant of works. Rather, "it was subservient and helpfull unto them, to attaine the end of the former covenant of grace which God had made with them in their fathers."[75]

Hypothetical, Formal Republication

The next type of formal republication is, perhaps, the most commonly recognized. The covenant of works was republished hypothetically in coordination with the pedagogical principle above. Ball says those who la-

71. Rutherford, *Covenant of Life*, 60, 63.
72. Ball, *Covenant of Grace*, 141–42, 135.
73. Blake, *Covenant of God*, 213.
74. Bridge, *Christ and the Covenant*, 64.
75. Bulkeley, *Gospel Covenant*, 62–63.

bor to explain further and clarify the administrative differences between the Old and New Testaments teach: "The old testament doth promise life eternall plainly under the condition of morall obedience perfect, that is under condition altogether impossible, together with an heavy burden of legal rites and a yoke of most strict pollicie, but covertly under the condition of repentance and faith."[76] This is a hypothetical offer of salvation by works for pedagogical purposes, unlike what might be found in the New Testament.[77] While there Christ, on a personal level, offered the rich young ruler an impossible offer of salvation by works to humble him, in the old covenant this hypothetical offer was an actual accessory of the covenant administration. The purpose of this hypothetical offer was to meet and break down pride, since the Israelites "swelled with mad assurance in themselves, saying, 'All that the Lord comandeth we will do,' and be obedient, Exod. xix. 8."[78]

This hypothetical principle reflects, generally speaking, the pedagogical use of the law. Louis Berkhof explains, "It is customary in theology to distinguish a three-fold use of the law." The first use is civil or political, in which God's law, as a means of common grace, helps restrain sin in secular society. The second use is pedagogical, in which "the law serves the purpose of bringing man under conviction of sin, and of making him conscious of his inability to meet the demands of the law. In that way the law becomes a tutor to lead him to Christ."[79] The third use is the normative use, in which the law is a guide for believers to understand God's revealed will, and a means of sanctification. When systematic theologians discuss the threefold use of the law, they do not necessarily have in mind what is unique about the Mosaic, legal economy, but what is continuous about the moral law in every dispensation since the fall. The hypothetical principle appears to reflect a specific example of the second use of the law in operation within the Mosaic structure.

76. Ball, *Covenant of Grace*, 96. See also Vos, "The Doctrine of the Covenant in Reformed Theology," in *Redemptive History*, 254–55.

77. Calvin, *Four Last Books of Moses*, 202–5; Calvin, *Romans*, 387; Mark Karlberg, "The Mosaic Covenant and the Concept of Works in Reformed Hermeneutics: A Historical-Critical Analysis with Particular Attention to Early Covenant Eschatology," Th.D. diss., Westminster Theological Seminary, 1980, 172. I call this the hypothetical works principle, but this language is not to be confused with Obadiah Sedgwick's similar terminology. He speaks of an absolute covenant and a hypothetical covenant. An absolute covenant is a monergistic, unconditional covenant, which requires no reciprocal response from man, exemplified in the covenant God made with Noah. A hypothetical covenant is a conditional covenant, which requires a response from man, either of works or faith. The covenants of works and grace are both hypothetical covenants according to Sedgwick's use of this terminology. See Sedgwick, *Bowels of Tender Mercy*, 6–7.

78. Boston, *Complete Works*, 205.

79. Berkhof, *Systematic Theology*, 614.

Typological, Formal Republication

Some people explain the works principle in a typological fashion. The heavy works burden, which is pressed upon the Jewish people, is a shadow of Jesus being born under the law to fulfil actively all its precepts in behalf of sinners. In the same way that the sacrifices foreshadow Jesus' passive obedience in suffering the curse-sanctions of the law, the do-this-and-live principle foreshadows his active obedience in keeping the precepts of the whole law. Samuel Bolton describes this view as held by some of the divines, writing, "There is another interpretation, and that is, that Doe this and live, though it was spoken to them immediately, yet not terminatively, but through them to Christ, who hath fulfilled all righteousnesse for us, and purchased life by his own obedience."[80] In the same way that Paul says God's covenant promise to Abraham was really spoken to Christ (Gal. 3:16, 19), God's covenant requirement of obedience upon Israel was really placed on Christ.

Bolton lists this interpretation as existing among the views of the divines of his day. For instance, William Strong says the "giving of the law . . . did darkly shadow and set forth unto them the Covenant of Grace made with Christ, and therefore it was not only delivered unto them as rule of righteousness, but in the form and terms of a Covenant, this do and thou shalt live."[81] Thomas Collier (ca. 1600s) says, "They had a righteousness commanded, which was a righteousness of doing, which they could not attain, a representation of the righteousness of Christ who was to fulfill all, and so become the end of the law for righteousness to everyone that believeth."[82]

Witsius gives expression to the hermeneutic behind such a view. Explaining the function of typology in the Old Testament, he writes, "Enoch walked with God, that is, according to the apostle, Heb. xi. 5. *pleased God.* This also Christ perfectly did, 'in whom the Father was well pleased.'" He also says, "Noah was a *just man in his generation*; Christ was *holy, harmless, undefiled*, and separate from sinners, knew no sin, neither was guile found in his mouth; nay, he is Jehovah our righteousness." Further along Witsius typologically compares Isaac's obedience to Abraham to Christ's obedience

80. Bolton, *True Bounds*, 156.
81. Strong, *Two Covenants*, 88; see also Meredith Kline, *God, Heaven, and Harmagedon: A Covenant Tale of Cosmos and Telos* (Eugene, OR: Wipf and Stock, 2006), 79, 127–28; idem, *Kingdom Prologue: Genesis Foundations for a Covenantal Worldview* (Eugene, OR: Wipf and Stock, 2006), 220–36; Vern Poythress, *The Shadow of Christ in the Law of Moses* (Phillipsburg, NJ: Presbyterian and Reformed, 1991), 72–73, 77; Michael Horton, *God of Promise: Introducing Covenant Theology* (Grand Rapids: Baker, 2006), 31–32.
82. Thomas Collier, *A Discourse of the True Gospel Blessedness in the New Covenant* (London, 1659), 22, 31.

to God the Father.[83] More recently Vos and Meredith Kline (1922–2007) incorporate this approach, aligned with the national principle of works inheritance.[84]

I should point out that the authors mentioned above, while accepting the typological principle of works, do not all agree on the organic question. For instance, unlike Kline and Vos, Collier, Witsius, and Strong view the Mosaic covenant as distinct and independent of the covenant of grace.[85]

Complex, Formal Republication

Thomas Boston (1676–1732) expresses a double republication view, which may be called complex, formal republication. The covenant of works *and* the covenant of grace were republished on Mount Sinai. "I conceive the two covenants to have been both delivered on Mount Sinai to the Israelites. First, the covenant of Grace made with Abraham. . . . Secondly, the covenant of works made with Adam."[86] In this quote Boston is distinguishing his own view from that of Edward Fisher who promotes formal republication. Andrew McGowan is mistaken when he writes, "Boston argues, the Mosaic covenant was simply the republication of the covenant of works first made in the garden with Adam."[87] Boston argues that the Ten Commandments were not "simply" a republication of the covenant of works, but rather a complex republication of the covenant of works and grace. This is notable only because Boston goes out of his way to distinguish his own view from the position McGowan attributes to him.

Conclusion

How does the Mosaic covenant relate to the covenant of works? The Reformed tradition recognizes a material and/or a formal relationship. As material, the precepts are continuous. As formal, the covenant itself is re-

---

83. Witsius, *Economy*, 2:196–97, 201.

84. Vos, *Biblical Theology*, 127; Meredith Kline, *Treaty of the Great King: The Covenant Structure of Deuteronomy* (Grand Rapids: Eerdmans, 1963), 65, 124–25; see also Mark Karlberg, *Covenant Theology*, 48.

85. "The New Covenant . . . was nevertheless a renewal of the Mosaic Covenant. It belonged to the familiar administrative pattern of periodic covenant renewal . . . and renewal is the exponent of continuity" (Kline, *By Oath Consigned*, 75). Vos calls abandoning the "positive, vital continuity" between the Old and New Testaments "the Gnostic position" (*Biblical Theology*, 129). "The covenants of the old and new testament are not one, as some imagine, but two . . . clearly to be distinguished, and not confounded together, no more than light and darkness" (Collier, *True Gospel Blessedness*, 4). In relation to the covenants of works and grace, the Mosaic covenant "was formally neither the one nor the other" (Witsius, *Economy*, 2:186). "Therefore, the apostle makes it [the Mosaic covenant] a distinct covenant from the covenant of grace" (Strong, *Two Covenants*, 90).

86. Boston, *Works*, 197.

87. Andrew McGowan, *The Federal Theology of Thomas Boston* (Carlisle: Paternoster, 1997), 10–11.

vived with an adjusted function in keeping with the covenant of grace; namely, to reveal those who are in Adam (the relative principle), to teach them about their moral ineptitude (the pedagogical principle), by presenting an impossible offer of salvation by works (the hypothetical principle), which only Christ has fulfilled (the typological principle), coupled with the relief and offer of grace and forgiveness by Christ's mediation (the complex principle). While few have attempted to incorporate all of these principles into a single position, and many theologians argue against one or another of them, the principles themselves appear complementary.

The Mosaic Covenant and the Covenant of Grace

> Here at first we meet with great difficulty, How, and whether at all the Covenant of Grace, was manifested by Moses?[88] —John Ball

How does the Mosaic covenant relate to the covenant of grace? Competing views may be divided into two general categories. First, the Mosaic covenant is an organically integrated administrative part of the covenant of grace or, second, the Mosaic covenant is a separate covenant, distinct from the covenant of grace, while nevertheless serving the purposes of the covenant of grace.

Administrative Covenant

The administrative view appears to have been the majority position among the seventeenth-century divines.[89] Stress is laid on the notion that the Mosaic covenant is an organic part of the covenant of grace. This position does not, however, preclude finding the covenant of works republished in the Mosaic covenant in some manner. For example, Calvin and others believed that the hypothetical principle of works inheritance was covenantally published in the accessories of the Mosaic covenant.[90]

As seen above, Calamy goes so far as to say that the Mosaic covenant is not a covenant at all. For him it is nothing more than a rule of life given to the Jews. It is not a covenant of grace. It is not a covenant of works. It is not a mixed covenant, or a subservient covenant, or a national covenant (all described below), or any kind of covenant. "Some . . . say the law at Mount Sinai was a covenant of grace, and others say it was a covenant of works,

---

88. Ball, *Covenant of Grace*, 95.
89. Ibid., 95; Bolton, *The True Bounds*, 146; Owen, *Hebrews*, 71.
90. Calvin, *Romans*, 386–87; Bridge, *Christ and the Covenant*, 64; Strong, *Two Covenants*, 88; Turretin, *Institutes*, 2:227; Vos, *Redemptive History*, 254–55.

but I shall prove that it was neither, but only given to those that were in covenant as a rule of obedience."[91] This position is coordinated with recognizing the differences between the old and new covenants as administrative rather than substantive (discussed above). Since both the old and new covenants are administrations of the same covenant of grace, there is no fundamental antithesis between them, only accidental, administrative differences.

Distinct Covenant

The second category of opinions finds the Mosaic covenant *organically* distinct from the covenant of grace (and the new covenant). There are at least six variations of this view among Reformed writers. All of the views below agree that there is a natural breach on the substantive level between the Mosaic covenant and the covenant of grace, as if to say that the Mosaic covenant *is not* a mere internal administration of the covenant of grace, but another covenant altogether. The Mosaic covenant is external to the covenant of grace. What remains among these views is to identify the nature of the Mosaic covenant as it stands alone.

A Distinct Covenant of Works

First, the Mosaic covenant is a distinct covenant of works. Edward Fisher (1627–55) says the Mosaic covenant "was added by way of [external] subserviency [not internal ingrediency as he describes earlier] and attendance to better advance and make effectual the covenant of grace." He quotes from Amandus Polanus (1561–1610), William Pemble (1592–1623), and John Preston (1587–1628) to show his agreement with them.[92] Jeremiah Burroughs (1600–1646) believed in three distinct covenants: a covenant of works with Adam, *a covenant of works with Israel*, and a covenant of grace made at the incarnation of Christ.[93] James Pope (mid-1600s) believed in two covenants: a covenant of works made with Israel, and a covenant of grace made in the death of Christ.[94] In the minds of some, any manner of

91. Calamay, *Two Solemne Covenants*, 8.
92. Boston, *Works*, 200. See also Bolton, *True Bounds*, 128–29; Ward, *God and Adam*, 128–29; "And foure hundred and thirty yeeres after the Law was added with great terrour upon Mount Sinai, not as part of this Covenant, but as the apostle saith expressely, it was added . . ." (Marshall, *Baptizing of Infants*, 10).
93. Calamay, *Two Solemne Covenants*, 1.
94. Ibid.; James Pope, *The Unveiling of the Antichrist* (London, 1646). Pope describes the following differences between the two covenants. First, the covenant of works was made at the time of the exodus, the covenant of grace at the time of the crucifixion (2–3). Second, the first covenant "was made with Israel after the flesh; the second as they are considered in spiritual relation to Christ" (3). Third, the covenant of works only promised temporal blessings and curses, but the covenant of grace concerned spiritual promises (4). Fourth, the mediators were, first, Moses, second Christ (4). Fifth, the blood of animals belonged to the first, and the blood of Christ belonged to the second

formal republication of the covenant of works requires extracting the Mosaic covenant from the body of the covenant of grace, resulting in this view. One must still identify the manner of formal republication as surveyed above (i.e., relative, pedagogical, hypothetical, typological, etc.).

Covenant of Grace

Others describe the Mosaic covenant as a distinct covenant of grace. Anthony Burgess writes that the Mosaic covenant was a covenant of grace, saying, "Some . . . make it a covenant of works, others a mixt covenant, some a subservient covenant; but I am perswaded to goe with those who hold it to be a covenant of grace."[95] Another member of the Westminster Assembly, Edmund Calamay, disputes with Burgess who Calamay says holds "that the law at Mount Sinai was a covenant of grace, implying that there is more than one covenant of grace, and this is affirmed by Mr. Anthony Burgesse in his Vindication of the Morall Law."[96] Burgess, however, appears to be misrepresented by Calamay, because further along Burgess affirms that the Mosaic covenant *is not* a distinct covenant of grace, but an organic part of the single covenant of grace.[97] In other words, Burgess does not belong in this category, though Calamay infers that he does.

This is the only view the Westminster Confession (7.6) explicitly denies: "There are not therefore two covenants of grace, differing in substance, but one and the same, under various dispensations."[98] Why? Likely because of the implication that there would be two methods of salvation. Tobias Crisp, reputed to be an antinomian, also held this view but in such a manner as to affirm two different orders of salvation (see n. 8).[99]

Mixed Covenant of Works and Grace

A third proposal finds the Mosaic covenant mixed of works and grace. George Walker (1581–1651) says, "For that Covenant is a mixt Covenant, partly of the Covenant of Workes, which is the old covenant, partly of the

---

(4). Sixth, the law was written on stone in the first covenant, but on the heart in the second (4). Seventh, one is obscure while the other is plain (5). Eighth, the worship in the first covenant was typological, but the worship in the second is spiritual (5). Ninth, "the first covenant is done away, that the second might be established" (5). The remainder of Pope's treatise makes application of these differences (5–26). For example, on the basis of difference number two he does not consider infants born to believing parents in the New Testament as "federaly holy" (6–7).

95. Burgess, *Morall Law*, 232.
96. Calamay, *Two Solemne Covenants*, 1.
97. Burgess, *Morall Law*, 246.
98. *Articles*, 15–16.
99. Crisp, *Christ Alone*, 31–68. See also, Ward, *God and Adam*, 132–33; Ernest Kevan, *The Grace of Law: A Study in Puritan Theology* (London: Carey Kingsgate, 1964), 25–28, 31–36.

Covenant of Grace, which was made after the fall."[100] Thomas Boston's view expressing complex republication also seems consistent with this.

National Covenant of Sincere Piety
Witsius describes Sinai as neither a covenant of works nor of grace, "but a covenant of sincere piety which supposes both." He also calls it "a national covenant between God and Israel." He explains that the obedience supposed in the national covenant is imperfect, and so dependent on the covenant of grace to achieve the promised reward. Witsius also says the terror accompanying the Mosaic covenant testifies to the reality of the covenant of works, which in turn "excited" Israel "to embrace the covenant of God."[101] Importantly, he explains that the reward for obedience to this national covenant is received in both this life and the next, benefiting both body and soul, which distinguishes his view from the next.

Subservient Covenant
Drawing from the teaching of John Cameron (1579–1625), Samuel Bolton promotes what he calls the subservient covenant. This view is similar to Witsius's national covenant, reflecting the influence of the covenants of works and grace. Yet reward is restricted to the temporal sphere of earthly life only. He explains that the subservient covenant "was temporary, & had respect to Canaan & God's blessing there, in obedience to it, and not to heaven."[102] Bolton calls this third covenant a subservient covenant because it is pedagogically subservient to soteric grace. Owen also promotes this view of the Mosaic covenant, stressing that it is not a spiritually saving covenant or a spiritually condemning covenant.

> This covenant thus made, with these ends and promises [not exceeding the temporal boundaries of Canaan], did never save or condemn any man eternally. All that lived under the administration of it did attain eternal life, or perished forever, not *by virtue of this covenant*, as formally such. It did, indeed, revive the commanding power and sanction of the first covenant of works. . . . And on the other hand, it directed also unto the promise, which was the instrument of life and salvation unto all that did believe. But as unto what it had of its own, it was confined unto things temporal.[103]

100. Walker, *Manifold Wisedome* (London, 1640), 66. See also Bolton, *True Bounds*, 128; Ward, *God and Adam*, 131–32.
101. Witsius, *Economy*, 2:186.
102. Bolton, *True Bounds*, 353–401, 145. Bolton translates and publishes Cameron's work on the Mosaic covenant as an appendix titled "Certain Theses, or Positions of the Learned John Cameron, concerning the Three-fold Covenant of God with Man."
103. Owen, *Hebrews*, 85.

"Bastard" Covenant

A notable view distinguishes itself from those above in that they all propose covenants that are established by God. David Dickson explains that the carnal Israelites devised a covenant of their own making on Sinai, which Dickson calls a "counterfeit, bastard covenant of works." In this covenant the carnal Israelites turn the covenant of grace "whereunto God was calling them, into a covenant of works of their own framing." Namely, they seek justification through external, ceremonial obedience. "And all these sorts of covenants of mens framing," writes Dickson, "we call bastard-covenants, because God will not admit any other Covenant of works than that which requireth perfect personal obedience." Dickson also adds that a bastard covenant was entertained in the New Testament, insofar as men joined their own works to their faith for justification. He identifies the error of the false apostles among the Galatians and also the Arminians.[104]

Conclusion

Is the Mosaic covenant part of the covenant of grace? Those who answer yes, like Calvin and Kline, consider it an "administration" of the covenant of grace. Those who answer no consider it a distinct covenant, and must go on to describe the nature of this distinct covenant as another covenant of works, or another covenant of grace, or a mixed covenant of works and grace, or a national covenant, or a subservient covenant.

Conclusion

> This is a subject wrapped up in much obscurity, and attended with many difficulties.[105] —John Owen

I hope to have given the reader a clear outline of Reformed trajectories on the place of the Mosaic covenant in the history of redemption. I have explained the problem of antithesis, the principle of republication, and the organic question. An attempt to interact with the Reformed tradition regarding the problem of antithesis should consider the function of the substance-accidents distinction, the civil-ceremonial-moral distinctions, the law-gospel emphases, the national principle of works, the redemptive-historical perspective, the principle of abstraction, the softer contrast, and the principle of misinterpretation. An attempt to interact with the Reformed tradition

---

104. Dickson, *Therapeutica Sacra*, 82–83, 108–9. See also Karlberg, *Covenant Theology*, 33; Ward, *God and Adam*, 138–39.
105. Owen, *Hebrews*, 60.

regarding the principle of republication should consider Paul's use of Leviticus 18:5, the distinction between material and formal republication, along with the formal principles of relativity, pedagogy, hypothetical, typological, and complex republication. An attempt to interact with the Reformed tradition regarding the organic question should consider the distinction between an administration and a distinct covenant; and among the latter, recognize further distinctions between works, grace, complex, national, subservient, and bastard covenants.

Works in the Mosaic Covenant:
A Reformed Taxonomy of the Order of the Covenants

	Five	Four	Four	Four	Four	Three	Three	Three	Three	Three	Two	Two	Two	One
How many covenants?	Five	Four				Three					Two			One
When is each covenant established?	Prelapsarian Prelapsarian Postlapsarian Postlapsarian Postlapsarian	Pre Post Post Post	Pre Pre Post Post	Pre Pre Post Post			Pre Post Post			Pre Pre Post	Post Post	Post Post	Pre Pre	Post
What kind of covenants are they, respectively?	Redemption Works Grace OT "Bastard" NT "Bastard"	Works Works Grace Grace	Redemption Works Grace Temporal	Redemption Works Grace National	Grace Works Works Temporal	Works Works Grace	Works Grace Grace	Nature Grace Subservient	Grace Works Mixed	Redemption Nature Grace	Works Grace	Grace Works	Grace Works	Grace
With whom is each covenant made, respectively?	Christ Adam Believers OT Legalists NT Legalists	Adam Israel Abraham Jesus	Christ Adam Believers Israel	Christ Adam Believers Israel	Christ Adam Israel Israel	Adam Israel Christ	Adam Israel Believers	Adam Believers Israel	Christ Adam Israel	Christ Adam Believers	Israel Believers	Abraham Moses	Christ Adam	Believers
How does the Mosaic covenant relate to the covenant of grace?	Administration	Distinct	Distinct	Distinct	Distinct	Distinct	Distinct	Distinct	Distinct	Administration	Distinct	Administration	Administration	Administration
Who represents this position?	Dickson[1]	Simpson[2]	Owen[3]	Witsius[4]	Fisher[5]	Burroughs[6]	Crisp[7]	Cameron,[8] Bolton	Boston[9]	Turretin[10]	Pope,[11] Collier	Calvin[12]	Calamay[13]	Murray[14]

1. David Dickson, *Therapeutica Sacra* (London, 1664), 22, 71, 86, 82, 108. For Dickson the "bastard" covenants are man-made.

2. Edmund Calamay, *Two Solemn Covenants between God and Man* (London, 1646), 1.

3. John Owen, *The Works of John Owen*, ed. William H. Goold, vol. 12, *The Mystery of the Gospel Vindicated* (Johnstone and Hunter, 1850–53; repr., Carlisle, PA: Banner of Truth, 1999), 507; John Owen, *The Works of John Owen*, ed. William Goold, vol. 22, *An Exposition of the Epistle to the Hebrews*, vol. 6 (Johnstone and Hunter: 1855; repr., Carlisle, PA: Banner of Truth, 1991), 60, 62, 63, 85, 86.

4. Herman Witsius, *The Economy of the Covenants*, vol. 2 (London, 1822; repr., Kingsburg: den Dulk Christian Foundation, 1990), 186.

5. Thomas Boston, *Complete Works of Thomas Boston*, vol. 7, *The Marrow of Modern Divinity with Notes* (Stoke-on-Trent: Tentmaker, 2002), 182, 184, 192, 171, 173, 198, 199, 204, 216, 196–98.

6. Calamay, *Two Solemn Covenants*, 1.

7. Tobias Crisp, *Christ Alone Exalted; in Seventeen Sermons*, vol. 2 (London, 1643), 39, 40, 42, 43, 44, 45, 47, 48, 50.

8. Samuel Bolton, *The True Bounds of Christian Freedome . . . whereunto Is Annexed a Discourse of the Learned John Camerons, Touching the Threefold Covenant of God with Man*, trans. Samuel Bolton (London, 1645), 356.

9. Thomas Boston, *The Complete Works*, vol. 8, *A View of the Covenant of Grace from the Sacred Records* (Stoke-on-Trent: Tentmaker, 2002), 397; vol. 11, *A View of the Covenant of Works from the Sacred Records*, 178; vol. 7, *The Marrow of Modern Divinity with Notes*, 197, 200.

10. Francis Turretin, *Institutes of Elenctic Theology*, trans. George Musgrave Giger, ed. James T. Dennison Jr, 3 vols. (Phillipsburg, NJ: P&R, 1992–97), 2:174–257; 1:574–78.

11. Calamay, *Two Solemn Covenants*, 1; James Pope, *The Unveiling of the Antichrist* (London, 1648); Thomas Collier, *A Discourse of the True Gospel Blessedness in the Newe Covenant* (London, 1659).

12. John Calvin, *Calvin's Commentaries*, vol. 21, *Commentaries on the Epistles of Paul to the Galatians and Ephesians*, trans. William Pringle (Grand Rapids: Baker, 1999), 97, 98; John Calvin, *Institutes of the Christian Religion*, ed. John T. McNeil, trans. Ford Lewis Battles, 2 vols., Library of Christian Classics 21–22 (Philadelphia: Westminster, 1960), 1:450.

13. Calamay, *Two Solemn Covenants*, 8.

14. John Murray, *Collected Writings*, vol. 2, *Select Lectures in Systematic Theology* (Carlisle, PA: Banner of Truth, 1996), 47–59; John Murray, *The Covenant of Grace* (1953; repr., Phillipsburg, NJ: P&R, 1988).

PART TWO

BIBLICAL STUDIES

4

LEVITICUS 18:5 AND DEUTERONOMY
30:1–14 IN BIBLICAL THEOLOGICAL
DEVELOPMENT

*Entitlement to Heaven Foreclosed
and Proffered*

BRYAN D. ESTELLE

The main theme of this book has to do with the republication of the covenant of works in the Mosaic covenant. Therefore, it touches (albeit indirectly) upon the contemplated legal outcome of the covenant of works: the promise of life or what I am calling *entitlement to heaven*.[1] This essay will demonstrate that the biblical evidence teaches that one way of obtaining entitlement to heaven has been foreclosed and another proffered. This book also touches profoundly (directly and indirectly) upon the doctrine of justification. Regarding that doctrine, entitlement to heaven has been an underdeveloped aspect. That fact has probably contributed to misunderstandings of texts—Scripture and otherwise—in the academy, to many sophomoric debates inside and outside of church courts and theological

1. See Westminster Confession of Faith 7:2.

journals, and perhaps even to an impoverishment among God's people with regards to their understanding of the benefits already possessed by virtue of their standing before God.

This chapter will deal with a very specific tension, not directly resolved within the Old Testament itself (with small exception): interpreting the significance of the Mosaic law in its own context does not automatically leave the impression of easily fitting a Pauline or New Testament paradigm. When these perspectives converge, seriously examined against their own immediate and following contexts, they raise a number of profound questions. For example, since obedience and disobedience are clearly tied to sanctions of blessing and curse, what measure of obedience and disobedience triggers the sanctions as recorded at the end of Deuteronomy and elsewhere in the Torah? Furthermore, is the obedience/disobedience that triggers the sanctions corporate (or representative) or individual? The blessings and curses clearly represent life and death, but life and death in what sense? Is the life/death reference literal, temporal, physical-temporal, or spiritual and eschatological? When we come to Paul's use of these terms and explore the context in which he understood the promise of life conditioned upon obedience, he clearly parsed that "life" as "the life of eternity" or "the world to come."[2] In short, this chapter examines the tension evident between the immediate context of the Torah's proleptic and anticipatory knowledge of the climactic event of salvation and the apostle Paul's *a posteriori* knowledge of it.

My thesis in this essay is as follows: although these two passages (Lev. 18:5 and Deut. 30:12–14) are quoted in antithetical relationship to one another by the apostle Paul, who was working within an established and increasingly "eschatologizing" exegetical tendency in both the Hebrew Bible and early Judaism (200 BC–AD 200), paradoxically they have the same *final* goal: entitlement to heaven. Furthermore, although both passages communicate two very different means of obtaining life, both passages placed in juxtaposition to one another serve very important purposes for describing the nature of the Mosaic covenant and clarify how one may obtain entitlement to heaven. Additionally, these passages have the final goal of entitlement to heaven that God alone will accomplish through his grace since man cannot through his impotence. Finally, these passages in their canonical development and context teach that God initiated and definitively obtained the goal of entitlement to heaven through the work of Jesus Christ which man may now possess by faith and not through his own works.

---

2. This is evident in *Targum Onkelos* and in Rabbinic Hebrew as well as the apostle's own argumentation apart from these possible contextual influences.

Before we discuss the role of the law and the meaning of "life" in the context of the original audience of Leviticus, let it be stated clearly that the law's function and its rewards are somewhat different before the fall.[3] The contemplated reward of eternal life offered in the garden is based upon the condition of perfect, personal obedience to the command.[4] The just and legal outcome of obedience was entitlement to heaven, plain and simple. The goal of the law and the function of works were different before the fall.[5] Life, in the sense of life consummated through eschatological blessing, hence entitlement to heaven, was the reward promised following the fulfilment of the command (Gen. 2:16–17) in the garden.[6] Eschatology, in this sense, preceded soteriology.[7]

But what about Leviticus 18:5 and Deuteronomy 30 in their original contexts and then in the citations of Paul (Rom. 10 and Gal. 3)? Does Paul understand "life" in these passages as eternal life? Does he understand that it is eternal life but in such a way that it is not exclusive of temporal life? Or is it the life promised in the covenant of works, that is, entitlement to heaven held out in the covenant of works?[8] Or is another alternative open before us?

3. See Johannes Wollebius, "*Compendium Theologiae Christianae*," in *Reformed Dogmatics: J. Wollebius, G. Voetius, F. Turretin*, ed. and trans. John W. Beardslee III (New York: Oxford University Press, 1965), 76–77. "v. Therefore, if we would be saved, a twofold satisfaction is required of us. The law requires both punishment and obedience; the one in its warnings and the other in its promises. It is false to separate these, and say that we are bound either to obedience or to punishment. The law requires both of us, and there is no other road to eternal life than the fulfillment of the law, concerning which Christ said, 'Do this and live' (Luke 10:28). Therefore, even if we were completely free from the guilt and punishment of transgression, we could not attain eternal life without fulfilling the law. vi. We can offer neither satisfaction in ourselves, but must seek both in Christ. vii. After the fall the law was re-established by God for the above end, as by a return to the former status [*ius postliminii*]. The law was given and inscribed within the first man, so that by his own obedience, if he willed, eternal life could follow; it is offered to fallen man in order that, lacking all faculty of fulfilling the law, he may fulfill it through Christ. (Rom. 10:4: 'The end of the law is Christ, for justification, to him who believes.') viii. Therefore, the promulgation of the law to Israel on Mount Sinai was a very gracious act."

4. Westminster Confession of Faith 19.1.

5. Francis Turretin, *Institutes of Elenctic Theology*, trans. George Musgrave Giger, ed. James T. Dennison Jr., 3 vols. (Phillipsburg, NJ: P&R, 1994), 2:190–91, §12.4.7, is lucid on this point, "As to works, they were required in the first [covenant] as an antecedent condition by way of a cause for acquiring life; but in the second, they are only the subsequent condition as the fruit and effect of the life already acquired. In the first, they ought to precede the act of justification; in the second, they follow it."

6. See Louis Berkhof, *Systematic Theology* (Grand Rapids: Eerdmans, 1984), 213; J. Gresham Machen, *The Christian View of Man* (London: Banner of Truth, 1965), 154; Turretin, *Institutes*, 1:585, §8.6.13; Robert L. Dabney, *Lectures in Systematic Theology* (Grand Rapids: Zondervan, 1972), 303; Herman Witsius, *Economy of the Covenants between God and Man: Comprehending a Complete Body of Divinity*, trans. William Crookshank, 2 vols. (1822; Phillipsburg, NJ: Presbyterian and Reformed, 1990), 1:75, §1.4.7.

7. Geerhardus Vos, *The Pauline Eschatology* (Phillipsburg, NJ: Presbyterian and Reformed, 1979), 325 n. 1; idem, *Biblical Theology* (Grand Rapids: Eerdmans, 1948), 22; Witsius, *Economy*, 1:75, §1.4.7.

8. Guy Waters argues in this volume that the answer for Paul's views is found in Rom. 5:12–21.

These are very complex and important questions that involve intertextual reading.[9] Intertextuality is interested in the dependence of one text upon another. It is concerned with how a received biblical text (a *traditum*) is engaged by later biblical literature and its reinterpretations (*traditio*).[10] This can be viewed along a spectrum of explicitness.[11]

The two passages with which this essay is most interested, Leviticus 18:5 and Deuteronomy 30:1–14 and their development in their various contexts, are arguably some of the most important and difficult texts in all of Scripture. Additionally, it is generally agreed that they are central texts for understanding the apostle's view of the law and the gospel. These passages have received immense discussion in the secondary literature, and therefore this essay will have to be necessarily selective in what it covers.

Since I plan to hone in on only certain issues, it may be best stated up front what my intentions are with regards to selectivity, especially with regard to conceptions in the Hebrew Bible of what exactly led to the eventual extirpation of the Israelites from the land of Canaan. Clearly for Leviticus, holiness is indispensable for the attainment of life. But holiness is integrally united to the concept of cleanness in Leviticus, a difficult subject that has attracted significant attention especially since the pioneering and influential work of Mary Douglas.[12] The demands of God and the dangers associated with potential extirpation from the land, therefore, are related to a complex matrix of ritual/moral obligations, a debated subject that I cannot engage here but plan to consider at some future date.[13] Needless to say, the pollu-

9. This is fundamental to my argument. As Danna Nolan Fewell, *Reading between Texts: Intertextuality and the Hebrew Bible*, ed. Danna Nolan Fewell (Louisville: Westminster John Knox, 1992), reminds us: "A lone voice produces a particular sound, and issues a particular communication. To recognize that the voice is not lone after all, but in dialogue with another voice, or host of voices, is what intertextual reading is all about. A dialogue communicates differently than a soliloquy. In a dialogue all voices help to shape meaning. Each single voice is reinterpreted in light of the others" (p. 12).

10. Brian D. Russell, *The Song of the Sea: The Date and Composition and Influence of Exodus 15:1–21* (New York: Peter Lang, 2007), 97. See also, for example, the seminal book in New Testament studies by Richard S. Hays, *Echoes of Scripture in the Letters of Paul* (New Haven: Yale University Press, 1989), and for examples in Old Testament inner-biblical interpretation, see Michael Fishbane, *Biblical Interpretation in Ancient Israel* (Oxford: Oxford University Press, 1985); Benjamin D. Sommer, *A Prophet Reads Scripture: Allusion in Isaiah 40–66* (Stanford: Stanford University Press, 1998).

11. See the insightful little book by John Hollander, *The Figure of an Echo: A Mode of Allusion in Milton and After* (Berkeley: University of California Press, 1981), and Hays, *Echoes*, especially 23–24.

12. Mary Douglas, *Purity and Danger: An Analysis of the Concepts of Pollution and Taboo* (London: Routledge and Kegan Paul, 1966).

13. See Jacob Neusner, *The Idea of Purity in Ancient Judaism* (Leiden: Brill, 1973); Jonathan Klawans, *Impurity and Sin in Ancient Judaism* (Oxford: Oxford University Press, 2000); Jonathan Klawans, *Purity, Sacrifice, and the Temple: Symbolism and Supersessionism in the Study of Ancient Judaism* (Oxford: Oxford University Press, 2006); Walter Houston, *Purity and Monotheism: Clean*

tion of the land by impurity was seen as a grave danger and a major threat to Israel and its privilege of occupation.[14]

There is a better-known explanation for extirpation from the land, which existed alongside of the one just mentioned but was not tantamount to it: the "legal paradigm of misdeed and punishment."[15] It is clear that obedience (and also disobedience) were clearly connected to the sanctions of blessings and curses of the covenant (see Deut. 28 and Lev. 26). Obeying God's laws is clearly the preeminent demand on God's people as a condition of holiness and God's continuing to dwell in her midst.[16]

In the first section of this essay, I discuss Leviticus 18:5. Next, I will discuss Deuteronomy 30:1–14. Finally, I will examine briefly how the apostle Paul brings these two passages together, yielding a meaningful interpretation of the Mosaic covenant and solutions to the issues raised in that epoch from one who stood at the climactic end of a long progression of development.

Leviticus 18:5 and Its Contexts

Leviticus 18:5 is only one of two passages from the book of Leviticus which the apostle Paul cites. As New Testament scholar Francis Watson states, it "encapsulate[s] the very essence of the law, summing up the law's entire rationale and content in a single lapidary utterance . . . a statement that concerns the law's goal and rationale."[17] Despite this fact, a thorough

---

and Unclean Animals in Biblical Law, Journal for the Study of the Old Testament Supplement 140 (Sheffield: Sheffield Academic Press, 1993). For a recent treatment aimed toward a college and seminary audience, see Gerald A. Klingbeil, *Bridging the Gap: Ritual and Ritual Texts in the Bible,* ed. Richard S. Hess, Bulletin for Biblical Research Supplement 1 (Winona Lake, IN: Eisenbrauns, 2007). Klawans is critiquing Neusner who maintains that purity and impurity were strictly cultic whereas Klawans suggests that purity/impurity is related to real moral obligations and that certain transgressions defile the people and therefore the land. As Klawans points out, the prophets utilize the language of purity/impurity in an ethical sense, and this seems to be the burden of the New Testament as well. This is all related, as is clearly apparent, to the topics of this essay, and I hope to do future work integrating the findings of Klawans (who might have overstated matters) and others, including treatment of these issues in Targum Jonathan.

14. Scott A. Swanson, "Fifth Century Patristic and Rabbinic Ethical Interpretation of Cult and Ritual in Leviticus," Ph.D. diss., Hebrew Union College, 2004, 172–81; I also am grateful to my pastor, Zach Keele, for pointing me to Tikva Frymer-Kensky, "Pollution, Purification, and Purgation in Biblical Israel," in *The Word of the Lord Shall Go Forth: Essays in Honor of David Noel Freedman in Celebration of His Sixtieth Birthday,* ed. Carol L. Meyers and M. O'Connor (Winona Lake, IN: Eisenbrauns, 1983), 399–414, especially 408; Klawans, *Impurity and Sin,* 119, states the obvious, when he notes that the final verses of this chapter (Lev. 18) give one of the clearest descriptions of the morally defiling character of sin, and the land ultimately spewing out the sinful inhabitants.

15. Frymer-Kensky, "Pollution," 409.

16. See Lev. 19:2ff.; Lev. 20:7ff.; Num 15:39–40.

17. Francis Watson, *Paul and the Hermeneutics of Faith* (London: T&T Clark, 2004), 314–15.

examination of Leviticus 18:5 has strangely been missing from scholarly discussion until recently.[18] This article will not engage the issue of source analysis for the book of Leviticus but works with Leviticus as a whole, as the received canonical text.[19]

The Issue of How Far the Prohibitions Extend

Leviticus 18:1–5 is primarily concerned with urging the Israelites not to follow the sexual practices of the Egyptians and Canaanites.[20] For the topic of this book, two of the most important issues in this passage and its context are determining how far the demands and promises of Leviticus 18:5, our central text, extend, and in what manner life is inherent in obeying those laws and what is meant by the "life" proffered there.[21] Leviticus 18:5 reads as follows:[22]

ושמרתם את־חקתי ואת־משפטי אשר יעשה   You must keep my statutes and my
אתם האדם וחי בהם אני יהוה   ordinances, which, if one does them, he shall
live by them: I am the LORD. (Lev. 18:5)

First, notice that the command is given in positive form. The one who does them shall live by them.[23] Secondly, this verse raises a very important question for our topic: do these demands extend to only those in the land, that is, only to Israel, or to a wider audience? Determining to whom the referent *hā'ādām* ("one" = "man") is attributed in this passage is important and is debated. The addressee is not defined as Israel per se, but as *hā'ādām* (i.e.,

---

18. See Preston Sprinkle, "Law and Life: The Interpretation of Leviticus 18:5 in Early Judaism and in Paul," Ph.D. diss., Aberdeen University, 2007; S. Gathercole, "Torah, Life and Salvation: Leviticus 18:5 in Early Judaism and the New Testament," in *From Prophecy to Testament: The Function of the Old Testament in the New*, ed. C. A. Evans (Peabody, MA: Hendrickson, 2004), 126–45; Friedrich Avemarie, "Paul and the Claim of the Law according to the Scripture: Leviticus 18:5 in Galatians 3:12 and Romans 10:5," in *The Beginnings of Christianity: A Collection of Articles*, ed. Jack Pastor and Menachem Mor (Jerusalem: Yad Ben-Zvi, 2005), 125–48.

19. Although I will not engage the issue of source analysis in detail, before entering into a discussion of Leviticus 18:5, it is worth noting the customary manner of dividing the book of Leviticus with regard to source analysis. August Klostermann, in the nineteenth century, was the first to call, roughly speaking, the chapters in Lev. 17–26 the Holiness Code (*Heiligkeitsgesetz*, from here on "H"), and chapters 1–16 the Priestly strand. Most scholars follow Julius Wellhausen who placed H before P (Postexilic). This construction is not accepted by all and has been challenged by some, including Jacob Milgrom.

20. Jacob Milgrom, *Leviticus*, 3 vols., Anchor Bible 3–3B (Garden City, NY: Doubleday, 1998–2001), 2:1739.

21. Ibid., 2:1522.

22. Unless otherwise indicated, Scripture quotations in this chapter are my translations.

23. Relating to the issue of republication, notice that this command is given in the opposite form from the original covenant of works (Gen. 2:16–17). There, the positive implications are perfectly clear even though the command is in negative form. Here, the negative implications are perfectly clear even though the command is in positive form.

"the man"). Notice the switch from the second person to the third person in this passage. This should not be passed over lightly. In view of the conceptual and lexical overlap between verse 5 and verse 26, which reads,

ושמרתם אתם את־חקתי ואת־משפטי ולא
תעשו מכל התועבת האלה האזרח
והגר הגר בתוככם

You must keep my statutes and my ordinances and you must not do any of these abominations, neither the native, nor the alien who sojourns in your midst. (Lev. 18:26)

it seems plausible that *hā'ādām* should include the *gēr* (sojourner or alien) as well as the Israelite, and urges the observance of God's law upon both.[24]

Joosten suggests that "Lev. 18:5 intimates the universal tenor of the OT message, which is expressed in Gen. 1:27 and in different terms in Gen. 12:3, etc."[25] This would seem to imply the universal implications for the works principle stated in Leviticus 18:5: the one who does them can expect to live, which will be discussed further below.[26]

Jacob Milgrom thinks this is carrying the language of the passage too far,[27] and Baruch Schwartz also disagrees with this line of Joosten's reasoning.[28] Even so, because of his exegetical sensitivities to the entire chapter, Schwartz recognizes the individualizing tendencies (focusing on the individual referents vis-à-vis corporate aspects) here in verse 5 in light of verse 29, although he still sees the application only to Israel.[29] Not without significance, Milgrom identifies the "person" in verse 5 as the *gēr* in verse 26. My own opinion, consequently, is that the point should not be missed that there is a kind of democratization of the law here: it is necessary that all, Jew and sojourner alike, keep these laws and avoid the morally defiling consequences of sin. This seems to fit with Paul's argument in Romans 10:5 also. When the apostle quotes Leviticus 18:5, as Guy Waters comments, there is an *a*

24. J. Joosten, *People and Land in the Holiness Code: An Exegetical Study of the Ideational Framework of the Law in Leviticus 17–26*, Vetus Testamentum Supplement 67 (Leiden: Brill, 1996), 77. Joosten says, "According to Lev. 18:24–30 even the previous inhabitants of the land were in a sense subject to these laws: it is because they did not observe them that they were vomited out by the land."

25. Ibid., 77.

26. David VanDrunen has argued in another essay in this book and in a forthcoming scholarly book that the *imago dei* entails inherent knowledge of covenantal sanctions, both promises and threats being part of man's natural knowledge.

27. Milgrom, *Leviticus*, 2:1522.

28. Baruch J. Schwartz, "Selected Chapters of the Holiness Code—A Literary Study of Leviticus 17–19," Ph.D. diss. (in Hebrew), Hebrew University, 1987, 67.

29. Ibid., 66, comments: "A man, which means every individual, as becomes clearer from v. 29, where we see the reward of the doers in comparison with the punishment of the lawbreakers: 'for who does any of these abominations will be cut off from the midst of their people'" (my translation).

priori presumption of a universal audience in Romans.[30] Romans 2 may also extend the logic of Leviticus 18:5 universally.[31] Since the New Testament is ultimately normative for interpreting the Old, I think that the previous evidence makes plausible the "universal tenor" (at least in an inchoate form) of the message here.

Law Observance, a Condition of Life, but Life in What Sense?

This expectation for obedience to God's law is a requirement for priests and laypersons alike.[32] In Leviticus, not only is there a democratization of the obligations of the law incumbent upon both Jews and sojourners, there seems to be a democratization of expectations for holiness within the Torah incumbent upon priests and laypersons: it is seminal in Leviticus but full-blown in Paul. Let me explain.

Leviticus 18 and 20 are integrally related and artistically arranged.[33] One may, for example, notice this in the intended echoes. Consider Leviticus 20:7–8:

והתקדשתם והייתם קדשים כי אני יהוה	You shall sanctify yourselves and be holy, for I am
אלהיכם ושמרתם את־חקתי ועשיתם	the LORD your God. You must keep my statutes
אתם אני יהוה מקדשכם	and do them: I am the LORD who sanctifies you. (Lev. 20:7–8)

These verses, and the opening verb (the *Hitpa'el*), make clear that "Israel can achieve holiness only by its own efforts. YHWH has given it the means: Israel makes itself holy by obeying YHWH's commandments."[34] Furthermore, these verses are once again reminiscent, or evocative, of 18:26 and 18:1–5. Since Leviticus 18:5 has a universalizing tendency even latent in its immediate context, what exactly is the nature of the life promised as a result of obedience?[35]

30. See Waters's essay in this volume. Interestingly, the apostle may take another approach in the form of the Leviticus citation in Gal. 3:12, where a subtle substitution and omission may be driven by a concern to steer the text away from application to Gentile Galatians. For details, see Sprinkle, "The Interpretation of Leviticus 18:5," 144–46.

31. See Watson's discussion of Josephus and related matters in *Paul and the Hermeneutics of Faith*, 344.

32. Milgrom, *Leviticus*, 2:1741.

33. Milgrom, *Leviticus*, 2:1739, states, "I submit that chaps. 18–20 were subjected to an artful H redaction: chap. 20 was chiastically balanced with chap. 18, thereby setting chap. 19 as the center of Leviticus (if not the entire Torah) and necessitating a corresponding symmetry between the flanking chaps. 18 and 20. . . . Thus the sexual prohibitions of 20 had to be supplied with opening and closing exhortations (vv. 1–8, 22–26) to match those of chap. 18 (vv. 1–5, 24–30)."

34. Milgrom, *Leviticus*, 2:1739–40.

35. Even the immediate context of the sexual laws in Lev. 18 throws light on the reward of life. Building on Mary Douglas's work, Doug C. Mohrmann, "Making Sense of Sex: A Study of Leviticus 18," *Journal for the Study of the Old Testament* 29.1 (2004): 57–79, says, "Sexuality was thus not

It is clear that in Leviticus, obedience with its entailed results, that is, "life," means mundane blessings, beatitude if you will, especially in a sense that would be manifest and meaningful to a society largely involved with agricultural concerns. For the Old Testament, "life" often means material life and blessing.[36] But what is being expressed in the immediate context of Leviticus?

Preston Sprinkle has recently outlined the various proposals for the meaning in Leviticus 18:5b of וָחַי ("he will live").[37] He marshals five arguments in support of those positions which may be called "result" views, noting that the results of curses and blessings in this chapter are always related to *dwelling in the land*. He tentatively concludes that "life" in this Leviticus context is: "A result of doing the 'statutes and ordinances' according to the author of H. And if Leviticus 18:5 can be read in connection with the blessings of 26:3–14 [blessings for obedience that are essentially temporal], as convincingly argued by Watson, then we can refer to the 'life' of 18:5 as a covenantal blessing of 'life.'"[38]

There is some unusual syntax expressed in Leviticus 18:5 by the words וָחַי בָּהֶם, "he shall live by them." Milgrom argues that the preposition בְּ is *beth instrumenti* and means that life is built into these laws. In other words, they have the power inherently to grant life.[39] This notion is expressed in chapters 18 and 20. Notice that the focus is not on the obligations of the commands here in these verses as much as on the "outcome of their keeping."[40] In a

---

only a constituent part of life, it also functioned as a *metaphor* for life: its fruit was a blessing, so it was part of living; its violation produced a curse, so it was part of dying" (p. 79).

36. Gordon J. Wenham, *The Book of Leviticus*, New International Commentary on the Old Testament (Grand Rapids: Eerdmans, 1979), 253. Wenham comments, "For the OT writers life means primarily physical life. But it is clear that in this [he is commenting on Lev. 18:5] and similar passages more than mere existence is being promised. What is envisaged is a happy life in which a man enjoys God's bounty of health, children, friends, and prosperity. Keeping the law is the path to divine blessing, to a happy and fulfilled life in the present (Lev. 26:3–13; Deut. 28:1–14)."

37. Sprinkle, "The Interpretation of Leviticus 18:5," 32–36.

38. Ibid., 35.

39. Milgrom, *Leviticus*, 2:1522–23. Schwartz, "Selected Chapters," 67. This seems to be a better option than taking the בְּ as meaning "in them" (the locative view), that is, "in accordance with them." Although there is some slight support in 18:4 for this view, the preponderance of the evidence for the meaning of וָחַי discussed above definitely tips the scales in favor of understanding this as "by them," preserving the view of the life promised as a result. For detailed exegesis of this position, see Sprinkle, "The Interpretation of Leviticus 18:5," 35–36. Note the connection here with VanDrunen's recent theological work mentioned in n. 26.

40. Schwartz, "Selected Chapters," 67, says: "The argumentation is not about the command to keep God's statutes but about the outcome of their keeping. This outcome can fall on those who keep them even though they are not commanded to do so. This idea is established with the words of preaching at the end of the chapter. Indeed, there is no punishment of 'cutting off' but of 'vomiting' alone, but the concept is one. The outcome of committing the abominations and avoidance of their performance can fall on a 'man,' because this outcome flows from them, as the phrase 'by them' teaches" (my translation of the author's Hebrew).

word, the life promised upon condition of performing the statutes and judgments in its immediate context in Leviticus here is "the covenantal blessing of abundant (and long) life in the land of Israel."[41]

But there is another view of life that comes as a result of obedience to the law that I am labeling *entitlement to heaven* (eschatological life). The law points forward, following successful fulfilment of its obligations perfectly, in Pauline terms "to eternal life" for the one who fulfils the stipulations contained therein.[42] Even so, to the one who fails in performing through concrete actions the stipulations set forth by the law, the curse of sanctions lies in wait.

One should not stop here, however, for these potential temporal blessings (and we might add potential curses as well) were intended only as an incremental step or sign of something far greater, what has recently been called "temporal blessings and curses with an eye to Christ."[43] My own position is that the temporal life promised in the Mosaic covenant portended and typified the greater "eternal life," which seems the clear position argued by the apostle Paul.[44] In this arrangement, there is typology, but not *mere* typology. This is crucial for instruction in the church and not too difficult even for simple young people if handled carefully. But now I get ahead of myself.[45] Reformed biblical scholars have been bringing to the attention of

41. Sprinkle, "The Interpretation of Leviticus 18:5," 36.

42. Wenham, *Leviticus*, 253, comments on Lev. 18:5, "But what about life after death? The OT envisaged life continuing in Sheol, a shadowy, depressing version of life on earth. And better existence in the presence of God himself (e.g., Ps. 73; Dan. 12:1–3). But it is Jesus and Paul who insist that the full meaning of life is eternal life. If anyone can keep the law, he will enjoy eternal life (Matt. 19:17; Rom. 10:5; Gal. 3:12). In John's Gospel man must keep the new law— the word of Christ. 'If anyone keeps my word, he will never see death' (John 8:51)."

43. R. Fowler White and E. Calvin Beisner, "Covenant, Inheritance, and Typology," in *By Faith Alone: Answering Challenges to the Doctrine of Justification*, ed. Gary L. W. Johnson and Guy Prentiss Waters (Wheaton, IL: Crossway, 2006), 147–70.

44. The apostle clearly understood Lev. 18:5 to refer ultimately to eternal life.

45. In other words, to talk *merely* and *exclusively* about a typological arrangement, where Israel must have some measure of obedience in order to maintain tenure in the land, and in that sense it is a covenant of works, would seem to falsify somewhat the biblical data. Rather, it is from the Mosaic perspective itself, therefore, that we do not have a crystal clear picture with lucid categorical distinctions (which is exactly what one would expect at this period in redemptive history). It is only from the later Pauline perspective, as will be discussed below, that these distinctions become clear and fully eschatologized. For example, in the context of the Old Testament itself, there is often the assumption that the law can be kept in some measure and indeed has been kept by certain generations, such as the generation of Joshua and Caleb. As redemptive history progresses, there is an inevitable slide toward disobedience with curse sanctions necessarily following. Another complicated question and issue at stake here is whether obedience or disobedience triggering sanctions is along corporate or individual lines. My own view is that individual righteousness and expectations for individual obedience are there mixed with expectations for corporate righteousness and obedience from the start (this too develops), but this is a matter beyond the scope of this essay. Lastly, let it be noted that there is indeed some eschatology already present there in Deuteronomy itself, for example, Deut. 4:30.

the church that the Westminster Larger Catechism, for example, could have done more with respect to demonstrating how typology pointing to Christ in the Old Testament works.[46]

There is a real connection that exists between the obedience/disobedience of Israel and tenure in the land. Indeed, according to Deuteronomy, "its [Israel's] right of occupation is therefore contingent on its actions."[47] On this former point, the biblical evidence is incontrovertible. Of course law-keeping never provided—this side of the fall of Adam into sin—the meritorious grounds of life in the eternal sense. Since the fall of mankind, no mere man could obtain that goal.[48]

Increasing Individualization Connected with Curse and Blessing

The Bible asserts and scholars have recognized that pollution and defilement of the land could build up and reach intolerable states, triggering the sanctions and leading to banishment.[49] Not only exile is in view, but also ultimate extirpation symbolized in the destruction of the Herodian temple in AD 70 and the potential rejection of the chosen people, not irrevocably but for a purpose (Rom. 11:11). What is important for our considerations is the growing focus on the individual in other spheres. This contributes to the apostle's understanding of our passages. This is due in part to the influence of two major forces: Pharisaism and Hellenism.

Pharisaism was arguably the most influential religious movement within Judaism during 150 BC to AD 70.[50] According to some authorities, we should "consider Pharisaism as normative Judaism, not because all *lived* according to Pharasaic halakah [rabbinical discussion of law, fusing Scripture and Mishnah] but because Pharisaism was acknowledged by the majority as

46. See Robert Cara, "Redemptive-Historical Themes in the *Westminster Larger Catechism*," in *The Westminster Confession of Faith into the 21st Century: Essays in Remembrance of the 350th Anniversary of the Westminster Assembly*, ed. J. Ligon Duncan III, vol. 3 (Fearn, Ross-shire: Christian Focus, forthcoming).

47. Frymer-Kensky, "Pollution," 408, tersely states, "According to Deuteronomy, it was not the goodness of Israel that caused God to give it the land, but the evil of the nations living there (Deut. 9:4–5). Its right of occupation is therefore contingent on its actions. Israel is warned against performing the abominations of the nations that God dispossessed: passing children through fire, and engaging in magic, divination, and necromancy (Deut. 18:9–12)."

48. Westminster Confession of Faith 7.3 reads: "Man, by his fall, having made himself uncapable of life by that covenant, the Lord was pleased to make a second, commonly called the covenant of grace; wherein he freely offereth unto sinners life and salvation by Jesus Christ; requiring of them faith in him, that they may be saved, and promising to give unto all those that are ordained unto eternal life his Holy Spirit, to make them willing, and able to believe."

49. Frymer-Kensky, "Pollution," 408.

50. Roland Deines, "The Pharisees between 'Judaisms' and 'Common Judaism,'" in *Justification and Variegated Nomism*, vol. 1: *The Complexities of Second Temple Judaism*, ed. D. A. Carson, Peter T. O'Brian, and Mark A. Seifrid (Grand Rapids: Baker, 2001), 442–504, esp. 503.

the legitimate and authentic interpretation of the divine will for the chosen nation."[51]

The second force that probably became influential for increasing individualizing notions, historically speaking, was hellenization. More specifically, this may have been connected with the rise of the Maccabeans, whose surprising victory was followed by zealous obedience to the laws of Moses.[52] These trends will become significant for our understanding of Paul's exegesis of Leviticus 18:5 and Deuteronomy 30:1–14. Now, however, I will explain the later echoes of Leviticus 18:5 found in Ezekiel and Nehemiah.

Citations, Allusions, and Echoes: Ezekiel and Nehemiah

Leviticus 18:5's influence on Ezekiel is of paramount importance.[53] The purpose of these echoic allusions in Ezekiel is to show that what Israel has failed to do, God will do.[54] This has been demonstrated clearly in a recent article by Sprinkle.[55] Sprinkle successfully argues that the previously stated principle about the reversal of fortunes based on divine initiative becomes conspicuously clear when Leviticus 18 allusions are seen throughout the entire book of Ezekiel and not merely restricted (as often) to chapter 20 of Ezekiel where three citations of Leviticus 18:5 have frequently been noted.

After arguing that the phrase "walking in my statutes and observing my judgments" is connected to the more explicit Leviticus 18:5 citations, "the person who does these things [the statutes and ordinances] will live by them," Sprinkle demonstrates the significance of this for the literary framework of the book. In short, there is a "composition connection between the unfulfilled 'statutes and ordinances' in chapters 18 and 20 with their fulfillment in 36.27 and 37.24; likewise, there is a connection with the 'life' unattained by Israel in chapters 18, 20, and 33 and Israel's 'life' in 37.1–14."[56] Whereas Israel's failure to fulfil the stipulations is highlighted repeatedly in Ezekiel 1–24, there is a dramatic reversal of this failure through divine initiative and fulfilment in Ezekiel 36–37. Sprinkle illustrates this in figure 1.[57]

---

51. Ibid., 501.
52. See ibid., 460–61.
53. Milgrom, *Leviticus*, 2:1522.
54. Walter Brueggemann, *Theology of the Old Testament: Testimony, Dispute, Advocacy* (Minneapolis: Fortress, 1997), 646, sees this as a prophetic tilt toward eschatology, with the banishment of "the Mosaic 'if' from the possibility of horizon," and rooted in "Yahweh's circumstance-defying capacity to work newness."
55. See Preston Sprinkle, "Law and Life: Leviticus 18:5 in the Literary Framework of Ezekiel," *Journal for the Study of the Old Testament* 31.3 (2007): 275–93. Details may also be found in his dissertation, quoted previously.
56. Sprinkle, "Law and Life," 279.
57. Ibid.

Fig. 1

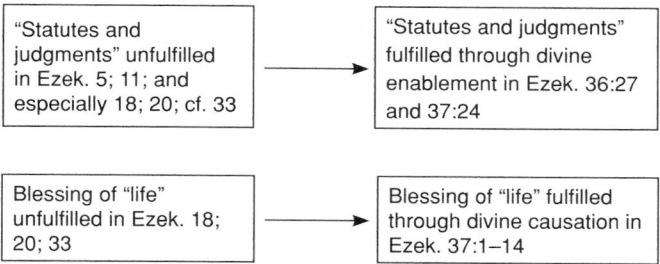

Sprinkle also argues plausibly for a string of connections between chapters 18, 20, and 33 of Ezekiel and chapters 36 and 37, especially regarding the "life" language associated with Leviticus 18:5. In short, divine causation replaces the conditions incumbent upon the people. What they are unable to perform in and of themselves, Yahweh will accomplish through his own divinely appointed agency. Again, Sprinkle summarizes illustratively in figure 2.[58]

Fig. 2

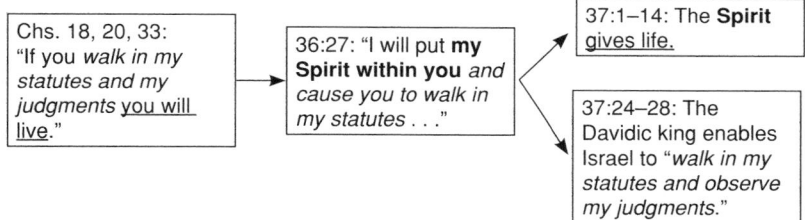

Another echo of Leviticus 18:5 occurs in the long prayer of Nehemiah 9 as well:

ותעד בהם להשיבם אל־תורתך והמה הזידו
ולא־שמעו למצותיך ובמשפטיך חטאו־בם
אשר־יעשה אדם וחיה בהם ויתנו כתף
סוררת וערפם הקשו ולא שמעו

You admonished them in order to turn them to your law, but they acted presumptuously and did not heed your commands, and your judgments they sinned against, *by which if a man does them he shall live by them*, and turned a stubborn shoulder, and their necks they stiffened and they would not obey. (Neh. 9:29)

Leviticus 18:5 is "alluded to" in this prayer, which is probably based on the pattern of Judges.[59] Interestingly, the prayer goes on to describe divine

---

58. Ibid., 292.

59. Again, I am indebted in the following analysis and summary to Preston Sprinkle, "The Interpretation of Leviticus 18:5," 46–49.

judgment in the form of exile. There are similarities between Ezekiel 20 and Nehemiah 9, and the important question here is to ask what the function of Leviticus 18:5 is in this prayer. Sprinkle notes several important points. First, he remarks that the allusion occurs in the context of prayer. Second, with regard to Israel's rebellious past, it functions negatively.[60] He also argues that special note should be taken of how the allusion is functioning here in contrast to its original setting. In its original setting, it was used apodictically, that is, to state what Israel *should* do. In contrast, the function of the reference in the prayer in Nehemiah is negative: it describes rebellion and what she *did not* do. As M. Gilbert has carefully noted, the law as a source of life is a frequent theme in the Hebrew Bible, but that emphasis has largely disappeared here in Nehemiah. The focus is on Israel's rebellion (cf. Neh. 9:16).[61]

Sprinkle also describes the major difference in the way in which "life" is used in the two passages. Life in Ezekiel is accomplished through divine initiative whereas in Nehemiah's prayer the community cries out for relief but there is no "life" or "restoration" in what follows. My own hypothesis is that this is purposeful. This silence (no answer) with respect to the cry for "life" and restoration functions as a kind of silent scream. The New Testament and Paul will answer that scream and make clear that Jesus is the life and the way to life (read = entitlement to heaven), and this will shatter the silence. I now will explain the other passage with which the article is concerned.

Deuteronomy 30:1–14 and Its "Contexts"

According to Francis Watson, Deuteronomy 30 is not only a hermeneutical key to the entirety of Scripture; it is more narrowly "integral to the theology of Deuteronomy as a whole."[62] In Deuteronomy 28:64–65, we have a description of dispersion, utter hopelessness, and the forlorn status of Israel scattered among the nations. Even so, Deuteronomy looks beyond this cursed exile to a restoration hope in the new covenant. As with the treatment of Leviticus, so also with the treatment of Deuteronomy, detailed engagement with the discussion of source analysis and composition history is outside the purview of this article.[63] Before discussing briefly the function

---

60. Here, Sprinkle is building upon the recently published article by Joel Willitts, "Context Matters: Paul's Use of Leviticus 18:5 in Galatians 3:12," *Tyndale Bulletin* 54.2 (2003): 105–15.

61. Maurice Gilbert, "La place de la Loi dans la prière de Néhémie 9," in *De la Tôrah au Messie*, ed., J. Doré, P. Grelot, and M. Carrez (Paris: Desclée, 1981), 307–16, esp. 314.

62. Watson, *Paul and the Hermeneutics of Faith*, 470–71.

63. Some have seen this passage as the hand of a Deuteronomistic editor in the exile. For example, H. W. Wolff, "Das Kerygma des deuteronomistischen Geschichtswerkes," *Zeitschrift für die alttestamentliche Wissenschaft* 73 (1961): 171–86. See also Frank Moore Cross, *Canaanite Myth and Hebrew Epic: Essays in the History of the Religion of Israel* (Cambridge: Harvard University Press,

of Paul's citation of Deuteronomy 30, I will first explain my understanding of the text in its original context.

Future Orientation of Deuteronomy 30:1–14 as a Prophecy of the New Covenant

Many commentators understand Deuteronomy 30:1–10 as speaking of the future restoration of Israel after the exile, and therefore they construe the text as an interpolation.[64] Few recognize verses 11–14 with future orientation but usually construe these verses as a shift back to the present time, an exhortation for the audience gathered on the plains of Moab. Some, however, recognize almost the entire section from 29:2 to 31:6 as oriented toward the distant future.[65] Others, more recently, see Deuteronomy 30:12–14 as a prophetic promise to be fulfilled in Christ.[66]

The crucial verses in which we are interested are Deuteronomy 30:1–14 and more specifically verses 12–14, since these are the verses to which the apostle alludes in Romans 10:5–8. Verses 12–14, however, may not be considered in isolation from the first eleven verses. The first thing to notice in these verses (vv. 1–10) is the predominance of the future orientation throughout the passage. My point is that this future orientation should be carried through all the way to the end of verse 14. I am in substantial agreement with Steven R. Coxhead that "reading 11–14 in the future tense seems to be the most natural reading in the context."[67]

1973), 278. Cross contends that Wolff has not given an adequate account of the promises to David in the book of Kings in his paradigm. Cross posits on page 287 a second hand in the Deuteronomistic history: "Deuteronomy 30:1–10, promising return from captivity, must be coupled with Deuteronomy 4:27–31 as an Exilic addition in a style distinct from the hand of the primary Deuteronomistic author." Dennis T. Olson, "How Does Deuteronomy Do Theology?" in *A God So Near: Essays on Old Testament Theology in Honor of Patrick D. Miller*, ed. Brent A. Strawn and Nancey R. Bowen (Winona Lake, IN: Eisenbrauns, 2003), 201–4, esp. 202, sees a theological strategy of paradox and juxtaposition "evident in 29–32 [which] serves to reframe the older Deuteronomic material (chapters 5–28) in light of the theological crisis brought on by the Babylonian exile of 587 B.C.E."

64. See, for example, Jeffrey H. Tigay, *Deuteronomy* (Philadelphia: Jewish Publication Society, 1996), 32.

65. See Robert Polzin, "Deuteronomy," in *The Literary Guide to the Bible*, ed. Robert Alter and Frank Kermode (Cambridge: Harvard University Press, 1987), 92–101, who on page 92 says: "Temporally, Moses' first address (1:6–4:40) looks mostly to the past events and statements, his second (5:1b–28:68) to the future; and in the rest of the book that future, both immediate and distant, is his main concern. . . . Thus, for example, in his third address (29:2–31:6), whenever Moses quotes others directly, it is their *future* utterances he reports, coinciding with the almost complete orientation of this address toward the distant future."

66. See Akio Ito, "The Written Torah and the Oral Gospel: Romans 10:5–13 in the Dynamic Tension between Orality and Literacy," *Novum Testamentum* 48.3 (2006): 234–60. I do not concur with some aspects of Ito's argument.

67. For a beginning bibliography, see Steven R. Coxhead, "Deuteronomy 30:11–14 as a Prophecy of the New Covenant in Christ," *Westminster Theological Journal* 68 (2006): 305–20, esp. 308.

In short, this amazing passage anticipates ahead of time the plight in which the Israelite nation will find itself, destitute and unable to fulfil the stipulations of the covenant *on its own*. It also describes the new measure of obedience—accomplished *by divine initiative*—in which they will satisfy the conditions hanging over them. Finally, when Paul creatively brings these two significant passages (i.e., Lev. 18:5 and Deut. 30) into closer proximity to one another, the mystery of the divine plan for fulfilment emerges from the shadows and into the light. The pedagogical function of both passages in the Old Testament becomes clearer.

Therefore, note that the passage begins by saying that all these words of blessing and curses will come on you.

(Deut. 30:1) והיה כי־יבאו עליך כל־הדברים האלה הברכה והקללה

According to the text, this will happen when the Lord gathers his people from the nations in which he has scattered them.

בכל־הגוים אשר הדיחך יהוה אלהיך שמה⁶⁸

In verse 2 of Deuteronomy 30, the future orientation of this passage is noted again, "When you will return to the Lord your God."

ושבת עד־יהוה אלהיך

The language here is not conditional. The writer goes on to say, "You will heed his voice in all that I am commanding you today."

ושמעת בקלו ככל אשר־אנכי מצוך היום⁶⁹

The phrase for today (היום) is not to be taken in the literal sense but rather as "now."⁷⁰ This language of obedience is couched in terms of new covenant idiom—you will do this "with all your heart and with all your soul."

בכל־לבבך ובכל־נפשך

---

68. Some construe the syntax of vv. 1–5 with vv. 1–2 forming the protasis (read conditional) and vv. 3–5 forming the apodosis once conditions were met. See, for example, Werner E. Lemke, "Circumcision of the Heart: The Journey of a Biblical Metaphor," in *A God So Near: Essays on Old Testament Theology in Honor of Patrick D. Miller* (Winona Lake, IN: Eisenbrauns, 2003), 299–319.

69. יום occurs at least 167 times in Deuteronomy although not all the occurrences are related to parenesis. In the immediate context, the formula אשר אנכי מצוך היום, "which I command you this day," occurs in vv. 2, 8, 11, 16.

70. Moshe Weinfeld, *Deuteronomy and the Deuteronomic School* (Oxford: Clarendon, 1972), 174–75.

Although what is implicit here becomes explicit in verse 6, even here two points are noteworthy: the Lord takes the initiative to accomplish this, and it is through the unconditional promises of God that this will be fulfilled. The idiomatic language of the new covenant permeates this forecasted blessing.

In verse 3, for example, the interesting phrase "the LORD your God will turn your turning,"

ושב יהוה אלהיך את־שבותך

seems to reinforce and signify that it is divine initiative and sovereign grace that will accomplish these promises when restoration occurs. This phrase means a decisive turn.[71]

Further prophetic idiom, prophetic promise if you will, is evidenced in the language that the Lord will turn and have compassion (ורחמך), and he will turn and gather the exiles from all the peoples.

ושב וקבצך מכל־העמים אשר הפיצך יהוה אלהיך שמה

In verse 4, we have yet further prophetic idiom. The Hebrew text says:

אם־יהיה נדחך בקצה השמים משם יקבצך
יהוה אלהיך ומשם יקחך

Even if your dispersed ones are at the ends of heaven, from there the LORD your God will gather you, and from there he will take you. (Deut. 30:4)

In Deuteronomy 10:16, the people are commanded to circumcise the foreskin of their hearts and not stiffen their necks any longer:

ומלתם את ערלת לבבכם וערפכם לא
תקשו עוד

You must circumcise the foreskin of your hearts and you must stiffen your necks no more!

Verse 6 of Deuteronomy 30, however, is no mere allusion to that passage! On the contrary, new covenant language and imagery permeate this Deuteronomy passage because it is clear that divine initiative will supersede human impotence. Notice the shift from the second person subject of action in Deuteronomy 10:16, where the Israelites are the agents, to the third person subject of action in Deuteronomy 30:6 where the Lord is the ultimate agent of enabling so that they may live:[72]

71. S. R. Driver, *Deuteronomy*, International Critical Commentary (Edinburgh: T&T Clark, 1895), 329.
72. See Westminster Confession of Faith 10.1, where under the effectual call of God, we read of his "taking away their heart of stone, and giving them a heart of flesh; renewing their wills,

וּמָל יהוה אלהיך את־לבבך ואת־לבב זרעך   Moreover, the Lᴏʀᴅ your God will circumcise
לאהבה את־יהוה אלהיך בכל־לבבך   your heart and the heart of your progeny
ובכל־נפשך למען חייך   in order to love the Lᴏʀᴅ your God with all
your heart and all your soul so that you
might live.[73]

Consequently, it is God himself who will accomplish this circumcision on their behalf.

This is the ultimate remedy of Deuteronomy 30:6. An extraordinary intervention—divine in its origin—will accomplish this, as others have recognized.[74] This is an extraordinary reversal of the earlier literature of the Hebrew Bible and the motifs found in Egyptian literature as well.[75]

Verse 8 declares that when God himself circumcises hearts, "*you* [fronted in the Hebrew] will repent and you will obey the voice of the Lᴏʀᴅ and you will do all his commandments." This will happen with the coming of the Spirit in the gospel age.[76]

In the next few verses of Deuteronomy 30, we note that the blessings and prosperity envisaged are enumerated in various physical manifestations with the curses of the covenant falling on those who are the enemies of Israel. Verse 10 recapitulates the same theme that the people will indeed obey. The only plausible explanation for the function of כִּי here seems to be "because."[77] This brings us to the verses that Paul will quote in Romans 10.

---

and, by his almighty power, *determining them to that which is good*, and effectually drawing them to Jesus Christ: yet so, as they come most freely, being made willing by his grace" (emphasis added).

73. This may be a strong echo of the Shema in Deut. 6:4–5; see Olson, "How Does Deuteronomy Do Theology?" 208.

74. Dennis T. Olson, *Deuteronomy and the Death of Moses: A Theological Reading*, Overtures to Biblical Theology (Minneapolis: Fortress, 1994), 128, says, "God ('the suzerain') transforms the curse into blessing, the command into promise, and the stipulation into gift. God's love transcends the quid pro quo of imperial powers and exchange. God forgives and loves even when the people do not love in return. More than that, God creates a love and empowers an obedience within the hearts of the people and community that humans on their own cannot attain."

75. See N. Shupak, "Some Idioms Connected with the Concept of 'Heart' in Egypt and the Bible," in *Pharaonic Egypt: The Bible and Christianity*, ed. Sarah Israelit-Groll (Jerusalem: Magnes, 1985), 202–12. I am grateful to Zach Keele for drawing my attention to this stimulating article. Though I am not necessarily positing direct borrowing on the part of the Hebrew Bible, what we do seem to have is adaptation and transformation, one step removed at best. Although in the Egyptian literature a "heart of stone" was considered a virtue symbolizing self-control, in the biblical material—as is so often the case with images and concepts of contiguous cultures—the image is turned on its head: the Pentateuch uses it to describe the pharaoh as the paradigmatic figure exemplifying stubbornness, thus taking on negative connotations, and then the prophets (Ezekiel in this case) use the image to symbolize full-blown stiffness and recalcitrance.

76. Note J. Gresham Machen's apt comments in *What Is Faith?* (London: Hodder and Stoughton, 1925), 192: "The gospel does not abrogate God's law, but it makes men live it with all their hearts." Also, Christ has redeemed us so we might be "zealous of good works" (Titus 2:14).

77. This could mean "if," "when," or "because." J. G. McConville, *Deuteronomy*, Apollas Old Testament Commentary (Leicester: Inter-Varsity, 2002), 428, comments that the latter two

In both verses 11 and 14, the important but elusive particle כִּי appears. As mentioned above, the most important issue is the interpretation of tense in these verses. Up to this point we have been talking about the future, so that the appropriate tense to apply here is the future, not the present. Even so, in verses 1–10 as well as here, it is important to weigh carefully the translational value of כִּי. Even a cursory glance at various English translations of these verses will note the diversity of translations of this particle throughout our passage. Since small particles can convey significant meaning, glossing this correctly is important. Although I formerly understood it as emphatic ("indeed," "verily," or "surely"), which is attractive to my overall understanding of Deuteronomy 30:1–14, I now realize that recent research is reducing this option for many contexts.[78] Despite the fact that originally verse 11 was the start of a new paragraph,[79] the causal meaning makes the most overall sense to my understanding.

The fact of the matter is that verses 11–14 are full of verbless clauses that need to have their tense supplied from the context.[80] Up to this point (vv. 1–10), we have been talking about the future messianic age. I interpret the temporal frame here as future although I realize this runs against the grain of majority opinion. Even so, there is new evidence to support the future and prophetic aspect of these verses.[81] The tension we feel discerning the future tense here may also be due to the manner in which Deuteronomy expresses its theology by using time and literary juxtaposition.[82]

---

options seem more suitable "because the point of the verse is to establish a correspondence between blessing and obedience, which is never lost in Deuteronomy, yet here remains under the strong influence of Yahweh's initiatives in vv. 3–7. The first option seems to be at odds with the former context unless Moses is enjoining the Israelites to obedience once again. Coxhead, "A Prophecy of the New Covenant," 307, comments, "God has just spoken through Moses in vv. 1–10 that Israel would finally return to him in renewed obedience; there can be no 'ifs and buts' about Israel returning to the Lord."

78. Anneli Aejmelaeus, "Function and Interpretation of כִּי in Biblical Hebrew," *Journal of Biblical Literature* 105.2 (1986): 193–209, esp. 204–8. Therefore, I am presently persuaded that the causal meaning "for" (even though perhaps misleading in "biblical English") is probably the more likely sense, meaning something close to the idea that Israel will return to the Lord *because* the law will have been written on her heart. See Coxhead, "A Prophecy of the New Covenant," 307–8. Although, as M. O'Connor and Bruce K. Waltke assert, it is probably worth noting the dangers of the translation "for" in "biblical English" and the fact that "the two clausal uses [the emphatic and the logical] . . . should not be too strictly separated"—*Biblical Hebrew Syntax* (Winona Lake, IN: Eisenbrauns, 1990), 665.

79. Marked at the end of v. 10 by פ, an abbreviation in the text for פְּתוּחָא, an "open" space in the Hebrew Masoretic Text which signaled the commencing of a new line. This does not seem to exclude the particle being causative here.

80. Coxhead, "A Prophecy of the New Covenant," 306.

81. Ibid. Also see Aki Ito, "The Written Torah."

82. See Olson, "How Does Deuteronomy Do Theology?" 208–10.

Verse 11 continues to say that the commandment will not be beyond their "ability" or "reach."

לא־נפלאת הוא ממך ולא־רחקה הוא[83]

It will not be "too wonderful" in the sense of not too baffling for them to understand.[84] Moshe Weinfeld eloquently explains this "intellectual accessibility" view from the standpoint of wisdom, biblical and otherwise, in its ancient Near Eastern context.[85]

If Deuteronomy 30:1–14 is a prophecy of the new covenant, then it would be teaching that at that time obedience would not be beyond Israel's capacity or ability. Once God circumcises a believer's heart, meeting the demands of his law will no longer be beyond one's ability, albeit still performed imperfectly.[86] The Spirit's presence in sanctification enables the person's will to be God's will. This is parsed beautifully by the Westminster divines.[87] Since Christ will have descended in the new covenant age to usher in the promises, the people will have no need to say, "who will go up for us heavenwards?"

מי יעלה־לנו השמימה

Verses 12 and 13 continue after the spatial language of verse 11 with the desired result, "so that he may cause us to do it," expressed a couple of times. Here then שמע means "heed" in the sense of doing it. Notice the frustration addressed: they are not longing for mere information, they are longing for power and ability! This section of Deuteronomy is addressing the ability to do the commands. They know what God wants them to do; they have the knowledge, they need the ability. If one does not recognize this as a prophecy of the new covenant, then a host of unconvincing exegetical conclusions follow.[88]

In verse 13, "who will cross beyond the sea" may possibly be an allusion to contemporary epic literature with its quest for the secret of life and immor-

---

83. נפלאת is probably the contracted feminine participle form. See *Gesenius' Hebrew Grammar*, ed. E. Kautzsch, A. E. Cowley, §74i.

84. Tigay, *Deuteronomy*, cites Eccl. 7:23 in support of "not beyond their intellectual grasp." Moreover, he cites a use of the same root (פלא), in Deut. 17:8, where it is stated that a legal case is not too difficult for judges to grasp.

85. Weinfeld, *Deuteronomy and the Deuteronomic School*, 257–60.

86. See Heidelberg Catechism 114 and Westminster Shorter Catechism 82.

87. See Westminster Larger Catechism 75.

88. For example, Patrick D. Miller, *Deuteronomy* (Louisville: John Knox, 1990), 216, says, "God's word in all these commandments and statutes is not in fact too difficult for human beings to carry out. Nor is it inaccessible. It is readily available in the teaching of Moses; when taught and studied and learned, that teaching can become appropriated and made a part of one's life ('in your mouth and in your heart')."

tality.[89] Again, if the passage is read as a prophecy of the new covenant, then verse 14 describes the people of the new covenant who have experienced this sort of thing. This whole matter just described (הדבר) will be near unto you, "in your mouth and in your heart, to do it."

בפיך ובלבבך לעשתו

It will be internalized in the heart. The main matter here is the source of power being the Spirit, as will be evidenced from the echoes of this passage below. Is it any wonder Paul will say, "Believe in your heart and profess with your mouth unto salvation" (Rom. 10:9–10)?

In verses 15–20, a section of the book which many see as the climax, the tone reverts to the present time and conditionality comes to the fore again with the dominant and pervasive themes of "life" and "death" placed in counterpoint and the immediate climactic kerygma placed before the people on the plains of Moab.[90]

Echoes, Citations, and Allusions: Jeremiah and Ezekiel

Just as Leviticus 18:5 is taken up in later biblical allusions and echoes, so also is this Deuteronomy passage. In Jeremiah 31:31–34, the language of the new covenant that was cloaked in the circumcision of the heart metaphor is unveiled in this classic passage:

הנה ימים באים נאם־יהוה וכרתי את־בית
ישראל ואת־בית יהודה ברית חדשה לא
כברית אשר כרתי את־אבותם ביום החזיקי
בידם להוציאם מארץ מצרים אשר־המה
הפרו את־בריתי ואנכי בעלתי בם נאם־יהוה
כי זאת הברית אשר אכרת את־בית ישראל
אחרי הימים ההם נאם־יהוה נתתי את־תורתי
בקרבם ועל־לבם אכתבנה והייתי להם
לאלהים והמה יהיו־לי לעם ולא ילמדו
עוד איש את־רעהו ואיש את־אחיו לאמר
דעו את־יהוה כי־כולם ידעו אותי למקטנם
ועד־גדולם נאם־יהוה כי אסלח לעונם
ולחטאתם לא אזכר־עוד

Behold, the days are coming, declares the LORD, when I will make with the house of Israel and the house of Judah a new covenant, and it will not be like the covenant which I cut with their fathers when I took them by their hand to bring them out from the land of Egypt, my covenant which they broke though I was a husband to them,[91] thus says the LORD. But this is the covenant I will make with the house of Israel after these days, declares the LORD, I will put my law in their midst and on their hearts I will write it. Then, I will be their God and they will be my people. No longer will they need to teach each man his neighbor and each man his brother, know the LORD! For all of them from the least to the greatest will heed me, for I will forgive their iniquities and no longer remember their sins. (Jer. 31:31–34)

---

89. See Tigay, *Deuteronomy*, 286 and endnotes for many references.

90. For details, see McConville, *Deuteronomy*, 429–30.

91. The Septuagint and the Masoretic Text (ואנכי בעלתי) differ here. The Septuagint reads, "and I loathed (or rejected) them," καὶ ἐγὼ ἠμέλησα αὐτῶν, as in Heb. 8:9. Either way, the thought

I argued above that Deuteronomy 30:1–14 is a predictive prophecy of the new covenant, and, therefore, all that was implicit there becomes explicit in Jeremiah 31. In verse 31, Jeremiah says this will happen in ימים באים ("in the coming days"), and in verse 33 he says,

אחרי הימים ההם

("after these days"); both refer to the new covenant, messianic days.

This new covenant, however, is going to be unlike the old covenant with respect to breaking. The old covenant was a breakable covenant, it was made obsolete; indeed, the promises in the Abrahamic covenant entailed that the old covenant would pass away: it was a planned obsolescence.[92] The reader is obliged to say that a works principle in the old covenant was operative in some sense because the text clearly states that it was a fracturable covenant, "not like the one *they broke*."[93] Here indeed was a covenant that was susceptible to fracture and breakable! They broke it at Sinai (Ex. 32), and they did it time and again until that old covenant had served its purposes. For the one who holds to a high view of God directing history, there must be something else going on here.

The contrast between the old and new covenants is clearly being made since the reference to the covenant which God made with the fathers when he brought them out of Egypt can be none other than the Sinaitic covenant. There is continuity between them; however, there is a major difference stated particularly in terms of the principle of works operative in this period.

Of course there is a sense in which individuals can break the new covenant. If one is a member of the covenant community and proves himself or herself to be a hypocrite, he is broken off from the vine, but the trunk still stands. Here, however, the point is that the whole old covenant order will be annihilated, it will be wiped out, and it will go down in judgment as a *modus operandi*. The new covenant is not like that: it is not subject to breaking because it is built upon God's initiative to complete it and Christ's satisfaction in his penalty-paying substitution and his probation keeping. His merit is the surety of the new covenant promises, and therefore it cannot fail. The old Sinaitic covenant by way of contrast is built upon a

---

is that this was a works arrangement; it was broken and, therefore, it resulted in the curses of the covenant.

92. See especially Heb. 8:13. On the necessity of the Sinaitic covenant passing away, see T. David Gordon's essay in this book and Olson, *Deuteronomy and the Death of Moses*.

93. From this passage alone it seems evident that the Scriptures considered this works principle operating realistically and not just hypothetically. I register here only this point. How and why the works principle was functioning is another matter.

very fallible hope, and therefore is destined to fail since Israel individually and corporately could not fulfil its stipulations. The principle of works is republished at Sinai for a purpose: to drive one to faith, trusting in God's initiative and provision to accomplish the goal, that is, entitlement to the land of heaven.

Deuteronomy 30:6 declared that God would circumcise their hearts; now this is rephrased in Jeremiah to explain that God will put the law in their midst and write the law upon their hearts (v. 33).[94] This is followed by the standard God-people formula. In verse 34, the author makes plain that God will forgive them on the basis of grace. More passages along these same lines could be examined if space permitted; however, we turn to Ezekiel to notice his unique contribution to this discussion.[95]

Ezekiel speaks similarly of consolation and of God's initiative in this regard:

ונתתי להם לב אחד ורוח חדשה אתן
בקרבכם והסרתי לב האבן מבשרם
ונתתי להם לב בשר

I will give to them one heart, and a new spirit I will put in your midst, and I will take the heart of stone out of their flesh, and I will give them a heart of flesh. (Ezek. 11:19)

As N. Shupak has pointed out, this idea is echoic[96] of passages in both Deuteronomy and Jeremiah.[97] Remember that Ezekiel and Jeremiah were contemporaries. Generally speaking, Jeremiah is the prophet to the people in the Land, and Ezekiel is the prophet to the people in Babylon. We would therefore expect similarity in the concepts and language used to describe the new covenant during this period of redemptive history.

After declaring in the immediately preceding verses that the Lord will gather the people from all the lands where they have been scattered, and that they will turn from their detestable idols and abominations, the Lord says that he will give them one heart. They will walk now in his statutes and commandments, and they will do them. As previously described, this will happen because God takes the initiative to make his people willing. Likewise, other passages could be observed in Ezekiel to illustrate the same

94. This is probably what Paul had in mind in 2 Cor. 3.

95. I have in mind especially Jer. 32:37–41. The distinctive contribution of that passage to the present discussion is similar prophetic language to describe the regathering of God's people in security, the God-people covenant formula again, and an undivided heart with respect to obedience. That is, there will be a full-souled love for the Lord, fearing of the Lord, a wholehearted commitment, and the establishing of an *eternal covenant* (note: unbreakable!). The Lord, through a wonderful anthropomorphism, says *he* will accomplish it with all his heart and soul!

96. See N. Shupak, "The Concept of 'Heart,'" 202–12.

97. Deut. 10:16; 30:6; Jer. 4:4; 9:25ff.

point (especially Ezek. 36:24–26).[98] We turn now to Paul's use of Leviticus 18:5 and Deuteronomy 30 in what are arguably his most important doctrinal epistles: Galatians and Romans.

The Use of Leviticus 18:5 and Deuteronomy 30 in Paul

Paul develops meanings in these juxtaposed Old Testament texts that go beyond what is recoverable when these texts are taken in isolation from one another in the context of their immediate environment. In other words, strictly grammatical-historical exegesis of the Old Testament texts severed from their New Testament context leaves us bereft of understanding.

The attempts to understand Paul's approach to these two passages fall into one of two categories: a view that posits a correlative understanding, which understands the citation of these texts as supportive of one another,[99] or an antithetical understanding, which understands these texts as cited in opposition to one another. In the conclusion of this essay, I suggest that the Old Testament evidence and its own developmental history support the position that Paul placed these passages (Lev. 18:5 and Deut. 30:1–14) in juxtaposition to one another in Romans 10 for a clear and specific reason: to communicate an antithesis. Moreover, Paul uses Leviticus 18:5 in Galatians 3 in a manner similarly juxtaposed to his quote from Habakkuk to demonstrate the same principle: a fundamental antithesis of works and grace. In short, in the apostle's understanding of the nature of the Mosaic covenant, there was a works principle operative in this administration of the covenant of grace.[100] This was intentionally present for specific reasons, and unless the categories are rightly understood in their own and their

---

98. Similar language and concepts are repeated with respect to the new heart and regathering and restoration, but the distinctive advancement here is the use of ritual language to talk about righteousness, "I will sprinkle you with clean water, and you will be clean from all your uncleanness . . . from all your idols I will cleanse you" (v. 25).

99. I am indebted to Sprinkle for this language from a paper, "Paul's Use of Leviticus 18:5 and Deuteronomy 30:12–14 in Romans 10:5–8: Conflicting Paradigms of Restoration," delivered at the British New Testament Conference, Sept. 2006. For the following classifications and bibliography (see below on Rom. 10:5), I acknowledge my indebtedness to him. Often the correlative approach understands this compatibility of these two texts as Paul's citing Deut. 30 to redefine the Lev. 18:5 citation. On this, see Sprinkle, "The Interpretation of Leviticus 18:5," 181 and following.

100. Even acknowledging this operative principle of works, with the confession I maintain that the Sinaitic covenant should be called an administration of the covenant of grace (Westminster Confession of Faith 7.5) due to the apostle's interpretation in Romans 10, among other reasons. See the historical analysis by Brent Ferry in this book demonstrating the various ways in which Reformed exegetes and theologians have dealt with this issue.

canonical context, this will entail systemic toxicity in one's theological system.[101]

Since almost all agree that Paul's letter to the Galatians was written first, we will explore that before turning to Romans. Paul's quote of Leviticus 18:5 juxtaposed with Habakkuk 2:4, "the just shall live by faith," is found in Galatians 3:

ὅσοι γὰρ ἐξ ἔργων νόμου εἰσὶν ὑπὸ κατάραν εἰσίν· γέγραπται γὰρ ὅτι Ἐπικατάρατος πᾶς ὃς οὐκ ἐμμένει πᾶσιν τοῖς γεγραμμένοις ἐν τῷ βιβλίῳ τοῦ νόμου τοῦ ποιῆσαι αὐτά. ὅτι δὲ ἐν νόμῳ οὐδεὶς δικαιοῦται παρὰ τῷ θεῷ δῆλον, ὅτι Ὁ δίκαιος ἐκ πίστεως ζήσεται· ὁ δὲ νόμος οὐκ ἔστιν ἐκ πίστεως, ἀλλ᾽ Ὁ ποιήσας αὐτὰ ζήσεται ἐν αὐτοῖς.

For as many as are of the works of the law, they are under a curse; for it stands written, "Cursed is everyone that does not abide by all the things written in the book of the law by doing them."[102] But that in the law no one is justified with God is clear, because "the just shall live by faith"; but the law is not of faith but "he who does them shall live in them." (Gal. 3:10–12)

Paul has two arguments in these verses. His first argument is in verse 10 in the form of an abbreviated syllogism.[103] Stated most simply, the argument of Galatians 3:10 assumes the following form:[104]

PREMISE: Cursed is everyone who does not observe and obey all the things written in the book of the law.

CONCLUSION: All who rely on the works of the law are under a curse.[105]

101. Watson, *Paul and the Hermeneutics of Faith*, states it well throughout his book but especially on 330 when he says: "Paul here creates a hermeneutical framework for the right interpretation of scripture as a whole, in its differentiated though ultimately convergent testimony to God's saving action in Christ. The unity and harmony of this scriptural testimony can only be grasped if one understands the inner-scriptural antithesis which Paul's oppositional testimony seeks to identify."

102. The citation from Deut. 27:26, which is the apostle's proof for his conclusion, does not fully correspond to either the Septuagint or the Masoretic Text. See Hans Dieter Betz, *Galatians: A Commentary on Paul's Letter to the Churches in Galatia*, Hermeneia (Philadelphia: Fortress, 1979), 144–45. For a collection of a massive amount of data and how Paul handled citations, see Christopher D. Stanley, *Paul and the Language of Scripture: Citation Technique in the Pauline Epistles and Contemporary Literature*, Society for New Testament Studies Monograph Series 69 (Cambridge: Cambridge University Press, 1992), esp. 238–43.

103. See Bryan Estelle, "The Covenant of Works in Moses and Paul," in *Covenant, Justification, and Pastoral Ministry: Essays by the Faculty of Westminster Seminary California*, ed. R. Scott Clark (Phillipsburg, NJ: P&R, 2007), 89–135, esp. 124–33, and the forthcoming chapter in a collection of essays on relevance theory—idem, "The Riddle of Galatians 3:10 and Its Context: Revisited Again."

104. The following reconstruction of Paul's argument is adopted from A. Andrew Das, *Paul, the Law, and the Covenant* (Peabody, MA: Hendrickson, 2001), 145–70.

105. It is possible that Paul associates the law in this context not only with a curse and with the flesh (5:18), but also with the Egyptian bondage rather than freedom. See William N. Wilder,

The implied reconstructed minor premise would then possibly look like this:

> All who rely on the works of the law do not observe and obey all the things written in the book of the law.[106]

Paul then goes on to make another argument in verses 11 and 12, which stated most simply assumes the following form:[107]

MAJOR PREMISE: The one who is righteous by faith shall live (v. 11b).

MINOR PREMISE: The law is not ἐκ πίστεως (v. 12a, reinforced by v. 12b).

CONCLUSION: No one is justified (= receives life) by law (v. 11a).

Let the reader understand the apostle's line of reasoning here. After stating the cursed condition of every person in his first argument (v. 10), the apostle states the conclusion of his second argument first (v. 11a—"no one is justified, i.e., receives entitlement to heaven, by law") and then asserts justification is by faith (v. 11b), and furthermore, law and faith are antithetical (read = incompatible, 3:12). The logic is lucid and insuperable: Habakkuk 2:4 and Leviticus 18:5 are "two mutually exclusive *soteriological* statements."[108] J. Gresham Machen stated this classic formulation years ago with unsurpassed eloquence and simplicity (obviously reflecting the standard theological formulation of justification).[109]

Echoes of the Exodus Narrative in the Context and Background of Galatians 5:18, Studies in Biblical Literature 23 (New York: Peter Lang, 2001), 76.

106. Kjell Arne Morland, *The Rhetoric of Curse in Galatians*, Emory Studies in Early Christianity 5 (Atlanta: Scholars, 1995), 203–4, says that it is difficult to identify exactly the omitted premise. He gives a summary of the way recent scholars have construed the missing premise. His reconstruction is, "All who rely on the works of the law do not abide by all things written in the book of the law and do them."

107. Building on Stanley and Das, see Sprinkle, "The Interpretation of Leviticus 18:5," 146–47, for recent bibliography and discussion.

108. Sprinkle, "The Interpretation of Leviticus 18:5," 148. The Canons of Dort, Heads III & IV, Article 5 states, "In the same light are we to consider the law of the Decalogue, delivered by God to His peculiar people the Jews by the hands of Moses. For though it discovers the greatness of sin, and more and more convinces man thereof, yet as it neither points out a remedy nor imparts strength to extricate him from misery, and thus being weak through the flesh leaves the transgressor under the curse, man cannot by this law obtain saving grace." Translation from *Reformed Confessions Harmonized: With an Annotated Bibliography of Reformed Doctrinal Works*, ed. Joel R. Beeke and Sinclair B. Ferguson (Grand Rapids: Baker, 1999), 130.

109. J. Gresham Machen, *Machen's Notes on Galatians, and Other Aids to the Interpretation of the Epistle to the Galatians from the Writings of J. Gresham Machen*, ed. John H. Skilton (Philadelphia: Presbyterian and Reformed, 1972), 178: "You might conceivably be saved by works or you might be saved by faith; but you cannot be saved by both. It is 'either or' here not 'both

N. T. Wright has recently suggested that there is a narrative substructure of exile and end of the exile in this passage.[110] Here I have to be briefer than one would like to be, for this definitely warrants further comment. If one were to consider the natural setting of the citations and the sequence of biblical books in the above passage, there may indeed be in the apostle's mind some notion of exile and end of exile; a *historia salutis* substructure may be present.[111] If that should be proved true, it would not negate the presence of republication of the works principle in the Mosaic covenant (although Wright would concede that it is definitely more along corporate lines than individual); rather, it would demonstrate that what Wright wishes to categorize under narrative substructure has been previously observed under the concept of republication by many Reformed exegetes.

However, what I wish to emphasize here in Galatians is that Habakkuk 2:4 and Leviticus 18:5 are also presented by the apostle as two different ways to obtain life that is *eschatological life*.[112] In the previously quoted passage of Galatians, ζήσεται ("will live") corresponds to either a benefit flowing forth from justification or the event of justification itself.[113] My own preference is for the latter view based on the apostle's correlation between justification and eschatological life in the immediate context (v. 21): "For if a law was given which was able to make alive (ὁ δυνάμενος ζωοποιῆσαι), then righteousness (ἡ δικαιοσύνη) would have been through the law." Therefore it seems clear that the following predication may be made with respect to our doctrine of justification: *it is biblically warranted to say that justification includes the element of entitlement to heaven.*

One further note needs to be emphasized before we turn from Galatians to Romans. Paul clearly saw *both a principle of works and a principle of grace* operating within the old covenant, that is the Sinaitic covenant; otherwise

---

and.' But which shall it be, works or faith? The Scripture gives the answer. The Scripture says it is faith. Therefore it is *not* works."

110. See especially N. T. Wright, *The Climax of the Covenant: Christ and the Law in Pauline Theology* (Minneapolis: Fortress, 1993), 137–56.

111. I am indebted to my friend John Fesko for drawing this point to my attention. In other words, there may be something to Paul quoting Deut. 27:26 first, which comes from the beginning of Israel's inheritance of the land, continued tenure of which is conditioned upon their obedience/disobedience to the stipulations, which is analogous to Adam's probative tenure in Eden. The subsequent quote from Hab. 2:4, which comes at the end of Israel's occupation in the land, so to speak, may highlight the narrative history of Israel's failure as God's son to be obedient to the stipulations and thus bring about the blessing sanctions of occupation. Of course, if this observation has merit to it, then it points typologically to the need of Christ's obedience, as the true Son of God, that will earn the entitlement of eschatological rest in the land of heaven itself.

112. Sprinkle, "The Interpretation of Leviticus 18:5," 148. I am gratefully indebted to Sprinkle for drawing the following exegetical nuances to my attention and helping me see the clear connection the apostle makes here between justification and eschatological life.

113. See ibid., 149, for bibliography on these options.

he would not have made the statement he did in verse 17: "The law [which demands concrete acts of obedience], which came 430 years afterward, does not annul a covenant [i.e., the covenant of grace] previously ratified by God, so as to make the promise void." The distinct necessity for obedience played a somewhat different function under the old covenant than the new with respect to our survey of these texts thus far and what it teaches as far as Israel's rights to possession in the land. In the old covenant there was the need for compliance so that this would be the ground for Israel's continuance in the land, the typological kingdom. This has become evident in the understanding of Leviticus 18:5 with respect to the temporal blessings of life that would ensue following the fulfilment of the stipulations.

That specific function of obedience has now changed in the New Testament.[114] In this regard, the necessity for obedience plays a somewhat different role under the old covenant. Although the substance of the covenant of grace is the same in both testaments, in the old covenant there was the need for compliance so that this would be the meritorious grounds for Israel's continuance in the land, the typological kingdom. Here we see the pressing need to pay particular attention to the so-called principle of periodicity, or successive covenant-makings at this point, if one wants to avoid mistakes.[115] God does not call the New Testament church to obedience in exactly the same way as he did the Old Testament saints in the Sinaitic covenant or for the same purpose, and neither should we: the promise of tenure in the land is over. There is no longer this necessity of obedience for the sake of maintaining tenure in the land since the purpose of that period of God's redemptive plan has been served. Israel's disobedience has triggered the curse sanctions. Therefore, the new covenant context has essentially changed matters here. The new context of Christ having come has changed matters. Now there is no longer any need for the typological land since it has fulfilled its designated purpose.[116] The final rest

114. *Pace* John Murray, *Principles of Conduct* (Grand Rapids: Eerdmans, 1957), 199–200, who writes, "In all this the demand of obedience in the Mosaic covenant *is principally identical* with the same demand in the new covenant of the gospel economy"(emphasis mine). On the following page, Murray further explains and cites for support Geerhardus Vos, *Biblical Theology: Old and New Testaments*, at a point where Vos himself could definitely have been clearer and done better in his analysis of the Sinaitic covenant and legal merit. In my judgment, Vos handled the covenant of works and the intratrinitarian matters with their analogous themes much better, for example, in "The Doctrine of the Covenant in Reformed Theology," in *Redemptive History and Biblical Interpretation: The Shorter Writings of Geerhardus Vos*, ed. Richard B. Gaffin Jr. (Phillipsburg, NJ: Presbyterian and Reformed, 1980), 234–67, and idem, "The Alleged Legalism in Paul's Doctrine of Justification," also in *Redemptive History and Biblical Interpretation*, 383–99.

115. See Geerhardus Vos, *Biblical Theology: Old and New Testaments* (Grand Rapids: Eerdmans, 1948), 16.

116. J. Gordon McConville, *Grace in the End: A Study in Deuteronomic Theology* (Grand Rapids: Zondervan, 1993), 89–90, writes, "There is no strand of 1, 2 Kings that imagines that the future lies along the path of a restored monarchy. It is significant that the prayer of Solomon, the

has been secured (Heb. 4). The need for perfect obedience is there (as always) for gaining eschatological life. The need for grateful obedience (the so-called third use of the law) is still there and was there in the old covenant.[117] But the demand for sincere obedience,[118] relative obedience (albeit imperfect) which would showcase an appropriate measure of readable obedience before the surrounding nations, has passed.[119] The whole system was planned obsolescence. Israel had served her purpose.[120] The temporary had given way to permanence. What was prototypical has been eclipsed by what is antitypical.

The Air That the Apostle Breathes

With Paul there is a radical break with the past and in some sense with his contemporaries. From Paul's perspective, there is no way that the works of the law can provide a mechanism for one to earn life, and particularly life defined as entitlement to heaven. The strands that were disconnected in the Old Testament have come together in the New Testament.

Paul has radicalized the Leviticus interpretation but not in the sense of mishandling it; rather, in its fullest meaning the Leviticus quote is now marshaled forth as an important part of the apostle's understanding of the demands of the law and their satisfaction through Christ's work. This may

---

most articulate expression of hope for the future in the books, anticipates no such thing, *not even a return to the land*. The two books of Kings issue a call to repent and leave open the question how God might then respond in Grace."

117. Westminster Confession of Faith 19.6–7; Westminster Larger Catechism 97; Heidelberg Catechism 115. See, e.g., Ps. 119:1–6, 101, 104, 128; Mic. 6:8.

118. Witsius, *Economy*, 2:184: "God did not require perfect obedience from Israel, as a condition of this covenant, as a cause of claiming the reward; but sincere obedience, as an evidence of reverence and gratitude." For more discussion on Witsius's development of the typology here, see John Fesko's essay, "Calvin and Witsius on the Mosaic Covenant," in this volume.

119. See Meredith G. Kline, *Kingdom Prologue* (Overland Park, KS: Two Age Press, 2000), 322–23: "The Israelite people corporately could maintain their continuing tenure as the theocratic kingdom in the promised land only as they maintained the appropriate measure of national fidelity to their heavenly King. Failure to do so would result in the loss of the typological kingdom and their very identity as God's people in that corporate, typological sense. . . . The standard of judgment in this national probation was one of typological legibility, that is, the message must remain reasonably readable that enjoyment of the felicity of God's holy kingdom goes hand in hand with righteousness. Without holiness we do not see God."

120. M. G. Kline, *Treaty of the Great King: The Covenant Structure of Deuteronomy* (Grand Rapids: Eerdmans, 1963), 65, states, "Israel's continued enjoyment of a habitation in God's land, like Adam's continued enjoyment of the original paradise, depended on continued fidelity to the Lord. Certain important distinctions are necessary in making such a comparison. Flawless obedience was the condition of Adam's continuance in the Garden; but Israel's tenure in Canaan was contingent on the maintenance of a measure of religious loyalty which needed not to be comprehensive of all Israel nor to be perfect even in those who were the true Israel. There was a freedom in God's exercise or restraint of judgment, a freedom originating in the underlying principle of sovereign grace in his rule of Israel. Nevertheless, God did so dispense his judgment that the interests of the typical-symbolical message of Israel's history were preserved."

have something to do with the very air he was breathing. For example, *Targum Onkelos* (Pentateuch) says:[121]

ותיטרון ית קימי וית דיני דאם יעביד יתהון	You must keep my law and my statutes which,
אנשא ייחי בהון <u>בחיי עלמא</u> אנא יוי	if a man obeyed, he would live in them *in the life of eternity*,[122] I am the Lord. (Lev. 18:5)

The Targum understands the reward to be eternal life, not merely temporal blessings. *Targum Jonathan* (The Former and Latter Prophets) similarly translates Leviticus 18:5 where it is cited (i.e., referring to eternal life).[123] This is the air that the apostle breathed, and he understood the reference as *eternal* life. It is not just in the Targum that such an eschatologizing tendency has occurred but throughout the literature of the Second Temple period.[124] This evidence flies in the face of the recent trends of interpreting Leviticus 18:5 in Paul and the literature of the Second Temple period.[125]

Correlative with this eschatologizing tendency is a parallel development with focus on individual soteriology as discussed above. The picture is more complicated than often presented. Although there is this growing movement toward a more individualistic model of retribution in the history of Israel, it does not negate, as Joel Kaminsky has ably demonstrated, that corporate responsibility and divine retribution toward individuals stand side by side even in the earliest periods of Israel's history.[126] Nevertheless, there is development along individualistic lines.

One could note the following polarities:[127]

---

121. See the following for language and dating issues connected with Targum Onkelos and Jonathan: Moshe Goshen-Gottstein, "The Language of Targum Onqelos and the Model of Literary Diglossia in Aramaic," *Journal of Near Eastern Studies* 37 (1978): 169–79; Stephen A. Kaufman, "On Methodology in the Study of the Targums and Their Chronology," *Journal for the Study of the New Testament* 23 (1985): 117–24; Abraham Tal (Rosenthal), *The Language of the Targum of the Former Prophets and Its Position with the Aramaic Dialects*, Texts and Studies in the Hebrew Language and Related Subjects 1 (Tel-Aviv: Tel-Aviv University, 1975).

122. Rabbinic Hebrew often expresses this עולם הבא "in the world to come."

123. The addition is lacking in Targum Neofiti and Fragment Targum, however, as noted by Friedrich Avemarie, "Paul and the Claim of the Law," in *The Beginnings of Christianity*, ed. Jack Pastor and Menachem Mor (Jerusalem: Yad Ben-Zvi, 1997), 125–48, esp. 124.

124. Gathercole, "Torah, Life and Salvation," and also Sprinkle, "The Interpretation of Leviticus 18:5."

125. I have in mind especially the regulatory view of the law proposed by J. D. G. Dunn, *The Theology of Paul the Apostle* (Grand Rapids: Eerdmans, 1998), 152–53; idem, *The New Perspective on Paul: Collected Essays*, Wissenschaftliche Untersuchungen zum Neuen Testament 185 (Tübingen: Mohr Siebeck, 2005), 13, 65.

126. See Joel S. Kaminsky, *Corporate Responsibility in the Hebrew Bible*, Journal for the Study of the Old Testament Supplement 196 (Sheffield: Sheffield Academic Press, 1995), 116–38.

127. I would like to acknowledge my debt to my former advisor and good friend, Dr. Doug Gropp, for a lengthy conversation in his home several years ago in which he set these polarities before me and caused me to begin thinking about this issue in depth.

A	B
Corporate	Individual
Physical/temporal	Spiritual/eschatological

In this chapter, I have tried to show in general terms how there is an increasing accent upon column B in these polarities. Hellenization and Pharisaism, as mentioned above, brought greater emphasis on the individual. Other extrabiblical literature demonstrates this same directional shift (as successfully argued by Simon Gathercole and Sprinkle). I suggest that Paul shared this eschatological perspective of his contemporaries that would lead to a greater freighting of the concerns in column B.

The Final Solution in Romans 10: Moses' Promise Prediction Speech Interpreted as Entitlement to Life through Faith, Not Man's Works

Two approaches to this text have been present in the scholarly literature: the correlative approach and the antithetical approach.[128] The correlative approach attempts to make these texts (Lev. 18:5 and Deut. 30) compatible, and the effect of that move is often to redefine the meaning of Leviticus 18:5 in the process.[129] Speaking generally, the antithetical approach sees a sharp opposition between two mutually exclusive soteriologies expressed in these two passages.[130] One is by works, the other by faith. One is active,

128. In what follows, for the terms "correlative" and "antithetical," and for the typology of various views within each approach, I am largely indebted to Preston Sprinkle's work, especially in his dissertation.

129. The correlative approach is followed by Leander Keck, *Romans* (Nashville: Abingdon, 2005), 254; Friedrich Avemarie, "Paul and the Claim of the Law according to the Scripture: Leviticus 18:5 in Galatians 3:12 and Romans 10:5," in Jack Pastor and Menachem Mor, eds., *The Beginnings of Christianity: A Collection of Articles* (Jerusalem: Yad Ben-Zvi, 2005), 125–48 (142–47); N. T. Wright, *Romans*, New Interpreter's Bible (Nashville: Abingdon, 2002), 645–46, 655, 658–63; J. Ross Wagner, *Heralds of the Good News: Isaiah and Paul "In Concert" in the Letter to the Romans* (Leiden: Brill, 2002); Edith Humphrey, "Why Bring the Word Down? The Rhetoric of Demonstration and Disclosure in Romans 9:30–10:21," in *Romans and the People of God: Essays in Honor of Gordon D. Fee*, ed. N. T. Wright and S. Soderlund (Grand Rapids: Eerdmans, 1999), 129–48; Hays, *Echoes*. Another approach is to see that Christ is the one who "does these things" (10:5); see, for example, Christopher Bryan, *A Preface to Romans: Notes on the Epistle in Its Literary and Cultural Setting* (New York: Oxford University Press, 2000), 168; C. E. B. Cranfield, *Romans 9–16*, International Critical Commentary (Edinburgh: T&T Clark, 1979), 522; S. Stowers, *A Rereading of Romans: Justice, Jews, and Gentiles* (New Haven: Yale University Press, 1994), 308–9; Johannes Munck, *Christ and Israel: An Interpretation of Romans 9–11*, trans. Ingeborg Nixon (Philadelphia: Fortress, 1967), 86–89; A. J. Bandstra, *The Law and the Elements of the World* (Kampen: Kok, 1964), 103–5; Karl Barth, *Church Dogmatics*, vol. II/2, ed. G. W. Bromiley and T. F. Torrance (Edinburgh: T&T Clark, 1951), 245.

130. As Sprinkle points out, within this taxonomy of the antithetical approach, there are a variety of approaches: some say the Leviticus formulation is wrong because it is legalistic, others suggest that it illustrates a law-gospel contrast, still others argue that the contrast is between divine agency and human agency. See Rudolf Bultmann, *Theology of the New Testament* (New York: Scribner, 1951), 1:259–69 (especially 264); Bultmann, "Christ the End of the Law," in

the other is receptive. A refutation of the correlative approach is too large for proper consideration here. It is important to try to sketch at least a positive presentation of the antithetical view at the conclusion of this essay. To my way of thinking, the antithetical approach is the more plausible view based upon the biblical evidence.

There are different ways to interpret the antithetical approach: some have seen the sense of the passage as referring to those who seek righteousness marked by regular obedience to the law; others see what is expressed in this antithesis as two different modes of action, one human and the other divine; and still others see it as a legalistic means of self-righteousness, that is, perfect obedience is required in light of Paul's pessimistic anthropology: life may not be achieved by human beings, weak as they are.

I have argued previously for the antithetical approach in Galatians 3:10. Even those vying for a correlative approach in Romans 10 usually recognize an antithetical approach in Galatians.[131]

Μωϋσῆς γὰρ γράφει τὴν δικαιοσύνην τὴν ἐκ [τοῦ] νόμου ὅτι ὁ ποιήσας αὐτὰ ἄνθρωπος ζήσεται ἐν αὐτοῖς.	For Moses writes about the righteousness which is of the law, that "the man who does them shall live by them."[132] (Rom. 10:5)

Bultmann, *Essays Philosophical and Theological* (London: SCM, 1955), 36–60; Hans Hübner, "Was Heisst bei Paulus 'Werke des Gesetzes'?" in *Glaube und Eschatologie*, ed. E. Grässer and O. Merk (Tübingen: Mohr, 1985), 123–33; Hübner, *The Law in Paul's Thought*, trans. James C. G. Greig, ed. John Riches (Edinburgh: T&T Clark, 1984); John Murray, *Epistle to the Romans*, New International Commentary on the New Testament (Grand Rapids: Eerdmans, 1960), 51, 249–51; Stephen Westerholm, *Perspectives Old and New on Paul: The "Lutheran" Paul and His Critics* (Grand Rapids: Eerdmans, 2004), 326–30; Eduard Lohse, *Der Brief an die Römer* (Göttingen: Vandenhoeck and Ruprecht, 2003), 209–10; Douglas Moo, *The Epistle to the Romans*, New International Commentary on the New Testament (Grand Rapids: Eerdmans, 1996), 627; J. S. Vos, "Die hermeneutische Antinomie bei Paulus (Galater 3.11–12; Römer 10.5–10)," *New Testament Studies* 38 (1992): 254–70; Otfried Hofius, "Das Evangelium und Israel: Erwägungen zu Römer 9–11," in *Paulusstudien I* (Tübingen: Mohr Siebeck, 1989), 178–84; idem, "Zur Auslegung von Römer 9.30–33," in *Paulusstudien I*, 155–56; Watson, *Paul and the Hermeneutics of Faith*; E. E. Johnson, *The Function of Apocalyptic and Wisdom Traditions in Romans 9–11*, Society of Biblical Literature Dissertation Series 109 (Atlanta: Scholars, 1989); Sprinkle, "The Interpretation of Leviticus 18:5."

131. Alain Gignac, "Citation de Lévitique 18.5 en Romains 10.5 et Galates 3.12. Deux lectures différentes des rapports Christ Torah?" *Église et Theologie* 25.3 (1994): 367–404, especially 387 and 401–3.

132. There is a significant text-critical issue in this verse with regard to where ὅτι belongs, immediately before ὁ ποιήσας or following γράφει. I am following the former reading. Details may be found in Andreas Lindemann, "Die Gerechtigkeit aus dem Gesetz: Erwägungen zur Auslegung und zur Textgeschichte von Römer 10 5," *Zeitschrift für die neutestamentliche Wissenschaft* 73 (1982): 231–50; Bruce M. Metzger, *A Textual Commentary on the Greek New Testament* (Stuttgart: UBS, 1971), 524–25. Although Lindemann and Metzger both follow the reading given above, Lindemann is not in agreement with all the reasons given by Metzger for the reading.

There are other good reasons for holding to an antithetical position between these two citations in Romans 10:5 and following.[133] Here I list only a few. First, very strong grammatical evidence is seen in the contrastive manner and sense of the two phrases in Romans 10:5–6, that is, a contrast between the righteousness by law and the righteousness by faith. It is clear here and elsewhere (Rom. 4:16; 9:30, 32 etc.) that the apostle intends a contrast when he construes his words this way (e.g., righteousness ἐκ πίστεως with δὲ as the linking word is put alongside righteousness ἐκ something else). As Dunn himself recognizes (I have almost cited his language here), this seems to suggest a contrast.[134] Additionally, Paul in other places in his epistle to the Romans sets "the law" in direct opposition to the "righteousness of faith" (e.g., Rom. 4:13). Also, as is well known, the apostle Paul suppresses the "doing" language in his citation of Deuteronomy 30 (on this, more below), which suggests he had in mind a contrast between the two citations.

This citation of the works principle in Romans 10:5 is not, strictly speaking, typological of what Christ has done. Too many readers collapse law into gospel in some manner here and elsewhere.[135] In other words, the law is not here functioning as a "proleptic manifestation of God's grace in Christ," and "Paul does not see the giving of the law as a manifestation of grace typological of the grace manifested in Christ."[136] Although the active obedience of Christ imputed to believers is a proper biblical category,[137] and indeed one could say that "the Mosaic law was necessary as the covenantal administration of a works principle for the Second Adam to fulfill,"[138] the apostle's point here about the law is its condemning character (Rom. 3:21; 4:15; 5:20; 7:10; 8:2–3).[139] My point is that the apostle is understanding Deuteronomy

133. Sprinkle, "The Interpretation of Leviticus 18:5," 183–85, marshals six arguments.
134. For further detail, see ibid., 184.
135. See, for example, how Mark Seifrid, "Paul's Approach to the Old Testament in Rom 10:6–8," *Trinity Journal* 6 (1985): 3–37, concludes his lengthy article by saying "Paul finds in the theology of Deuteronomy, and more specifically in the giving of the law, a correspondence to the grace which has come in Jesus Christ" (36).
136. Sprinkle, "The Interpretation of Leviticus 18:5," 193–94.
137. See R. Scott Clark, "Do This and Live: Christ's Active Obedience as the Ground of Justification," in *Covenant, Justification, and Pastoral Ministry: Essays by the Faculty of Westminster Seminary California*, ed. R. Scott Clark (Phillipsburg, NJ: P&R, 2007), 229–66; and David VanDrunen, "To Obey Is Better than Sacrifice: A Defense of the Active Obedience of Christ in the Light of Recent Criticism," in *By Faith Alone: Answering the Challenges to the Doctrine of Justification*, ed. Gary L. W. Johnson and Guy P. Waters (Wheaton, IL: Crossway, 2006), 127–46.
138. See S. M. Baugh, "Galatians 3:20 and the Covenant of Redemption," *Westminster Theological Journal* 66 (2004): 49–70, esp. 66. Baugh says, "For it was the righteousness of the law which Christ fulfilled (Matt. 3:15; 5:17–29; Rom. 3:21–22, 31; 5:12–21; 8:4; etc.) and it was the specific curse of the Mosaic law which he took upon himself in the stead of the seed of Abraham ([Gal.] 3:13, see John 8:46; 2 Cor. 5:21; 1 Peter 3:18) as guarantor and mediator of the new covenant (esp. Heb. 7:22; 8:6; 9:14–15)."
139. Similar to what the apostle had set forth in Gal. 3:13, 19, 22; 4:5.

30:12–14 as prophetic, what Christ would come to do; that is not the case with his use of Leviticus 18:5 in this immediate context.

As in Galatians, so also here the life envisioned in Romans 10:5 by ζήσεται, as Sprinkle deftly notes, "probably corresponds to σωτηρία (10:1, 9, 10) and δικαιοσύνη (Rom. 9:30–32; 10:3, 5, 6, 10) to refer to the present experience of salvation in Christ; but this salvation and life is not yet fully manifested (Rom. 2:7, 10; 5:10, 21; 6:22; 8:11, 18–23)."[140] This distinction seems to support the notion stated previously that our doctrine of justification should include the element of entitlement to heaven.

Recently, others suggest that Paul has "comprehensively rewritten" Deuteronomy in light of the Christ event.[141] This is a natural step when one assumes the conditionality of Deuteronomy 30:12–14 instead of the exegesis above that suggests conditionality starts at verse 15, not verse 11. For those who want to say Paul has rewritten Moses, Christ's coming has rendered "Moses' [conditional] exhortation out of date since the promise of life was realized through divine action."[142] In my view, Moses' unconditional exhortation (vv. 12–14) has now come into its own and has been realized through divine action.

Paul's eschatological position does not compel him to rewrite Deuteronomy 30: Paul's eschatological position entails that he writes about fulfilment. This is supported not only by the initial exegesis of Deuteronomy offered above, but by the increasingly eschatological (and individualized) exegetical milieu in which the apostle finds himself.[143]

Paul emphasizes in this passage the sheer gracious manner in which entitlement to heaven is now offered through two considerations that would have been obvious to the original audience: the impossibility of entitlement to heaven through works, and the introduction of the Deuteronomy quotation in verse

---

140. Sprinkle, "The Interpretation of Leviticus 18:5," 210. Sprinkle helpfully makes the further important point that to recognize the already/not yet aspect of this eschatological life is very different from other interpreters in Second Temple Judaism who also recognize an already/not yet aspect of obtaining eschatological life but predicate the obtainment of that life upon the works and achievements of man as a necessary precondition.

141. Watson, *Paul and the Hermeneutics of Faith*, 336–41, 439, 475; followed by Sprinkle, "Law and Life," 195, 197.

142. Sprinkle, "The Interpretation of Leviticus 18:5," 194. Sprinkle writes, "We suggest that Paul is not citing Deut. 30 as a proof text, but is rewriting the text to reconfigure its original message. As such, Paul's exegetical result is a theological point that is antithetical both to Lev. 18:5 and *the original context of Deut 30* [original emphasis]. In the context of Deut. 30:11–20, Moses stands on the plains of Moab exhorting Israel to 'choose life that you may live' (30:19), to keep God's commandments in order to have life (30:16). Conditionality accentuates the entire passage: life is available to Israel only if they do these things. . . . Deut. 30 must be rewritten in light of the Christ event."

143. That there may have been a growing movement toward a more individualistic model of retribution is not to suggest that individualized retribution was not there in the ancient community of Deuteronomy. See Joel S. Kaminsky, *Corporate Responsibility in the Hebrew Bible*.

6 with the warning "Do not say in your heart" from Deuteronomy 8:17–18 and 9:4–6.[144] The apostle is probably making lexical analogies through linking verbal phrases between various texts, a technique called *gezerah shawa* in rabbinic exegetical procedures and probably having precedent in the Hebrew Bible itself.[145] A cursory glance at just a portion of these passages in their original context demonstrates that Paul's audience would understand this to be a stern rebuke to those relying on their own achievements:

μὴ εἴπῃς ἐν τῇ καρδίᾳ σου Ἡ ἰσχύς μου καὶ τὸ κράτος τῆς χειρός μου ἐποίησέν μοι τὴν δύναμιν τὴν μεγάλην ταύτην.	*Do not say in your heart,* "My strength and the power of my hand did for me this great mighty deed."[146] (Deut. 8:17, Septuagint)
μὴ εἴπῃς ἐν τῇ καρδίᾳ σου, ἐν τῷ ἐξαναλῶσαι κύριον τὸν θεόν σου τὰ ἔθνη ταῦτα ἀπὸ προσώπου σου, λέγων, Διὰ τὰς δικαιοσύνας μου εἰσήγαγέν με κύριος κληρονομῆσαι τὴν γῆν τὴν ἀγαθὴν ταύτην. ἀλλὰ διὰ τὴν ἀσέβειαν τῶν ἐθνῶν τούτων κύριος ἐξολεθρεύσει αὐτοὺς πρὸ προσώπου σου. οὐχὶ διὰ τὴν δικαιοσύνην σου οὐδὲ διὰ τὴν ὁσιότητα τῆς καρδίας σου σὺ εἰσπορεύῃ κληρονομῆσαι τὴν γῆν αὐτῶν.	*Do not say in your heart* when the Lord your God destroys these nations from your face, "Because of my righteousness the Lord led me in to inherit this good land." Rather because of the ungodliness of these nations the Lord will destroy them before your face. Not because of your righteousness nor because of the holiness of your heart may you enter to inherit their land.[147] (Deut. 9:4–5a, Septuagint)

Entitlement to heaven itself is not based upon some achievement of mere humans, nor is it based upon some later postregeneration congruent merit of believers. Paul is driving home the point that salvation is by grace based upon the grounds of Christ's satisfaction alone.

This becomes conspicuously clear when we see the apostle's threefold deliberate suppression of the "doing" language when he quotes the actual passage from Deuteronomy 30:11–14. He begins by employing the very apt powerful rhetorical device of personification.[148]

144. Although many have recently commented on this, for an extensive detailed discussion see John Paul Heil, "Christ, the Termination of the Law (Romans 9:30–10:8)," *Catholic Biblical Quarterly* 63 (2001): 484–98.

145. See Heil, "Christ, the Termination," 493–95; Michael Fishbane, *Biblical Interpretation in Ancient Israel* (Oxford: Clarendon, 1985), 157 and 249; Coxhead, "Deuteronomy 30:11–14," 313–15, also comments on the use of *gezerah shawa* but sees only Deut. 9:4 coming into play in the apostle's citation. He also thinks that "their own righteousness" in Rom. 10:3 and 5 refers to national Israel and not the individual, contrary to Moo, *Epistle to the Romans*, 649–51.

146. The translation, a very literal one, is Heil's.

147. Again, Heil's translation.

148. I say "apt" because it is a form of metaphor whereby an author groups particulars from the multiplicity of humanity's concrete experiences of this world and drives it to the universal. See, for details, Claudia V. Camp's profound study, *Wisdom and the Feminine in*

After introducing Leviticus 18:5 as coming from Moses in Romans 10:5, again setting forth the principle of works as operative in the Mosaic covenant, Paul uses an interpretive quote from Deuteronomy 30:11–14 with some changes in Romans 10:6–8. I quote the Septuagint side by side with the apostle's allusion so that it becomes obvious what he is doing:[149]

Deuteronomy 30:11–14 LXX	Romans 10:6–8
	[6]ἡ δὲ ἐκ πίστεως δικαιοσύνη οὕτως λέγει,
[11]ἡ ἐντολὴ αὕτη . . .	
[12]οὐκ ἐν τῷ οὐρανῷ ἐστιν λέγων·	Μὴ εἴπῃς ἐν τῇ καρδίᾳ σου,
τίς ἀναβήσεται ἡμῖν εἰς τὸν οὐρανὸν . . .	Τίς ἀναβήσεται εἰς τὸν οὐρανόν;
καὶ ἀκούσαντες **αὐτὴν** *ποιήσομεν.*	τοῦτ' ἔστιν **Χριστὸν** καταγαγεῖν·
[13]οὐδὲ πέραν τῆς θαλάσσης ἐστὶν	[7]ἤ,
λέγων· τίς διαπεράσει ἡμῖν	Τίς καταβήσεται
εἰς τὸ πέραν τῆς θαλάσσης	εἰς τὴν ἄβυσσον;
καὶ λήμψεται ἡμῖν **αὐτήν**;	τοῦτ' ἔστιν **Χριστὸν** ἐκ νεκρῶν ἀναγαγεῖν.
καὶ ἀκούσαντες **αὐτὴν** *ποιήσομεν.*	
	[8]ἀλλὰ τί λέγει;
[14]ἐγγύς σου ἐστιν τὸ ῥῆμα σφόδρα	Ἐγγύς σου τὸ ῥῆμά ἐστιν,
ἐν τῷ στόματί σου	ἐν τῷ στόματί σου
καὶ ἐν τῇ καρδίᾳ σου	καὶ ἐν τῇ καρδίᾳ σου·
	τοῦτ' ἔστιν τὸ ῥῆμα τῆς πίστεως
	ὃ κηρύσσομεν.
καὶ ἐν ταῖς χερσίν σου αὐτὸ *ποιεῖν.*	

A translation of Paul's text would read: "But the righteousness from faith says thus, '*Do not say in your heart*, "Who will ascend into heaven?" (that is, to bring Christ down), or "Who will descend into the abyss?" (that is, to bring Christ up from the dead).' Rather, what does it say? 'The word is near you, in your mouth and in your heart; this is the word of faith which we are preaching.'"

From the citation, it becomes clear that Paul suppresses the "doing" language from Deuteronomy. Since Christ has descended and been raised to usher in the promises (indirect allusions to the incarnation and resur-

---

the Book of Proverbs, Bible and Literature Series 11, ed. David Gunn (Decatur, GA: Almond, 1985), 209–22.

149. I am obliged to J. Ross Wagner, *Heralds*, 163, for the layout of the chart here that helps make the differences so clear. He follows the correction of the Göttingen edition suggested by John William Wevers, *Notes on the Greek Text of Deuteronomy*, Society of Biblical Literature Septuagint and Cognate Studies (Atlanta: Scholars, 1995), 482–85.

rection of Christ),[150] the people have no need to say, "who will go up for us heavenwards?" Christ himself has gone through a death passage because he is the real Israel and the second Adam who has done everything that is necessary on our behalf: the obedience of *the* Son has rendered satisfaction. The quest is over—definitively—for those that will receive the answer by faith.

Conclusion

Entitlement to heaven is not some separate benefit of justification which is based upon the meritorious or even the demonstrative works of believers after they are justified. Rather, entitlement to heaven is something won by the satisfaction of Christ.

What Walter Kaiser writes, "The alleged antithesis then is only in the misconception of Paul's generation of Jews,"[151] is wrong on two counts: the antithesis is not alleged and it is not a misconception of Paul's contemporary generation of misguided Jews.[152]

In the garden of Eden, the probation was put in negative terms with an implicit positive promise, eschatological life. In the Mosaic economy, that was reversed: the probation was put in positive terms (temporal blessings) with an explicitly stated punishment: extirpation from the land. Additionally, it was obvious that no mere man could earn life, gain entitlement to heaven that is, since he was only able always to sin. Nevertheless, God was well pleased to hold out the promise of life, with its temporal blessings, in order to teach the Israelites that there was an entitlement to a land beyond any geopolitical sphere. They could enter the rest of heaven, and a greater Joshua could lead them there one day, a true son of Israel (Heb. 4). Entitlement to heaven can be secured only by grace through faith, not works, not mere human works, that is.[153]

This is related to another very important question that necessarily issues from this present study: what about the final judgment for the believer

---

150. See Joseph A. Fitzmyer, *Romans*, Anchor Bible 33 (Garden City, NY: Doubleday, 1993), 590.

151. Walter C. Kaiser, "Leviticus 18:5 and Paul: 'Do this and you shall live' (eternally?)," *Journal of the Evangelical Theological Society* 14 (1971): 19–28, esp. 27.

152. This faulty view is hamstrung by the apostle himself (see Gal. 4:24–26 and 2 Cor. 3:6–9).

153. As Sprinkle, "The Interpretation of Leviticus 18:5," 217, comments, "For Paul, God's saving act in Christ grants eschatological life to 'the one who does not work but believes on the one who justifies the ungodly' (Rom. 4:5); as such, divine saving action in Christ cannot be correlated with the Lev. 18:5 principle. No one can gain, should try to gain, or will gain through the law the eschatological life that has been given by God in Christ."

once that person enters the community of faith? What are Paul's and early Judaism's views on this?[154] Are they identical, similar, or radically different? Recent scholarly works which deal with this subject, for example, Chris VanLandingham's,[155] and Kent Yinger's,[156] demand a response at least in the form of a scholarly monograph if not a book. We are now ready to ask what the preceding detailed treatment teaches us.

In sum, if Paul, under the influence of increasing eschatologizing exegetical tendencies (both in the Hebrew Bible and early Judaism), understood the reward of human obedience leading to life as offered in Leviticus 18:5 as eternal life which was necessarily contrary to fact because of man's impotence; and if Deuteronomy 30:1–14 is a predictive prophecy suggesting that faith in Jesus Christ is the only answer to that prophecy which earns life; then, life in the Pauline mind-set leads to entitlement to eschatological life, that is, heaven, through the faith principle and in no other way. There has been a divine reversal. What mere man could not accomplish, God has. Moses says no mere man may gain entitlement to heaven through the works principle, but the righteousness of faith says that Jesus has won entitlement to heaven and now the principle of faith receives that gratuitous gift. It is grace in the end. As Machen so aptly states in another context, "For what the Apostle is concerned to deny is any intrusion of human merit into the work by which salvation is obtained. That work, according to the Epistle to the Galatians and according to the whole New Testament, is the work of God and of God alone."[157]

154. Ibid., 217–18, raises this relevant question and suggests a path for more exploratory work in both Paul and early Judaism.

155. See Chris VanLandingham, *Judgment & Justification in Early Judaism and in the Apostle Paul* (Peabody, MA: Hendrickson, 2006), 334–35. In answer to the question, "What must one do to receive eternal life?" he writes that Paul agrees with many Jewish texts of his time that one's eternal destiny is decided finally according to one's deeds. . . . The last judgment is not a judgment over the work of Christ or even over what the Holy Spirit has done in the believer; it is a judgment over the individual and what he or she has done."

156. See Kent L. Yinger, *Paul, Judaism, and Judgment according to Deeds*, Society for New Testament Studies Monograph Series 105 (Cambridge: Cambridge University Press, 1999), deals with the issue of judgment according to deeds and justification by faith in Paul and Second Temple Jewish sources.

157. Machen, *What Is Faith?* 192–93.

5

The King, the Law, and Righteousness in the Psalms

A Foundation for Understanding the Work of Christ

RICHARD P. BELCHER JR.

At first glance it seems implausible to use the psalms to understand the work of Christ in securing salvation for his people. Such a study seems fraught with exegetical, hermeneutical, and theological difficulties. How does one establish that the psalms do speak of Christ? How does one argue that the psalms speak of the work of Christ? More specifically, is it possible that the psalms even speak of the obedience of Christ in fulfilment of the law, traditionally called the active obedience of Christ? These questions are important in light of recent discussions concerning the covenant of works, justification by faith, and the role of works in salvation. For example, Peter Leithart argues that justification is not just a secret act of declaration of righteousness by God, but it is also something worked out in history when God demonstrates faithfulness to his covenant by delivering his people from their enemies. He argues this on the basis of certain psalms,

such as Psalms 7 and 26. Thus justification is defined as a favorable verdict
from God rendered through deliverance from enemies. It is broader than
the judicial, forensic meaning in that it describes loyalty within a covenant
relationship. Justification is thus a process that is worked out in human history whenever God vindicates his people by delivering them.[1]

It is not surprising that such a redefinition of justification also includes a
denial of the covenant of works and the active obedience of Christ. Instead
of arguing that Christ has satisfied the demands of the law, to which all
people are bound but are unable to perform, and has thus made it possible
to receive his righteousness imputed through faith alone, some are arguing
that the fulfilment of the law has no place in salvation.[2] The result is that
salvation is no longer by faith alone, but faith includes one's nonmeritorious
covenantal obedience in justification.[3] However, the way the psalms present
the king, the law, and righteousness supports the principle of works as a
basis of justification, not the works of any human being but the works of
Christ the king.

It is beyond the scope of this chapter to get into the foundational hermeneutical questions concerning which psalms speak of Christ, but the assumptions of such an approach must be laid out. First, without taking away the
necessity of understanding the psalms in their original Old Testament context, it is appropriate to argue that all the psalms relate to the person and/or
work of Christ. Although some psalms are more direct in their connection
to Christ, the so-called messianic psalms, the rest of the psalms indirectly
relate to Christ's person (his humanity and deity) and/or his work as prophet,
priest, and king.[4] Second, it is common to argue that the psalms that deal
with the king have a connection to Christ because of the promises in the
Davidic covenant and because Christ clearly comes as the "Son of David."[5]

1. Peter Leithart, "'Judge Me, O God': Biblical Perspectives on Justification," in *The Federal
Vision*, ed. Steve Wilkins and Duane Garner (Monroe, LA: Athanasius, 2004), 203–36.
2. James Jordan denies there is a covenant of works that operates according to merit in God's
relationship with Adam. Instead, the key to understanding Adam, as well as Christ, is the idea of
growing from childhood to maturity. His conclusion is that Christ does not fulfil the law on our
behalf and that there is no merit theology in the Bible ("Merit versus Maturity: What Did Jesus Do
for Us?" in *The Federal Vision*, 151–202).
3. Steve Schlissel, "Justification and the Gentiles," in *The Federal Vision*, 243. See also two
unpublished essays by Richard Lusk in 2003: "Future Justification to the Doers of the Law" and
"The Tenses of Justification." For critical evaluations of these views see Guy Waters, *The Federal
Vision and Covenant Theology: A Comparative Analysis* (Phillipsburg, NJ: P&R, 2006), and
Brian M. Schwertley, *Auburn Avenue Theology: A Biblical Analysis* (Saunderstown: American
Presbyterian Press, 2005).
4. For the hermeneutical justification for such an approach see Richard P. Belcher Jr., *The
Messiah and the Psalms* (Fearn, Ross-shire: Christian Focus, 2006).
5. The following is a partial listing of those who would see a connection between the psalms
that deal with the king and Christ: John Calvin, *Psalms 36–92*, trans. Henry Beveridge, Calvin's

Third, recent work on the structure of the Psalter and the implications of that structure for interpreting the individual psalms has opened many paths of beneficial study;[6] for example, do the kingship psalms[7] or the torah psalms[8] have a role in the final editing of the Psalter? Do the kingship psalms and the torah psalms have any relationship to each other in the Psalter, and if so, does that teach us anything about the relationship between the king and the law?[9] Such a pursuit raises the question whether there is any connection between the psalms and Deuteronomy.[10]

Finally, it is legitimate to ask how the relationship between the king and the law relates back to Adam and forward to Christ. What connections are there to Adam who was to reign in the garden in obedience to God's word? Are there implicit or explicit connections that can be made between the relationship of the king to the law and the work of Christ? More specifically, what relationship does the king have to the law in the Psalter, and how does that relationship help in understanding the work of Christ? Can appropriate connections be made to what has traditionally been called the

Commentaries 5 (Grand Rapids: Baker, 1996); Walter Kaiser, *The Messiah in the Old Testament* (Grand Rapids: Zondervan, 1995); Gerard Van Groningen, *Messianic Revelation in the Old Testament* (Grand Rapids: Baker, 1990); Brevard Childs, *Introduction to the Old Testament as Scripture* (Philadelphia: Fortress, 1979), 504–25; James L. Mays, *The Lord Reigns: A Theological Handbook to the Psalms* (Louisville: Westminster John Knox, 1994); and David C. Mitchell, *The Message of the Psalter: An Eschatological Programme in the Book of Psalms*, Journal for the Study of the Old Testament Supplement (Sheffield: Sheffield Academic Press, 1997).

6. The following are some of the works that explore the implications of the structure of the Psalter: Gerald H. Wilson, *The Editing of the Hebrew Psalter* (Chico, CA: Scholars, 1985); J. Clinton McCann, ed., *The Shape and Shaping of the Psalter* (Sheffield: JSOT, 1993); David M. Howard Jr., "Recent Trends in Psalms Study," in *The Face of Old Testament Studies*, ed. David W. Baker and Bill T. Arnold (Grand Rapids: Baker, 1999), 329–50; and Jamie A. Grant, *The King as Exemplar: The Function of Deuteronomy's Kingship Law in the Shaping of the Book of Psalms* (Atlanta: SBL, 2004).

7. Kingship psalms are also called royal psalms and are defined on the basis of content rather than structure. They focus on the king or concepts and activities related to the king, such as his conquests or his reign. The problem of identifying the royal psalms as a separate genre is that they sometimes fit the other genre categories of complaint, thanksgiving, and hymn (Herman Gunkel, *Introduction to the Psalms: The Genres of the Religious Lyric of Israel*, trans. James D. Nogalski [Macon, GA: Mercer University Press, 1998]; and Erhard S. Gerstenberger, *Psalms*, Part 1, The Forms of the Old Testament Literature [Grand Rapids: Eerdmans, 1988], 19).

8. Torah psalms are usually placed under the category of wisdom psalms. Although James L. Crenshaw (*The Psalms: An Introduction* [Grand Rapids: Eerdmans, 2001], 87–95) denies that there are wisdom psalms, most acknowledge a wisdom category based on content (the two ways, retribution, torah, creation) and literary characteristics (the term "blessed," numerical sayings, "better than" sayings, and admonition); see especially Roland Murphy, "A Consideration of the Classification 'Wisdom Psalms,'" in *Congress Volume: Bonn, 1962*, Vetus Testamentum Supplement 9 (Leiden: Brill, 1963), 159–60, which is also found in *Studies in Ancient Israelite Literature*, ed. James Crenshaw (New York: KTAV, 1976), 456–567.

9. James L. Mays, "The Place of Torah-Psalms in the Psalter," *Journal of Biblical Literature* 106 (1987): 3–12, and Grant, *The King as Exemplar*.

10. Patrick D. Miller, "Deuteronomy and Psalms: Evoking A Biblical Conversation," *Journal of Biblical Literature* 118.1 (1999): 3–18.

active obedience of Christ, defined as "Christ perfectly fulfilling the law as our covenant head as a condition for granting eternal life"?[11]

The Structure of the Psalter and the Kingship Psalms

One of the most fruitful areas of recent studies in the Old Testament is the structure of the Psalter. Is there a rationale for the placement of the psalms in the Psalter, and does the structure of the Psalter have significance for the meaning of the individual psalms? Augustine himself wrote, "The arrangement of the Psalms, which seems to me to contain a secret of great mystery, has not yet been revealed to me."[12] A certain Jewish rabbi, who commented that the psalms were not presently in their right order, went on to say that if a person could determine that order, that person could raise the dead and do miracles.[13] Without claiming to have miraculous powers, some light can be shed on this subject by examining the structure of the Psalter.

G. H. Wilson's book *The Editing of the Hebrew Psalter* was a landmark work that laid the methodological foundation to move psalm studies away from concentrating on the historical and cultic origin of individual psalms to studying the Psalter as a literary work. He focused on what the placement of the psalms within the Psalter can teach us about the editorial shaping of the book, and what such editorial shaping says about the concerns of the final editors of the Psalter.[14] The evidence for general editorial activity in the Psalter includes the division of the psalms into five books, each ending with a doxology, and the way the Psalter begins and ends. Psalms 1–2 seem to introduce the book, and Psalms 145–50 are Hallelujah psalms that end the book in a "fireworks of praise."[15] Wilson showed that there is a distinct difference between Books 1–3 (Pss. 1–89) and Books 4–5 (Pss. 90–150), the former having a significantly higher number of superscriptions attributing authorship to the psalms, which is much different from Books 4–5, where out of 61 psalms only 19 bear superscriptions attributing authorship.[16] The psalms in Book 1 are virtually all Davidic psalms, with another Davidic col-

11. Louis Berkhof, *Systematic Theology* (Grand Rapids: Eerdmans, 1941), 379–81.

12. Quoted in both Mitchell, *The Message of the Psalter*, 14, and Grant, *The King as Exemplar*, 1, from *Enarrationes in Psalmos* 150.i.

13. The statement is attributed to Rabbi Eleazar in James Limburg, "Review of Klaus Koenen, *Jahwe wird kommen, zu herrschen über die Erde: Ps 90–110 als Komposition,*" *Journal of Biblical Literature* 116 (1997): 543.

14. Wilson, *Editing of the Hebrew Psalter*, 1–6.

15. Tremper Longman III, *How to Read the Psalms* (Downers Grove, IL: InterVarsity, 1988), 45. See below for further discussion on the role of Psalms 1–2.

16. Wilson, *Editing of the Hebrew Psalter*, 155–58.

lection in Book 2 (Pss. 51–71). Other designations include the sons of Korah (Pss. 42–49, 84–85, 87) and Asaph (Pss. 50, 73–83).

Kingship psalms also occur at the seams of the books in Books 1–3. Psalm 2, at the beginning of the Psalter, sets forth the coronation[17] of the king: "You are My son; today I have begotten you" (Ps. 2:7). The victory of the king over the nations is set forth. Psalm 72 occurs at the end of Book 2 and sets forth the results of the reign of a righteous king, which includes justice for the poor and an outpouring of great material blessings. Psalm 89 closes Book 3 and celebrates the faithfulness of God in the covenant promises that God has made to David (Ps. 89:4, 21–30).[18] Even if future descendants break the covenant by not keeping the commandments of God, the promise is that God will be faithful to his covenant promises (Ps. 89:31–38). However, something has gone terribly wrong because God is angry with his anointed (Ps. 89:39), has allowed enemies to defeat the king (Ps. 89:43–44), and has cut short the days of his youth (Ps. 89:46). Psalm 89 ends with questions imploring God to remember his covenant promises to David (Ps. 89:47–52). Thus the kingship psalms in Books 1–3 move from the promise of the anointed king's victory over his enemies in Psalm 2, to the glorious benefits of the reign of a righteous king in Psalm 72, to the defeat of the king in Psalm 89.

It is apparent that Books 4–5 reflect the concerns of the exilic and postexilic community. Book 4 may be an answer to the questions concerning kingship at the end of Book 3. Psalm 90 takes the people back to their foundation with a psalm of Moses, Psalm 91 is the strongest psalm of confidence in the Psalter, and Psalm 92 gives thanks to God first for his covenant faithfulness, lamented at the end of Psalm 89, and then for the downfall of the enemies of God's people. Psalms 93–100 proclaim that Yahweh reigns so that even if the monarchy is in trouble, Israel still has a king.[19] However, the proclamation of Yahweh as king does not mean that the Davidic kingship is no longer viable, for Psalm 101 is a psalm attributed to David, who sings of the covenant faithfulness of Yahweh. God's promises to David are not dead yet.[20]

17. Willem VanGemeren, *Psalms*, Expositor's Bible Commentary, 12 vols. (Grand Rapids: Zondervan, 1991), 5:64, and Peter Craigie, *Psalms 1–50*, Word Biblical Commentary (Dallas: Word, 1983), 64, use the term coronation.

18. The verses in the psalms are given according to the Hebrew versification, which sometimes is one verse different from the English translation. For example, Ps. 89:4 in Hebrew is Ps. 89:3 in English.

19. For an analysis of this group of psalms see David M. Howard Jr., *The Structure of Psalms 93–100* (Winona Lake, IL: Eisenbrauns, 1997).

20. Gerald H. Wilson, "Shaping the Psalter: A Consideration of Editorial Linkage in the Book of Psalms," in *The Shape and Shaping of the Psalter*, 81, argues that the emphasis on Yahweh as king in Books 4–5 signifies the demise of human kingship in Israel, but Howard (*Structure of*

Book 4 closes with two psalms that review the history of Israel. Psalm 105 emphasizes the great things God has done for his people in his faithfulness to them. Psalm 106 emphasizes the sin of Israel and ends with a plea for God to gather his people from the nations (v. 47). Thus Book 4 reflects the exile and emphasizes that Yahweh is king, but gives a glimmer of hope that God has not forgotten his covenant promises to David with two psalms of David (Pss. 101, 103).

Book 5 presents the concerns of the postexilic community. The prayer at the end of Psalm 106 that God would gather his people from the nations is answered in Psalm 107, the first psalm of Book 5, which gives thanks for the fact that God has gathered his people from the nations (v. 3). There are two groups of Davidic psalms in Book 5, Psalms 108–10 and 138–44, which essentially frame Book 5. These psalms set forth a model of the type of king the people need and show the ultimate triumph of the Davidic king. The final psalm in each group is particularly significant. Psalm 110 renews the hope of the triumph of the Davidic king over all his enemies, and Psalm 144 locates the final triumph of the Davidic king.[21]

These key kingship psalms set forth an interesting progression from coronation and promise of victory, to the righteous reign of the king, to the defeat of the king, to the initial triumph of the king, and finally to the ultimate triumph of the king. The editors of the Psalter seem to be setting forth their hopes related to a coming Davidic king. Although there are aspects of these psalms that can refer to both the first and second coming of Christ, the progression of these kingship psalms follows the work of Christ the king. Psalm 2:7 is used at his baptism where he is proclaimed publicly to be the Son of God. The righteous reign of Psalm 72 is reflected in his works. The gospel of Christ is good news to the poor because he delivers from oppression (Matt. 11:5) and brings forth the blessings of creation in material abundance. It is interesting that after the multitudes are fed the people come to make Jesus king (John 6:15). Do they recognize the connection between material blessing and the coming reign of the righteous king? Psalm 89 sets forth the defeat and humiliation of the king. Much of what is said about the king in verses 39–45 relates to Christ. He was cast off and rejected. The full wrath of God was against Christ, not for his own disobedience, but for the disobedience of his people. He was the scorn of those around him, and the right hand

---

Psalms 93–100, 200–207) shows the deficiency of this argument, partly based on the placement of Davidic psalms in Books 4–5.

    21. See Jinkyu Kim, "Psalm 110 in Its Literary and Generic Contexts: An Eschatological Interpretation," Ph.D. diss., Westminster Theological Seminary, 2003, for an analysis of how Pss. 110 and 144 function in Book 5.

of his enemies seemed to triumph over him; however, the enemies did not triumph over him. The king/priest is raised in triumph and sits at the right hand of God (Ps. 110:1, 4) until his enemies are made a footstool for his feet. The ultimate triumph is then set forth in Psalm 144, which will occur at his second coming. Not only do individual kingship psalms relate to Christ, but the progression of key kingship psalms in the Psalter also relates to the work of Christ.[22]

The Structure of the Psalter and Torah Psalms

Although there are not as many psalms that deal explicitly with the torah as there are kingship psalms, many have recognized the significance of the placement of the torah psalms for the Psalter.[23] The psalms that deal explicitly with torah are 1, 19, and 119. It also appears that these psalms are strategically placed in the Psalter. Psalm 1 is the very first psalm, which not only shows that the following psalms are to be studied and meditated upon, but it also lays out two destinies that will be worked out in the Psalter itself.[24] Psalm 1 sets forth the stability and fruitfulness of the person who meditates on the תורה (torah)[25] of God over against the instability of the wicked. At the beginning of the Psalter is the reminder that the righteous will triumph, but the wicked will perish. Psalm 19 is also strategically placed at the center of Book 1 (see below for more discussion of this). It sets forth God's revelation in creation and in the torah and lays out not only the character of the torah, but also its effects in the lives of God's people, which reinforces the benefits of meditating on it.[26]

22. For more on how each of these psalms relates to Christ, see Belcher, *The Messiah and the Psalms*, 117–56.
23. Mays, "The Place of Torah-Psalms," 3–12; Grant, *The King as Exemplar*; and P. D. Miller Jr., "Kingship, Torah Obedience, and Prayer: The Theology of Psalms 15–24," in *Neue Wege der Psalmenforschung: Für Walter Beyerlin*, ed. K. Seybold and E. Zenger (Freiberg: Herder, 1994), 127–42.
24. Childs, *Introduction*, 513, and Patrick D. Miller Jr., *Interpreting the Psalms* (Philadelphia: Fortress, 1986), 85. The Psalter also gives evidence that psalms were used in the worship of Israel. A dichotomy does not need to be drawn between these different emphases in the Psalter because the psalms can be profitably used as texts for meditation and instruction, as prayers, and as songs sung by God's people.
25. For a discussion of how תורה should be translated see Grant, *The King as Exemplar*, 272–73, who argues that there is no single English word that conveys the various aspects of torah. The translation "instruction" is good because it captures the didactic function of torah, but it does not convey connections to the covenant and leaves a take-it-or-leave-it attitude in our contemporary society. The translation "law" maintains the didactic, binding function of the word, but torah includes much more than what is commonly associated with "law." Grant believes the best solution is to translate with "law" and to clarify that translation by way of footnotes.
26. Grant, *The King as Exemplar*, 94, 99–100.

Psalm 119 is a massive psalm dealing with torah. It shows the longing of the psalmist[27] for God's torah and the blessing of the torah for the life of the psalmist in a variety of circumstances.[28] The acrostic nature of Psalm 119, with each verse of stanza one beginning with the consonant aleph, and each verse of stanza two beginning with beth, and so forth for twenty-two stanzas, may emphasize that the torah deals with everything from "A to Z," so to speak,[29] or that the life of the person who commits himself to the torah will be as stable as this psalm. It seems that with each psalm dealing with torah there is an expansion on the nature of the torah and the benefits of the torah for life, which demonstrates the fruitfulness of meditating on the torah.

The placement of Psalm 119 at the center of Book 5 of the Psalter is also significant. Earlier it was shown how two groups of Davidic psalms frame Book 5 (Pss. 108–10 and 138–44). Inside those two groups of kingship psalms are also two groups of psalms that deal with worship. Psalms 111–17 are the Hallel psalms used in connection with Passover, and Psalms 120–34 are Songs of Ascents used by pilgrims who travel to the feasts at Jerusalem. Psalm 119 stands at the center of these groupings of psalms. The placement of these psalms shows that the postexilic community was concerned with kingship, worship, and the role of the torah.

The Juxtaposition of Kingship and Torah Psalms

There has been some debate concerning whether the kingship psalms or the torah psalms should receive priority in the structure of the Psalter,[30] but perhaps one does not have to choose between the two. It is noteworthy that the torah psalms are closely associated with kingship psalms, so that when one thinks of torah the issue of the king is not very far removed. Perhaps the two are meant to be taken together.[31]

27. The term "psalmist" is used as a general designation of the author of the psalm and does not preclude the fact that the author or speaker may be the king. The term "psalmist" leaves open the possibility that anyone can use the psalm.

28. Grant comments that Psalm 119 is in and of itself an act of meditation upon the torah (*The King as Exemplar*, 167).

29. J. Clinton McCann Jr., *Psalms*, New Interpreter's Bible 4 (Nashville: Abingdon, 1996), 1166.

30. Wilson ("Shaping the Psalter," 78–81) argues for a royal covenantal frame, consisting of Psalms 2, 72, 89, and 144, and a final wisdom frame, consisting of Psalms 1, 73, 90, 107, and 145. He argues that the wisdom frame takes precedence over the royal covenantal frame so that the Psalter is a book of wisdom emphasizing Yahweh's instruction and his kingship. Human kingship is ultimately abandoned. For a response to Wilson's view that human kingship was no longer seen as important see Howard, *Structure of Psalms 93–100*, 200–207, and Mitchell, *Message of the Psalter*, 78–82.

31. Grant (*The King as Exemplar*, 1–4) argues that the final editors of the Psalter placed the kingship and torah psalms together as a reflection of the law of the king in Deut. 17:14–20 in order to shape the eschatological hope in a Davidic king and to model a type of devotion to Yahweh.

Although there has been some debate concerning the role of Psalms 1–2 in the Psalter, the best approach is to see them as introductory psalms to the whole book.[32] These two psalms are set apart by the fact that they do not have a superscription, which is different from most other psalms in Book 1 (Pss. 1–41). Psalms 1–2 are also bound together by literary connections. For example, both contain the term אַשְׁרֵי ('ashre, "blessed"). Psalm 1 begins with "Blessed is the man" and Psalm 2 ends with "Blessed are all who take refuge in him." The term אַשְׁרֵי ('ashre) acts as an inclusio setting the two psalms apart from the other psalms. Both psalms use the word הָגָה (hagah), which in Psalm 1:2 is usually translated "meditate" in relationship to the torah, and in Psalm 2:1 is translated "plot" in relationship to the rebellion of the nations against God. Both psalms end with the idea of אָבַד ('abad, "perish"). In Psalm 1:6, the way of the wicked will perish, and in Psalm 2:12, those who do not bow before the king will perish. Thus, Psalms 1–2 are bound together through a lack of superscription and through literary connections.[33] Both psalms serve as an introduction to the whole book.

Psalm 19, which stands at the center of Book 1, is also surrounded by kingship psalms (Pss. 18, 20–21). These psalms speak about the deliverance of the king. Psalm 18 is a psalm spoken by the king recounting his deliverance. Psalm 20 is a prayer that the Lord would deliver the king in the day of battle, and Psalm 21 recounts that deliverance.

Psalm 119 stands at the center of Book 5 and deals with the torah. Psalm 118 has traditionally been connected to the Hallel psalms (111–17), but Jamie Grant argues that Psalm 118 is best understood as independent from the Hallel psalms.[34] It is a thanksgiving song offered by an individual as part of a procession up to the temple; thus, it has both communal and individual elements. There is some discussion as to whether or not the individual is a king, which makes sense if it is a song of thanksgiving for military victory (vv. 10–12).[35] Grant argues that the juxtaposition of Psalm 118 with 119 makes it likely that the speaker in Psalm 118 is the king

32. Wilson ("Shaping the Psalter," 87) argues that Psalm 1 alone introduces the Psalter with Psalm 2 as the first psalm of Book 1, but it is better to understand Psalms 1–2 together as an introduction to the Psalter (see Howard, *Structure of Psalms 93–100*, 202–4).

33. Grant has an excellent discussion of how to identify psalm groupings within the Psalter (*The King as Exemplar*, 225–26).

34. Although Psalm 118 was included in the Hallel psalms in rabbinic literature, there are textual reasons for separating Psalm 118 from the Hallel psalms, such as the fact that it does not have הַלְלוּ יָהּ ("hallelujah") at the beginning or the end and that it does not reflect the exodus themes of the other Hallel psalms (*The King as Exemplar*, 123–24).

35. Leslie C. Allen, *Psalms 101–150*, Word Biblical Commentary (Dallas: Word, 1983), 123, calls it a royal psalm of thanksgiving for military victory.

who leads the people in antiphonal acts of worship as their representative before Yahweh.[36]

The Significance of the Juxtaposition of the Torah and Kingship Psalms

If the editors of the Psalter have placed together the torah and kingship psalms, what possible implications can be drawn from this association? The binding together of Psalms 1–2 on a literary level as an introduction to the Psalter invites one to connect their content. Psalm 1 positions the contrast between the righteous and the wicked, describing the stability and the fruitfulness of הָאִישׁ (ha'ish, "the man") who meditates on the torah, which is contrasted with the instability of the wicked. Psalm 2 moves out into the public domain and sets forth the enmity between the rebellious nations and God. The plotting of the nations is in vain because God has established his king in Zion who will conquer the nations (Ps. 2:7–9). "The man" in Psalm 1 who meditates on the torah and is fruitful is the son, and the king, who will conquer the nations. In other words, the king himself will be victorious and fruitful as he meditates on the law of God. It is interesting that this is the picture that Deuteronomy 17:14–20 paints of the king, who is to keep for himself a copy of the law and read it all the days of his life. The relation between "the man" in Psalm 1 and the king in Psalm 2 opens up a connection with Adam as a ruler in the garden, especially in light of the appeal of Psalm 8 to Genesis 1:26–28 in its reflection on the role of mankind in God's creation. Psalm 8, which reflects on Genesis 1:26–28 with royal terminology ("crowned with glory and honor"), is used by the author of Hebrews to refer to Jesus, whose exaltation as man is "the reinstatement of the originally intended divine order for earth, with man properly situated as God's vicegerent."[37] Thus it is appropriate to associate the rule of Adam in the garden, the reign of the king, and the work of Jesus Christ.

The juxtaposition of torah and king at the beginning of the Psalter will have implications for understanding the rest of the Psalter, but it needs to be stressed that the connection between "the man" and the king does not take away from the legitimacy of reading the Psalter as an individual member of God's people or from using the psalms in the worship of God's people. The king himself is presented as an example of piety that the people are to follow.[38]

---

36. Grant, *The King as Exemplar*, 118–25.
37. Dan G. McCartney, "Ecce Homo: The Coming of the Kingdom as the Restoration of Human Vicegerency," *Westminster Theological Journal* 56 (1994): 2.
38. Grant, *The King as Exemplar*, 117, 286–88.

Psalm 19, a torah psalm, is surrounded by kingship psalms (Pss. 18, 20–21), which speak about the deliverance of the king. It becomes clear that the king himself is a part of those who are blessed because they take refuge in Yahweh (Ps. 2:12; 18:3). As a result the king defeats his enemies (Pss. 2:9; 18:41–43). Psalm 20 is connected to Psalm 2 by the use of the term משיח (mashiah, "anointed"). The king is victorious because he trusts in Yahweh (Pss. 20:8; 21:8). There is also an emphasis in Psalm 18:21–23 on the role of the torah in the king's life: he kept the ways of the Lord (Ps. 1:6), and the torah was always before him (Ps. 1:2; Deut. 17:18–20). The king is blessed because he takes refuge in Yahweh, keeps the torah, and so defeats his enemies.

Not only is it significant that Psalm 19 stands near the center of Book 1 of the Psalter and is surrounded by kingship psalms, but the grouping of Psalms 15–24 also seems significant for the relationship of the king to the torah,[39] especially in terms of the king's relationship to the righteousness of the torah. There is a concentric pattern in Psalms 15–24, with Psalms 15 and 24 asking a similar question concerning the person who is able to come into the presence of God in worship. Psalms 16 and 23 are psalms of confidence, Psalms 17 and 22 are lament psalms, and Psalms 18 and 20–21, which surround Psalm 19, are kingship psalms.[40]

The questions in Psalms 15 and 24 concerning "who shall dwell on your holy hill?" (15:1) or "who shall stand in his holy place?" (24:3) are answered in both psalms with a description of the character of the person who is allowed to come into God's presence. Such a person reflects the characteristics of the law laid out in Psalm 19. In Psalm 19:8 the law is תמימה (tamimah, "blameless"), a word which means to be whole or to be without blemish.[41] This word is translated as "perfect" in some translations[42] because the law is a reflection of the perfect character of God.[43] In Psalm 15:2 the person who may enter the presence of God is also described as תמים (tamim, "blameless"), which refers to a wholeness or integrity in life and an attitude of the heart desirous of pleasing God.[44] Such wholeness is a reflection of the law. In Psalm 19:9 the law is also ברה (barah, "pure"), and in Psalm 24:4 the one who may come into God's presence has a בר־לבב (bar-lebab, "pure

39. Miller, "Theology of Psalms," 15–24.
40. Grant, The King as Exemplar, 236.
41. J. P. J. Olivier, "תמם (tmm)," in New International Dictionary of Old Testament Theology and Exegesis, ed. Willem VanGemeren, 5 vols. (Grand Rapids: Zondervan, 1997), 4:306–8.
42. See the NASB, NIV, ESV; Craigie, Psalms 1–50, 178.
43. VanGemeren comments that God's word reflects God's integrity, uprightness, and fidelity (Psalms, 5:182).
44. VanGemeren, Psalms, 5:150.

heart"). In Psalm 19:10 the law is אֱמֶת (*'emet*, "true" or "trustworthy"), and in Psalm 15:2–3 the one who may enter God's presence speaks אֱמֶת (*'emet*, "truth") in his heart, which is reflected in his words. In Psalm 19:10 the law is צָדַק (*tsadaq*, "righteous"), and in Psalm 15:2 the person acceptable to God פֹּעֵל צֶדֶק (*po'el tsedeq*, "does right"). Bringing together Psalms 1, 15, 19, and 24, it is clear that the person who meditates on the law will reflect the character of the law in his life. This is the kind of person who may enter into God's presence.

Similar concepts are found in Psalm 18, where in verses 21–23 the psalmist affirms, "I have kept the ways of Yahweh," "his ordinances [מִשְׁפָּט, *mishpat*][45] were before me," and "his statutes [חֻקָּה, *huqqah*] I did not put away from me." The psalmist affirms that Yahweh rewarded him "according to my righteousness" [צֶדֶק, *tsedeq*] and "according to the cleanness [בֹּר, *bor*] of my hands" (Ps. 18:21). His life reflects the character of the law, and so he is one who may enter into the presence of God, whose prayers are answered by God, and whose life is rewarded by God in being delivered from his enemies. The same ideas are found in other places of Book 1. In Psalm 7:9 the psalmist asks God to judge (שָׁפַט, *shapat*) him "according to my righteousness" (צֶדֶק, *tsedeq*), and in Psalm 26:1 the statement is "Vindicate [שָׁפַט, *shapat*][46] me . . . for I have walked in my integrity [תֹּם, *tom*]." In both cases the word שָׁפַט (*shapat*) is used because the psalmist is asking God to render a judgment in a particular situation where the enemies of God are trying to bring him down. Such a judgment by God will result in deliverance, which will act as vindication in this particular situation. This is in line with Psalm 1 where the way of wickedness will be destroyed and the way of the righteous will be established.

Psalm 118 reflects some of the same concepts that are in Psalms 15 and 24 as the king comes to seek entrance into the temple to offer thanks to God for deliverance (vv. 10–12, 19–21). He seeks entrance into the gate of Yahweh through which the righteous enter. The fact that Yahweh is on his side and has delivered him is evidence of his righteousness.[47]

---

45. This word has a variety of meanings in the OT, including the process of settling a dispute, the actual verdict itself, a breach of justice, and the commands of the law. There is a distinct judicial connotation to the word (see Peter Enns, "מִשְׁפָּט [*mishpat*]," in *New International Dictionary of Old Testament Theology and Exegesis*, 2:1142–44). It is translated a number of ways by the English versions: "judgments" (NKJV), "ordinances" (NASB, NRSV), "laws" (NIV), "rules" (ESV), "regulations" (NLT). The word "ordinance" has a variety of meanings that to some degree overlaps the meanings of מִשְׁפָּט.

46. Richard Schultz ("שָׁפַט [*shapat*]," *New International Dictionary of Old Testament Theology and Exegesis*, 4:214) notes that when this verb refers to a specific activity, it can be translated "deliver" or "rescue." Many English translations use "vindicate" (NKJV, NASB, NIV, ESV) to refer to the rendering of a judgment in favor of the psalmist.

47. Grant, *The King as Exemplar*, 128–29.

Although the character of the king as a basis for entry is not emphasized in Psalm 118, as it is in Psalms 15 and 24, similar terms are used of both the law and the psalmist in Psalm 119. The psalm begins in verse 1 with אשרי תמימי־דרך ('ashre temime darek), a blessing on those who are blameless, identified in the next clause as those who walk in the law of the Lord. In Psalm 119:80 the psalmist requests, "May my heart be blameless [תמים, tamim] in your statutes [חקה, huqqah]." Not only are the precepts (פקודים, piqqudim) of Yahweh considered right (the verb ישר [yashar] in Psalm 119:128 and the adjective ישר [yashar] in 19:9), but the heart of the psalmist in Psalm 119:7 is also ישר (yosher, "upright"). The psalmist also affirms that he has kept the ways of Yahweh (119:168), but the strong statements of being rewarded according to "my righteousness" are missing. The focus is more on God's steadfast love and righteousness that is demonstrated in the torah. The psalmist delights in the torah (119:24, 35), hopes in the torah (119:43), and seeks the beneficial results of the torah in his life (119:11, 72, 98–100). The law revives the psalmist (119:25, 37, 107) and leads to life (119:144).

The King, the Law, and Deuteronomy

The bringing together of king and law in the Psalter reminds one of the presentation of the king in Deuteronomy 17:14–20. The role of the king is limited within the theocracy of Israel in the context of other leaders (Deut. 16:18–18:22) and in the prohibitions of not acquiring horses, women, and money. The king is also to keep a copy of the law and read it all the days of his life so that he will keep the law and learn how to fear Yahweh (Deut. 17:18–20). This picture of the king fits with the presentation of "the man" who meditates on the law in Psalm 1 and seeks the benefits of the law for his life in Psalms 19 and 119.

The relationship between the king and the law in the psalms and Deuteronomy raises the question whether there might be other connections between the Psalter and Deuteronomy. The latter is a covenant document that sets forth the stipulations and the sanctions of the covenant in the blessings and curses of the covenant.[48] The stipulations of the covenant are reflected in the torah psalms in the terms used of the torah. The basic term for the law, תורה (torah), is used in both the psalms and Deuteronomy,[49] and other major terms for the law used in Deuteronomy are also found in Psalms 19 and

---

48. Meredith Kline, *Treaty of the Great King* (Grand Rapids: Eerdmans, 1963).
49. See n. 25 above for a discussion on how to translate the term תורה (torah).

119.[50] The blessings of the covenant, which entails fruitfulness and abundance in every area of life, including children, crops, and livestock (Deut. 28:4–6), victory over enemies (Deut. 28:7), and life itself (Lev. 18:5), are also reflected in the psalms. Psalm 1 sets forth the fruitfulness and stability of the one who meditates on the torah in the image of a tree planted by the rivers of water. Although Psalms 19 and 119 stress more the benefit of the law for the spiritual life of the psalmist, they also affirm that the law is more valuable than gold (Pss. 19:11; 119:72) and that in keeping the law there is great reward (Ps. 19:12), including life (Ps. 119:144). Psalm 91 specifically sets forth the blessings of the Mosaic covenant in its strong affirmations of confidence in God's deliverance and protection. In fact, one wonders if Psalm 91 promises too much. For example, it affirms that "no evil shall be allowed to befall you, no plague come near your tent" (v. 10), "a thousand may fall at your side, ten thousand at your right hand" (v. 7), and "with long life I will satisfy him" (v. 16). The tremendous promises in verses 3–13 must be understood in light of the covenant that God made with his people, for they are a reflection of those covenant promises, which can be seen in a comparison of Psalm 91 and the blessings of the Mosaic covenant:

Mosaic covenant	Psalm 91
not afraid (Lev. 26:6)	verse 5
chase thousand/ten thousand (Lev. 26:7–8)	verse 7
God's dwelling (Lev. 26:11)	verse 9
beasts removed or let loose (Lev. 26:6, 22)	verse 13
deliverance from pestilence (Lev. 26:5; Deut. 28:21)	verse 3
deliverance from boils, diseases of Egypt (Deut. 28:34, 59)	verse 10[51]

Psalm 91 is setting forth the blessings of the Mosaic covenant, the security that comes with those blessings, and the confidence that God will pour out those blessings upon his people.

The curses of the Mosaic covenant (Deut. 28:15–68; Lev. 26:14–45) are also reflected in a general sense in the psalms. The lament psalms that seek God's deliverance from enemies, death, and destruction are psalms that appeal to the covenant faithfulness of God. The curses of the covenant normally come because of the disobedience of the nation.[52] When there

---

50. See Grant (*The King as Exemplar*, 157–59) for a discussion of the synonyms of תורה (*torah*).

51. For further discussion see Belcher, *The Messiah and the Psalms*, 58–60. Some of the blessings in Psalm 91 are stated over against the curses of the covenant listed in Deut. 28:15–68 and Lev. 26:14–45.

52. There is not always a one-to-one relationship between the curses of the covenant and the hardships of God's people, as is evidenced in some of the trials of David's life even though he is

is a situation of a defeat in battle or the destruction of the temple, there is also a wrestling as to why the disaster has occurred. Psalm 74, which is a response to the destruction of the sanctuary, is a plea for God to remember the covenant and to defend his cause (vv. 20–23). Psalm 79, which reflects a similar situation, is more explicit concerning the sins of the people (vv. 8–9). It is clear in light of the history of rebellion in Psalm 106 that the exile has come to God's people because of their sin in accordance with the curses of the Mosaic covenant, which specifically mentions exile from the land (Lev. 26:32–33; Deut. 28:64–67).

The King, the Law, and Righteousness

The juxtaposition of the kingship and torah psalms not only brings into focus the relationship of the king to the law in terms of his responsibility to meditate on it, but it also brings into focus the responsibility of the king to keep the law. Thus there are statements that speak of the king keeping the law or desiring to keep the law. The character of the king and his righteousness come into play in the statements of Psalm 18 and its relationship to the entrance liturgies of Psalms 15 and 24 (see the discussion above). How is the terminology of law, righteousness, and the judgment of God to be understood in relationship to the king?

There are two different kinds of statements in the Psalter that relate to the law and righteousness. A less prominent theme is that no one is righteous before God, which is specifically stated in Psalm 143:2. The psalmist requests that God not enter into judgment with him because "no one living is righteous [צדק, tsadaq] before you." The lament of Psalm 143 is a request for God to answer the prayer of the psalmist for deliverance from his enemies based on God's faithfulness and righteousness. The transition from verse 1 to verse 2 sets in contrast God's righteousness with the lack of righteousness in the psalmist. Because the psalmist is not righteous, he does not want God to enter into judgment (משפט, mishpat) with him on that basis. A similar idea is expressed in Psalm 130:3, "If you, Yahweh, should mark iniquities, O Lord, who could stand?" The next verse goes on to state that there is forgiveness with the Lord. Everyone stands condemned before God and is in need of forgiveness because of sin.

---

not living in disobedience to God. Individual suffering cannot always be blamed on disobedience. However, in relation to Israel as a nation, there is a closer connection between the curses of the covenant and the disobedience of the nation. Thus Israel loses the land because of her disobedience, which gives evidence of a principle of works operating within the Mosaic covenant (Lev. 18:5; Rom. 10:5); see Meredith G. Kline, *Kingdom Prologue* (Overland Park, KS: Two Age Press, 2000), 6, 109–15.

Other psalms set forth the opposite sentiments in terms of the psalmist's relationship with righteousness and God's judgment. Whereas Psalm 143:2 asks God not to enter into judgment (מִשְׁפָּט, *mishpat*) with the psalmist, Psalm 26:1 requests that God would "judge" (שָׁפַט, *shapat*) him because he has walked in integrity (תֹּם, *tom*). Whereas Psalm 143:2 asks God not to enter into judgment because "no one living is righteous [צָדַק, *tsadaq*] before you," Psalm 7:9 requests God to judge (שָׁפַט, *shapat*) the psalmist "according to my righteousness [צֶדֶק, *tsedeq*]." These expressions are also reflected in Psalm 18:21–23 where the psalmist affirms, "I have kept the ways of Yahweh," "his ordinances [מִשְׁפָּט, *mishpat*] were before me," and "his statutes [חֻקָּה, *huqqah*] I did not put away from me." Thus the psalmist declares that Yahweh rewarded him "according to my righteousness" (צֶדֶק, *tsedeq*) and "according to the cleanness [בֹּר, *bor*] of my hands" (Ps. 18:21).

It seems obvious that the different statements concerning God's judgment and righteousness arise due to different stances of the psalmist to the law. On one level the law condemns because no one is able to keep it, which is expressed in Psalm 143, and is evident in the statement concerning Abram in Genesis 15:6: "he believed Yahweh, and he counted it to him as righteousness [צְדָקָה, *tsedaqah*]." Here the law shows the need of Christ to fulfil the law[53] and is pertinent for discussions of justification by faith. The other statements of the law in the Psalms are positive expressions of the benefits of the law in the life of God's people in guiding them in how to live for God, which has traditionally been called the third use of the law.[54] In these situations the law helps in the growth or sanctification of the believer.[55]

The emphasis on growth or sanctification is prominent in the Psalter. First of all, the law in Psalm 1 is not something that condemns the psalmist, but it is a delight because it brings blessing, fruitfulness, and stability. The way of the righteous is the way of submission to the law of God, and the way of the wicked is the way of rebellion against God and his law. The delight of the law comes out in Psalm 19 in the desirability of the law over gold and honey because in keeping the law there is great reward.

53. This use of the law is sometimes referred to as the second use of the law (see Berkhof, *Systematic Theology*, 614–15).

54. Berkhof, *Systematic Theology*, 614–15. John Calvin, *Institutes of the Christian Religion*, ed. John T. McNeil, trans. Ford Lewis Battles, 2 vols., Library of Christian Classics 21–22 (Philadelphia: Westminster, 1960), 1:360; 2.7.12, calls the third use the principal use of the law.

55. Confusion results when the distinction between justification and sanctification is not kept in view as in Peter Leithart, "'Judge Me, O God': Biblical Perspectives on Justification," in *The Federal Vision*, 203–36.

Secondly, the character of the person who is able to come into the presence of God in Psalms 15 and 24 reflects the character of the law (see the discussion above). Such a person is blameless, which is used in Psalm 19:14 in the context of being free from presumptuous sins and being innocent of great transgression. The sanctifying process of the law of God has produced its godly effect in the life of the believer.

Thirdly, when the psalmist calls for God to vindicate him or judge him according to his righteousness (Ps. 7:9; 26:1), or to reward him according to his own righteousness (Ps. 18:21), he is calling on God to be faithful to his covenant promises in delivering him. This is vindication in the sense that the psalmist is on the side of righteousness and has tried to live out that righteousness in his life. Psalm 18:22 specifically says, "For I have kept the ways of Yahweh, and have not wickedly departed from my God." He is walking in the paths of the righteous and not in the way of the wicked (Ps. 1). In Psalm 7:9, where the psalmist asks God to judge him according to his righteousness, the parallel phrase says "according to my integrity." The word תם (*tom*, "integrity" or "blameless") also occurs in Psalm 26:1, "Vindicate me . . . for I have walked in my integrity." The parallel phrase in 26:1 is "I have trusted in Yahweh." The psalmist is walking in the ways of the Lord, trusting God for each step. In Psalm 18:21 the phrase "according to my righteousness" is parallel with "according to the cleanness of my hands," a concept that in Psalm 24:4 refers to a particular character of life.

The theme of Psalm 26 is the integrity of the psalmist in the midst of false accusations, which is then the basis for the plea of vindication and the certainty that the situation will turn out right for the psalmist. There is much discussion concerning the setting of Psalm 26 and the situation that led to these assertions of integrity.[56] It is hard to be certain because so much of the language of the psalm is general enough to be used in a number of situations.[57] It may just be the general prayer of a person who is unjustly accused and appeals to God for vindication.[58] The psalm is framed by assertions of integrity (vv. 1–3, 11–12). In the body of the psalm the psalmist affirms his integrity in relation to the wicked (vv. 4–5, 9–10) and in relation to wor-

56. Hans-Joachim Kraus, *Psalms 1–150* (Minneapolis: Augsburg, 1988), 1:325–26, takes Psalm 26 as the prayer of a falsely accused person who has fled to the temple to find asylum from his accusers and pursuers. At the temple he affirms his innocence and asks Yahweh to judge his case and vindicate him, as in 1 Kings 8:31–32. Craigie (*Psalms 1–50*, 224) takes Psalm 26 as an entrance liturgy at the temple, very much like Psalms 15 and 24, where the worshipers are met by priests and must affirm their integrity for entrance into the temple.

57. Mays (*Psalms*, 127–28) argues that the language is formulaic and traditional, which means it is open to a variety of situations.

58. John Calvin, *Psalms 1–35*, Calvin's Commentaries 4 (Grand Rapids: Baker, 1979), 437.

ship (vv. 6–8). Thus many see a chiastic structure to Psalm 26: (A) walking in integrity (vv. 1–3), (B) relationship to the wicked (vv. 4–5), (C) relationship to worship (vv. 6–8), (B') relationship to the wicked (vv. 9–10), and (A') walking in integrity.[59] The psalmist asserts his integrity by describing his way of life: "I have walked in my integrity" (v. 1) and then "I walk in your truth" (v. 3). This is not a statement of perfection or sinlessness but a description of the general tenor of his life.[60] In the context of being falsely accused, it is a response to a specific charge that has been brought against him.[61] He proclaims his innocence of the charge by asserting the integrity of his life and his devotion to Yahweh. The verb הלך (halak, "walk") connotes a whole life that is devoted to Yahweh, which is emphasized in the rest of the psalm with the mentioning of heart and mind (v. 2), eyes (v. 3), hands (v. 6), and foot (v. 12). His integrity encompasses his whole being.[62] An attitude of trust looks away from oneself to God for vindication in light of the false charges that have been brought against him.[63]

Psalm 40, which occurs toward the end of Book 1, also brings together the king, as it is a psalm of David, and the law. Not all the issues of this psalm can be covered here, but verses 7–9 are used in the book of Hebrews to refer to Jesus Christ. The psalm begins with a song of thanksgiving for God's deliverance (vv. 1–4), which would normally be celebrated by the offering of a sacrifice. However, there is something more basic than the offering of a sacrifice, and that is the offering of oneself to God.[64] The psalmist presents himself in verses 8–9 as willing to do the will of God from an internal compulsion ("your law is within my heart"). In this way obedience is better than mere sacrifice (1 Sam. 15:22–23; Ps. 51:18–19). There is debate concerning the meaning of במגלת־ספר (bemiglat-seper, "in the scroll of the book") in verse 8 and whether one can determine what is written in that scroll.[65] In light of the juxtaposition of the kingship and

59. For different ways to state the chiastic structure of the psalm see McCann, Psalms, 4:782; Konrad Schaefer, Psalms, Berit Olam (Collegeville, MN: Liturgical, 2001), 64; and VanGemeren, Psalms, 5:238.

60. Craigie, Psalms 1–50, 225; Mays, Psalms, 129; and Gerald H. Wilson, Psalms, vol. 1, The NIV Application Commentary (Grand Rapids: Zondervan, 2002), 472.

61. McCann, Psalms, 4:783.

62. Ibid., 4:782.

63. Ibid., 4:783.

64. These statements should not be seen as a repudiation of the sacrificial system but as stressing the importance of an inner willingness to do God's will (VanGemeren, Psalms, 5:320, and Craigie, Psalms 1–50, 315).

65. Suggestions include the law of the king in Deut. 17:14–20, the law of Moses, revelation up to the time of David, and an account of the deliverance itself, which would include the song of thanksgiving in Psalm 40. Wilson (Psalms, 1:641) lists most of these while Walter C. Kaiser (The Uses of the Old Testament in the New [Chicago: Moody, 1985], 136) stresses 2 Samuel 7 and revelation up to the time of David.

the torah psalms in the Psalter, it is possible to see the scroll as a reference to the law that the king is to keep before him (Deut. 17:14–20). The king, as leader of God's people, is to lead the way in being willing to keep the law of God from the heart (vv. 7–9), which leads to the public praise of God (vv. 10–11).

The King, the Law, Righteousness, and Christ

It is significant that the kingship psalms and the torah psalms play a role in the editing of the Psalter and that they occur side by side, which has implications for how the king relates to the law. In light of the fact that Books 4–5 reflect the concerns of the exilic and postexilic community, the group of Davidic psalms in Book 5 and the juxtaposition of Psalm 118 with Psalm 119 show what is significant to that community: they are still looking for a righteous king who will obey the law and reign in righteousness. Part of the reason for the exile was the rejection by the kings of the law of God and the prophetic word. The hope was kept alive that a righteous king would come. This king would be one "like his brothers" (Deut. 17:15), a human being from the line of David, but there are also clear statements that this king is the adopted son of God (Ps. 2:7),[66] who is closely identified with God (Ps. 45:7),[67] and who will take on the character of God himself, as other Scriptures call him Emmanuel (Isa. 7:14) and "mighty God" (Isa. 9:6). These concepts come together in the person of Jesus Christ, who is son of David (Matt. 1:1; Rom. 1:3) and Son of God (John 1:34; Rom. 1:4). Thus it is appropriate to reflect on how the concepts that have been examined in the psalms relate to Christ.

There are at least three ways that the relationship of the law to Christ can be explored. First of all, the New Testament clearly teaches that Christ is a human being who has experienced what it is like to be a human being, including being tempted, yet without sin (Heb. 4:15). Even though his human

---

66. The use of "son" in relationship to the king is rooted in the Davidic covenant (2 Sam. 7:12–16). The king is "begotten" (ילד, *yalad*) by God (Ps. 2:7), which is not a physical or mythological relationship, as in Egypt (Kraus, *Psalms 1–150*, 1:130–31), but a legal relationship, described as adoption (VanGemeren, *Psalms*, 5:70). The king is declared to be son of God, and as son he represents the covenant relationship between God and the people of Israel. Israel was God's son in Egypt, even his firstborn (Ex. 4:22). The terms son (בן, *ben*) and firstborn (בכור, *bekor*) could be used of both the king (2 Sam. 7:14; Ps. 89:27) and the people (Ex. 4:22), so that the king represented the people.

67. For the different approaches to Ps. 45:7 see Belcher, *The Messiah and the Psalms*, 130–32. Although the king is never considered to be divine in the OT, there is a close relationship in Ps. 45:7 between the king and God so that the king's throne is God's throne. Further revelation begins to show that the coming king is more than human (Isa. 7:14; 9:6).

nature was perfect, he developed in his humanity by growing in favor with God and man, and by learning obedience (Luke 2:40; Heb. 5:8). The law would have had an important part to play in this growth and development by setting forth the true standard of righteousness. As Jesus meditated on the law, he would have been able to affirm of himself all the statements in the psalms related to the benefit of the law. The fruitfulness that comes from the law would have been a part of his life. The character of the one seeking entrance into the temple (Pss. 15 and 24) would have been true of his human nature: blameless, doing what is right, speaking truth in his heart, and clean hands. Like the psalmist, he too would have prayed for deliverance as "in the days of his flesh, Jesus offered up prayers and supplications, with loud cries and tears, to him who was able to save him from death, and he was heard because of his reverence" (Heb. 5:7). He could state, "Yahweh recompensed me according to my righteousness; according to the cleanness of my hands he rewarded me" (Ps. 18:24). He would have delighted in the law of Yahweh and kept his way pure according to its precepts (Ps. 119:9, 97). He would have been vindicated because of his integrity (Ps. 26:1).

Secondly, the New Testament presents Christ as one who has come to fulfil the law. Hebrews 10:5–10 places Psalm 40:7–9 (Septuagint Ps. 39:7–9) in the mouth of Jesus so that Christ affirms, "Behold, I have come to do your will, O God, as it is written of me in the scroll of the book." These verses demonstrate the willing obedience of Christ to do the will of God. The author of Hebrews uses these words to show that Christ was willing to be the sacrifice that ends all sacrifices. Christ fulfils Psalm 40 in his priestly work by bearing the punishment of sin on the cross and by abolishing the sacrificial system of the Old Testament. This relates to what has been called the passive obedience of Christ, which has been defined as his bearing on the cross the punishment for sin.[68] However, the passive obedience and the active obedience of Christ cannot be separated from each other but are integrally related.[69] When Christ bears the punishment of sin on the cross, he does so through an act of obedience to the law. He fulfils the law by becoming a sacrifice for sin, thereby taking away the punishment for sin.

Thirdly, Christ is the king who perfectly keeps the law for us. Jesus came to fulfil all righteousness (Matt. 3:15), to keep the commandments (John 15:10), and to be born under the law that he might redeem those under the law (Gal. 4:4–5). Thus the righteousness of Christ is received through faith,

68. Berkhof, *Systematic Theology*, 381.
69. Berkhof (ibid., 379) comments that the active and passive obedience of Christ accompany each other at every point in the Savior's life and that it was part of Christ's active obedience that he subjected himself voluntarily to sufferings and death.

not on the basis of the works of the law (Phil. 3:9), because he has fulfilled the law for his people.

It is appropriate to understand the statements in the psalms that relate to the sanctification of the believer as absolute statements in relationship to Christ. In other words, the obedience of sanctification typologically relates to the perfect obedience of Christ. The sacrificial system always stood as a background to those who came to worship, allowing them to come into God's presence even though they were sinners. But Christ has fulfilled the sacrificial system as the perfect sacrifice, and he is able to enter into God's presence on the basis of his own righteousness. He is blameless (Pss. 15:2; 18:24) in a complete sense because he has no sin. He has been rewarded according to his righteousness and according to the cleanness of his hands (Ps. 18:25). His character reflects the character of the law as laid out in Psalm 19 because he is himself the word of God. Thus he is perfect, sure, right, pure, clean, true, and righteous (Ps. 19:8–10). Jesus could assert his integrity in relationship to his whole life. He was put to the test (Ps. 26:2) in the wilderness temptations and was tempted in all ways common to humanity yet without sin (Heb. 4:15). Jesus' integrity is affirmed by the witness of the Father (John 8:12–18). He is vindicated on the third day when he is raised from the dead. He is admitted into the presence of the heavenly temple (Pss. 15, 24) in his ascension on the basis of his righteous work and character.[70]

The righteousness of the king is granted to his people as an "alien righteousness" that does not come from the law but through faith in him (Phil. 3:9). Romans 5:19 reminds us that "as by the one man's disobedience the many were made sinners, so by the one man's obedience the many will be made righteous." Where Adam failed in keeping the law of God, resulting in the imputation of his sin to his posterity, Christ perfectly kept the law of God, resulting in the imputation of his righteousness to those who are in him. It appears that kingship, torah, and righteousness in the Psalter lay a foundation for the coming of the king who will satisfy the just demands of the law by fulfilling all righteousness. If not for Christ's active obedience and righteousness, received through faith alone, no one would receive eternal life. Thus life is

---

70. Although the psalmist requests that God not enter into judgment with him because no one living is righteous before God (Ps. 143:2), Christ is righteous and can stand before the judgment of God on the basis of his own righteousness. In other words, he can be declared righteous because of his own righteousness. This raises questions as to how Christ can pray a psalm like Ps. 143:2, or other psalms of confession, such as Ps. 51. For the justification that the psalms are the prayers of Christ and that the psalms that confess sin can be prayed by Christ as our priest and representative, see Belcher, *The Messiah and the Psalms*, 36–38, 83–88.

granted on the basis of works, not the works of any human being but the works of Christ the king and mediator, who fulfils the law for his people.

Conclusion

This study has tried to show that the kingship and torah psalms lay a basis for understanding the work of Christ as the king who fulfils the law in every way for his people. Several different arguments have been set forth to substantiate this view. The role of the kingship psalms in the Psalter is significant in showing the foundation of kingship in the Davidic covenant, in demonstrating the problems of kingship in its failure, and in setting forth the hopes of kingship for the future.

Although there are only three torah psalms (1, 19, 119), they are strategically placed in the Psalter, with each successive psalm reinforcing and expanding the concepts of the previous torah psalm(s), culminating in Psalm 119. Psalm 1 is an introductory psalm setting forth the importance of the torah for the life of the righteous. Psalm 19 is strategically placed in Book 1 so that the characteristics of the torah are also a reflection of the life of the one who is able to enter into God's presence (Pss. 15, 24). Psalm 119 is strategically placed in Book 5, being surrounded by groups of Davidic psalms and liturgical psalms, setting forth what the postexilic community sees as foundational for their future: the law, worship, and a king.

It is also significant that the torah psalms are juxtaposed with kingship psalms. Bringing together the king and the torah fits the description of the king in Deuteronomy 17:14–20. "The man" of Psalm 1 who meditates on the torah is the anointed king of Psalm 2. The character of the torah laid out in Psalm 19 is also reflected in the character of the king in Psalm 18, so that the king himself reflects the character of the one who is able to enter into God's presence (Pss. 15, 24). Similar ideas occur in Psalms 118 and 119, with emphasis in Psalm 119 on the benefit of the torah for the life of the psalmist.

The relationship of the king to the torah is important. The king meditates on the torah and desires to keep the torah. The king declares that his life is a reflection of the righteousness of the torah in that he is blameless. Thus the king is able to ask God to judge him according to his righteousness because his life is a reflection of the righteousness of the torah. All the statements in the psalms related to the benefit of the law would have been true of Jesus' sinless human life. He would have delighted in the law and kept his way pure according to its precepts. In this way he not only fulfils the role of the king in relationship to the law, but he also fulfils the original role of mankind in creation as the one who rules over God's creation in obedience to the word of God.

Thus Christ fulfilled the law in every way. As the perfect sacrifice he fulfils the sacrificial system and bears on the cross the punishment for sin (the passive obedience of Christ). But he also perfectly keeps the requirements of the law so that he is allowed into the presence of God on the basis of his own righteousness (the active obedience of Christ). His righteousness is imputed through faith alone, and apart from his righteousness all are condemned. The statement of Machen as he neared death is so pertinent: "I am so thankful for [the] active obedience of Christ. No hope without it."

6

HOSEA 6:7 AND COVENANT-BREAKING LIKE/AT ADAM

BYRON G. CURTIS

והמה כאדם עברו ברית שם בגדו בי

vehemmah ke'adam 'aberu berit sham bagedu bi

D oes Israel's prophetic literature support the republication thesis? One important thrust of this thesis is the claim that the covenant of Moses—in regard to the question of Israel's tenure in the Promised Land—is a contextualized restatement of the covenant of works. The republication thesis acknowledges that in its greater biblical context, the Mosaic covenant is the older administration of the covenant of grace; but in regard to the question of how Israel shall retain possession of the Promised Land, the republication thesis claims that it functioned as a covenant of works. Few texts in the prophetic books are designed to address such a specific question. Hosea 6:7 is perhaps the great exception, and is perhaps the only Old Testament text that explicitly connects the person Adam to the biblical covenants. Hence, in the history of covenant theology, Hosea 6:7 has played a small but important role in supporting two theological claims: (1) that despite the lack of the covenant term in Genesis 1–3, God's arrangement in Eden with the first humans, in biblical perspective, was indeed a "covenant," and (2) that the Mosaic covenant is in some important sense analogous to the Adamic covenant. Can this text bear this theological weight?

The Prophets, Moses, and the Land

One of the most obvious conclusions regarding Israel's prophetic litera-ture[1] is that it is deeply concerned with Israel's tenure in its land, a tenure conditioned by Israel's obedience to the will of Yahweh, Israel's God.[2] The prophetic books routinely relate Israel's land tenure to Israel's obedience. O. Palmer Robertson counts just shy of two hundred prophecies about exile and restoration, and speaks of the "permeating character" of this discourse in the prophetic books. He accordingly denotes exile-and-restoration as "the core event of Israel's prophetic movement."[3] Thus Amos declares of Israel:

> You have lifted up Sakkut your king,
>   Kaiwan your star-god,
>   your images which you have made for yourselves.
> Therefore I will send you into exile beyond Damascus
>   —says Yahweh,
>   whose name is the God of the heavenly armies. (Amos 5:26–27)[4]

And Isaiah announces of Judah:

> They [the Judeans] have no regard for the deeds of Yahweh,
>   no respect for the work of his hands.
> Therefore my people will go into exile
>   for lack of understanding;

1. Of the many important works on the theological interpretation of Israelite prophetic litera-ture I shall mention here only a few from various perspectives: Donald E. Gowan, *Theology of the Prophetic Books: The Death and Resurrection of Israel* (Louisville: Westminster John Knox, 1998); James Luther Mays and Paul J. Achtemeier, eds., *Interpreting the Prophets* (Philadelphia: Fortress, 1987); O. Palmer Robertson, *The Christ of the Prophets* (Phillipsburg, NJ: P&R, 2004); Marvin A. Sweeney, *The Prophetic Literature*, Interpreting Biblical Texts (Nashville: Abingdon, 2005); Willem A. VanGemeren, *Interpreting the Prophetic Word* (Grand Rapids: Zondervan, 1990).

2. On the issue of Israel's land tenure, see the important biblical-theological discussions in Walter Brueggemann, *The Land: Place as Gift, Promise, and Challenge in Biblical Faith*, Overtures to Biblical Theology (Philadelphia: Fortress, 1977); and in W. D. Davies, *The Territorial Dimension of Judaism* (Berkeley: University of California Press, 1982), 6–28. See also Charles H. H. Scobie, "Land and City" in *The Ways of Our God: An Approach to Biblical Theology* (Grand Rapids: Eerdmans, 2003), 541–66, whose debt to Brueggemann is evident.

3. Robertson, *Christ of the Prophets*, 454. For another often fruitful perspective on exile and the prophets, see Peter R. Ackroyd, *Exile and Restoration: A Study of Hebrew Thought of the Sixth Century B.C.*, Old Testament Library (Philadelphia: Westminster, 1968).

4. Unless otherwise indicated, translations in this chapter are my own.

their men of rank will die of hunger
  and their masses will be parched with thirst. (Isa. 5:12–13)

And the book of Jeremiah declares:

But if you do not listen, I will weep in secret because of your pride;
  my eyes will weep bitterly, overflowing with tears,
  because Yahweh's flock will be taken captive.
Say to the king and to the queen mother,
  "Come down from your thrones,
  for your glorious crowns will fall from your heads."
The cities in the Negev will be shut up,
  and there will be no one to open them.
All Judah will be carried into exile,
  carried completely away. (Jer. 13:17–19)

And the book of Ezekiel has the prophet fulfil this sign-action: "Therefore, mortal man, pack your belongings for exile and in the daytime, as they watch, set out and go from where you are to another place. Perhaps they will understand, though they are a rebellious house" (Ezek. 12:3). What is the background to this relation between obedience and land tenure in the prophets?

Israel's prophetic literature presents the prophets as mediators of the will of Yahweh, intimates of this God, revelators who knew what this God wants, and who also knew how Israel so often failed to follow that revealed will. While there is much that may be called innovative in the prophetic literature, a literature that possesses no full parallel in the ancient world, Israel's prophets were not innovators in regard to the core values they most prized and promoted.[5] These values, they believed, came from Yahweh himself in generations long past, during times that were for them already

5. Examples of prophet-like figures and revelatory mediation in the literature of ancient Mari and of Neo-Assyria really are no match for Israel's prophets. For comparisons, see the collected essays in Martti Nissinen, *Prophecy in Its Ancient Near Eastern Context: Mesopotamian, Biblical, and Arabian Perspectives*, Society of Biblical Literature Symposium Series 13 (Atlanta: SBL, 2000), in particular the essay by Herbert B. Huffmon, "A Company of the Prophets: Mari, Assyria, Israel" (47–70) and Nissinen's essay on "The Socio-Religious Role of the Neo-Assyrian Prophets" (89–114). In the case of the Neo-Assyrian oracles, the tests of authentication seem to focus on whether the declarations were favorable to the royal house—hardly a criterion that would please Amos or Hosea. For the Neo-Assyrian texts, see Simo Parvolo, *Assyrian Prophecies* (Helsinki: Helsinki University Press, 1997); most of the extant texts address Esarhaddon or Ashurbanipal. For a more diverse collection, one that includes the Mari texts also, see Nissinen, *Prophets and Prophecy in the Ancient Near East*, Writings from the Ancient World 12 (Atlanta: SBL, 2003). The surviving Mari texts typically address Zimri-Lim. Comparisons with Israel's prophetic literature are valuable, but limited in scope. For another comparative approach, employing twentieth-century African prophetic figures and the biblical prophet Zechariah ben-Iddo, see Byron G. Curtis, *Up the*

antique, the times of Israel's origins. As a famous oracle of Jeremiah's puts it: "Stand at the crossroads, and look, and ask for the ancient paths, where the good way lies; and walk in it" (Jer. 6:16 NRSV). The prophets were in this sense, then, ardent traditionalists, defenders of an ancient ideal. That ancient ideal was drawn from a repository of divine revelation, the Torah of Moses.

In the history of scholarship this sense of the prophets as guardians of an earlier and ancient Mosaic tradition has not always been recognized. Nineteenth-century German criticism, as embodied in the work of Karl Heinrich Graf (1815–69) and Julius Wellhausen (1844–1918), reversed the order: not the law and the prophets, but the prophets and the law, with the prophets as the innovators and inventors of the distinctive ideas of Israelite monotheism.[6] The law was created later by the Deuteronomists of the late seventh century (D), and (worse) by the ruling priests of the postexilic age (P), who abandoned their rich inheritance of "the ethical dynamism of the prophets" and traded it for the pottage of "legalistic and ritualized behavior," to become (and to mix metaphors) a mere shadow of its former glory.[7] However, as Robertson has observed, "Wellhausen's wholesale isolation of law from the prophets could not stand the test of time."[8]

Suspicion in critical circles that Graf and Wellhausen had wrongly suppressed the Mosaic antecedents of Israelite prophecy may be said to begin with Bernhard Duhm's 1916 opus *Israels Propheten*, a work which still held that the law came later, but which at least accorded Moses recognition as Israel's first and founding prophet.[9] With the development of tradition criticism, the prophets were increasingly seen as dependent upon Israel's traditions of worship, and as associated with local or centralized cult centers. This perspective is especially characteristic of Gerhard von Rad, whose early essay "The Form-Critical Problem of the Hexateuch," a far-reaching and programmatic piece, explored (among other things) "The Sinai Tradition as a Cult-Legend," and theorized that "the declamation of divine commandments and the binding of the assembly under obedience to them must have

---

Steep and Stony Road: The Book of Zechariah in Social Location Trajectory Analysis, Academia Biblica 25 (Atlanta: Society of Biblical Literature, 2006).

6. See Julius Wellhausen, *Prolegomena to the History of Ancient Israel* (New York: Meridian, 1957); reprint of *Prolegomena to the History of Israel*, trans. J. Sutherland Black and Allan Menzies (Edinburgh: Adam and Charles Black, 1885); trans. of *Prolegomena zur Geschichte Israels*, 2nd ed. (Berlin: G. Reimer, 1883).

7. G. T. Sheppard, "Biblical Interpretation in the 18th & 19th Centuries," in *Historical Handbook of Major Biblical Interpreters*, ed. D. K. McKim (Downers Grove, IL: InterVarsity, 1997), 257–80.

8. Robertson, *Christ of the Prophets*, 126.

9. See the discussion in R. E. Clements, *One Hundred Years of Old Testament Interpretation* (Philadelphia: Westminster, 1976), 56.

formed a major element of a cultic occasion in ancient Israel."[10] Such occasions were more ancient than the prophets. If cult provided the background to the prophets, then so did law, even if in some attenuated form.

It was the exegetical work of von Rad among others that permitted Walter Brueggemann forty years ago to begin his first scholarly book, a study of Hosea,[11] with a declaration that would have drawn withering fire from Graf and Wellhausen: "A central fact in the study of the eighth-century prophets of the Old Testament has come clear in recent times. The prophets can only be understood in the context of the ancient historical and legal traditions of the Pentateuch."[12]

Here Brueggemann does not actually assert that it was the canonical Torah to which Israel's prophets looked; it was rather "the ancient historical and legal traditions" enshrined in the Torah. Hosea was not "copying a document," but "drawing perceptively and creatively upon the [oral] traditions of the community."[13] Some practitioners of literary critical methods may still want to defend Graf and Wellhausen, but the decay of this approach has advanced much over the last forty years of scholarship.[14]

Nonetheless, Douglas Stuart's 1987 Hosea commentary begins with the still somewhat shocking sentence, "Understanding the message of the book of Hosea depends upon understanding the Sinai covenant."[15] In the broader

10. Gerhard von Rad, "The Form-Critical Problem of the Hexateuch," in *From Genesis to Chronicles: Explorations in Old Testament Theology*, ed. K. C. Hanson, Fortress Classics in Biblical Studies (Minneapolis: Fortress, 2005), 16, 19. This essay first appeared in German in 1938.
11. Brueggemann's dissertation, "A Form-Critical Study of the Cultic Material in Deuteronomy: An Analysis of the Nature of Cultic Encounter in the Mosaic Tradition," Ph.D. diss., Union Theological Seminary, 1961, was apparently never published. The title alone suggests how this work became foundational for Brueggemann's later writings.
12. Walter Brueggemann, *Tradition for Crisis: A Study in Hosea* (Richmond: John Knox, 1968), 13.
13. Ibid., 43.
14. Note, for example, Klaus-Dietrich Schunck, who discusses the rather Wellhausenian proposal that the ninth and tenth Commandments may be the "youngest links" of the Decalogue, attested first (?) by the eighth-century prophets. See Schunck, "Das 9. und 10. Gebot—jüngstes Glied des Dekalogs?" *Zeitschrift für die alttestamentliche Wissenschaft* 96.1 (1984): 104–9. On the decay of the Graf-Wellhausen approach, see, among others, Rolf Rendtorff, "The Paradigm Is Changing: Hopes—and Fears," *Biblical Interpretation: A Journal of Contemporary Approaches* 1.1 (1993): 34–53. See also the newly published *A Farewell to the Yahwist: The Composition of the Pentateuch in Recent European Interpretation*, ed. Thomas B. Dozeman and Conrad Schmid (Atlanta: Society of Biblical Literature, 2007).
15. Douglas Stuart, *Hosea–Jonah*, Word Biblical Commentary 31 (Waco: Word, 1987), 6. Hans Walter Wolff agrees that Hosea's theology is a covenantal theology. See his *Hosea*, trans. Gary Stansell, ed. Frank Moore Cross et al., Hermeneia (Philadelphia: Fortress, 1974), 50–51, where he identifies Hosea 2:20 as the earliest announcement in the prophets of an eschatological new covenant (*berit*) for the sake of Israel; and 121–22 and 137–38, where he expounds 6:7's and 8:1's *berit* references as an Exodus-based *berit* resulting in *torah* (8:1) and *da'at 'elohim*, "knowledge/acknowledgment of God" (6:6). *Berit* appears elsewhere in Hosea only as civil or political treaties (10:4; 12:2). For a contrary view, eliminating the Sinai *berit* from Hosea as a later redactional addition in 8:1 and

field of the Book of the Twelve Prophets, Stuart argued his case mainly by categorizing twenty-seven types of covenant curses and ten types of restoration blessings all found in the Pentateuch, and allusively utilized by the Twelve.[16] While he overstates his case with the (again) shocking sentence, "True prophecy and true originality were mutually exclusive in ancient Israel," the sentence nonetheless makes a telling point.[17] The Pentateuch is the necessary backdrop for the prophets; the prophets are exponents of the Sinai covenant.[18]

This brings us back to my main text for this study, Hosea 6:7, a text about covenant violation in the land.[19] If the prophets are exponents of the Sinai covenant, do they also expound an Adamic covenant? Hosea 6:7 might signal such a connection; however, an exegetical block is wedged between my text and that Adamic assertion. This text has proven difficult to translate. No consensus translation exists; two main approaches are evident in modern versions, one reading אדם (*'adam*) as the personal name Adam, the other reading it as a reference to the Jordan valley town of Adam mentioned elsewhere only in Joshua 3:16. How should we translate Hosea 6:7, and does this troublesome text provide support for the republication thesis?[20]

---

reading *berit* in 6:7 as a political treaty, see Lothar Perlitt, *Bundestheologie im Alten Testament*, Wissenschaftliche Monographien zum Alten und Neuen Testament 36 (Neukirchen-Vluyn: Neukirchener Verlag, 1969), 129–55. For Perlitt, theological "covenant" is the later invention of the Deuteronomists. This approach looks like doctoring the evidence to fit the theory. Against Perlitt's approach, see John Day, "Pre-Deuteronomic Allusions to the Covenant in Hosea and Psalm 78," *Vetus Testamentum* 36 (1986): 1–12; Ernest C. Lucas, "Covenant, Treaty, and Prophecy," *Themelios* 8.1 (1982): 19–23; and Gordon J. McConville, *"berit," New International Dictionary of Old Testament Theology and Exegesis* 1:747–55. For critical review, see Ernest W. Nicholson, *God and His People: Covenant and Theology in the Old Testament* (Oxford: Clarendon, 1986); for a review of more recent work on the biblical covenants, see Scott Hahn, "Covenant in the Old and New Testaments: Some Current Research (1994–2004)," *Currents in Biblical Research* 3.2 (2005): 263–92. McConville, *"berit,"* 1:750, astutely notes that *berit* is uncommon also in the postexilic prophets; hence, the problem is not specific to the eighth-century books.

16. Stuart, *Hosea–Jonah*, xxxi–xlii.

17. Ibid., xxxi.

18. Aside from the massive commentary literature on Hosea, see the following useful exegetical articles: Elizabeth Achtemeier, "The Theological Message of Hosea: Its Preaching Values," *Review and Expositor* 72 (1975): 473–85, who correlates themes in Hosea with NT texts for preaching; R. E. Clements, "Understanding the Book of Hosea," *Review and Expositor* 72 (1975): 405–23, who, unfortunately, sees no hope in the original Hosea's message; the book's hope stems from a post-Hosean Judean redaction; David B. Wyrtzen, "The Theological Center of the Book of Hosea," *Bibliotheca Sacra* 141 (1984): 315–29, a brief but perceptive read of the book's major themes; and Karl A. Plank, "The Scarred Countenance: Inconstancy in the Book of Hosea," *Judaism* 32 (1983): 343–54.

19. Against Perlitt's nontheological understanding of Hosea 6:7's *berit*, see Nicholson, *God and His People*, 179–86.

20. In one recent evangelical work on biblical theology, P. R. Williamson can write, "Exegetical support for the posited 'covenant of works' or 'Adamic covenant' is sought in Hosea 6:7. This text, however, is open to a wide range of interpretations, the most likely of which reads 'Adam' as the

"Like a Man" or "Like Adam"?

The problem of the translation of Hosea 6:7 strikes the student of the Bible even from the earliest versions:

αὐτοὶ δέ εἰσιν ὡς ἄνθρωπος παραβαίνων διαθήκην.
ἐκεῖ κατεφρόνησέν μου. (Septuagint)

Ipsi autem sicut Adam transgressi sunt pactum;
Ibi praevaricati sunt in me. (Vulgate)

Here the nameless Septuagint translator renders the key phrase *ke'adam* as ὡς ἄνθρωπος, "like a man":

They [the Israelites] are like a man violating an agreement;
there they despised me.

Some other ancient versions follow suit. *Ke'adam* is read by the Peshitta as *'yk br nsh'*, "like a son of man," and by Targum Jonathan as *kdry' qdm'y*, "like earlier generations."[21]

Jerome's Vulgate on the other hand renders *ke'adam* as *sicut Adam*, "like Adam." The Douay-Rheims version of 1609/1610, a Latin-based English version, acceptably renders this Vulgate text as:

But they, like Adam, have transgressed the covenant;
there have they dealt treacherously against me.[22]

The various ancient versions, while differing among themselves, do not bear witness to a different Hebrew reading from what we find in the Masoretic text's *ke'adam*.

These two competing understandings given in the Septuagint and the Vulgate directed the course of ancient commentators. For example, the patristic

---

name of a geographical location and the event of an otherwise unrecorded breach of the Mosaic covenant by Israel. Given the exegetical difficulties with the key phrase, Hosea 6:7 is a rather tenuous basis on which to construct the otherwise unattested concept of a 'covenant of works' with Adam." See "Covenant" in *New Dictionary of Biblical Theology*, ed. T. Desmond Alexander et al. (Downers Grove, IL: InterVarsity, 2000), 421.

21. Cited in A. A. Macintosh, *Hosea*, International Critical Commentary (Edinburgh: T&T Clark, 1997). George Lamsa renders the Peshitta text as "But they like men have transgressed my covenant; there have they dealt treacherously against me." See http://www.aramaicpeshitta.com/OTtools/LamsaOT/28_hosea.htm.

22. Many of the Bible versions that are quoted in this article are accessible through the Bible Tool website, cosponsored by the Society of Biblical Literature, the American Bible Society, and the Crosswire Bible Society, at: http://www.crosswire.org/study/index.jsp.

commentator Theodore of Mopsuestia (ca. AD 350–428) apparently made no attempt to go beyond the local Antiochian version of the Septuagint available to him, accepting the story of Septuagintal origins told in the Letter of Aristeas, and arguing that it contained the sole apostolically approved text.[23] Missing the *'adam* reference altogether, absent as it was from his text, Theodore's sole comment on 6:7 is: "You [Israelites] persisted in your transgression, showing no regard for the pact you made with me in the beginning, despising me completely to the point of killing those of the prophets who reminded you of this."[24]

On the other hand, we find Cyril of Alexandria (d. AD 444), whose early works are surprisingly irenic (given the vitriol which he could later spew against various heresiarchs).[25] In writing his early *Commentary on the Twelve Prophets*, Cyril regularly consulted Jerome's earlier commentary to ascertain the differences between the Greek texts available to him and what Jerome called the *Hebraica veritas*.[26] Accordingly, he comments on Hosea 6:7 as follows:

> We should at all points be very zealous in investigating the truth; in this case we need to say that in place of *like someone* the Hebrew text says 'like Adam' *breaking a covenant*, so that we may understand that the *breaking* by the people of Israel was like that committed by Adam. . . . While it was granted to him . . . to be regaled with the delights of paradise, he paid no heed to the divine commandment [and was] deprived of his former condition. So, too, with *them*, the people of Israel. . . . Like the first man—Adam, that is—they fell headlong into apostasy.[27]

These two approaches—the Septuagint's and the Vulgate's—directed the future course of translators and annotators of Hosea 6:7 for a long time to come. For example, one important early Protestant version, the

23. See Robert C. Hill, "Introduction," in *Theodore of Mopsuestia: Commentary on the Twelve Prophets*, ed. Thomas P. Halton et al., Fathers of the Church 108 (Washington: Catholic University of America Press, 2004), 6.

24. *Theodore*, 66.

25. See Robert C. Hill, "Introduction," in *Cyril of Alexandria: Commentary on the Twelve Prophets*, ed. Thomas P. Halton et al., Fathers of the Church 115 (Washington: Catholic University of America Press, 2007), 3.

26. Hill, "Introduction," in *Cyril*, 6–7.

27. *Cyril*, 143. After this historical interpretation of the text (not characteristic of Cyril's fellow Alexandrians), Cyril typically launches into a spiritual, christological interpretation, applying the text to the Jews of Jesus' day and their rejection of the Christ. Citing the parable of the wicked tenants (Matt. 21), he gives their rejection of Jesus a covenantal interpretation: "They [first-century Jews] *broke* the Father's *covenant* by depriving him [Christ] of his inheritance as far as it lay with them" (144).

Geneva Bible of 1560, in the main perpetuates the interpretation found in the Septuagint:

> But they like men have transgressed the covenant:
> there have they trespassed against me.[28]

The Geneva Bible, famous for its Puritan interpretive notes, glosses the word "men" with this comment: "That is, like light and weak persons," a comment clearly in line with the Septuagint rendering. This understanding comports with the one put forth by the most famous Genevan, John Calvin, in his lectures on the twelve minor prophets, published the previous year, 1559. After rejecting the anonymous proposal that the word 'adam is in the genitive, "the covenant of man," that is, Israel had rejected God's covenant as if God were a mere human,[29] Calvin writes, "'They as men have transgressed the covenant,' [that is,] they showed themselves to be [mere] men in violating the covenant."[30]

Here, as in many places, the 1611 King James Version is similar to the Geneva Bible:

> But they like men[31] have transgressed the covenant:
> there have they dealt treacherously against me.

This is the same general understanding put forth long after by another Protestant of Geneva, Louis Segond, in his 1910 French translation:

28. Nonstandard spellings in older versions are, with a few exceptions, modernized here.

29. Jeremiah Burroughs identifies Vatablus (François Vatable, d. 1547) and Tremellius (1510–80) as propagators of this rejected view. See his *Commentary on the Prophecy of Hosea* (1643; Beaver Falls, PA: Soli Deo Gloria, 1989), 334. Calvin may have encountered Vatable's opinion when he was a student at the Collège Royal, 1531–32, where Vatable taught Hebrew. On Calvin and Vatable see W. de Greef, *The Writings of John Calvin*, trans. Lyle D. Bierma (Grand Rapids: Baker, 1993), 22. See also David L. Puckett, *John Calvin's Exegesis of the Old Testament* (Louisville: Westminster John Knox, 1995), 76 n. 44. John Immanuel Tremellius was a Jewish convert, first to Catholic Christianity, under the influence of Cardinal Reginald Pole in 1540, and then the following year to Protestantism, under the preaching of Peter Martyr Vermigli, in whose monastery he had been teaching. Fleeing Italy like Vermigli in 1541, he taught Hebrew and Bible in universities in Strasbourg, Cambridge, Hornbach, Heidelberg, and Sedan, declining Calvin's 1558 invitation to teach in the newly forming Geneva Academy. On Calvin and Tremellius, see de Greef, *Writings of John Calvin*, 54. Tremellius arrived in Strasbourg in 1542, the year after Calvin's departure from that city. For the Calvinizing influence of Tremellius's new Latin Bible, see Kenneth Austin, "Immanuel Tremellius' Latin Bible (1575–79) as a Pillar of the Calvinist Faith," in *Print and Power in France and England 1500–1800*, ed. David Adams and Adrian Armstrong (Aldershot: Ashgate, 2006). For more on Tremellius, see Kenneth Austin, "From Judaism to Calvinism: The Life and Writings of Immanuel Tremellius (1510–1580)," Ph.D. diss., University of St. Andrews, 2002.

30. John Calvin, *The Minor Prophets*, Calvin's Commentaries 6 (Grand Rapids: Associated Publishers and Authors, n.d.), 100.

31. KJV footnote reads, "Or, *like Adam.*"

> Ils ont, comme le vulgaire, transgressé l'alliance;
> C'est alors qu'ils m'ont été infidèles.

This can be rendered in English as,

> They, like the vulgar masses, have transgressed the covenant;
> that is when[32] they proved unfaithful to me.

Curiously, Calvin, fledgling covenant theologian that he was,[33] likewise rejected the "covenantal" understanding found in the Vulgate: "They have transgressed as Adam the covenant." Calvin says, "This exposition is frigid and diluted," and, he suggests, unworthy of further refutation.[34]

Nonetheless, "as Adam" was the understanding put forth by many others. In his German *Bibel* of 1545, Luther translates:

> Aber sie übertreten den Bund wie Adam;
> darin verachten sie mich.

This can be rendered into acceptable English as:

> But they have transgressed the covenant like Adam;
> thus they despised me.

In the tradition of English translation of the Bible, the Wycliffe translation stands out:

> But thei as Adam braken the couenaunt;
> there thei trespassiden ayens me. (1395)

Miles Coverdale's version of 1535 is similar:

---

32. Segond takes the Hebrew םש, *sham*, "there," as a reference to time, a remote possibility in Hebrew syntax (Macintosh, *Hosea*, 236 n. 2). Calvin likewise takes the *sham* as other than literal: it here means "in *that* particular you have acted perfidiously" (Calvin, *Minor Prophets*, 100). Waltke-O'Connor's *Biblical Hebrew Syntax* (Winona Lake, IN: Eisenbrauns, 1990) allows that *sham* may sometimes be used temporally, but cites no example (§31.3.1.h). On the other hand, C. F. Keil states outright that "there is no foundation for the temporal rendering 'then.'" See his *Minor Prophets*, vol. 10, in C. F. Keil and F. Delitzsch, *Commentary on the Old Testament*, trans. James Martin (Grand Rapids: Eerdmans, 1975), 100.

33. On Calvin's fledgling covenantalism, see Peter A. Lillback, *The Binding of God: Calvin's Role in the Development of Covenant Theology* (Grand Rapids: Baker, 2001). Lillback stops short of calling Calvin a "federalist," but he does demonstrate what he calls the "pivotal" character of Calvin's covenantalism (Lillback, *Binding*, 311).

34. Calvin, *Minor Prophets*, 100.

But euen like as Adam dyd,
so haue they broken my couenaunt,
and set me at naught.

The Bishops' Bible of 1568 likewise follows in the Vulgate tradition.[35]

But even as Adam did, so have they broken my covenant.

It was this general "Adamic" understanding of Hosea 6:7 that was used by the early covenant theologians.[36] This fact shows that later Calvinists were not slavish followers of John Calvin. For example, in sermons published in 1643, the famous Puritan independent preacher and member of the Westminster Assembly, Jeremiah Burroughs,[37] understood the text to refer directly or "immediately" to the Sinai covenant, and indirectly or "mediately" to the covenants of works and of grace. Thus according to Burroughs, Adam, Abraham, and Moses are all in view in this text: Adam is named, the Israelite covenant is the one given at Sinai, but "the covenant at large" is also in view, that is, the covenant of grace initiated formally with Abraham. Moreover, "these [Israelites], as they have old Adam in them, so they have dealt with me [God] as he did; and as he for his sin was cast out of Paradise, so these men have deserved to be cast out of the good land."[38] Thus Burroughs gives a brief but hearty nod to an important aspect of the republication principle. This interpretation stands soundly in the historical-christological exegetical tradition of Cyril of Alexandria.

35. Rowland S. Ward claims that the Bishops' Bible contains "the first known British usage of the term 'covenant' in relation to Adam." Rather, the connection can be traced at least as far back as Wycliffe's Hosea 6:7, printed above. For the claim, see Ward's *God and Adam: Reformed Theology and the Creation Covenant* (Wantirna: New Melbourne Press, 2003), 56. Despite the quite minor lapse, this book is an able historical survey of important issues in the topic of the covenant of works. One wonders whether the anonymous fifteenth-century poet of "Adam lay y-bounden," may have thought not only of Adam's bond of sin, but also of Adam's bond of covenant: "Adam lay bounden, bounden in a bond. Four thousand winter thought he not too long. And all was for an apple, an apple that he took. As clerkes finden written in their book. Ne, ne, had the apple taken been. Ne had never our ladie abeen heav'ne queen. Blessed be the time that apple taken was; therefore we moun singen Deo gracias" (British Museum, *Sloane Manuscript* 2593).
36. Francis I. Andersen and David Noel Freedman, *Hosea*, Anchor Bible 24 (Garden City, NY: Doubleday, 1980), 439, write, "Since . . . it is a commonplace of prophetic thought that Israel kept on acting like their unfaithful ancestors, the covenant-breaking theme could easily have been extended back to the beginnings of humanity."
37. See the biographical sketch of Burroughs given in William S. Barker, *Puritan Profiles* (Fearn, Ross-shire: Mentor, 1996), 80–84.
38. Jeremiah Burroughs, *Hosea*, 334. The nineteenth-century facsimile title page calls this work *An Exposition of the Prophecy of Hosea*.

"Like Adam" or "In [the Town of] Adam"?

Bible translations of Hosea 6:7 remained within these parameters—"like men" or "like Adam"—until the late nineteenth century, with some taking the text as support for a covenant theology for both Adam and Israel, and others resisting that claim.[39] Then in the 1890s the debate changed. At that time Wellhausen published a small but highly influential book, *Die Kleinen Propheten*, a work that consisted of a new German translation of the Book of the Twelve, followed by brief textual and interpretive notes. In his new translation, as was his sometime practice for noting what he judged to be doubtful texts, Wellhausen left blank the place where the word *'adam* would have appeared:

> Sie haben in . . . den Bund gebrochen,
> dort sind sie von mir abgefallen. [40]

> They have in . . . broken the covenant,
> there they have deserted me.

However, in the following "*Noten*" section, he writes:

> 6,7. Lies בְאָדָם [be'adam], wegen des folgenden שׁם [sham] und der Lokalisirung der Sünde auch in den sich anschliessenden Versen.[41]

Which means:

> 6:7. Read בְאָדָם [*be'adam*] because of the following שׁם [*sham*], and because of the localization of the sins in the adjoining verses.

Wellhausen seems to have been the first to propose this apparently minor emendation, reading *bet* instead of *kaf* for the opening letter: "In [the town of] Adam" (בְאָדָם, *be'adam*), rather than "like Adam" (כְאָדָם, *ke'adam*).[42]

---

39. Benjamin B. Warfield has an able article that in the main surveys the arguments for these two understandings of Hosea 6:7. See his "Hosea 6.7: Adam or Man?" in *Selected Shorter Writings of Benjamin B. Warfield*, ed. John E. Meeter, 2 vols. (Nutley, NJ: Presbyterian and Reformed, 1970), 1:116–29. This article originally appeared in 1903. Warfield favored "like Adam."

40. Julius Wellhausen, *Die Kleinen Propheten*, 3rd ed., ed. Rudolf Smend (Berlin: Georg Reimer, 1898), 14. The first edition of this work was 1892. I have not been able to see the first edition to check its Hosea 6:7 reading.

41. Wellhausen, *Die Kleinen Propheten*, 116.

42. According to A. A. Macintosh, de Rossi Codex 554 also contains this perhaps otherwise unattested reading, See his *Hosea*, 236. Bernardo de Rossi collated more than seven hundred Hebrew biblical manuscripts and published this text-critical work in the 1780s. In 1903 Warfield noted

In support of the emendation, one may note that *bet-kaf* confusion is a commonplace of textual corruption. In the square script that became the standard for transmission of Hebrew biblical texts (sometimes called Aramaic square, or Assyrian script), the two letters are very similar, distinguished mainly by the presence of a *tittle* in the lower right side of the *bet* (ב, versus tittleless כ).[43] But even in Paleo-Hebrew, or the later scripts of Elephantine and the Samaritan tradition, *bet-kaf* confusion is readily possible (ᛒ, versus ᛦ).[44]

But in what sense can there be said to have been a violation of the covenant in this obscure little town? Adam, likely to be identified as *Tell ed-Damiyeh*, located on the southeastern side of the confluence of the Jabbok and Jordan rivers and opposite Wadi Fari'a, is some twenty-six miles (forty-one km.) north of biblical Jericho, a little more than a third of the distance from the Dead Sea toward the Sea of Galilee.[45] This town's name is rare, appearing in the unemended Masoretic text only once, in Joshua 3's story of Israel's crossing the Jordan:

> Now the Jordan is at flood stage all during harvest. Yet as soon as the priests who carried the ark reached the Jordan and their feet touched the water's edge, the water from upstream stopped flowing. It piled up in a heap a great distance away, at a town called *Adam* in the vicinity of Zarethan, while the water flowing down to the Sea of the Arabah (the Salt Sea) was completely cut off. So the people crossed over opposite Jericho. (Josh. 3:15–16 NIV)

This small but important text-critical emendation would prove to bear great weight in twentieth-century translations of Hosea. Wellhausen's emendation was modest—a single stroke of a single letter—and plausible; it made sense of the second clause's שם, *sham* ("there"), a word that had troubled commentators, giving it a clear geographical antecedent. However, it left unsolved the question of what had allegedly happened "at Adam" to merit such a ringing denunciation. I shall return to this question below.

Many biblical scholars soon endorsed Wellhausen's proposal, including it in their versions, or in the notes and commentaries they produced. For

several similar emendations proposed by early textual critics, none identical to Wellhausen's, and, I think, none as elegant. See Warfield, "Hosea 6.7," 122–24.

43. For description of these scripts, see Emmanuel Tov, *Textual Criticism of the Hebrew Bible* (Minneapolis: Fortress, 1992), 218–19. For a chart showing the actual scripts, see 410, plate 30.

44. The paleo-Hebrew script in the parentheses is copied from potsherds found at the Iron Age II site of Lachish. For examples of *bet-kaf* confusion in biblical texts, see Tov, *Textual Criticism*, 248.

45. Mark J. Fetz, "Adam (place)," *Anchor Bible Dictionary*, 1:64.

example, in his commentary on the Book of the Twelve, George Adam Smith published Hosea 6:7 as:

> But they in Adam (?) have broken the covenant.
> There have betrayed Me![46]

Similarly, Julius Bewer in *Harper's Annotated Bible* sometimes presents the reader with a slightly revised KJV text. On Hosea 6:7 Bewer prints the KJV unrevised; but in the textual notes he writes that the town of Adam is "probably" meant, and thus translates, "They have transgressed the covenant at Adam."[47]

What Smith and Bewer marked as tentative grew more boldly asserted by later translators and editors. The 1952 Revised Standard Version unapologetically read the text this way:

> But at Adam they transgressed the covenant;
> there they dealt faithlessly with me.

This rendering is mostly retained in the 1989 New Revised Standard Version:

> But at[48]Adam they transgressed the covenant;
> there they dealt faithlessly with me.

Other modern translations followed suit. *La Bible de Jérusalem* reads:

> Mais eux, à Adam, ont transgressé l'alliance,
> là, ils m'ont trahi. (1998 revision)[49]

> (But they at Adam have transgressed the covenant,
> there they betrayed me.)

The English renditions of the Jerusalem Bible followed the same approach:

> But they have violated the covenant at Adam,
> they have proved unfaithful to me there. (JB, 1968)

---

46. *The Book of the Twelve Prophets*, 2nd ed., 2 vols. (New York: Harper & Brothers, 1928), 1:289. The first edition of volume 1 of this work appeared in 1896; I have not been able to check its Hosea 6:7 reading.

47. *The Book of the Twelve Prophets*, 2 vols., Harper's Annotated Bible (New York: Harper & Brothers, 1949), 49.

48. NRSV footnote reads, "Cn [='conjectural']: Heb. *like*."

49. I have not been able to see the 1956 French original.

The "at Adam" rendering became so well accepted in many circles that Else Kragelund Holt in her 1995 monograph on Hosea could simply adopt the emendation, without argument, by merely asserting, "reading [be'adam] with BHS, as has been customary since Wellhausen."[50]

Unlike the Revised Standard and the Jerusalem Bible and its transla-tional family, the New English Bible and its Revised English Bible revision follow Wellhausen part of the way, and then strike off on their own. These translators emend or repoint 'adam to read 'admah, a reference to the Val-ley of Siddom town in Genesis that was destroyed along with Sodom and Gomorrah, and referred to elsewhere in Scripture only in Deuteronomy and in Hosea 11:8.[51]

> At Admah they have broken my covenant,
> there they have played me false. (Hos. 6:7 NEB, 1970)

> At Admah they violated my covenant,
> there they played me false. (Hos. 6:7 REB, 1992)[52]

The NEB/REB translators apparently decided that "Adam" was too ob-scure a town for such an impressive accusation; hence they opted for a town name already found elsewhere in the Masoretic text of Hosea, and a notorious one. The emended consonantal text might differ by only two letters from the Masoretic text, the initial bet (= in) and Admah's final he, which could be safely omitted by certain Hebrew scribes as a *mater lectio-*

50. Else Kragelund Holt, *Prophesying the Past: The Use of Israel's History in the Book of Hosea*, Journal for the Study of the Old Testament Supplement 194 (Sheffield: Sheffield Academic Press, 1995), 54 n. 8. BHS refers to the present standard academic Hebrew Bible, *Biblia Hebraica Stuttgartensia*, ed. K. Elliger and W. Rudolph (Stuttgart: Deutsche Bibelgesellschaft, 1984). Since 1905, the various reigning editions of Rudolph Kittel's *Biblical Hebraica* (BHK) have played host to a wide variety of textual emendations. Earlier versions proposed a vast number of conjectural emendations; later editions scaled down the speculation. The 1973 BHK lists two proposals for Hosea 6:7's difficult phrase: the abbreviated Latin code of the textual apparatus translates as "read probably ba'aram [='in Aram/Syria'] (cf. sham); perhaps be'adam." The Aram proposal would sug-gest the interpretation of Hos. 6:7's *berit*/covenant as a political treaty involving a foreign power, but the general tenor of Hosea stands against this approach. Few have followed BHK up the road to Aram. See *Biblia Hebraica*, ed. R. Kittel, P. Kahle, A. Alt, and O. Eissfeldt, 16th ed. (Stuttgart: Württembergische Bibelanstalt, 1973), 901. The successor to BHK, the 1984 BHS, dropped the Aram suggestion, and includes only the be'adam reading.

51. The other references are Gen. 10:19; 14:2, 8; and Deut. 29:23. The name is missing from the story of Sodom and Gomorrah's overthrow in Gen. 19, and it is Deut. 29:23 alone that reports Admah and Zeboyim as "overthrown" with Sodom and Gomorrah in Yahweh's "fierce anger." References to Sodom and Gomorrah are much more frequent: the pair appear together twenty-three times in Scripture; nineteen times in the Masoretic text, of which eight are in the latter prophets (Isa. 1:9, 10; 13:19; Jer. 23:14; 49:18; 50:40; Amos 4:11; Zeph. 2:9).

52. Both the NEB and REB give a footnote that reads, "At Admah: *prob. rdg.*; Heb. Like Adam."

nis, an optional aid to reading. But in what sense could this non-Israelite town be meaningfully said to have violated a *berit*, a covenant? Hosea's only other reference to Admah does not contribute any real help to this proposal:

> How can I give you up, Ephraim?
>> How can I hand you over, Israel?
> How can I treat you like Admah?
>> How can I make you like Zeboyim? (11:8)

Here Admah and its partner-in-crime, Zeboyim, are reprobate, rejected, precisely not covenant partners with Israel's God. Hence, most translators have eschewed the Admah alternative.

Another minority report appears in the 1970 New American Bible, a Roman Catholic production that benefited enormously from the surge of Catholic biblical scholarship in the twentieth century:

> But they, in their land, violated the covenant;
> there they were untrue to me.

Unlike most, the New American Bible translators saw fit to publish the list of their text-critical emendations, the study of which is instructive. For Hosea 6:7 they emended the Masoretic text's כְּאָדָם, *keʾadam*, "like Adam," to read בְּאַדְמָתָם, *beʾadmatam*, "in their land."[53] This emendation assumes not only Wellhausen's *bet-kaf* confusion, but also a lost *tav-mem* pair, to be explained by supposing that the scribe's eye passed from the first *mem* to the second, thus omitting the overlooked letters. Like Wellhausen, this serves to provide a clear antecedent for that troublesome שָׁם, *sham* ("there").

The New American Bible antecedent, "their land," may bear a better plausibility than the obscure town of Adam, until one notices, as Wellhausen did, the local geography of the context: the "city" Gilead (6:8), probably either Ramoth Gilead or Jabesh Gilead, and "the road to Shechem" (6:9). If *Tell-ed-Damiyeh* is biblical Adam, it is located at the southern extremity of Gilead, beside a major ford of the Jordan River, and opposite Wadi Fariʾa, the major valley whose Iron Age road leads up toward Shechem in the Ephraimite hills.[54] Thus, if Hosea 6:7 requires a place name, the town of

---

53. The NAB scholars further reference Amos 9:15; Joel 4:20 (=MT 4:19); and Isa. 2:8, all of which contain either *ʾadamah* or *ʾerets* ("land") with various syntaxes, but none of which reproduces their emendation.

54. See the rendering of the Iron Age road crossing at Adam and leading up to Wadi Fariʾa in *The Holy Land Satellite Atlas*, ed. Richard Cleave (Nicosia: Rohr Productions, 1999), 1:127, map 3.1.

Adam is much more suitable than the New American Bible's generic "their land."[55]

The Good News Bible more fully exploits the geographical interpretation than any other English version I have seen:

> But as soon as they entered the land at Adam,[56]
> they broke the covenant I had made with them. (GNB, 1976)

The suggestion that Israel transgressed the covenant from its very entrance into the land "at Adam" is intriguing, and matches the characterization in the book of Joshua that Israelites had persistently worshiped other gods, even during the heady days of Joshua's leadership (24:14). Second Chronicles 36:21 also implies a lengthy disobedience, beginning 490 years before the exile, which if taken at face value pushes disobedience back to the time of Samuel. Likewise, the book of Ezekiel speaks of a lengthy disobedience for the northern kingdom, 390 years, symbolized by the strange command for the prophet to lie on his left side for 390 days (4:4–5). Ezekiel's years take the reader back to the very inception of the northern kingdom. Obviously these numbers are meant to be taken as suggestive, schematic, rather than literal; but they generally concur with the sense given in the Good News Bible.

The Good News Bible rendering "at Adam" for Hosea 6:7 also suggests a clever use of the line's first verb, 'abr, "cross/transgress." Israel crossed ('abr) the Jordan at Adam (Josh. 3:14, 17); Israel transgressed ('abr) the covenant at Adam (Hos. 6:7), a double entendre. One is tempted to say "double-crossed." I will deal with this at greater length below.

However, the suggestion in the Good News Bible that Israel's tradition spoke of entering the land by crossing the Jordan *at Adam* is not sustained by the narrative in the book of Joshua, which reports that the water piled up by the town of Adam, "a great distance away," while Israel crossed "opposite Jericho" (Josh. 3:16).[57] Adam, despite its important ford, was not the crossing site.

---

55. Other place name suggestions include Michaelis's proposal of Edom (אדום, 'edom), cited in Warfield, "Hosea 6.7," 121–22; and Adamah (אדמה), named only once, in a list of cities in Naphtali territory (Josh. 19:36). Edom is elsewhere spelled *defectio* (אדם), and so identically to Adam, only in the personal name Obed-Edom, who appears as a character in Samuel and Chronicles (2 Sam. 6:10–12). In Amos 1:9, the terms "Edom" and "covenant" (*berit*) appear together, but the broken covenant in question is one between Israel and Tyre, not with Edom.

56. GNB footnote reads, "*Probable text* But . . . at Adam; *Hebrew* But like Adam."

57. Landslides near Adam have blocked the Jordon on several occasions in recorded history, most recently in 1906 and 1927; see R. K. Harrison, *Old Testament Times* (Grand Rapids: Eerdmans, 1970), 172. See also the note on Josh. 3:13 in *TNIV Study Bible*, ed. Kenneth L. Barker

One translation that attempts an alternative understanding of the *ke'adam* phrase, as well as an alternative understanding of the geographic referent *sham* ("there"), is the new Jewish Publication Society's version:

> [7]But they, to a man, have transgressed the Covenant.
> This is where they have been false to Me:
> [8]Gilead is a city of evildoers,
> Tracked up with blood. (NJPS, 1999)

Here the New Jewish Publication Society's version works with the unemended Masoretic text, seems to take the *ke-* of *ke'adam* as distributive ("to a man" = "every one of them"), and tracks that troublesome *sham* as *preceding* its referent in the discourse. Both of these involve, I think, precarious syntactical decisions.[58]

Meanwhile most evangelical versions continued to print "like Adam." I present a sample, in order of appearance, from the old hyper-literal American Standard Bible, to the New International Version, the "update" revision of the New American Standard Bible, the New Living Translation, the English Standard Version, *The Message*, and the Holman Christian Standard Bible:

> But they like Adam have transgressed the covenant:
> there have they dealt treacherously against me. (ASV, 1901)

> Like Adam,[59] they have broken the covenant—
> they were unfaithful to me there. (NIV, 1984)

> But like Adam[60] they have transgressed the covenant:
> there have they dealt treacherously against Me. (NASB, 1995)

> But like Adam,[61] you broke my covenant
> and betrayed my trust. (NLT, 1996)

(Grand Rapids: Zondervan, 2006), 302. Perhaps a well-timed landslide blocked the Jordan in the event recorded in Joshua 3.

58. I can find no distributive use of *ke-* in Waltke-O'Connor's *Biblical Hebrew Syntax* (§11.2.9). And, on every other occasion of the adverb *sham* ("there") in Hosea, the referent precedes it: see 2:15 (where the referent is the "wilderness" of 2:14); 6:10; 9:15; 10:9; 12:4; and 13:8. The same is true of Hosea's contemporaries Amos and Micah. See Amos 6:2; 7:12; 9:3, 4; and Micah 2:3 and 4:10.

59. The NIV footnote reads, "Or *As at Adam*; or *Like men*."

60. The NASB footnote reads, "Or *men*."

61. The NLT footnote reads, "Or *But at Adam*." The New Living Translation is a vast improvement over the old Living Bible, often following a functional equivalence approach to translation.

But like Adam they transgressed the covenant;
there they dealt faithlessly with me. (ESV, 2001)

You broke the covenant—just like Adam!
You broke faith with me—ungrateful wretches! (*The Message*, 2002)

But they, like Adam,[62]
have violated the covenant;
there they have betrayed Me. (HCSB, 2003)

Most of these fairly footnote Wellhausen's text-critical proposal as a possibility, but print a rendering of the unemended Masoretic text.

The recent trend in evangelical Bible translation to print "like Adam" for Hosea 6:7 is broken by the newish Today's New International Version, which accepts Wellhausen's geographical interpretation and prints it as the main text, while relegating the "Adamic" reading to the footnotes:

As at Adam, they have broken the covenant—
they were unfaithful to me there. (TNIV, 2001)[63]

The TNIV's text-critical decision, and the recent evangelical trend to print a Wellhausenian footnote, show that it is hard to choose between the two main options. Both have something to commend them. Benjamin Warfield even "frankly confessed" that reading *'adam* as a place name is "very attractive."[64] But both readings also have a mark against them with which I must deal.

Difficulty A: Adam and Pentateuchal Intertextuality in Hosea

If *'adam* is taken to denote the first human, this choice creates a difficulty, for no other prophet seems to name Adam. Indeed, outside of Genesis, Adam is hardly named at all in the Masoretic text: The genealogy in

62. The HCSB footnote reads, "Or *as at Adam*, or *they, like men*." The lesser-known HCSB is mainly a Baptist project published by Broadman and Holman. This version is advertised as following an "optimal equivalence" translational method, occupying the netherworld between formal equivalence and functional equivalence. In my judgment the main result is, however, a formal equivalence version. The editors state, "form . . . should not be changed . . . unless comprehension demands it." See the HCSB "Introduction," p. vii.

63. The TNIV footnote reads, "Or *Like Adam*; or *Like human beings*." The commentary note in the *TNIV Study Bible* further says, "The allusion in 'Like Adam,' . . . is uncertain since Scripture records no covenant with Adam," ed. Kenneth L. Barker (Grand Rapids: Zondervan, 2006), 1476. This sentence is identical to one in the *NIV Study Bible*.

64. Warfield, "Hosea 6:7: Adam or Man?" 124.

1 Chronicles 1:1 is the only certain example.[65] Indeed, this observation, marshaled along with many other claims, helped establish the historical-critical theories of the origins of the Pentateuch in nearly all the leading universities of the West. However, uniquely among the prophets, Hosea shows an unusual propensity for knowledge of Genesis. Passage after passage resonates with the details of the Genesis stories.

Genesis Stories Evoked in Hosea[66]

Hosea 1:9: "You are not my people and I am not your *'ehyeh* [I AM]" evokes the covenant formula found first in the canon in texts such as Genesis 17:7–8 and Exodus 6:7.[67]

Hosea 1:10: "Israelites . . . like the sand on the seashore which cannot be counted" certainly evokes the Abrahamic promise in Genesis 22:17. The idiom "like sand on the seashore" appears ten times in the Masoretic text, but only three times of Israel's numerous population: the third reference is 1 Kings 4:20, itself also dependent upon the patriarchal promise, and written as a testimony to its fulfilment under Solomon's reign.

Hosea 2:20 (ET 2:18): "I will make a covenant for [Israel] with the beasts of the field, the birds in the sky, and the creatures that move along the ground" evokes the Noahic covenant with creation in Genesis 9:10, as well as the creation account of Genesis 1, while at the same time pushing the promised covenantal event into the eschaton as a kind of "new" covenant, as noticed by Wolff.[68]

---

65. Job 31:33 and Ps. 82:7 are the other possibilities, with Job 31:33 the more plausible case. Interestingly, both texts read *ke'adam*, just as in Hos. 6:7. Iain M. Duguid tentatively suggests that the personal name Adam may also be in mind in Ezekiel 34:31, rendering this text, "You will be 'Adam' and I will be your God." This is a perplexing text syntactically. The syntactical difficulty and the absence of an equivalent term in the Septuagint lead both the historical critic Walther Zimmerli and the evangelical inerrantist Daniel Block to suppose that there *'adam* is an unoriginal gloss. If a gloss, it is perhaps based on Ezek. 36:37–38 where in the final state of blessedness "flocks of people" (*tso'n 'adam*) will inhabit the land. See Duguid, "Covenant Nomism and the Exile," in *Covenant, Justification, and Pastoral Ministry: Essays by the Faculty of Westminster Seminary California*, ed. R. Scott Clark (Phillipsburg, NJ: P&R, 2007), 70 and n. 21; cf. 73. See also Zimmerli, *Ezekiel 2*, ed. Paul D. Hanson, trans. James D. Martin, Hermeneia (Philadelphia: Fortress, 1983), 211, 221; and Block, *The Book of Ezekiel, Chapters 25–48*, ed. R. K. Harrison and Robert L. Hubbard, New International Commentary on the Old Testament (Grand Rapids: Eerdmans, 1998), 308.

66. The scholarly literature on the nature of inner-biblical exegesis and inner-biblical citation and allusion has grown considerably. For a foundational discussion, see Michael Fishbane, *Biblical Interpretation in Ancient Israel* (New York: Oxford University Press, 1985).

67. On the covenant formula, see the excellent study by Rolf Rendtorff, *The Covenant Formula: An Exegetical and Theological Investigation*, trans. Margaret Kohl, Old Testament Studies (Edinburgh: T&T Clark, 1998), esp. 14 n. 20.

68. Wolff, *Hosea*, 50–51. See also the excellent exegetical article by Michael DeRoche, "The Reversal of Creation in Hosea," *Vetus Testamentum* 31.4 (1981): 400–409, which strongly ties the language of Hosea 2:20 and 4:1–3 to Genesis.

Hosea 2:25 (ET 2:23): "You are my people . . . you are my God" certainly repeats the covenant formula seen also in Genesis 17:7–8 and Exodus 6:7.

Hosea 4:3: "beasts of the field, birds in the sky, and fish in the sea" echoes Genesis 1:28, 30.[69]

Hosea 5:14: "I will be . . . like a lion to Judah" may evoke Genesis 49:9.

Hosea 6:2: "on the third day he will restore us that we may live" may evoke the third day restoration of Isaac in Genesis 22 (cf. 22:4), or perhaps the third day theophanic revelation of Exodus 19:15.

Hosea 6:8–9: "Gilead is a city of wicked men, stained with footprints (*'aqubbah*) of blood; as troops of robbers (*gedudim*) lie in ambush for a man, so do bands of priests; they murder on the road to Shechem, committing shameful crimes." This passage evokes the blessing on Gad in Genesis 49:19; there *gedud*, "troops," appears together with the *'aqab* root (note the *gimel-dalet* combination in Gilead, Gad, and *gedudim*). Gad's Transjordanian territory included the southern part of Gilead.

Hosea 8:9: "they have gone . . . like a wild donkey (פֶּרֶא) wandering alone" may evoke Ishmael's lonely fate in Genesis 16:12 (פֶּרֶא).

Hosea 9:6: "briers and thorns will overrun their tents" may evoke Genesis 3:18's curse upon the ground.

Hosea 9:16: "Ephraim is blighted, their root is withered, they yield no fruit" employs the same Ephraim/fruitful (אֶפְרַיִם/פְּרִי, *pri/'efrayim*) pun found first in Genesis 41:52 (cf. Gen. 49:22).[70]

Hosea 10:1: "Israel was a spreading vine; he brought forth fruit for himself. As his fruit increased, he built more altars" evokes the same "fruitful" pun in 9:16 and Genesis 41:52.

Hosea 10:8: "thorns and thistles will grow up and cover their altars" evokes Genesis 3:18's thorn-and-thistles curse on the land more clearly than the similar reference in Hosea 9:6, since it reproduces the exact terms in Genesis 3.

Hosea 11:8: "How can I treat you like Admah? How can I make you like Zeboyim?" certainly evokes the fire-and-brimstone judgment of Genesis 19's story of Sodom and Gomorrah (cf. also Gen. 10:19; 14:2, 8; and Deut. 29:23), where Admah and Zeboyim are also named. Hosea can make use of even *rarely* mentioned elements of the Pentateuchal traditions.

Hosea 12:3–6 (ET 12:2–5) deserves special treatment because of the way it transforms the underlying patriarchal story into an indictment. The text reads:

---

69. Again, see DeRoche, "The Reversal of Creation in Hosea," 400–409.

70. The name Ephraim, Joseph's second son, sounds like the Hebrew for "double-fruit" or "twice fruitful."

> Yahweh has a charge to bring against Judah;
>> he will punish Jacob according to his ways . . .
> In the womb he grasped his brother's heel;
>> and in his manhood he struggled with God.
> He struggled with the angel and overcame him;
>> he wept and begged for his favor.
> At Bethel he found him,
>> and there he spoke [*yedabber*] with him—
> Yahweh of the heavenly armies,
>> Yahweh is his name of renown!

Here the Jacob story is evoked in an intriguingly elegant manner: heel-grasping birth (Gen. 25:26), theophany-wrestling at Peniel (Gen. 32:24–30), and God-dreaming at Bethel (Gen. 35:9–15, where the emphasis of 35:14 is that God had *spoken* [*dibber*] to Jacob/Israel, with possible reference back to the original Bethel theophany in Gen. 28:10–22). Is it that the Bethel and Peniel stories are here conflated into the same event? Holt, who devoted a monograph to Hosea's reuse of Israel's history, reads the passage (rightly) as an indictment (*riv*) against Jacob's Israelite descendants, and concludes that "the Jacob traditions . . . were known" to Hosea's audience, and thus "did not require narrative elaboration."[71] Accordingly, the story is allusively/elusively retold in barest minimum. Michael Fishbane rightly concludes, "Hosea 12 applies events in the individual biography of Jacob to the nation as a whole."[72] Thus the indictment is rooted in Israel's archetypical past.

Hosea 12:13 (ET 12:12): "Jacob fled to the land of Aram; Israel served to get a wife, and to pay for her he tended sheep" evokes the Jacob-Laban story of Genesis 28–30.

If my interpretation of these texts is correct, there are sixteen references to the Genesis stories in Hosea's fourteen chapters, excluding Hosea 6:7. He seems to know the creation of beasts, birds, and fish; the curse of thorns and thistles; the Noahic covenant with the animals; the Abrahamic covenant formula; the Abrahamic promise of uncountable offspring; the solitary fate of Ishmael; the far more severe fate of the rarely mentioned Admah and Zeboyim; the many particulars of the Jacob story; the fruit/double-fruit puns on Ephraim's name; the Lion of Judah; and Jacob's blessing on Gad. Some

---

71. Holt, *Prophesying the Past*, 34.
72. Fishbane, *Biblical Interpretation*, 377. While noting some differences, Fishbane lists Hosea 12's many parallels to Genesis in note 149. See also René Vuilleumier, "Les traditions d'Israël et la liberté du prophète: Oséa," *Revue d'histoire et de philosophie religieuses* 59 (1979): 491–98, who argues that all the traditions are in some measure transformed in Hosea, except for the rock-solid Exodus tradition.

of these are uncertain, and some such as Judah's Lion might perhaps be ana-
lyzed as pointing, alongside Genesis, to some other source of traditions told
also in Genesis. But the compound effect of so many connections, including uncommon ones, is sufficient, in my judgment, to sweep the objections
aside. Hosea knows the book of Genesis in something quite like the form in
which we know it. He knows it well, and he uses its stories like well-honed
weapons against his Israelite audience. But there is more.

Other Pentateuchal Traditions

Hosea 1:9: "You are not my people and I am not your *'ehyeh* [I AM]"
certainly is meant—and shockingly so—to evoke the *'ehyeh 'asher 'ehyeh*
("I am that I am") encountered in the story of the burning bush (Ex.
3:14).

Hosea 2:14: "I will lead her into the wilderness" evokes the wilderness
experience of Israel in Exodus–Numbers.

Hosea 2:15: "as in the days she came up out of Egypt" evokes the exodus
event.

Hosea 4:2: "cursing, lying, murder, stealing, and adultery" evokes the
Decalogue of Exodus 20 and Deuteronomy 5.

Hosea 5:6: "when they go with their flocks and herds to seek the LORD"
may evoke Israel's request to Pharaoh in Exodus 10:9, 24–26.

Hosea 7:1: "they practice deceit, thieves break into houses, bandits rob
in the streets" may again evoke the Decalogue.

Hosea 8:1: "the people have broken my covenant, and rebelled against
my law" evokes the Sinai covenant of Exodus–Deuteronomy.

Hosea 8:12: "I wrote for them the many things of my law" certainly
evokes the law of Sinai, and probably evokes the specific statement that the
Decalogue was inscribed "by the finger of God" (Ex. 31:18; cf. 34:1).

Hosea 8:13: "They will return to Egypt," and 9:3: "Ephraim will return
to Egypt" both evoke the exodus tradition, and perhaps the rebellion story
found in Numbers 14 (cf. 14:4). The Ephraim reference may also include
the remembrance that Ephraim, son of Joseph and Asenath, was born in
Egypt.

Hosea 9:10: "When I found Israel, it was like finding grapes in the desert"
again evokes the wilderness tradition of Exodus–Deuteronomy.

Hosea 9:10: "But when they came to Baal Peor, they consecrated themselves to that shameful idol" certainly repeats the story of apostasy told in
Numbers 25.

Hosea 9:15: "Because of all their wickedness in Gilgal I hated them there,"
according to Wolff, may either evoke the conquest travel itinerary from Peor

to Gilgal in Numbers 25–Joshua 5; or the coronation of Saul as king, related in 1 Samuel 11:15 (cf. 15:12, 21, 33).[73]

Hosea 11:1: "Out of Egypt I called my son" certainly echoes the exodus events, even down to the detail that "Israel is my son; let my son go that he may worship me" (Ex. 4:22–23).

Hosea 11:5: "Will they not return to Egypt?" or perhaps "they will return to Egypt,"[74] again evokes the wilderness traditions of Exodus–Deuteronomy and perhaps again Numbers 14:4.

Hosea 12:14 (ET 12:13): "By a prophet Yahweh brought Israel up from Egypt and by a prophet he cared for him" perplexingly omits all reference to the name of Moses, leading some exegetes into tortuous attempts to identify the "prophet" as someone other than Moses. But who else can be meant?

Hosea 13:1: "When Ephraim spoke, people trembled; he was exalted [a prince?] in Israel. But he incurred guilt by Baal worship and so he died" evokes the individual Ephraim as a leader in Israel, with possible allusive reference, according to Wolff, to the Ephraimites Joshua and Jeroboam I. The Baal-worship reference may refer to the Baal-Peor incident of Numbers 25 in which a deadly plague of divine wrath strikes the Israelite camp because of Baal worship.

Hosea 13:4–6: "I am Yahweh your God [who brought you up] out of Egypt. You shall acknowledge no God but me, no Savior except me. I knew you in the desert, in the land of burning heat. When I fed them, they were satisfied; when they were satisfied, they became proud; therefore they forgot me." This text powerfully evokes the Exodus-Sinai tradition.

Here I find seventeen references to features in Exodus–Deuteronomy. Again, some are less secure, and may perhaps be explained in alternative ways, but the combined effect is the same as in the first set. Hosea knows the stories in some detail, and he knows many of them: the burning bush, the escape from Egypt, the prophet-leadership of the unnamed Moses, the giving of the Decalogue, the wilderness testing, the miraculous feeding in the desert, the threat to return to Egypt, and the Baal-Peor incident. Moreover, he gives prominence through repetition to significant elements in the Pentateuch, especially the departure from Egypt, and the desert trials and travails.[75]

---

73. Wolff, *Hosea*, 167.
74. The proper delineation of the lines and syntax of the negative *lo'* is in doubt. See *Biblia Hebraica Stuttgartensia*.
75. Vuilleumier, "Les traditions d'Israël," 491–98.

Other Early Israelite Traditions

Hosea 2:15: "I will make the Valley of Achor a door of hope" evokes Joshua 7:26, the sin of Achan, and his execution at Achor.

Hosea 8:4: "They set up kings without my consent" evokes the ancient tradition of Yahweh choosing the Israelite kings, going back to the days of Saul (1 Sam. 8–9) and David (1 Sam. 16), and later, Jeroboam (1 Kings 11).[76]

Hosea 9:9: "They have sunk deep in corruption as in the days of Gibeah," as H. W. Wolff argues, probably refers to the "appalling crime" committed by Benjamites against a traveling Levite and his concubine as related in Judges 19–21, and with which the book of Judges horrifyingly concludes.[77] Alternatively, the text could evoke the apostasy of Saul, whose capital Gibeah was.

Hosea 13:10–11: "Where is your king, that he may save you? Where are your rulers in all your towns, of whom you said, 'Give me a king and princes'? So in my anger I gave you a king, and in my wrath I took him away" evokes 1 Samuel 8:5–7 and perhaps 1 Samuel 15:23, on the selection and rejection of King Saul.

Hence, we have the Achan/Achor story of Joshua, the "appalling crime" against the Levite's concubine, the ancient stories of the origins of kingship in Israel, and the rejection of Saul. Considering all three of the above lists of Pentateuchal and early Israelite history, probably well over twenty individual stories are evoked by the eighth-century Hosea.[78]

The point of all this citation and correlation is to show the likelihood that if Hosea knew all these other stories, he probably knew the Adam story too.[79] Since Hosea was well apprised regarding the Genesis stories and other

---

76. Hos. 8:5–6: "your calf-idol of Samaria" (*'egelek shomeron*) may evoke perhaps either the golden calf of Ex. 32:4 (*'egel*) or of the Jeroboam story in 1 Kings 12:28, 32. On the other hand, a textual reference is really not necessary since the object itself was sufficient to evoke Hosea's denunciation.

77. Wolff, *Hosea*, 158.

78. For a strong argument for early dates for the Samuel literature, especially 2 Samuel, see Baruch Halpern, *David's Secret Demons: Messiah, Murderer, Traitor, King*, The Bible in Its World (Grand Rapids: Eerdmans, 2001), 57–72.

79. If for the purpose of argument one were to grant to the Wellhausen school its identification of the Pentateuchal strands J, E, D, and P, and its assigned dates, one notes that the Adam/fall story of Gen. 2:4b–3:24 derives from the earliest of the sources, the Yahwist, a ninth- or tenth-century source, according to the classic expositors of the hypothesis. Thus as Andersen and Freedman write, "The J corpus was settled long before Hosea wrote, and there seems to be no reason why Hosea should not have known and used it, in some form" (*Hosea*, 439). On the Yahwist, see Otto Eichrodt, *The Old Testament: An Introduction: The History of the Formation of the Old Testament*, trans. Peter R. Ackroyd (New York: Harper & Row, 1965), 199–200. Biblical minimalism pushes these dates much later. For now-classic statements in favor of exilic dating, see H. H. Schmid, *Der sogenannte Jahwist: Beobachtungen und Fragen zur Pentateuchforschung* (Zurich: Theologischer Verlag, 1976), and John Van Seeters, *Abraham in History and Tradition* (New Haven: Yale University Press, 1975). For a more comprehensive statement of minimalism, see Philip R. Davies, *In*

Israelite traditions shown in preexilic sources, then it may be nothing other than antitheological prejudice when some scholars judge that Hosea could not or would not have mentioned the Adam of Genesis. The Adam reference is rather elegantly theological. If Hosea wrote of the first human, he compared his dismal deed with the deeds of Israel, and thus brought together into one text important ideas from the Torah and the prophetic traditions. Was Hosea capable of such elegance? Was Hosea a theologian? There is no compelling reason to deny such a capability to him, and strong reasons—especially in the evocative reuse of the Jacob tradition in Hosea 12—to attribute to him a strong literary mind steeped in Torah. Hosea knows how to use literature and tradition in subtle, clever, theological ways. Did he do so in Hosea 6:7?

Moreover we have in Hosea 2:20 (ET 2:18) the equally elegant theological point that Yahweh will make for Israel a covenant in the eschaton "with the beasts of the field, the birds in the sky, and the creatures that move along the ground."[80] In other words, a creation-covenant with Adam in 6:7 might be matched with a new-creation covenant in 2:20. The creation parallel in Hosea 2:20 strengthens the case that Hosea 6:7 refers to the first human, and in a covenant with God.

Difficulty B: Adam as a Place Name in Hosea

We may deal with Difficulty B with brevity. If someone favoring the "at Adam" interpretation objects to the "like Adam" translation, on the grounds that the person Adam is never named elsewhere in the prophets, this same brush can paint both fences. The town of Adam is likewise never named elsewhere in the prophets. Indeed, it is named only once: Joshua 3:16. Hence, the argument cuts both ways and (on these grounds) neither translation is likely at all, let alone more likely than the other. So we are dealing with a *hapax legomenon* in the prophets, no matter which way we go.[81]

Search of "Ancient Israel," Journal for the Study of the Old Testament Supplement 146 (Sheffield: Sheffield Academic Press, 1992). For brief, temperate appraisals of the minimalists, see K. Lawson Younger, "Early Israel in Recent Biblical Scholarship," in *The Face of Old Testament Studies: A Survey of Contemporary Approaches,* ed. David W. Baker and Bill T. Arnold (Grand Rapids: Baker, 1999), 176–206; and Gary T. Knoppers, "The Historical Study of the Monarchy: Developments and Detours," in Baker and Arnold, *The Face of Old Testament Studies,* 207–35. For a longer, engagingly intemperate response, see William G. Dever, *What Did the Biblical Writers Know & When Did They Know It? What Archaeology Can Tell Us about the Reality of Ancient Israel* (Grand Rapids: Eerdmans, 2001).

80. DeRoche, "The Reversal of Creation in Hosea," 400–409.

81. The term *hapax legomenon* refers to a term or expression appearing only once in a given body of literature. *Hapax legomena* understandably bear peculiar difficulties for translators and commentators.

On the other hand, there is that troublesome adverbial particle *sham* (שָׁם) in the second clause of Hosea's sentence: "there (*sham*) they betrayed me." The adverb almost certainly requires a referent in the text. The New Jewish Publication Society Version takes the referent to be the place name in the next verse, Gilead: "Gilead is a city of evildoers tracked up with blood" (6:8). However, such referents precede *sham* everywhere else in Hosea, Amos, and Micah, the set of the eighth-century books in the Twelve Prophets. This fact renders the geographical understanding of Hosea 6:7's *'adam* again, as Warfield noted, "very attractive."

Moreover, locating trouble in the Transjordan town of Adam makes good sense of the geopolitics and military situation of Hosea's time. When interpreters have dared to render a specific historical judgment about the alleged event at Adam that Hosea is supposed to have denounced, several possibilities come up: one is the career of Pekah.[82] Twenty years are given for Pekah's rule in 2 Kings 15:27 (ca. 752–732 BC). It seems, however, that we must count some of these years as a rival rule in Gilead (ca. 752–740), overlapping the regnal years of Menahem (ca. 752–742) and his son Pekahiah (ca. 742–740), whom Pekah opposed.[83] Second Kings informs us that Pekah with a gang of fifty men crossed from Gilead and assassinated Pekahiah in Samaria. We are not informed of the location of Pekah's Gileadite headquarters, but one likely travel route from Gilead for such an expedition would be the ancient crossing at Adam, up into the Ephraimite hill country via the ancient road at Wadi Fari'a, which opens opposite Adam, passing through Shechem, and on to the city of Samaria. This scenario links the site of Adam (v. 7) with the "city" of Gilead (v. 8, perhaps either Ramoth Gilead or Jabesh Gilead), the road to Shechem (v. 9), and a crime of bloodshed (vv. 8–9). Such a correlation between Hosea 6:7–8 and the assassination story in 2 Kings 15:25 can only be the most tentative of hypotheses, but it does "work."

82. An alternative is the view of Albrecht Alt, who placed Hos. 5:5–6:6 during the Syro-Ephraimite War of ca. 734 BC. See John H. Hayes, *Amos, The Eighth-Century Prophet: His Times and His Preaching* (Nashville: Abingdon, 1988), 77; for bibliography, 66. Andersen and Freedman discount Alt's approach, because Alt thought that the attack was initiated by Judah against the north (Benjamin), and not the other way around. See their *Hosea*, 34.

83. See the reconstruction offered in J. Maxwell Miller and John H. Hayes, *A History of Ancient Israel and Judah* (Philadelphia: Westminster, 1986), 323–24, 328–29. Supporting this construction of Pekah's twenty-year reign (laid out in its main lines at length by Edwin Thiele, *The Mysterious Numbers of the Hebrew Kings* [Grand Rapids: Eerdmans, 1965]) in important particulars is Eugene H. Merrill, *A Kingdom of Priests: A History of Old Testament Israel* (Grand Rapids: Baker, 1987), 396–98. There are differences: Miller and Hayes interpret Pekah as a crony of the Syrians; Merrill suggests that he was an Israelite patriot opposed to the allegedly pro-Assyrian rule of the Menahem-Pekahiah dynasty. Both views have their merits. Andersen and Freedman lay out another variant in their *Hosea*, 36–37. In this variant, it is Pekah's military pressure that impels Menahem to seek against him Assyrian aid.

Alternatively, Andersen and Freedman opt for a more general thesis: (a) the town of Adam is more fully named Adam-Gilead; the place name is thus poetically distributed between two cola; (b) the place of the murder (of unknown victim[s]) is on the Adam-Shechem road, and therefore possibly even in Adam; (c) the murderers are a gang of wayward priests (v. 9).[84] Thus "Adam was the scene of terrible crime," "no ordinary murder," "a serious breach of covenant."[85] Again, the scenario "works," but the choice between them need not detain us, and other options also appear.

So, racking up the score, I find that there is an excellent reason *not* to follow *either* the human or the town interpretation of *'adam* in Hosea 6:7—either way is a *hapax*. On the other hand, I find that there is an excellent contextual reason for either the human or the town: translating *'adam* as the first man matches Hosea's affinity for the stories of Genesis and early Israel; translating it as the town matches Hosea's use of the place-adverb *sham*, "there," and may match the geopolitical significance of the ford-town. Is there a path beyond the impasse?

Toward a Solution for Hosea 6:7

Faced as we are with two unlikely choices (or is it two likely choices?), we are now ready to consider a third option: double entendre. I suggest that Hosea 6:7 is meant to be read polysemously, that both the man and the town would have readily suggested themselves to the prophet-poet's Israelite audience. This understanding requires no textual emendation either. The *ke'adam* phrase can be taken as a reference to the residents of Adam: "Like [the inhabitants of] Adam . . . they betrayed me there." This "inhabitants of" understanding, in fact, is the sense given in one of the more recent German translations of our text. The revision of the Elberfelder Bibel reads:

> Sie aber haben den Bund übertreten wie [die Bewohner von] Adam,
> haben dort treulos gegen mich gehandelt. (Elberfelder Bibel, 1985
>   revision)

The German can be acceptably rendered into English as:

> But they have transgressed the covenant like [the inhabitants of] Adam;
> there they have acted disloyally against me.

<hr>

84. See Andersen and Freedman, *Hosea*, 438–39.
85. Ibid., 436–37.

The full rendering that I propose is as follows:

והמה כאדם עברו ברית שם בגדו בי

vehemmah ke'adam 'aberu berit sham bagedu bi

Like [their ancestor] Adam, they broke the covenant;
Like [the residents of the town of] Adam, they double-crossed me there.

This rendering translates doubly the *ke'adam* phrase, for there is no more convenient way to bring out the polysemous character of the text. It recognizes that the phrase does double-duty, as is sometimes the case in Hebrew poetry.[86] When the reader encounters the *sham* ("there") of verse 7b, he or she is forced back to reconsider the sense of the *ke'adam*. This rendering also contains a subtle pun: since the town of Adam was the site of the Jordan-ford which one would "cross" (the usual verbal root for such crossings is *'br*), transgressing a covenant at Adam is likewise expressed as a "cross" (*'aberu*)—or better—a double-cross. Whatever atrocity happened at Adam, the perpetrators had double-crossed Yahweh. Recognizing this pun in the text strengthens the polysemous interpretation I have given the phrase *ke'adam*. The *'aberu* verb is further appropriate for the wordplay, for it is followed by a duplication of the *bet-resh* combination in the consonants of *berit*. But is a polysemous text likely in Hosea 6:7?

Wordplay in Hosea

Here I shall argue that Hosea exhibits an unusual propensity toward wordplay, especially wordplay on the meanings of names. This propensity makes it much easier to suggest that Hosea 6:7 is a polysemous wordplay. The foundational work devoted exclusively to the study of wordplay in the Hebrew Bible is the 1892 Johns Hopkins University dissertation by Immanuel Casanowitz, done under the direction of Paul Haupt.[87] In this work Casanowicz primarily identifies passages where sound-play (paronomasia) can

---

86. Another example of a double-duty term in Hosea is the *'appi* ("my anger"/ "my nose") of Hosea 8:5, as argued by Jack R. Lundbom, "Double-Duty Subject in Hosea 8:5," *Vetus Testamentum* 25.2 (1975): 228–30. Double-duty terms are far from rare in Hebrew poetry, as in the frequent line strategy a-b-c // b'c'.

87. Immanuel M. Casanowitz, *Paronomasia in the Old Testament* (Boston: J. S. Cushing and Co., 1894; repr., Jerusalem: Makor, 1970). See also the summary of Casanowicz in Jack M. Sasson, "Wordplay in the OT," *Interpreter's Dictionary of the Bible, Supplemental Volume* (Nashville: Abingdon, 1976), 970. For a sampling of puns in Genesis, see Scott B. Noegel, "Drinking Feasts and Deceptive Feats: Jacob and Laban's Double Talk," in *Puns and Pundits: Word Play in the Hebrew Bible and Ancient Near Eastern Literature*, ed. Scott B. Noegel (Bethesda, MD: CDL, 2000), 163–79.

be heard; some of his references also contain semantic tricks. The body of the book is a list of 502 examples of paronomasia, gleaned from multiple readings of the Hebrew Bible.

In all of the Old Testament, the minor prophets lead Casanowicz's list for the densest use—in descending order, Joel, Habakkuk, Micah, Zephaniah, Nahum, and Hosea; the bottom ranks were occupied by historical narrative books, except for Genesis, which ranked higher.[88] We should not think that Casanowicz's list is by any means exhaustive. New examples of wordplay are published regularly, and even new genres of wordplay have been proposed, with pivotal patterning or Janus parallelism perhaps the most recently added genre.[89]

Is Hosea a punster? Try Hosea 4:16:

> *kiy kefarah sorerah sarar yisra'el*
> Like a stubborn heifer Israel is stubborn.

Here the feature is the repetition of phonemes and root letters: the initial *kiy* is echoed by the *ke* in *kefarah*; the ending of *kefarah* links forward to the ending of *sorerah*; *sorerah* links forward to *sarar*; *sorerah* and *sarar* both link forward to the phonemically equivalent *s-r* of *yisra'el*.

A few lines later we find a syntactically difficult but paronomasically brilliant line, echoing at its outset the *s-r* phonemes of the previous example—

> *sar sabe'am hazneh hiznu 'ahabu hebu qalon maginneyha*
>
> When hard drinking runs dry, they play the harlot;
> her leaders love—yes, love—shame! (4:18)

Or, to preserve the paronomasic effect of the Hebrew, we might render the second of this pair as "her leaders love lust and lewdness" (4:18). The line begins with a pair of sibilants in *sar* and *sabe'am*, continues with root replication with the alliterative hiphil forms of *znh*, "play the harlot," as in *hazneh hiznu*, followed by root replication again in *'ahabu hebu*, a pair in which the second word appears to be simply a rhyming reduplication of the

---

88. His list for Hosea includes these nineteen texts: 1:6; 2:24, 25; 4:15, 18; 5:8; 8:7, 11; 9:6, 11, 16; 10:5, 10; 12:4, 12; 13:12, 15; 14:5, 9. See Casanowicz, *Paronomasia*, 90. I believe there are more in Hosea, but cannot fully pursue the question here.

89. Scott B. Noegel, *Janus Parallelism in Job*, Journal for the Study of the Old Testament Supplement 223 (Sheffield: Sheffield Academic Press, 1996). For more on biblical puns, see J. William Whedbee, *The Bible and the Comic Vision* (Cambridge: Cambridge University Press, 1998). See the cautions in the review of Whedbee by Scott B. Noegel, "Review of J. William Whedbee, *The Bible and the Comic Vision*," *Journal of Biblical Literature* 120.2 (2001): 393–95.

last two syllables of the first, in a hocus pocus–like effect.[90] The final word, *maginneyha*, is much debated: *magen* could mean "reward," as perhaps it does in Genesis 15:1; "shield," as it perhaps does in Psalm 47; or "ruler," as it does in Ugaritic and perhaps sometimes in the Old Testament.[91] Here I take it as "ruler," based in part upon the punning technique of the prophet. The first and last words of the line are suggestive: *sar*, spelled with initial *samek*, means "turn"; but *sar* spelled with initial *sin* means "chief," "ruler," "leader."[92] Such tricks are common in Hosea, as a detailed examination of its Hebrew text shows.

These examples should attune the reader to Hosea's propensities toward wordplay. This punning is apparent from the opening page of the book. There the opening oracular direction from Yahweh to "go, take a wife of harlotry" abounds in assonances and ironies. I transcribe the Hebrew to give the assonances most clearly:

> *lek qakh-leka 'eshet zenunim*
>   *veyalde zenunim*
> *kiy-zanoh tizneh ha'arets*
>   *me'akhare yhwh*

> Go, take for yourself a wife of harlotry
>   and [beget] children of harlotry,
> for the land has committed vile harlotry,
>   going astray from Yahweh. (Hos. 1:2)

Here the first three words *lamed-kaf*, *qof-khet*, *lamed-kaf* grate appropriately on the ear.[93] These are followed within the quatrain by four forms of the root *znh*, "have illicit intercourse."[94] The most intimate bond of familial love is (ironically) to be corrupted by adultery. Thus the book's arranger

---

90. Macintosh relates the *'ahabu hebu* to the rarely attested *pe'al'al* forms found in Lam. 2:11 and Ps. 45:3. See his *Hosea*, 169–70. Some others (see *Biblia Hebraica Stuttgartensia* critical note) identify the form as a textual corruption.

91. William Holladay, *A Concise Hebrew and Aramaic Lexicon of the Old Testament* (Grand Rapids: Eerdmans, 1988), 182.

92. Ibid., 354.

93. A possible case for a further wordplay here is the assonant similarity of this *lek qakh-leka* command to the original command to Abram in Genesis 12:1, *lek-leka*. Abram is called to leave the land of his birth, and is promised godly offspring though his wife Sarai; Hosea is called to quite a different fate: an adulterous wife and illegitimate children, resulting in the reversal of Abraham's journey: exile to Mesopotamia. With these words is Hosea presented as an ironic Abram, an Abram in reverse?

94. Holladay, *Concise Hebrew and Aramaic Lexicon*, 90.

signals the reader (and hearer) to attune an attentive eye and ear to the crafted, crafty language.

Like Genesis, the book of Hosea seems especially to revel in wordplay involving names.[95] There are about thirty proper names in the book of Hosea; a surprisingly large number of them are punned upon in various ways. We see this propensity already on page one of the book:

> Call him "Jezreel," for in a little while
>> I will punish the house of Jehu for the massacre at Jezreel,
>> and bring an end to the house of Israel's kingdom.
> On that day
>> I shall break Israel's bow in the valley of Jezreel. (Hos. 1:4–5)

Here the firstborn's name Jezreel is drawn from the Jezreel Valley town, the vacation capital of the northern kings, where the reigning Jehu dynasty got its start in bloodthirsty excess.[96] But "Jezreel" means "God sows," a reference to the vast grain fields of the Jezreel Valley, the breadbasket of Israel both today and in antiquity, sown as it were by the hand of God. Under Hosea's punning inspiration, Jezreel now bears the punitive meaning "God scatters"—scatters the power of the Jehu dynasty, and scatters Israel's people into exile. The broken bow alludes back to Jehu's king-killing archery (2 Kings 9:24). The name Jezreel is appropriate for this judgment oracle, similar in sound as it is to Israel itself: *yizre'e'l* versus *yisra'el*. Then, a few lines later it is said that these people shall be reunited and restored, for "great will be the day of Jezreel," that is, God will resow the people into their land (2:2 [ET 1:11]). Hence in the space of seven verses, there are five distinct meanings to Jezreel: the town, the boy, the valley, the exile, and the return.

The examples of Lo-Ruhamah and Lo-Ammi are better known, but bear brief repeating. Lo-Ruhamah is likewise a polysemous pun: "she who is not loved" is first a reference to the girl's suspected illegitimacy, and then to rejected Israel. In the narrative of Jezreel's birth it is at least said that Gomer bore "to him," to Hosea, a son (1:3). No such statement is made for Lo-Ruhamah (1:6), with ominous implications. *Ruhamah* is also a close cognate to the word for "womb," *rehem*. The child of the womb should be loved, but what if the womb is violated by another lover? All of this

95. For discussion of the Genesis puns, see Whedbee, *The Bible and the Comic Vision*. But care should be taken of this author's tendency to see wordplay as essentially comic. See Noegel, "Review of J. William Whedbee," 393–95.

96. Commissioned by Elisha's orders to wipe out the line of Ahab, Jehu also killed the Judean king—two kings killed at Jezreel—perhaps in a bid to become a new Solomon, king over all twelve tribes (2 Kings 9).

pertains also to Israel, bastard daughter that she is, no child of Yahweh's love, doomed. But like the name Jezreel, Lo-Ruhamah is reversed: Hosea will love this bastard girl, and Yahweh will love wayward Israel: "call her Ruhamah" (2:1 ET).[97]

The brutally abrupt "Lo-Ammi," "not my people," means both "he's no son of mine," and "Israel is no longer Yahweh's people." Lo-Ammi likewise is not born "to him" (Hosea) but only to Gomer, and so the name "not my people" (1:9) means, in effect, "bastard." Hence, Israel too is a bastard people, not the people of Yahweh.

Such names must be reversed: "Say of your brothers, 'Ammi' [my people]" (2:3 [ET 2:1]). Hosea must love this bastard son as if his own. The bastard names are not permitted to stand. Yahweh will re-create for himself a faithful and beloved people; Israel shall be renewed in divine love and compassion.

In 1:9 the reversal of the covenant formula employs another name-based pun, this time on the name Yahweh: "Call him lo-Ammi, for you are not my people and I am not your 'Ehyeh!'" "'Ehyeh" is, of course, the "I AM" name of Exodus 3:14, the source of the mysterious name Yahweh.[98] This reversal-pun must have sounded quite shocking to Hosea's audience.

Hosea 1:7 may contain yet another pun on the names in this family:

ve'et-beyt yehudah 'arahem vehosha'tim
But the house of Judah—I will love them and I will save them.

Here the roots raham (in 'arahem) and yasha' (in vehosha'tim) match the names of two members of the family, Lo-Ruhamah and Hoshea himself. If we simply had the root yasha' by itself, it would be hard to make this claim; matched as it is with raham, the claim is more conceivable. Perhaps the pairing is the author's signal.[99]

Such punning is present not only at the outset of the book, but is scattered throughout. If we found it only in chapters 1–3, and claimed it only for 6:7, the claim might be suspect, for Hosea 1–3 with its dominance of narrative

97. Gary Rendsburg proposes that Lo-Ruhamah also contains the polysemous play upon the word rhm, "rain," suggesting in the crisis of fertility cult religion that she who is not loved is also "not rained on." According to Rendsburg the pun recurs in Hos. 1:6, 7; 2:6; and 2:25. See Rendsburg, "Hebrew RHM = 'Rain,'" Vetus Testamentum 33.3 (1983): 357–61.

98. For an alternative understanding, based on a textual emendation from 'ehyeh lakem to 'eloheykem, see Carl S. Ehrlich, "The Text of Hosea 1:9," Journal of Biblical Literature 104.1 (1985): 13–19.

99. The root yasha', "save," is sparse in Hosea: only five times in four verses, twice in the verse cited above; and also in 13:4, 10, and 14:4 (ET 14:3). In none of these other cases is there any obvious wordplay.

may have a different transmission history from chapters 4–14 with their exclusively poetical discourse.[100] However, one finds such punning late in the book as well. I have already examined examples from Hosea 4:16 and 4:18 above. It goes far beyond the scope of this essay to render a complete survey of such plays and puns in Hosea, but let a few more examples of the kind of wordplay that we find in Hosea 6:7 suffice.

Hosea refers to the northern kingdom of Israel mainly by the tribal name Ephraim, for in his time much of the rest of the traditional ten-tribe territory had been eaten up by Syria and Assyria. In Genesis the child Ephraim (*'efrayim*) receives this name as a pun upon the fact that he is Joseph's second son; hence Joseph is doubly fruitful (Gen. 41:52). The word *peri* means "fruit," and the *-ayim* ending is the Hebrew dual plural, as in *shenayim*, "two." The pun is repeated, now of fruitful Joseph, in the blessing of Jacob in Genesis 49:22. In Hosea the pun is recurrent. Here are three examples:

> Ephraim is blighted,
>> their root is withered,
>> they yield no fruit [*peri*].
> Even if they bear children,
>> I will slay their cherished offspring. (9:16 NIV)

Here the reference to Ephraim's origins not only repeats the Genesis 41 "fruitful" pun but relates the judgment to the birth of Ephraim's own children, ironically reversing the blessing of Jacob (cf. Hos. 9:11). The pun recurs a few lines later:

> Israel was a spreading vine;
>> he brought forth fruit [*peri*] for himself.
> As his fruit [*lefiryo*, derived from *peri*] increased,
>> he built more altars;
> as his land prospered,
>> he adorned[101] his sacred stones. (10:1 NIV)

Here Ephraim's fruitfulness becomes but the fruitfulness of burgeoning idolatry in the confused Yahweh-Ba'al-bull cult of the northern kingdom. The solution to this spiritual crisis appears the last time the pun recurs, in the climax of the book's final chapter:

---

100. For an appraisal of this problem from a mainstream historical-critical perspective, see Joseph Blenkinsopp, *A History of Prophecy in Israel*, 2nd ed. (Louisville: Westminster John Knox, 1996), 82–90.

101. "Prospered" translates the noun *tob*; "adorned" translates the *hiphil* verb *heytiybu* from the same "good" root, *tob*.

> O Ephraim, what more have I to do with idols?
>> I will answer him and care for him [*'ashurennu*].
> I am like a flourishing juniper;
>> your fruitfulness [*peryeka*] comes from me. (14:8 TNIV; 14:9 Maso-
>> retic text)

Here the clever poet, one verse shy of the end of the book, makes his (or rather, Yahweh's) final and tender appeal: Ephraim must return to Yahweh, the true source of all blessing. Not even here does wordplay abandon him. The reference to Yahweh's tender care (*'ashurennu*) plays upon the close-at-hand reference to Assyria in 14:4 (ET 14:3), whom many of the north trusted to bring them deliverance:

> Say to him:
>> "Forgive all our sins
> and receive us graciously,
>> that we may offer the fruit [*farim*, derived from *peri*] of our lips.
> Assyria [*'ashur*] cannot save us; ·
>> we will not mount war-horses.
> We will never again say 'Our gods'
>> to what our own hands have made,
>> for in you the fatherless find compassion." (14:3–4 [ET 14:2–3] NIV)

'Ashur (Assyria) shall not *'ashur* (care for) Ephraim; only Yahweh can—and shall.

A partial list of proper names that are played upon in Hosea include: Achor/hope in 2:17 (ET 2:15); Admah/Ephraim in 11:8; Ashshur in 14:4 with 14:9; Beth-Arbel/Beth-El in 10:14–15; Beth-El = Beth-Aven ("house of sin") in 4:15; 5:8; 10:5 with 10:8; is Canaan punned on in 6:4's *ka'anan*, "like mist"?; Ephraim/lion (note the *f-r* in *'efrayim/kakkefir*) in 5:14; Ephraim/wild donkey (*alef-pe-resh* in *'efrayim* is metathesized in *pere'*: *pe-resh-alef*) in 8:9 (does this line evoke Ishmael's lonely *pere'*-fate in Gen. 16:12?); Gibeah/Ramah in 5:8 (both words mean "hill"); Gilead/Gilgal in 12:12 (ET 12:11); Gilead/gang of thugs (*gil'ad/gedudim*) in 6:8–9; Hosea (perhaps) in 1:7; Jacob/heel/heel-grabber in 6:8 ("footprints tracked with blood") and in 12:4 (ET 12:3); Judah/lion in 5:14; Judah is said to "be unruly" (note the emphatic *d*'s in *yihudah 'od rad*) "against God, against the faithful Holy One[s?]" (12:1), which perhaps evokes the Jacob-wrestling tradition (Gen. 32) evoked in the next lines of text (12:4–6)—does Judah want to wrestle with the Holy One(s?) too? Jezreel plays repeatedly in chapters 1–2; Israel/wrestling (*yisra'el/sarah*) with God in 12:4 (ET 12:3);[102] Lo-Ammi in chapters 1–2; Lo-Ruhamah in chapters 1–2.[103] The alphabetical list could continue.

The list of divine names played upon in Hosea includes: Ba'al/'Al (for *'Elyon*, "Most High") in 7:16 and 11:7 (unless *'Al* represents a textual corruption for *Ba'al*); Ba'ali/'Ishi ("my master" / "my husband") 2:18 (ET 2:16); Ba'al Shamem (Phoenician, "Baal of the Heavens") may be punned upon in the closing word of both 2:18 and 2:19, another example of a compound name becoming the elements of a parallel pair, where first *ba'ali* appears and then *shemam*, which in unpointed Hebrew would be identical with the Phoenician spelling of the Tyrian Baal, *ba'al shamem*, who (ironically) the text says shall not be named in future;[104] and *'ehyeh/Yahweh* in 1:9.

The point of all this citation is to demonstrate two matters beyond reasonable doubt: (1) the book of Hosea is dense with wordplay; and (2) wordplay is especially common in regard to proper names. Hence, we should conclude that a wordplay in Hosea 6:7 upon the name *'adam* is (at least) well worth considering. But what kind of wordplay?

Pivotal Polysemous Parallelism or "Janus" Parallelism

One of the advances in recent decades has been the discovery and classification of various types of wordplays in the Hebrew Bible. It is not my intention to survey that material here, but to focus on one variety.[105] One of the newest types has been called pivotal polysemous parallelism, or, evoking the two-faced Roman god of entries and exits, "Janus" parallelism. Polysemy is unseemly business in discourse: "A pun is a menace to the textual coherence of the 'grammatical' text."[106] Such punning may serve to emphasize an element in the text, or to create a new secondary text, operating furtively, even subversively, beneath the main text. Or, the polysemy may

102. Note that Jacob "in the womb" grabbed his brother's heel, and "in his manhood" (*be'ono*, evoking *ba'avono*, "in his sin") wrestled with God (12:4).

103. The personal names in Hosea that do not seem to me to be played upon are Gomer, her father Diblaim, Benjamin, and Shalmaneser.

104. For discussion of the Tyrian Baal and other Baal deities, see John Day, *Yahweh and the Gods and Goddesses of Canaan*, Journal for the Study of the Old Testament Supplement 265 (Sheffield: Sheffield Academic Press, 2001), 68–90.

105. For a brief survey, see Edward L. Greenstein, "Wordplay, Hebrew," *Anchor Bible Dictionary* (New York: Doubleday, 1992), 6:968–71; Jack M. Sasson, "Wordplay in the OT," 968–70; for in-depth examination, see Noegel, *Puns and Pundits*. For an exposition of polysemy in biblical texts, see Daniel Grossberg, "Multiple Meaning: Part of a Compound Literary Device in the Hebrew Bible," *East Asia Journal of Theology* 4 (1986): 77–86.

106. Stefen Schorch, "Between Science and Magic: The Function and Roots of Paronomasia in the Prophetic Books of the Hebrew Bible," in *Puns and Pundits*, 206–7. See also James Barr's discussion of polysemy in *Comparative Philology and the Text of the Old Testament* (Oxford: Clarendon, 1968), 142–44, 154, which he takes up in a discussion of the problem of homonyms.

be sufficiently obvious that it is hard to choose which (if either) is the main text. The reader or hearer must ponder.[107]

In pivotal polysemous parallelism, nicknamed "Janus" parallelism, there may appear (for example) three lines or more of poetry, and a term in the middle line is delightfully or disturbingly ambiguous: it pivots. Tracked with a prior line, it takes one meaning; tracked with a following line, it takes another meaning. Such a case is labeled "symmetrical," that is, there is balance fore and aft. Some cases are labeled asymmetrical.[108] The asymmetrical sort might have only two lines, or in some other way lack the balance of the first type. The most famous example of Janus parallelism may be the one first cited by Cyrus Gordon:

> The blossoms have appeared in the land;
> the time of *zamir* has arrived,
> the call of the turtledove is heard in our land. (Song 2:12)

Here one notes that *zamir* could mean either "song" (2 Sam. 23:1) or "pruning" (cf. *tizmor* in Lev. 25:3). Hence, with the blossoming of the first line, "the time of pruning has arrived"; and with the final line's cooing turtledoves, "the time of singing has come." This example is clearly symmetrical.

Scott Noegel has devoted a monograph to Janus parallelism, focusing on the book of Job, wherein he finds no fewer than forty-nine "hitherto unrecognized" Januses.[109] In the book's appendices, he published proposals for an additional seven in Hosea.[110] He also discusses another dozen biblical examples proposed by other scholars, finding them faulty, while commending about twenty other proposed examples. Noegel's best Hosean example may be from 1:6–7:

> For I will no longer have mercy upon the house of Israel,
> *Kiy-naso' 'essa' lahem*
> but I will have mercy upon the house of Judah. (1:6–7)[111]

---

107. Schorch discusses emphatic, exegetic, and symbolic polysemy. I am not convinced by Schorch's third category. See the note above.

108. Noegel, *Janus Parallelism*, 26. The "Janus" term derives from Cyrus Gordon. Noegel cites Gordon's "New Directions," *Bulletin of the American School of Papyrologists* 15 (1978): 59–66.

109. Noegel, *Janus Parallelism*, 25.

110. Ibid., 151–54. Aside from the examples I shall cite below, his Hosean list of Janusly divinized words includes *tassig* in Hos. 2:8–9 ("fence about," "move away"); *damim* in Hos. 4:2–3 ("blood," "laments"); *'amir* in Hos. 4:7–8 ("exchange," "procure food"); *yir'em* in Hos. 4:16–17 ("he will pasture," "he will associate"); and *qeshet remiyyah* in Hos. 7:16 ("bow of deceit," "a bow that has shot its arrow"). Some of these need further argumentation to be entirely convincing.

111. Ibid., 151. According to Noegel, the terrifying ambiguity of this sentence seems to have been first noticed by Ibn Ezra.

Here the middle term, *kiy-naso' 'essa' lahem*, is disturbingly ambiguous, with danger either way. It may mean "for I will certainly carry them off." But it may also mean "that I should forgive them at all." Noegel opts for both meanings.

Another one of Noegel's Hosean examples happens to appear in our context, Hosea 6:7–9. He quotes the KJV:

> But they like men have transgressed the covenant:
>> there have they dealt treacherously against me.
> Gilead is a city of them that work iniquity,
>> and is *'aqubbah* with blood.
> And as troops of robbers (*gedudim*) wait for a man,
>> so the company of priests murder in the way by consent:
>> for they commit lewdness.[112]

Here the ambidextrous term *'aqubbah*, from the *'aqab* root famous for its Jacob-story punning, can be read both as "foot-tracked" and as "deceitful." Hence, Gilead is "deceitful" with bloodshed and treacherous against the covenant, or Gilead is foot-tracked with blood, like that band of murderous priests.[113]

These two examples suffice, I think, to show that pivotal polysemous parallelism is a sometime weapon in Hosea's poetical arsenal. Hosea knows of Janus. Given the long ambiguity of the translators over *ke'adam* in Hosea 6:7, a reasonable solution to this problematic text now appears evident. Translators need not choose between the two attractive options. Hosea 6:7 is an asymmetrical Janus parallelism. This leads us once again to my proposed translation:

והמה כאדם עברו ברית שם בגדו בי

vehemmah ke'adam 'aberu berit sham bagedu bi

Like [their ancestor] Adam, they broke the covenant;
Like [the residents of the town of] Adam, they double-crossed me there.

Summary and Conclusions

To summarize the argument, Hosea shows strong familiarity with ancient Pentateuchal traditions, especially those in Genesis; hence there can be no

112. Ibid., 153.
113. Moreover, as noted above in the list of evocations from Genesis, the *gedudim* term, "troops of robbers," appears together with the *'aqab* root (note the *gimel-dalet* combination in all three terms, Gilead, Gad, and *gedudim*) in Gen. 49:19's blessing of Gad.

powerful argument against his naming *'adam* as the first human. Hosea
also uses rarely mentioned traditions, such as Admah and Zeboyim; why
not Genesis's Adam, too? Hosea loves wordplay and employs it frequently,
in many different styles. Often he plays upon both personal names and
place names. My translation brings these two types of punning together.
Hosea uses Janus parallelism. Polysemous meaning accounts for the two
main approaches of 6:7's translation in twentieth-century Bible versions.
Hosea also showed himself to be a covenantal thinker in other texts (2:20
[ET 2:18]; 8:1). On the other hand the presence of the locative adverb
sham ("there") indicates a place name in the text; *'adam* is the best candidate for this place name, not the following occurrence of Gilead in 6:8.
He also punned upon the place name as a ford-site for crossing/double-
crossing. The double-cross pun strengthens the case for a geographic
reading of *'adam*. An asymmetrical pivotal polysemous parallelism, or
asymmetrical Janus parallelism, thus makes good sense of all the data. I
conclude that the most defensible understanding of Hosea 6:7 is that the
text involves an asymmetrical polysemous wordplay, in which are evoked
both the person Adam and the town Adam. So, with double entendre,
both schools of modern translators get their cake.

Moving now to theological considerations, I note that Hosea conceives
of Israel's relationship to Yahweh as a covenant. This fact ought to be clear
from the theological use of the term *berit* in Hosea (6:7, with *'aberu*, "cross/
transgress"; 8:1, with *torah*).[114] Hosea 2:20 (2:18 ET) even anticipates an
eschatological covenant that Yahweh shall arrange with the animals of creation—for Israel's sake—for all to dwell together in peace and safety. Hosea
is thus a covenantal theologian. The covenant in mind in Hosea 6:7 and 8:1
is the exodus-based Sinai covenant, a covenant now tragically violated by
Israel's heinous crimes and persistent idolatry, the latter likened to a spouse's
adultery, itself a violation of the marriage covenant as taught elsewhere in
the prophets (Mal. 2:14; cf. Prov. 2:17). This is covenantal treason.

Hosea conceives of Adam's relationship to Yahweh also as a covenant.
This creation-covenant may be matched in the book with the future "new"
covenant with the animals for Israel's sake in Hosea 2:20 (ET 2:18). Adam
violated his covenant with Yahweh; likewise Israel violated her covenant
with Yahweh.

This violation is likened as well to an unknown but probably murderous
event involving the Jordan Valley town of Adam. Perhaps this event can be
related (following Miller and Hayes) to the Gilead-based revolt of Pekah

114. Again, as argued, contra Perlitt, in Nicholson, *God and His People*, 179–88. I have reservations about some other aspects of Nicholson's argument.

and his assassination of the northern king Pekahiah (2 Kings 15:25); or (following Andersen and Freedman) to a gang of murderous priests somewhere on the Adam-Shechem road. Neither of these alternatives can be positively asserted, but they comport well with the textual evidence.

It is the tragic violation of the two covenants that provides the point of comparison between Adam the man, Adam the town, and Israel. Although not stated in so many words, such violations result in expulsion: Adam from Eden, Israel (including the Adamites) from Canaan. In larger biblical perspective, we see that the comparison pertains only to select features of the two relationships. Adam the man had been wholly innocent; Israel had not. Nonetheless, the question about the republication thesis in view in this paper is sustained. According to Hosea, the Sinai covenant can be likened to an Adamic covenant. In Hosea's covenantal comparison, both covenants were implicitly in part about land tenure: Eden or Canaan. Like Adam of old, Israel committed covenantal treason: especially idolatry and murder. As the Mosaic covenant had threatened, "if you defile the land, it will vomit you out as it vomited out the nations that were before you" (Lev. 18:28). Hosea 6:7 thus provides perhaps unexpected support for the "republication" thesis.[115]

---

115. After I completed this article, a colleague pointed out to me that Duane Garrett's 1997 Hosea commentary commends the same general interpretation as I defend here. See Garrett, *Hosea, Joel*, New American Commentary 19A (Nashville: Broadman and Holman, 1997), 162–63.

7

ROMANS 10:5 AND THE COVENANT OF WORKS

GUY P. WATERS

Romans 10:5 (Μωϋσῆς γὰρ γράφει τὴν δικαιοσύνην τὴν ἐκ [τοῦ] νόμου ὅτι ὁ ποιήσας αὐτὰ ἄνθρωπος ζήσεται ἐν αὐτοῖς) is the proverbial exegetical onion. To peel back a single layer of investigation is to uncover several more layers of equal or greater complexity. Of what righteousness does Moses speak? How does it relate to "the righteousness by faith" (ἡ δὲ ἐκ πίστεως δικαιοσύνη, 10:6)? How precisely does Paul define the term νόμος in this passage? How does Paul's affirmation at 10:5 relate to his claim that Christ is "the end of the law" (τέλος νόμου, 10:4)?[1]

One's answer to these questions in turn shapes the way one frames and resolves the looming question in Pauline study—how does the apostle understand the Mosaic covenant? How is one to account for the likely contrast Paul erects between his quotation from Leviticus and his quotation from Deuteronomy at 10:5–8? How does Paul's argument at 10:4–8 give expression to his claim that he does not "abolish the law through faith" (νόμον οὖν καταργοῦμεν διὰ τῆς πίστεως; μὴ γένοιτο· ἀλλὰ νόμον ἱστάνομεν, 3:31)?

1. Scripture quotations in this chapter are my translations.

How are these questions to be resolved? Many older commentators see Romans 10:5 as a witness to the standard of righteousness set forth in the covenant of works. This chapter will consider afresh that Paul's engagement of the Mosaic law at Romans 10:5 is, in fact, an engagement of the Mosaic law in one very specific but important respect. Paul considers the moral demands of the Mosaic law, in distinction from the gracious covenant in which they were formally promulgated, to set forth the standard of righteousness required by the covenant of works.[2] This is not to say that Paul believed that God placed Israel under a covenant of works at Mount Sinai. Nor is it to say that the apostle regarded the Mosaic covenant itself to have degenerated, by virtue of Israel's unbelief and rebellion, into a covenant of works. Nor is it to say that Paul understood that God gave the Decalogue specifically or the Mosaic legal code generally as a covenant of works separate from a gracious Mosaic covenantal administration.[3]

That Paul is here engaging the Mosaic law as it articulates the standard of righteousness set forth by the covenant of works is a venerable inter-

2. This position set forth in this chapter is essentially that argued by Anthony Burgess, "The Law (as to this purpose) may be considered more largely, as that whole doctrine delivered on Mount Sinai, with the preface and promises adjoyned, and all things that may be reduced to it; or more strictly, as it is an abstracted rule of righteousnesse, holding forth life upon no termes, but perfect obedience. Now take it in the former sense, it was a Covenant of grace; take it in the later sense, as abstracted from Moses his administration of it, and so it was not of grace, but workes," *Vindiciae Legis: Or, A Vindication of the Morall Law and the Covenants, from the Errours of Papists, Arminians, Socinians, and More Especially, Antinomians. In 30 Lectures, Preached at Laurence-Jury*, London, 2nd ed. (London, 1647), 235. Anthony Burgess was a member of the Westminster Assembly and served on the committee that drafted the Westminster Confession of Faith 19 ("Of the Law of God").

Consider the similar reflections of Francis Turretin, "The Mosaic Covenant may be viewed in two aspects: either according to the intention and design of God and in order to Christ; or separately and abstracted from him. *In the latter way, it is really distinct from the covenant of grace because it coincides with the covenant of works and in this sense is called the letter that killeth and the ministration of condemnation, when its nature is spoken of* (2 Cor. 3:6–7). But it is unwarrantably abstracted here [i.e., by those who would make the 'Sinaitic legal covenant . . . a certain third covenant distinct in species from the covenant of nature and the covenant of grace,' 262] because it must always be considered with the intention of God, which was, not that man might have life from the law or as a sinner might be simply condemned, but that from a sense of his own misery and weakness he might fly for refuge to Christ"—*Institutes of Elenctic Theology*, trans. George M. Giger, ed. James T. Dennison Jr., 3 vols. (Phillipsburg, NJ: P&R, 1992–97), 12.12.18 (2:267), emphasis mine.

3. That is, in the sense of what has been called a "mixed" covenant. See here the judicious comments of Patrick Fairbairn, *The Revelation of Law in Scripture* (Edinburgh: T&T Clark, 1869), 445–46, quoted *infra*. For options circulating among Reformed theologians and expositors in the seventeenth century regarding the relation of the Mosaic covenant to the covenant of grace, see Burgess, *Vindiciae Legis*, 233–35; Ernest Kevan, *The Grace of Law: A Study in Puritan Theology* (Grand Rapids: Baker, 1965), 109–34; and, most recently, Rowland Ward, *God and Adam: Reformed Theology and the Creation Covenant* (Wantirna: New Melbourne Press, 2003), 126–39. See also chapter 3 in this present volume.

pretation.[4] It is also one enshrined by the proof-texts of the Westminster Standards. The Assembly cited Romans 10:5 as proof for the following declaration: "God gave to Adam a law, as a covenant of works, by which He bound him and all his posterity, to personal, entire, exact, and perpetual obedience, promised life upon the fulfilling, and threatened death upon the breach of it, and endued him with power and ability to keep it" (Westminster Confession of Faith 19.1).[5] Tellingly, the Assembly does not cite Romans 10:5 here as proof for the covenant of works *simpliciter*. Romans 10:5 is proof, rather, for the moral law which lies at the heart of the covenant of works.[6] The identification in view, then, is not between the Mosaic covenant and the covenant of works as covenantal administrations. The identification is twofold. First, the moral law set forth in the covenant of works is substantially identical with the moral law set forth in the Mosaic covenant. Second, the connection between "obedience" and "life" expressed by the moral law in the covenant of works is an abiding one. The moral law set forth in the Mosaic covenant continues to express that connection.[7]

If this historical proposal is tenable, then it goes a long distance toward resolving a number of exegetical and theological difficulties that have attended recent study of the apostle Paul. The question at hand, then, is this—is this proposal exegetically tenable? In other words, is this what the apostle Paul is arguing at Romans 10:5?

Romans 10:5–8: Contrast or Continuity?

As recently as 1979, one respected commentator could claim that "a contrast between v. 5 and vv. 6–8" could be affirmed "without much fear of contradiction."[8] What could be assumed a generation ago must now be

4. John Brown [Haddington], *An Exposition of the Epistle of Paul the Apostle to the Romans* . . . (Edinburgh, 1776), 402–3; Thomas Wilson, *A Commentarie upon the Most Divine Epistle of S. Paul to the Romanes* . . . (London, 1614), 776–85.

5. See also the citations of Rom. 10:5 at Confession 7.2, Westminster Larger Catechism 20, 92, 93, and Westminster Shorter Catechism 40.

6. This is especially evident from the citation of Rom. 10:5 as proof in Westminster Larger Catechism 92: "Q. What did God at first reveal unto man as the rule of his obedience? A. The rule of obedience revealed to Adam in the estate of innocence, and to all mankind in him, besides a special command not to eat of the fruit of the tree of knowledge of good and evil, was the moral law."

7. Having spoken of the law given as a covenant of works (19.1), the Westminster divines proceed to say, "*This law*, after [Adam's] fall, continued to be a perfect rule of righteousness; and, as such, was delivered by God upon Mount Sinai, in ten commandments, and written in two tables: the four first commandments containing our duty towards God; and the other six, our duty to man" (19.2, emphasis mine).

8. C. E. B. Cranfield, *A Critical and Exegetical Commentary on the Epistle to the Romans*, 2 vols., International Critical Commentary (Edinburgh: T&T Clark, 1979), 2:520.

vigorously argued. The question concerns the relationship between Romans 10:5 and Romans 10:6–8.

Μωϋσῆς γὰρ γράφει τὴν δικαιοσύνην τὴν ἐκ [τοῦ] νόμου
  ὅτι ὁ ποιήσας αὐτὰ ἄνθρωπος ζήσεται ἐν αὐτοῖς.
ἡ δὲ ἐκ πίστεως δικαιοσύνη οὕτως λέγει,
  Μὴ εἴπῃς ἐν τῇ καρδίᾳ σου, Τίς ἀναβήσεται εἰς τὸν οὐρανόν;
    τοῦτ᾽ ἔστιν Χριστὸν καταγαγεῖν·
  ἤ, Τίς καταβήσεται εἰς τὴν ἄβυσσον;
    τοῦτ᾽ ἔστιν Χριστὸν ἐκ νεκρῶν ἀναγαγεῖν.
ἀλλὰ τί λέγει; Ἐγγύς σου τὸ ῥῆμά ἐστιν,
  ἐν τῷ στόματί σου καὶ ἐν τῇ καρδίᾳ σου·
  τοῦτ᾽ ἔστιν τὸ ῥῆμα τῆς πίστεως ὃ κηρύσσομεν.

What is the force of the particle δὲ (10:6)? Is this particle adversative ("but") as many commentators have maintained?[9] Or is this particle connective ("and") as many recent commentators have argued?[10] One's conclusion to this question has significant and determining implications for how he will relate the two "righteousnesses" in view (τὴν δικαιοσύνην τὴν ἐκ [τοῦ]

9. C. H. Dodd, *The Epistle of Paul to the Romans*, Moffatt New Testament Commentary (New York: Harper and Brothers, 1932), 165; Ernst Käsemann, *Commentary on Romans*, trans. Geoffrey Bromiley (Grand Rapids: Eerdmans, 1980), 286–87; Mary Ann Getty, "An Apocalyptic Perspective on Rom. 10:4," *Horizons in Biblical Theology* 4.5 (1982–83): 115; James D. G. Dunn, "'Righteousness from the Law' and 'Righteousness from Faith': Paul's Interpretation of Scripture in Romans 10:1–10," in *Tradition and Interpretation in the New Testament*, ed. Gerald Hawthorne and Otto Betz (Grand Rapids: Eerdmans, 1987), 222; Werner Führer, "'Herr ist Jesus,' Die Rezeption der urchristlichen Kyrios-Akklamation durch Paulus, Römer 10,9," *Kerygma und Dogma* 33 (1987): 137–49; E. Elizabeth Johnson, *The Function of Apocalyptic and Wisdom Traditions in Romans 9–11*, Society of Biblical Literature Dissertation Series 109 (Chico, CA: Scholars, 1989), 157; Christian Beker, "Echoes and Intertextuality: On the Role of Scripture in Paul's Theology," in *Paul and the Scriptures of Israel*, ed. Craig A. Evans and James A. Sanders, Journal for the Study of the New Testament Supplement 83 (Sheffield: Sheffield Academic Press, 1993), 64–69; Steven Richard Bechtler, "Christ, the Τέλος of the Law: The Goal of Romans 10:4," *Catholic Biblical Quarterly* 56 (1994): 304; Arthur Dewey, "A Re-Hearing of Romans 10:1–15," *Semeia* 70 (1997): 109; Jean-Noël Aletti, *Israël et la Loi dans la Lettre aux Romains*, Lectio Divina 173 (Paris: Cerf, 1998), 223.

10. For examples of "complementary" readings, see those discussed at Thomas Schreiner, "Paul's View of the Law in Romans 10:4–5," *Westminster Theological Journal* 55 (1993): 126 n. 52. Adherents include George Howard, "Christ the End of the Law: The Meaning of Romans 10:4ff.," *Journal of Biblical Literature* 88 (1969): 331–37; Cranfield, *Romans*; C. Thomas Rhyne, *Faith Establishes the Law*, Society of Biblical Literature Dissertation Series 55 (Chico, CA: Scholars, 1981), 106; Richard B. Hays, *Echoes of Scripture in the Letters of Paul* (New Haven: Yale University Press, 1989), 76; Alain Gignac, "Citation de Lévitique 18,5 en Romains 10,5 et Galates 3,12: Deux Lectures Différentes des Rapports Christ-Torah?" *Eglise et Théologie* 25 (1994): 367–403; J. Ross Wagner, *Heralds of the Good News: Isaiah and Paul "In Concert" in the Letter to the Romans*, Novum Testamentum Supplement 101 (Leiden: Brill, 2002), 159–61; cf. Wagner, "'Who Has Believed Our Message?' Paul and Isaiah 'In Concert' in the Letter to the Romans," Ph.D. diss., Duke University, 1999, 196–98; and N. T. Wright, *Romans*, New Interpreter's Bible 10 (Nashville: Abingdon, 2002), 660.

νόμου, 10:5; ἡ δὲ ἐκ πίστεως δικαιοσύνη, 10:6). If the complementary position is correct, then the two "righteousnesses" are in turn complementary.[11] If the antithetical position is correct, then the two "righteousnesses" are antithetical.

There is compelling evidence that the particle δὲ is adversative.[12] Paul is setting in juxtaposition two concepts that elsewhere in his correspondence are antithetical. First, there is a "close parallel" between Philippians 3:9 and Romans 10:5.[13] Both passages speak of a righteousness which is "from the law" (ἐμὴν δικαιοσύνην τὴν ἐκ νόμου, Phil. 3:9; τὴν δικαιοσύνην τὴν ἐκ [τοῦ] νόμου, Rom. 10:5), and a righteousness which is "by faith" (τὴν ἐκ θεοῦ δικαιοσύνην ἐπὶ τῇ πίστει, Phil. 3:9; ἡ δὲ ἐκ πίστεως δικαιοσύνη, Rom. 10:6). In Philippians 3:9, the two righteousnesses are set in indisputable contrast (ἀλλὰ). This lends considerable weight to the thesis that the particle δὲ is, in the context of Romans 10:4–6, adversative.[14]

Second, and contextually closer to his statement at 10:5, Paul also contrasts two righteousnesses at Romans 10:3. These righteousnesses are surely parallel with and defining of the righteousnesses of 10:5–8 (and in turn parallel with and defining of the righteousnesses of 9:30–32).[15] In what relation do these two righteousnesses stand to each other? At 10:3, there is the righteousness to which unbelieving Israel has not submitted: "the righteousness of God" (θεοῦ δικαιοσύνην . . . τῇ δικαιοσύνῃ τοῦ θεοῦ). There is also the righteousness for which they strive (τὴν ἰδίαν [δικαιοσύνην] ζητοῦντες στῆσαι). Paul sets these righteousnesses in contrast with respect to possession or origin. The righteousness for which Israel strives is their own (τὴν ἰδίαν). The righteousness they lack comes from God (τοῦ θεοῦ). That the righteousnesses of Romans 10:3 are thus set in contrast suggests therefore that the righteousnesses of 10:5–6 are similarly set in contrast.

A third reason that the particle δὲ at Romans 10:6 is adversative pertains to Paul's definitions of these righteousnesses at 10:5–6. The hallmark of

11. "[Deut. 30:12–14] offers . . . a fresh explanation, granted exile and return, for what 'do the law and live' might actually mean"—Wright, *Romans*, 660.

12. Although this line of reasoning will not be pursued here, see Stephen Westerholm's *reductio ad absurdum* of the complementary position, *Perspectives Old and New on Paul: The "Lutheran" Paul and His Critics* (Grand Rapids: Eerdmans, 2004), 327–28.

13. Thomas Schreiner, *Romans*, Baker Exegetical Commentary on the New Testament 6 (Grand Rapids: Baker, 1998), 553.

14. *Pace* Daniel P. Fuller, *Gospel & Law: Contrast or Continuum? The Hermeneutics of Dispensationalism and Covenant Theology* (Grand Rapids: Eerdmans, 1980), 66.

15. "Mit der 'Gerechtigkeit aus dem Gesetz' in 10.5 kann Paulus kaum etwas anderes meinen als die 'eigene Gerechitgkeit' in 10.3 und den Versuch aufgrund von Werken nach dem 'Gesetz der Gerechtigkeit' zu trachten in 9.31–2. Die in 9.31 als fascher Weg abgewiesene Werke korrespondieren mit dem in 10.5 genannten 'Tun'"—J. S. Vos, "Die hermeneutische Antinomie bei Paulus (Galater 3.11–12; Römer 10.5–10)," *New Testament Studies* 38 (1992): 259.

"the righteousness which is of the law" at 10:5 is that "the one who does these things will live by them" (ὁ ποιήσας αὐτὰ ἄνθρωπος ζήσεται ἐν αὐτοῖς). In other words, inextricably tied to this "law righteousness" is human performance or activity as its basis or ground.[16] The "righteousness by faith" (10:6) is a righteousness that is exclusive of human endeavor and is received through faith.

This reading is confirmed when one observes that Paul elsewhere in his discussions of "righteousness" juxtaposes performance and faith antithetically. At Romans 4:4–5, Paul contrasts "working" (ἐργαζομένῳ, 4:4) and "believing" (πιστεύοντι, 4:5) with respect to the righteousness of justification (εἰς δικαιοσύνην, 4:5; cf. 4:6, καθάπερ καὶ Δαυὶδ λέγει τὸν μακαρισμὸν τοῦ ἀνθρώπου ᾧ ὁ θεὸς λογίζεται δικαιοσύνην χωρὶς ἔργων). Paul similarly contrasts the language of faith and striving at 9:30–31. Paul speaks of Gentiles who have attained "righteousness" (δικαιοσύνην, 9:30)—not by striving (μὴ διώκοντα, 9:30), but through faith (ἐκ πίστεως, 9:30). By way of contrast, Israel precisely through striving (Ἰσραὴλ δὲ διώκων, 9:31) has failed to attain unto the "law [of righteousness]" (εἰς νόμον, 9:31). Whatever one concludes concerning the precise identity of the word νόμος in 9:31, the contrast between the "righteousness" (δικιαιοσύνη) connected with striving (διώκοντα, διώκων) and the "righteousness" (δικαιοσύνη) connected with faith (ἐκ πίστεως) is indisputable.[17] Paul's conclusion in 9:32 (ὅτι οὐκ ἐκ πίστεως ἀλλ᾽ ὡς ἐξ ἔργων), citing the familiar contrast "faith/works," simply cements the contrast he has been drawing in this argument and throughout the epistle.

A fourth reason why the particle δέ is adversative has to do with the passage that Paul adduces to demonstrate "law righteousness." Paul cites Leviticus 18:5 at Romans 10:5.[18] He has earlier cited Leviticus 18:5 at Galatians 3:10–13, and does so to support a contrast between the law (νόμος)

---

16. Brendan Byrne, *Romans*, Sacra Pagina 6 (Collegeville, MN: Liturgical, 1996), 317.

17. In this vein, compare Dunn's observation that "when Paul sets righteousness ἐκ πίστεως alongside ἐκ something else, with δέ as the linking word, he obviously intends his reader to understand a contrast between the two phrases (4:16; 9:30, 32; as well as Gal. 2:16 and 3:21–22)"— *Romans*, Word Biblical Commentary 38 (Waco: Word, 1988), 602. For discussions of the meaning of the phrase νόμον δικαιοσύνης, see Douglas Moo, *The Epistle to the Romans*, New International Commentary on the New Testament (Grand Rapids: Eerdmans, 1996), 622–27; and Schreiner, *Romans*, 536–38.

18. Few dispute that Paul intends to quote Lev. 18:5 at Rom. 10:5. Paul's use of the phrase Μωϋσῆς γὰρ γράφει signals a citation from Scripture, and the phrase in question (ὁ ποιήσας αὐτὰ ἄνθρωπος ζήσεται ἐν αὐτοῖς) substantially corresponds to the text of Septuagint Lev. 18:5b (ποιήσετε αὐτὰ ἃ ποιήσας ἄνθρωπος ζήσεται ἐν αὐτοῖς ἐγὼ κύριος ὁ θεὸς ὑμῶν). On the variations between Paul's text and the text of Septuagint Lev. 18:5 see Ulrich Wilckens, *Der Brief an die Römer*, Evangelisch-katholischer Kommentar zum Neuen Testament (Zurich: Benziger/Neukirchen-Vluyn: Neukirchener, 1980), 224 n. 1003. Further, Dunn, "'Righteousness from the Law' and 'Righteousness from Faith,'" 217, notes that Lev. 18:5 "was a text he had already used in Gal 3:12."

216

and faith (ἐκ πίστεως) in a passage that, similarly to Romans 10:4–6, "treat[s the question] whether righteousness is available by the law."[19] To those who object that Paul could not set two passages of Scripture in contrast, Galatians 3:12 offers compelling precedent.[20]

Scripture versus Scripture?

If Paul intends a contrast between the two righteousnesses of Romans 10:5 and Romans 10:6, the question arises whether Paul is pitting one passage of Scripture against another. Daniel Fuller asserts that to maintain an adversative relationship between Romans 10:5 and 10:6–8 necessitates "either (1) conced[ing] that the Pentateuch can state such opposites, or (2) that Paul, while holding to the intended meaning of Lev. 18:5 in Rom. 10:5, nevertheless ignored the intended meaning of Deut. 30:11–14."[21] Philip Vielhauer, however, not only maintains a contrast, but articulates it in the strongest of terms: "Paul here places two passages of Scripture against one another and pits the second against the first."[22] Is it true that Paul is playing one Scripture passage against the other, as Vielhauer asserts?[23]

Some respond to this question by affirming that Paul does not set one Scripture in contrast with another.[24] One proposed explanation is that Paul is said to set Leviticus against his imaginative reworking of Deuteronomy 30:12–14.[25] In other words, there is at Romans 10:6–8 not the text of Scrip-

19. Schreiner, *Romans*, 554. See also W. Schmithals, *Der Römerbrief: Ein Kommentar* (Gütersloh: Mohn, 1988), 372.

20. Dunn, *Romans*, 602. See further at Schreiner, "Paul's View of the Law," 132. It is in this regard surprising to see Wright, *Romans*, 659, assert, "It would be out of character for Paul to set up one passage of Scripture against another."

21. Fuller, *Gospel & Law*, 67.

22. "Hier stellt Paulus zwei Schriftworte einander entgegen . . . und spielt das zweite gegen das erste aus"—"Paulus und das Alte Testament" in *Oikodome: Aufsätze zum Neuen Testament*, Theologische Bücherei 65 (Munich: Kaiser, 1979), 2:214, quoted at Vos, "Die hermeneutische Antinomie bei Paulus," 254.

23. Similarly Byrne, *Romans*, 318, responds to the charge that Paul here "appears to pit scripture against itself in a way that has no foundation in the original" by affirming that "Paul is not so much 'proving' anything from scripture as 'finding' validation in scripture for the superiority of the new dispensation God has brought about through Jesus Christ."

24. What follows is condensed and adapted from Guy Prentiss Waters, "'Rejoice, O Nations, with His People': Deuteronomy 27–32 in the Epistles of Paul," Ph.D. diss., Duke University, 2002, 213–18. See also idem, *The End of Deuteronomy in the Epistles of Paul*, Wissenschaftliche Untersuchungen zum Neuen Testament II.221 (Tübingen: Mohr Siebeck, 2006), 163–66.

25. Dunn, *Romans*, 603, offers Sanday-Headlam, Zahn, Denney, and Barrett in a partial listing of scholars who do not see Paul engaging the text of Deut. 30:12–14 as Scripture at Rom. 10:6–8, to which list Hans-Joachim Eckstein adds P. Billerbeck, "'Nahe ist dir das Wort': Exegetische Erwägungen zu Röm 10.8," *Zeitschrift für die neutestamentliche Wissenschaft* 79 (1988): 211. For a more extensive listing of exegetes who accept this text as "a rhetorically construed paraphrase of the OT text," see Käsemann, *Romans*, 284; R. Badenas, *Christ the End of the Law*, Journal

ture but "an allusion" or "a constructed rhetorical figure."[26] Paul is sometimes understood to be "distinguish(ing) between the use of authoritative scriptural texts, and the use of scriptural texts in formulating thoughts of [his] own."[27] Joseph Fitzmyer sees Paul "not interpreting the OT in the strict sense," but "borrow[ing] phrases from Deuteronomy and appl[ying] them to Christ."[28] Although this position resolves the question by declaring its nonexistence, Paul does intend to quote Deuteronomy 30:12–14 as Scripture at Romans 10:6–8.[29] Paul introduces Romans 10:6 with a statement "appropriate to an introduction to a quotation."[30] The parallel between Romans 10:5 and 10:6, on the one hand, and Galatians 3:11 and 3:12, on the other, further compels the reader to the conclusion that Paul is deliberately engaging Deuteronomy 30:12–14 *as Scripture.*[31]

Ernst Käsemann has argued that Paul accepts both Leviticus 18:5 and Deuteronomy 30:12–14 as part of the Scripture, and sets them in contrast. He maintains, however, that Paul has "appl[ied] to Scripture too the distinguishing of spirits demanded of the prophets in 1 Cor. 12:10; 14:29ff." He does so on the basis of the criterion of "justification," namely, "the contrast between the old and new aeons under the banner of the law on the one side and of the promise and the gospel on the other."[32] Paul has, in other words, mounted a stringent critique of Leviticus 18:5. J. S. Vos has rightly observed, however, that Käsemann has misconstrued the spiritual discernment of the prophets. This discernment was not intended to establish a "canon within the canon," to establish or manifest degrees of authority within the Old Testament Scripture. It was, rather, to discern "whether a prophetical expression

---

for the Study of the New Testament Supplement 10 (Sheffield: JSOT Press, 1985), 125–26. For a comparable survey of opinion among critics active prior to 1900, see H. A. W. Meyer, *A Critical and Exegetical Handbook to the Epistle to the Romans* (New York: Funk & Wagnalls, 1884), 406. For scholars who see Paul driven to engage Deut. 30:12–14 as he has done by "Jewish polemic," see Eckstein, "Nahe ist dir das Wort," 210.

26. "Eine Anspielung," "eine . . . gebildete rhetorische Figure"—Ulrich Luz, *Das Geschichtsverständnis des Paulus,* Beiträge zur Evangelischen Theologie 49 (Munich: Chr. Kaiser, 1968), 91. Luz is describing the viewpoint of a number of scholars, but not necessarily his own viewpoint.

27. Johannes Munck, *Christ & Israel: An Interpretation of Romans 9–11* (Philadelphia: Fortress, 1967), 41. Seventeenth-century commentators were well aware of the complexities of this question and offered a substantial, nuanced discussion of it. See especially Andrew Willet, *Hexapla: That Is, A Six-folde Commentarie upon the most Divine Epistle of the holy Apostle S. Paul to the Romanes* . . . , 2 vols. (London, 1620), 1:458–59; and Matthew Poole, *Synopsis Criticorum Aliorumque S. Scripturae Interpretum,* 5 vols. (London, 1676), 4:226–27.

28. Joseph A. Fitzmyer, *Romans: A New Translation with Introduction and Commentary,* Anchor Bible 33 (New York: Doubleday, 1992), 588.

29. See Waters, "'Rejoice, O Nations,'" 215–18. See also Dunn, "'Righteousness from the Law,'" 217–18; Schreiner, *Romans,* 556; Wright, *Romans,* 658–60.

30. Waters, "'Rejoice, O Nations,'" 215.

31. Ibid., 215–16.

32. Käsemann, *Romans,* 286.

actually originated from God (cf. 1 John 4:1)."[33] One might further observe the incongruity of Paul—having earlier declared his purpose not to "destroy the law through faith" but to "establish the law" (Rom. 3:31)—proceeding to critique the law by means of the doctrine of justification by faith alone.

The "Righteousness Which Is of the Law"

If, then, Paul is quoting from Leviticus and from Deuteronomy as Scripture, and if these passages are set in antithesis, then what is the import of this antithesis? Precisely what is Paul contrasting against "the righteousness by faith"? To answer this question, one will need to determine what Paul means by "the righteousness which is of the law" (τὴν δικαιοσύνην τὴν ἐκ [τοῦ] νόμου, 10:5).

Boundary Markers?

Many recent interpreters have concluded that the "law righteousness" of which Paul speaks has fundamentally to do with Israel's zeal and privilege concerning her status as the covenant people of God.[34] James Dunn, who has claimed that Paul maintains a contrast between the "law righteousness" of 10:5 and the "righteousness by faith" of 10:6, has argued that Paul's objection to "law righteousness" does not consist in performance per se:

> "Righteousness out of the law" then is righteousness understood as sustained and dependent upon acts of lawkeeping, righteousness understood as marking out a relationship with God peculiar to the people of the law and documented and validated by their faithfulness to those ancestral customs in particular which gave them their distinctiveness among the nations.[35]

In other words, Paul is "*not* . . . condemning all 'doing' or 'good works' in general, but . . . characterizing that Jewish covenant zeal which restricted God's righteousness to ethnic Israel, to those who by doing what the law commanded lived within the law and identified themselves as God's people."[36] Israel's fault is that she has "confused" what Dunn terms "a

---

33. "Ob eine prophetische Äußerung tatsächlich von Gott stammt (vgl. 1 Joh 4.1)"—Vos, "Die hermeneutische Antinomie," 270.

34. One of the earlier of modern proponents of this view in connection with Rom. 10:4–8 is George Howard, "Christ the End of the Law."

35. Dunn, *Romans*, 2:612. For Dunn's more comprehensive treatment of this subject see his *The Theology of Paul the Apostle* (Grand Rapids: Eerdmans, 1998), 354–66.

36. Dunn, "'Righteousness from the Law,'" 223. Compare here the similar claim of Ragnar Bring, "Paul and the Old Testament: A Study of the Ideas of Election, Faith, and Law in Paul, with Special Reference to Romans 9:30–10:13," *Studia Theologica* 25 (1971): 44.

secondary righteousness" (that of 10:5) with the "primary righteousness" (that of 10:6), of which the secondary righteousness is its "fruit." She has expressed this confusion by pressing this secondary righteousness upon "Gentile believers as much as the primary righteousness."[37]

If Dunn is correct, then Paul's critique of unbelieving Israel is fundamentally sociological and not fundamentally soteriological. Two considerations, however, militate against Dunn's proposal. First, Paul here defines "law righteousness" primarily in terms of activity and not status or identity: "the one who does these things" (ὁ ποιήσας αὐτά, 10:5). Paul's concern is "doing." It is *activity* that constitutes the essence of the "law righteousness" of which Paul speaks.[38]

Second, the text form in which Paul presents Leviticus 18:5 highlights precisely this concern to underscore activity.

> καὶ φυλάξεσθε πάντα τὰ προστάγματά μου
> καὶ πάντα τὰ κρίματά μου
> καὶ ποιήσετε αὐτά. ἃ ποιήσας ἄνθρωπος ζήσεται ἐν αὐτοῖς. ἐγὼ κύριος ὁ
>   θεός ὑμῶν. (Lev. 18:5 Septuagint)

> ὁ ποιήσας αὐτὰ ἄνθρωπος ζήσεται ἐν αὐτοῖς. (Rom. 10:5)

Leaving aside the thorny text-critical questions attending the text of Romans 10:5, one may note that Paul's citation of Leviticus 18:5 omits the phrase "all of my decrees and all of my commands" (πάντα τὰ προστάγματά μου καὶ πάντα τὰ κρίματά μου).[39] Far from attempting to minimize or even to eliminate from consideration "all the decrees and commands" of God by excising this phrase, Paul encapsulates "all the decrees and commands" of God by a single word (αὐτά). In doing so, he assumes his readership's competency to discern the connection.[40]

When Paul encompasses Moses' phrase "all of my decrees and all of my commands" (πάντα τὰ προστάγματά μου καὶ πάντα τὰ κρίματά μου) in a single word (αὐτά), he is stressing a vital point. The righteousness which is of the law (τὴν δικαιοσύνην τὴν ἐκ τοῦ νόμου) is a righteousness which is based upon and demands perfect and entire obedience to all the commands

---

37. Dunn, *Theology of Paul the Apostle*, 516.
38. Meyer, *Epistle to the Romans*, 406.
39. On which see Cranfield, *Commentary on Romans*, 520–21, and Schreiner, *Romans*, 562–63.
40. John Paul Heil, "Christ, the Termination of the Law (Romans 9:30–10:8)," *Catholic Biblical Quarterly* 63 (2001): 491. So also Meyer, *Epistle to the Romans*, 406.

of God's law.[41] It is the meeting of *this* standard that is requisite for entrance into "life." There is at Romans 10:5, then, an important affirmation parallel to Paul's claim at Galatians 3:10 that failure to perform flawless obedience to the law results in coming under the law's curse ("for as many as are of the works of the law are under a curse, for it is written, 'Cursed is everyone who does not abide in everything which has been written in the book of the law, to do them'").[42]

The Righteousness ἐκ τοῦ Νόμου

Paul's citation form of Leviticus 18:5 focuses upon the doing of the commandments of the Mosaic law. This means that Paul understands "the righteousness which is of the law" (τὴν δικαιοσύνην τὴν ἐκ [τοῦ] νόμου, 10:5) to consist of perfect and flawless obedience to the demands of the law.

In the phrase "the righteousness which is of the law," does Paul in fact mean by the word "law" (νόμος) "commandments" or "precepts" specifically? C. E. B. Cranfield claims that by the word νόμος Paul generally means "the Old Testament Law (without distinguishing between the legal parts and the rest of the Pentateuch)."[43] Such a position gains plausibility, for instance, from Paul's argument at 4:1–25, where his defense of the law (3:31) is taken from the Abrahamic narrative of Genesis. It also rightly recognizes Paul's sensitivity to the narrative context within which his Pentateuch citations fall.[44]

---

41. "Paulus ändert kontextbedingt den Plural der Gebote in den Singular der Gesetzesgerechtigkeit"—Wilckens, *Der Brief an die Römer*, 2:224 n. 1003.

42. For a survey of discussion of this verse in the contemporary literature, see Christopher D. Stanley, "'Under a Curse': A Fresh Reading of Galatians 3.10–14," *New Testament Studies* 36 (1990): 481–86; James M. Scott, "For as Many as Are of Works of the Law Are under a Curse, (Galatians 3.10)," in *Paul and the Scriptures of Israel*, ed. Craig A. Evans and James A. Sanders, Journal for the Study of the New Testament Supplement 83 (Sheffield: JSOT, 1993), 188–94; and Norman Bonneau, "The Logic of Paul's Argument on the Curse of the Law in Galatians 3:10–14," *Novum Testamentum* 39 (1997): 60–62. For defenses of the position that Paul at Gal. 3:10 understands the law to require perfect obedience, see Thomas Schreiner, "Is Perfect Obedience to the Law Possible? A Re-examination of Galatians 3:10," *Journal of the Evangelical Theological Soceity* 27 (1984): 151–60; idem, "Paul and Perfect Obedience to the Law: An Evaluation of the View of E. P. Sanders," *Westminster Theological Journal* 47 (1985): 245–78; R. Gundry, "Grace, Works, and Staying Saved in Paul," *Biblica* 66 (1985): 1–38; and most recently, Bryan D. Estelle, "The Covenant of Works in Moses and Paul," in *Covenant, Justification, and Pastoral Ministry: Essays by the Faculty of Westminster Seminary California*, ed. R. Scott Clark (Phillipsburg, NJ: P&R, 2007), 124–33.

43. C. E. B. Cranfield, "St. Paul and the Law," *Scottish Journal of Theology* 17 (1964): 44, cited by Stephen Westerholm, *Israel's Law and the Church's Faith* (Grand Rapids: Eerdmans, 1988), 108.

44. For general "narrative" approaches to Pauline engagement of Old Testament Scripture generally, and of the Pentateuch specifically, see Richard B. Hays, *Echoes of Scripture*; N. T. Wright, *The Climax of the Covenant* (Minneapolis: Fortress, 1991); James M. Scott, *Adoption as Sons of God: An Exegetical Investigation into the Background of ΥΙΟΘΕΣΙΑ in the Pauline Corpus,*

Nevertheless, as Stephen Westerholm correctly observes, Cranfield's definition inadequately captures what Paul means by the term νόμος at a number of points in his epistles. Westerholm concludes that "the 'law' in Paul's writings frequently (indeed, most frequently) refers to the sum of specific divine requirements given to Israel through Moses." It is, in other words, "the Sinaitic legislation . . . accompanied by sanctions."[45]

It is, of course, not a general definition but the immediate context that provides one with Paul's meaning of νόμος at Romans 10:5. Paul's insistence that "law righteousness" is attained by performance (ὁ ποιήσας), and that the standard for entrance into life[46] (ζήσεται) continues to be perfect obedience (αὐτά, cf. Septuagint Lev. 18:5) certainly *could* accommodate Westerholm's definition.

Nevertheless, an objection surfaces at this very point. Does Paul understand Moses to teach that one ought to earn eternal life through obedience to the demands of the law? Does this mean that the Sinaitic administration required perfect obedience of the individual in order to attain to life? This question is heightened when one considers Leviticus 18:5 in its context. John Murray observes that "Lev. 18:5 is in a context in which the claims of God upon his redeemed and covenant people are being asserted and urged upon Israel. . . . [It] refers not to the life accruing from doing in a legalistic framework but to the blessing attendant upon obedience in a redemptive and covenant relationship to God."[47] If the Scripture teaches that the Mosaic administration is an administration of the covenant of grace, as the Westminster divines affirm (Westminster Confession of Faith 7.5), then how could Paul have interpreted Leviticus 18:5 as he has? How could he have taken a passage which, in context, appears to refer to the sanctificational works of a redeemed person within the covenant community, and apply this text

---

Wissenschaftliche Untersuchungen zum Neuen Testament 2.48 (Tübingen: Mohr-Siebeck, 1992); Carol Stockhausen, *Moses' Veil and the Glory of the New Covenant: The Exegetical Substructure of II Cor. 3, 1–4, 6*, Analecta Biblica 116 (Rome: Pontifical Biblical Institute, 1989); idem, "2 Corinthians 3 and the Principles of Pauline Exegesis," in Evans and Sanders, *Paul and the Scriptures of Israel*, 143–64; and James A. Sanders, "Paul and Theological History," 52–57.

45. Westerholm, *Israel's Law*, 108–9.

46. As shall be argued *infra*, the "life" in view in Paul's argument is not mere temporal life, but eternal life. See Poole, *Synopsis Criticorum*, 226; Willet, *Epistle to the Romanes*, 438; *Annotations upon All the Books of the Old and New Testament . . .* [=Westminster Annotations], 3rd ed. (London, 1657), ad loc.; Edward Leigh, *Annotations upon All the New Testament Philologicall and Theologicall* (London, 1650), 221; Thomas Wilson, *A Commentarie upon the Epistle to the Romanes*, 782.

47. John Murray, *The Epistle to the Romans*, 2 vols., New International Commentary on the New Testament (Grand Rapids: Eerdmans, 1959, 1965), 2:249. Compare the similar observations of Patrick Fairbairn, *The Revelation of Law in Scripture* (Edinburgh: T&T Clark, 1869), 444.

to individuals seeking the righteousness of justification on the basis of their performance?

One way of alleviating this difficulty is to argue that the one who performs in Romans 10:5 is not the sinner seeking justification, but Jesus Christ performing obedience to the law and thereby earning life for his people. This passage is said to teach the "achievement of the one Man who has done the righteousness which is of the law in His life and, above all, in His death, in the sense of fulfilling the law's requirements perfectly and so earning as His right a righteous status before God."[48] In this sense, one could argue that Leviticus 18:5 points to Jesus Christ typologically. It is, as Cranfield maintains, an illustration of what it means that Christ is the goal of the law (τέλος νόμου, 10:4).[49]

While one may dispute what it is that Cranfield maintains Christ to obtain in consequence of his obedience and death (mere "status"), it is unquestionably true that, for Paul, Christ by his obedience and death has accomplished the sole basis for the sinner's justification (Rom. 5:12–21).[50] Cranfield's point, in modified form, stands theologically. Nevertheless, it is not at all clear that Paul is advancing this point exegetically at Romans 10:5. There is no contextual reason requiring Christ to be the implied subject of Romans 10:5b (ὁ ποιήσας αὐτὰ). Furthermore, such a reading of Leviticus 18:5 would unexpectedly differ from Paul's reading of the same verse at Galatians 3:12—a quotation that surfaces in a context similar to that of Romans 10:5–8.[51]

To return to the question—has Paul misquoted Leviticus 18:5 at Romans 10:5? One must answer decidedly in the negative. First, Paul's interest in Leviticus 18:5 concerns precepts or commandments. By the quoted word αὐτὰ, Paul summons to the reader's mind "all [God's] decrees and commands" (πάντα τὰ προστάγματά μου καὶ πάντα τὰ κρίματά μου). Which precepts does Paul have in mind? Westerholm argues that Paul most frequently means by the word νόμος "the Sinaitic precepts." One may, however, press Westerholm's definition of the word νόμος as "Sinaitic precepts

48. Cranfield, *Romans*, 2:521. In support of this claim, Cranfield cites Karl Barth, *Church Dogmatics* II/2, *The Doctrine of God*, ed. G. W. Bromiley and T. F. Torrance (Edinburgh: T&T Clark, 1957), 521 n. 4.

49. Cranfield, *Romans*, 2:522.

50. Moo, *Romans*, 646–47. For Rom. 5:12–20 as defending the active and passive obedience of Christ as *the* righteousness imputed to the believer in justification, see Estelle, "Covenant of Works in Moses and Paul," 117–24; David VanDrunen, "To Obey Is Better than Sacrifice: A Defense of the Active Obedience of Christ in the Light of Recent Criticism," in Gary L. W. Johnson and Guy Prentiss Waters, eds., *By Faith Alone: Answering the Challenges to the Doctrine of Justification* (Wheaton, IL: Crossway, 2007), 142–45; John Piper, *Counted Righteous in Christ* (Wheaton, IL: Crossway, 2002), 90–114 ; and the discussion *infra*.

51. Moo, *Romans*, 647.

accompanied by sanctions." Paul, to be sure, will never separate Mosaic commandments from the Mosaic covenant, but he will distinguish or abstract them.[52] At Romans 10:5, Paul patently concerns himself with the commandments found within the Mosaic law. His immediate concern is not the Mosaic covenant per se.

While Paul concerns himself with the commandments found within the Mosaic law, he does not concern himself with commandments that are found *only* within the Mosaic law. This is evident from a few considerations. First, Paul's argument in 10:4–13 is universal in scope. Paul affirms at 10:4 that Christ is the "end of the law to everyone who believes" (τέλος νόμου . . . εἰς δικαιοσύνην παντὶ τῷ πιστεύοντι [emphasis mine]). The righteousness of justification is not restricted to Jews only. It belongs to "everyone who believes." This point is reinforced by Paul's repeated emphasis in Romans 10:6–13 upon the universality of preaching and reception of the "righteousness by faith." In other words, the gospel is proclaimed to all kinds of people, whether Jew or Gentile. The "righteousness by faith," as Paul stresses, is held out to all who are within the hearing of the preached word (10:8). Paul's addition of the word Πᾶς to his quotation of Isaiah 28:16 at Romans 10:11, and to his quotation of Joel 2:32 at Romans 10:13 (Πᾶς γὰρ ὅς ἂν ἐπικαλέσηται τὸ ὄνομα κυρίου σωθήσεται), stresses the universality of those to whom "righteousness by faith" is proclaimed and of those who receive it. Finally, Paul explicitly stresses at 10:12 the universality of the gospel (οὐ γάρ ἐστιν διαστολὴ Ἰουδαίου τε καὶ Ἕλληνος; cf. κύριος πάντων, πλουτῶν εἰς πάντας τοὺς ἐπικαλουμένους αὐτόν).

Second, if the solution is universal, it stands to reason that what has occasioned that solution (the "problem") is universal as well.[53] Why proclaim the "righteousness by faith" to individuals who stand in no need of it?[54] This

---

52. It is at this point that Westerholm and this author are agreed.

53. Universal, however, in a different respect. The problem of sin is numerically universal. Each ordinary son and daughter of Adam bears the guilt and pollution of sin. The solution of salvation, however, is generically universal. It is possessed by all kinds of people, but not all persons individually.

54. In other words, Paul's claims evidence that he not only argues, but also reasons at Rom. 10:4ff. from "plight" to "solution." Some scholars have argued that Paul reasons from "solution" to "plight," although he argues from "plight" to "solution"; see E. P. Sanders, *Paul and Palestinian Judaism* (Philadelphia: Fortress, 1977), 552; *Paul, the Law, and the Jewish People* (Philadelphia: Fortress, 1983), 70ff. For a review and critique of this thesis see Robert H. Gundry, "Grace, Works, and Staying Saved in Paul," *Biblica* 66 (1985): 1–38; Frank Thielman, *From Plight to Solution: A Jewish Framework to Understanding Paul's View of the Law in Galatians and Romans*, Novum Testamentum Supplement 61 (Leiden: Brill, 1989); and Guy Prentiss Waters, *Justification and the New Perspectives on Paul* (Phillipsburg, NJ: P&R, 2004), 64–72. N. T. Wright has retained the "plight" to "solution" framework but has argued that it does not concern fundamentally soteriological issues. For a response to this (chiefly) nonsoteriological construction of the plight-solution framework in the Pauline correspondence, see Waters, *Justification*, 151–90.

lends an *a priori* presumption to a universal audience at 10:5. Is this so? Paul does not explicitly identify the subject who "does these things" at 10:5. The subject, however, must be as extensively defined as the persons with whom Paul is interested in 10:6–13, namely "Jew[s] and Gentile[s] without distinction" (10:12). The problem that Paul identifies, then, is one to which Moses gives expression (Μωϋσῆς γὰρ γράφει, 10:5), but is not one that Paul limits or restricts to the Jews, the recipients of the Torah.

Gentiles and the Law?

Paul, however, has affirmed that it is to the "law" (νόμου) that the problem of Jews and Gentiles has reference. What does he mean when he says this? To answer this question, one must rehearse Paul's claims in the opening three chapters of Romans.[55]

That Paul understood the human problem of sin to be universal requires little argument. Paul labors to show in Romans 1:18–3:20 that Jews *and* Gentiles alike are "all under sin" (πάντας ὑφ' ἁμαρτίαν, 3:9). Paul is also careful to state the grounds of human culpability for Jews and Gentiles, respectively. On the one hand, Paul can affirm that "as many as have sinned apart from the law shall also perish apart from the law, and as many as have sinned by the law shall be judged through the law" (Ὅσοι γὰρ ἀνόμως ἥμαρτον, ἀνόμως καὶ ἀπολοῦνται, καὶ ὅσοι ἐν νόμῳ ἥμαρτον, διὰ νόμου κριθήσονται, 2:12). By the word νόμος, Paul at Romans 2:12 certainly means the "written law," the law codified, written, and given through the hand of Moses on Mount Sinai.[56] The Jews' moral culpability is assessed against the standard of the Mosaic law. The Gentiles, who lack that particular standard, are also morally culpable. But culpability, Paul argues, presupposes and even requires a standard ("but where there is no law, neither is there transgression," 4:15b [οὗ δὲ οὐκ ἔστιν νόμος οὐδὲ παράβασις]).[57] Paul will stress that

---

55. Friedrich Lang rightly expresses the connection between Paul's emphasis upon the perfect "doing" of the law at Rom. 10:5 and human inability to keep the law unto life argued at Rom. 1–3: "In diesem Zitat liegt der Akzent ganz eindeutig auf dem Tun der göttlichen Vorschriften und auf der vollständigen Einhaltung aller Anordnungen und Rechtsentscheidungen Gottes, worauf das doppelte πάντα hinweist. Nur der vollständigen Tora-Observanz, die aber kein Mensch vorweisen kann (Röm 1–3), wird das Leben, d.h. das Heil, zugesagt"—"Erwägungen zu Gesetz und Verheißung in Römer 10,4–13," in *Jesus Christus als die Mitte der Schrift*, ed. Christof Landmesser, Hans-Joachim Eckstein, and Hermann Lichtenberg, Beihefte zur Zeitschrift für die neutestamentliche Wissenschaft 86 (Berlin: Walter de Gruyter, 1997), 582.

56. Charles Hodge, *Commentary on the Epistle to the Romans*, rev. ed. (New York: A. C. Armstrong and Son, 1896), 81. Compare the similar comments of W. G. T. Shedd, *A Critical and Doctrinal Commentary upon the Epistle of St. Paul to the Romans* (New York: Charles Scribner's Sons, 1879), 43. See the extended defense of this position by Timothy Dwight at Meyer, *Romans*, 107–8.

57. Shedd, *Romans*, 43.

Gentiles not only know God as he has revealed himself in creation and providence ("therefore what is known of God is manifest to them," 1:19 [διότι τὸ γνωστὸν τοῦ θεοῦ φανερόν ἐστιν ἐν αὐτοῖς]; "although they knew God," 1:21 [γνόντες τὸν θεὸν]), but also know his righteous decree that evildoers are worthy of death (οἵτινες τὸ δικαίωμα τοῦ θεοῦ ἐπιγνόντες ὅτι οἱ τὰ τοιαῦτα πράσσοντες ἄξιοι θανάτου εἰσίν, 1:32).

Paul leaves his reader in no doubt concerning what that standard is. He says that the Gentiles who do not have the (Mosaic) law nevertheless do by nature what that law requires (2:14, ὅταν γὰρ ἔθνη τὰ μὴ νόμον ἔχοντα φύσει τὰ τοῦ νόμου ποιῶσιν). The reason this is so is that the work of the law is written on their hearts (2:15, οἵτινες ἐνδείκνυνται τὸ ἔργον τοῦ νόμου γραπτὸν ἐν ταῖς καρδίαις αὐτῶν). The result is that the consciences and thoughts of Gentile men and women, informed by this standard, alternately accuse or excuse their thoughts, words, and behavior (2:15b).[58]

What can be said of this "law" which is thus available to all men and women? This "law" can certainly be distinguished from the Mosaic law in its totality, since Gentiles are expressly said *not* to have the Mosaic law. Nevertheless, because Paul uses the term νόμος to describe this standard available to the Gentiles, neither may one separate it from the Mosaic law.[59] Wherein does the overlap consist? Paul answers this question explicitly in the first chapter. He gives a catalogue of transgressions committed by Gentile persons (1:25–32) for which transgressions they are culpable (1:32). Each of these transgressions is *moral* in nature. All of them are traceable to the moral law, which was "summarily comprehended" in the Ten Commandments of the Mosaic law.[60] What Paul is stressing is not simply the horizontal consequences of these sinful behaviors, but that these behaviors are transgressions of a divine, moral standard which is inescapably manifested to and known by every human being.[61] It is this law (νόμος)—the moral law—of which

58. See ch. 10 in this present volume. For a discussion of the biblical foundations of natural law, see David VanDrunen, *A Biblical Case for Natural Law* (Grand Rapids: Acton Institute, 2006).
59. *Pace* Westerholm, *Perspectives Old and New*, 414–17. Westerholm claims that Paul, in "depict[ing] the plight of all humanity in terms borrowed from, and (strictly speaking) appropriate only to, the Jewish situation ('under the law')," has made a "generalization" albeit "unconsciously."
60. Westminster Larger Catechism 98.
61. *Pace* Wright, *Romans*, 434. Wright states, "Paul's view of sin, once more, is not that it is the breaking of arbitrary divine rules but that it is subhuman or nonhuman behavior, deeds that are unfitting for humans to perform," and again, "[Paul] asserts that humans in general have an innate awareness that certain types of behavior are inherently dehumanizing, to their practitioners as well as to their victims." It is not simply that these behaviors are "inherently dehumanizing" (though they certainly are). Neither do they entail the breaking of "*arbitrary* divine rules" (emphasis mine). They are the breaking of divine laws to which the moral constitution of all rational creatures inescapably bears witness, and which necessarily express the moral perfection of God (1:20).

Paul speaks in Romans 2:12–16. Because Paul invokes a "law righteousness" pertaining to all kinds of people (Jew and Gentile) in Romans 10:5, it must be this same law that he has in mind there.[62]

How could Paul have derived a testimony regarding the moral law, revealed to Jews and Gentiles, from Leviticus 18:5? The answer is found in the overlap that exists between the moral law and the Mosaic law. Because of this overlap Paul can quote the Mosaic writings, deducing therefrom a principle that applies universally to Jews and Gentiles alike.

Do This and You Shall Live

Thus far it has been argued that the "law righteousness" of Romans 10:5 and the "righteousness by faith" of Romans 10:6 are set in contrast with one another; that the "law righteousness" of Romans 10:5 requires perfect obedience to commandments found in the Mosaic law; that the commandments in view are the moral law, formally promulgated in the Decalogue; and that the particular commandments that Paul has in mind are not unique to the Mosaic law but known, through conscience, by every human being. Paul, however, claims more at Romans 10:5. He argues that "life" is suspended upon perfect obedience to the commands of the law.[63] What precisely is this "life"? To be sure, Paul understands Moses to bear witness to an "obedience-life" connection. Does this connection, however, find precedent in the pre-Mosaic era?

Paul asserts that the one who flawlessly obeys the commands of the moral law shall live by them (ζήσεται ἐν αὐτοῖς). This life is clearly future, but how far into the future is this life located? Commentators have raised the question whether the "life" in view is "temporal" or "eternal." In other words, does this "life" consist of such this-worldly blessings as longevity, wealth, or victory over one's enemies? Or does it consist of eternal felicity and communion with God? This question was vigorously discussed in the seventeenth

---

62. At this point disagreement should be registered with Westerholm's analysis of this issue. Westerholm, *Perspectives Old and New*, 415, in arguing that those "under the law" (Rom. 3:19) are Jews only, maintains that the Gentiles being a "law to themselves" (2:14) does not warrant affirming the Gentiles to be "under law." One can affirm with Westerholm that Paul did not understand the Gentiles to have stood under the law defined as the Sinaitic administration (broadly) or the Sinaitic legal code (specifically). Paul's use of the word "law" at Rom. 2:12–16, however, seems to admit of more flexibility than Westerholm allows. By "law," Paul means here in substance the Decalogue, that is, the Decalogue less any adjuncts that were uniquely revealed to Israel.

63. This speaks against the claim of many New Testament scholars that "the attempt to live from the law in and of itself merits curse" ("der Versuch, aus dem Gesetz zu leben, als solcher fluchwürdig ist")— Schmithals, *Der Römerbrief*, 371, quoted at Schreiner, "Paul's View of the Law," 125.

century.[64] For at least one Reformed commentator, the "life" set forth by the law in Romans 10:5 is eternal but not altogether exclusive of temporal life.[65] Many seventeenth-century Reformed commentators, however, simply argued and concluded that the "life" of Romans 10:5 is "eternal."[66] Some did so by rightly appealing to Matthew 19:16–18 ("what good thing shall I do in order that I may have eternal life?" 19:16 [τί ἀγαθὸν ποιήσω ἵνα σχῶ ζωὴν αἰώνιον;]; "But if you want to enter into life, keep the commandments," 19:17b [εἰ δὲ θέλεις εἰς τὴν ζωὴν εἰσελθεῖν, τήρησον τὰς ἐντολάς].[67] At least one expositor made the claim that the life of Romans 10:5 is the eternal life held out in the covenant of works.[68]

Among contemporary commentators, one may find the same division. Some contend that Paul conceives "life" here to be essentially temporal,[69] and others that this "life" is essentially eternal.[70] Is the latter an exegetically tenable position?

One fruitful avenue in answering this question is to consider the alternative scenario that Paul describes. Just as obedience brings life, the apostle maintains in quoting Leviticus 18:5 at Galatians 3:12, disobedience brings curse (κατάρα, Gal. 3:10). Similarly, Paul has argued, those who disobey the moral law are "worthy of death" (ἄξιοι θανάτου, Rom. 1:32). Paul can also claim that sin's wage is "death" (ὀψώνια τῆς ἁμαρτίας θάνατος, 6:23a). This earned death is contrasted with the eternal life (ζωὴ αἰώνιος) which is a "gift" in Christ Jesus (6:23b). For Paul, then, the counterpart of "death" is the gift of "*eternal* life" in Christ. The "death" in view must also be eternal death. Is there any evidence that Paul likewise conceives at Romans 10:5 the "life" consequent upon perfect obedience to the law to be eternal?

The answer to this question is found in Paul's argument at Romans 5:12–21. In this section of Romans, Paul maintains a running comparison and contrast between Adam (5:14) and Christ. Adam is alternatively called "one man"

64. For commentators who took either side of the question, see the listing at Poole, *Synopsis Criticorum*, 226.

65. Poole, for instance, cites one commentator who argues that the temporal life of the Mosaic law set forth the eternal life set forth by the moral law in typological fashion ("[spirituali & aeterna] vita illa quae sub vita temporali typice continebatur"), *Synopsis Criticorum*, 226.

66. See n. 46 above.

67. Andrew Willet, *A Six-folde Commentarie*, 438; Thomas Wilson, *Romanes*, 783; Westminster Annotations, *ad* Rom. 10:5; Poole, *Synopsis Criticorum*, 226.

68. So Brown [Haddington], "That which the Lord promised in the covenant of works, upon condition of perfect and personal obedience, was not an animal life in paradise, or the continuance of his estate in paradise; but everything which conduceth to make a man truly happy, is comprehended under life, and so it takes in the happiness both of soul and body: *The man that doth these things shall live thereby*"—*An Exposition of . . . Romans*, 403a.

69. Although their proposals differ substantially, see Dunn, *Romans*, 601; and Schmithals, *Der Römerbrief*, 372, for examples.

70. Byrne, *Romans*, 317; Schreiner, *Romans*, 555.

(ἑνὸς ἀνθρώπου, 5:12, 19) and "the one" (τοῦ ἑνὸς, 5:15, 16, 17). Christ is, by comparison, also termed "one man" (ἑνὸς ἀνθρώπου, 5:15) and "the one" (τοῦ ἑνὸς, 5:17, 19). The comparison is not accidental. Adam is, Paul declares, a "type of the coming one" (Ἀδὰμ ὅς ἐστιν τύπος τοῦ μέλλοντος, 5:14).

Precisely how are Adam and Christ related? How does Adam's work look ahead to Christ's work? Paul concentrates upon the mode in which their respective actions came to bear on those whom they represent. Which action or actions of Adam's are in view? Paul points to the "transgression of Adam" (παραβάσεως Ἀδὰμ, v. 14), and speaks of it in pointed and definite terms. It is "*the* sin" (τὸ παράπτωμα, v. 15; emphasis mine) or "the one sin" (τοῦ ἑνὸς παραπτώματι, vv. 15, 17, 18). Paul can only have in mind the sin of Adam in eating the fruit of the tree of knowledge of good and evil—the fruit that God had forbidden him to eat (Gen. 2:16–17; 3:6). While Adam as a reasonable creature was bound to the whole of the moral law, this positive command was subsequently issued as a test of his obedience, and it was by disobedience to this command that he fell.[71]

This one sin has in turn impacted Adam's posterity. Paul expressly precludes the possibility that Adam's posterity have become sinners through imitation of his sinful deed (5:14, ἐπὶ τοὺς μὴ ἁμαρτήσαντας ἐπὶ τῷ ὁμοιώματι τῆς παραβάσεως Ἀδὰμ). How is it then that Adam's one sin has become the possession of his ordinary posterity such that they have died (5:15; cf. 5:17), stand condemned (5:16, 18), and are constituted sinners (5:19)?[72] The answer is that Adam's one sin has been imputed, reckoned, or accounted to those with whom he is united and whom he represents, his ordinary posterity.[73] Specifically, the guilt of his sin is counted theirs such that they justly enter into a state of condemnation and death.

Paul argues that the relationship between Christ and his people operates in an analogous way with respect to their justification. He delineates the mode of Christ's representative actions coming into the possession of his people in much the same way that he has delineated the mode of Adam's representative actions coming into the possession of humanity, namely imputation. Which action or actions of Christ's are in view? Paul describes his work variously in these verses. It is the "one righteous act" (ἑνὸς δικαιώματος, 5:18), the "obe-

71. Even so, Adam's sin entailed disobedience to the whole law. See n. 74 below.

72. The NASB translation of 5:19 ("the many were made sinners") is an imprecise translation of Paul's phrase "κατασταθήσονται οἱ πολλοί." The verb καθίστημι is best rendered "constitute, appoint" (see Piper, *Counted Righteous in Christ*, 106–9; Brian Vickers, *Jesus' Blood and Righteousness* [Wheaton, IL: Crossway, 2006], 116–22). The term, in other words, does not speak to a moral change within the descendant of Adam. It refers to the change in legal or forensic status of the descendant.

73. As Hodge, *Romans*, 280, rightly observes, "the ground of this [i.e., Adamic] imputation is the union between Adam and his posterity."

dience of the one man" (τῆς παρακοῆς τοῦ ἑνὸς ἀνθρώπου, 5:19). Paul has in mind in such statements the obedience of Jesus Christ to the law culminating in his death on the cross.[74] It is Christ's "perfect obedience and full satisfaction," then, that is imputed to believers for their justification.[75]

What benefits have accrued to Christ's people by virtue of what theologians have termed the imputation of his active and passive obedience?[76] Paul stresses that believers have received "justification" (δικαίωμα, 5:16), or "a justification leading to life" (δικαίωσιν ζωῆς, 5:18).[77] They have been "constituted" or "appointed righteous" (δίκαιοι κατασταθήσονται, 5:19). This

---

74. Dunn, *Romans*, 1:283, has argued that "to see in it [ἑνὸς δικαιώματος] a reference to Christ's whole life . . . weakens both the point of contrast (Adam's "trespass") and the echo of 3:24–26 (God's righteousness displayed in Christ's death as expiatory sacrifice)." Wright, *Romans*, 529, speaks of the "one act of righteousness" in terms of "Jesus' messianic action on the cross," and argues that Christ's "merits . . . [are] almost certainly not what Paul has in mind here." He will, however, claim that the "obedience" in view encompasses Christ's "obedience to God's commission . . . to the plan to bring salvation to the world." It is not, at any rate, "obedience to the law." For a helpful response to these objections raised by Dunn and Wright, see VanDrunen, "To Obey Is Better than Sacrifice," 143–45.

Recently, J. R. Daniel Kirk, "The Sufficiency of the Cross (I): The Crucifixion as Jesus' Act of Obedience," *Scottish Bulletin of Evangelical Theology* 24 (2006): 36–64, has argued that Paul, in Rom. 5:18–19, does not have Jesus' law-keeping in view. Kirk maintains that "the Fall narrative . . . along with Paul's interpretation of it in Romans 5, points particularly to the one *peculiar* command that God gave by which the fate of the many rested in Adam's hands: the command concerning the tree of the knowledge of good and evil. A comparison with Jesus would more naturally fall to the one *peculiar* command that God gave by which the fate of the many rested in his hands: the command concerning the tree on which Jesus died" (44–45). Kirk disallows that "Paul views Adam's *one* transgression as a transgression of the whole (moral?) law. The context of Romans 5 argues rather strongly against it" (44 n. 26).

Paul, however, claims that every human being—Jew and Gentile—is obliged to keep the commands of the moral law. This obligation rests on every reasonable creature qua reasonable creature. The covenant of works (Gen. 2) did not suspend or replace this obligation. Instead, it entailed the addition of a single positive command to the moral law to which Adam had already been bound. When Paul speaks of the "one act" of Adam's disobedience, he is not referring to the disobedient eating of the fruit *simpliciter*. He is referring to Adam's disobedience as a "violation of the whole law"—Turretin, *Institutes*, 2:450, quoted at Kirk, "Sufficiency (I)." In similar fashion, when Paul speaks of Christ's work in terms of the "one righteous act," he is not speaking of Christ's death to the exclusion of his life of obedience to the law. He is speaking, rather, of Christ's life of obedience to the law as it culminates in his death on the cross. That Christ's active obedience, in particular, is in view is evident from the way in which Paul speaks of what is bestowed upon believers—it is a "gift of righteousness" (τῆς δωρεᾶς τῆς δικαιοσύνης, 5:17) whereby they shall reign in life (ἐν ζωῇ βασιλεύσουσιν, 5:17). They have not received pardon only (which could not of itself entitle to life; see John Owen, *The Doctrine of Justification*, in *The Works of John Owen*, ed. William H. Goold [Edinburgh: Banner of Truth, 1965], 5:263), but they have received by imputation that "righteousness" which entitles them to life.

75. Westminster Larger Catechism 70.

76. For defenses of Rom. 4:4–5 as a Pauline testimony to the imputation of Christ's righteousness, see now D. A. Carson, "The Vindication of Imputation: On Fields of Discourse and Semantic Fields," in *Justification: What's at Stake in the Current Debates*, ed. Mark A. Husbands and Daniel J. Treier (Downers Grove, IL: InterVarsity, 2004), esp. 55–68; and Vickers, *Jesus' Blood and Righteousness*, 71–111.

77. For the latter rendering, see Murray, *Romans*, 1:202.

verdict of justification stands in direct contrast with the condemnation that by nature was theirs in Adam. The basis of the verdict of justification, Paul says, is the "abundance of . . . the gift of righteousness" that they have "received" (τὴν περισσείαν . . . τῆς δωρεᾶς τῆς δικαιοσύνης λαμβάνοντες, 5:17). It is this "righteousness" which entitles them, Paul affirms, to "reign in life" (τὴν περισσείαν . . . τῆς δωρεᾶς τῆς δικαιοσύνης λαμβάνοντες ἐν ζωῇ βασιλεύσουσιν), a "life" that Paul describes as "eternal life" (ζωὴ αἰώνιος, 5:21; 6:23).

The relation between the consequences of Adam's work and the consequences of Christ's work for those whom they represent may be charted as follows.

Adam	Christ
Condemnation (5:16, 18)	Justification [of life] (5:17–19)
Appointed sinners (5:19)	Appointed righteous (5:19)
[Reign of] death (5:14, 17)	[Reign in] life (5:17; cf. 18)

To be sure, Paul throughout Romans 5:12–21 stresses a disparity between Adam and Christ with respect to what comes to those whom they represent. Paul twice stresses the "how much more" of Christ's work (πολλῷ μᾶλλον, 5:15, 17). Although sin may "increase" (πλεονάσῃ), yet grace "superabounds" (ὑπερεπερίσσευσεν, 5:20). The difference, as Bryan Estelle has aptly put it, is one of "degree" (5:15) and "consequence" (5:19).[78] The disparity extends neither to the mode (i.e., imputation) of the work of Adam and Christ impacting those whom each represents nor to the "life/death" issues that were set before each federal head. The fact that Christ purchased eternal "life" for his own, and that he did so for those who were eternally "dead" in Adam means that Christ's work was intended to remedy what Adam had wrought (death), and to accomplish what Adam had failed to do (life). Paul emphasizes disparity in his argument precisely in order to underscore the breathtaking achievement of what Christ has accomplished in relation to what Adam has wrought.

This means that if Adam by his disobedience brought eternal death, then his obedience would have brought eternal life. In other words, Christ's "obedience" and its consequence ("eternal life") parallel what Adam ought to have done but did not do. The life that Adam ought to have attained would have been consequent upon Adam's continuing, during the period of his testing, in obedience to all the commands set before him, whether moral or positive. This life, it stands to reason, could be aptly described "eternal."

---

78. Estelle, "The Covenant of Works in Moses and Paul," 123.

How do these findings in Romans 5:12–21 relate to the study of Romans 10:5? Moses bore witness to the "obedience—life" connection by means of the commands of the moral law, Paul argues at Romans 10:5. The basis of this connection, Paul argues at Romans 5:12–21, is the moral law as it functions within the covenant of works.

Before offering a summarization of these findings, it is important for this study of Romans 10:5–8 to note that, while Paul illustrates Adam and Christ in *parallel* relationship in the respects outlined above, he highlights significant points of *difference* between Adam and the believer. What Adam and Christ attain comes to them in the sphere of achievement: Adam has achieved death, and Christ has achieved life. This is why the language of disobedience and obedience with respect to each one figures prominently in Paul's argument. For believers, however, the benefits that Paul outlines in Romans 5:12–21 (righteousness, justification, reigning in life) come not along the avenue of their performance but along the avenue of reception.

This is evident from Romans 5:15–21 in two ways. First, Paul underscores by means of repetition the language of gratuity throughout this passage. What believers possess is a "gift" (χάρισμα, 5:15, 16; δωρεὰ, 5:15; δώρημα, 5:16), the "gift of righteousness" (τῆς δωρεᾶς τῆς δικαιοσύνης, 5:17). It comes to them by the "grace of God" (ἡ χάρις τοῦ θεοῦ, 5:15); the "grace of the one man, Jesus Christ" (ἐν χάριτι τῇ τοῦ ἑνὸς ἀνθρώπου Ἰησοῦ Χριστοῦ, 5:15). Paul speaks in this connection of the "abundance of grace" (τὴν περισσείαν τῆς χάριτος, 5:17), or simply "grace" (χάρις, 5:20, 21). On at least ten occasions in these verses, then, Paul verbally highlights the gratuity of the believer's righteousness in justification. Second, Paul explicitly says that the "abundance of the grace and of the gift of righteousness" is something that believers "receive" (λαμβάνοντες). Although commentators differ, Paul is here likely referring to the reception by faith of the imputed righteousness of justification (as he has stressed earlier in the epistle).[79] What is undisputed is that Paul stresses that this righteousness has come to believers not on the basis of their performance, but by divine grace.

To summarize these findings in Romans 5:12–21: Adam and Christ are parallel in important respects. First, they both function in a representative

---

79. Murray, *Romans*, 1:198, following Meyer, argues that the reception in view "does not refer to our believing acceptance of the free gift, but to our being made the recipients, and we are regarded as the passive beneficiaries of both the grace and the free gift in their overflowing fullness." Other commentators see the reception of faith in view at 5:17: John Brown [Wamphray], *Exposition . . . of Romans*, 189; John Brown [Edinburgh], *Analytical Exposition of the Epistle of Paul the Apostle to the Romans* (New York: Robert Carter and Brothers, 1857), 78; and (likely) Moo, *Romans*, 340.

capacity. They are, in other words, public persons.[80] Second, both operate in the sphere of performance or achievement. Third, the works of each are reckoned, accounted, or imputed to those whom they represent. Christ's work ("obedience"), then, resulted in "righteousness," "justification," and, finally, "eternal life" for his people. In parallel fashion, Adam's earlier work ("transgression") resulted in "condemnation" and "death" for his ordinary posterity. Had Adam obeyed, however, eternal "life" would have been the result. This eternal "life" would have been the result of his performance. Believers' eternal "life" is based on Christ's work and therefore is of grace to them.

Romans 10:5 through the "Lens" of Romans 5:12–21

What does this mean for one's understanding of Romans 10:5? In Romans 10:5, Paul suspends "life" upon perfect obedience to the law. He found testimony to this principle in Leviticus 18:5. In Romans 5:12–21, however, Paul demonstrates that there is pre-Mosaic precedent for this principle: this principle is rooted in the covenant of works. This is why Paul sets the "righteousness by faith" (10:6) in such stern contrast against the "righteousness which is of the law" (10:5). Romans 10:5–8 is but one link in a running chain through this letter—the setting of "works" against "faith" in the sphere of justification (3:28; 4:4–5; 9:30–32). Romans 5:12–21 provides, historically although not rhetorically, the first link in this chain.

Romans 5:12–21 informs one's reading of Romans 10:5–8 in two respects. First, at Romans 10:5, Paul repudiates the suggestion that a fallen person can attain to righteousness and life by performance or obedience to the law. He does so simply by setting forth the principle that defines what is necessary to enter into life—perfect obedience to the law. Romans 5:12–21 explains *why* this is so. Justification (and thus life) cannot come on the basis of the deeds of the ordinary descendants of Adam. They are condemned and dead and are unable to meet the standard of performance necessary to see life. Justification and life can come to them only from without, on the basis of the performance of "the one who was to come" (5:14).

Similarly, at Romans 10:6–8, Paul stresses that righteousness comes by faith. The argument that follows stresses the receptivity of faith in justification. Paul's quotations from Deuteronomy 30:12–14 illustrate this point precisely.[81]

---

80. Westminster Larger Catechism 22.
81. On the text form of Deut. 30:12–14, see Waters, "'Rejoice, O Nations, with His People,'" 219–23; Christopher D. Stanley, *Paul and the Language of Scripture*, Society for New Testament

ἡ δὲ ἐκ πίστεως δικαιοσύνη οὕτως λέγει,

Μὴ εἴπῃς ἐν τῇ καρδίᾳ σου,

    Τίς ἀναβήσεται εἰς τὸν οὐρανόν;

      τοῦτ᾽ ἔστιν Χριστὸν καταγαγεῖν·

    ἤ, Τίς καταβήσεται εἰς τὴν ἄβυσσον;

      τοῦτ᾽ ἔστιν Χριστὸν ἐκ νεκρῶν ἀναγαγεῖν.

ἀλλὰ τί λέγει;

Ἐγγύς σου τὸ ῥῆμά ἐστιν

    ἐν τῷ στόματί σου καὶ ἐν τῇ καρδίᾳ σου,

    τοῦτ᾽ ἔστιν τὸ ῥῆμα τῆς πίστεως ὃ κηρύσσομεν.

Paul's focus in these verses is "the word of faith that we preach" (τὸ ῥῆμα τῆς πίστεως ὃ κηρύσσομεν, 10:8). "Righteousness by faith" does not require climbing into the heavens or plumbing the depths.[82] That work has been done by Christ.[83] To suggest otherwise is, quite literally, unspeakable (Μὴ εἴπῃς ἐν τῇ καρδίᾳ σου, 10:6). "Righteousness by faith" comes, rather, through the preached word (cf. 10:17). That word, Paul says in his citation of Deuteronomy, is "near" the hearer (ἐγγύς, 10:8).

If one asks *why* this is so, he need go no further than Romans 5:12–21. "Righteousness," "justification," and "life" come not in the way of performance, but in the way of reception. Faith, as Paul earlier argues at Romans 4:4–5, is unlike all other human activity in this respect: in justification, faith uniquely *receives* the righteousness of Christ. At Romans 10:6–8, Paul again stresses the receptivity of faith in justification. It is the proper alternative to performance in justification (Rom. 10:5).

Studies Monograph Series 74 (Cambridge: Cambridge University Press, 1992), 128–33; and Dieter-Alex Koch, *Die Schrift als Zeuge des Evangeliums: Untersuchungen zur Verwendung und zum Verständnis der Schrift bei Paulus*, Beiträge zur historischen Theologie 69 (Tübingen: Mohr Siebeck, 1986), 129–32.

82. It is at this point that proposals understanding continuity between the "law righteousness" of 10:5 and the "righteousness by faith" of 10:6 misconstrue the text's meaning. Felix Flückiger (quoted approvingly at Fuller, *Gospel & Law*, 70) claims that "the life which Moses promises according to [Rom.] 10:5 is therefore to be enjoyed by those who believe and confess. The obedience of faith thus becomes the proper fulfilling of the law, which requires righteousness and promises life to those who do righteousness." The problem with this reading is that Paul quotes Rom. 10:6–8 precisely in order to *exclude* (in the realm of justification) the activity of which Flückiger and Fuller speak.

83. "The design of this passage is to present the simplicity and suitableness of the gospel method of salvation, which requires only faith and confession, in opposition to the strict demands of the law, which it is as impossible for us to satisfy as it is to scale the heavens" (Hodge, *Romans*, 535). Compare William Sanday and Arthur Headlam, *A Critical and Exegetical Commentary on the Epistle to the Romans*, 2nd ed., International Critical Commentary (New York: Charles Scribner's Sons, 1896), 287; Moo, *Romans*, 655–56; Heil, "Christ, the Termination of the Law," 497.

Once Again, ΤΕΛΟΣ ΝΟΜΟΥ

These conclusions have bearing on another, related exegetical question. What does Paul say when he affirms at Romans 10:4 that Christ is "the end of the law unto righteousness for everyone who believes" (τέλος νόμου . . . εἰς δικαιοσύνην παντὶ τῷ πιστεύοντι)? To answer this question, one must define the word τέλος at 10:4. Scholars have for centuries debated the meaning of the term τέλος.[84] Does it mean "termination"?[85] Does it mean "goal"?[86] Does it combine these two senses?[87] The complexity of the debate is evident from Cranfield's comment that, while he adopts the meaning "goal," "it is tempting to settle for the view that both meanings were intended."[88]

This question is not without implications for one's exegesis of Romans 10:5–8. Arguing that Paul conceives Christ as the goal or fulfilment of the law at Romans 10:4, some scholars proceed to conclude that there is a presumption of compatibility between the two righteousnesses of 10:5–6.[89] In other words, since "goal" speaks to a fundamental compatibility between "Christ" and the "law," Paul's reflections in the following verses must surely

84. For helpful and brief taxonomies of the options circulating in the contemporary secondary literature, see George Howard, "Christ the End of the Law," 332; and, more recently, Thomas Schreiner, "Paul's View of the Law," 113–24; and Moo, *Romans*, 638. For a particularly helpful survey of the German literature, see Wilckens, *Der Brief an die Römer*, 2:222–24. For the discussion in the seventeenth century, see Poole, *Synopsis Criticorum*, 225–26 (Poole gives four major positions in the exegetical discussion contemporary to him). The most comprehensive work, however, is Badenas, *Christ the End of the Law*.

85. Brown (Edinburgh), *Romans*, 365; Hodge, *Romans*, 527–29; Frederic Godet, *Commentary on the Epistle to the Romans* (1883; Grand Rapids: Zondervan, 1956), 376; Meyer, *Romans*, 405; R. C. H. Lenski, *The Interpretation of St. Paul's Epistle to the Romans* (Columbus: Wartburg, 1945), 645; Murray, *Romans*, 2:49; Heinlich Schlier, *Der Römerbrief*, Herders theologiescher Kommentar zum Neuen Testament 6 (Freiburg/Basel/Vienna: Herder, 1979), 311; Leon Morris, *The Epistle to the Romans* (Grand Rapids: Eerdmans, 1988), 381; Dunn, *Romans*, 2:589–90; Moo, *Romans*, 638–42; Lukas Kundert, "Christus als Inkorporation der Tora: Röm 10, 4 vor dem Hintergrund einer erstaunlichen rabbinischen Argumentation," *Theologische Zeitschrift* 55 (1999): 76–89; Heil, "Christ, the Termination of the Law," 484–98. For other twentieth-century proponents of this view, see Cranfield, *Romans*, 518; and Fitzmyer, *Romans*, 584.

86. John Calvin, *Commentaries on the Epistle of Paul to the Romans* (Grand Rapids: Baker, 1996), 383–85; Burgess, *Vindiciae Legis*, 267–75; Owen, *Works* 5:342 (on the latter two of whom, see Badenas, *Christ the End of the Law*, 23); Badenas, *Christ the End of the Law*, esp. 38–80; Fitzmyer, *Romans*, 584; Wright, *Romans*, 655–57. For other twentieth-century proponents of this view, see Fitzmyer, *Romans*, 584.

87. Howard cites Leenhardt as an example of this view, "Christ the End of the Law," 332. See also the authors referenced at Dunn, *Romans*, 2:589. Note also Michel Quesnel, "La figure de Moïse en Romains 9–11," *New Testament Studies* 49 (2003): 328: "Les deux lectures ("arrêt, cessation"; "but, objectif") ne sont pas exclusives l'une de l'autre, le texte jouant sans doute sur l'un et l'autre sens du terme."

88. Cranfield, *Romans*, 519. Compare the comments of Shedd, *Commentary on Romans*, 313.

89. See Badenas, *Christ the End of the Law*, 118; Wright, *Romans*, 660.

follow suit. Other scholars argue that the word τέλος means, in context, "termination." Such scholars often proceed to argue that the two righteous-nesses of 10:5–6 are related antithetically.[90] Käsemann too rigidly affirms the connection between one's position on the meaning of the word τέλος and one's position on the relationship of the "righteousnesses" of 10:5–8.[91] He is surely correct, however, to remind the reader that these two questions are related.

So far as the definition of the word τέλος is concerned, formidable lexical arguments have been mounted for both the "termination" and the "ful-filment" positions.[92] Nevertheless, scholars have not achieved consensus. Sometimes overshadowed by the debate surrounding the meaning of the word τέλος is the equally important question of the meaning of the word νόμου. John Brown (Edinburgh) frames the question nicely:

> "The law" may be viewed as to its substance—the duties it enjoins; or as to its form—a covenant or method of justification, or a rule of conduct: it may mean law generally, or the Mosaic Law; and, supposing it to mean the latter, it may have especial reference either to its moral or its ceremonial stat-utes—either to it as an exhibition of duty to the Israelites, or as a temporary economy established for some particular purposes in the great scheme of the Divine moral government of mankind.[93]

Both parts of the phrase τέλος νόμου, then, pose significant challenges to the exegete. As Dunn rightly notes, this question cannot be resolved with-out sufficient attention to the context of the passage.[94] In the spirit of this observation, a question may be posed. Do the above conclusions concerning Romans 10:5–8 contribute to the resolution of this issue? In order to answer this question, one must first observe that the claim of Romans 10:4 is tied not only to the proposition that precedes it, but also to the proposition that follows it. In Romans 10:4 and 10:5, Paul inserts the postpositive particle γάρ. Consequently, as commentators frequently observe, Romans 10:4 must be explanatory of Romans 10:3, and Romans 10:5–8 must be explanatory

90. Although both present different readings of Rom. 10:4–8 in other respects, see the agree-ment of Lenski, *Romans*, 645–54; and Dunn, *Romans*, 589–91, 598, 602, 613.

91. See Käsemann, *Romans*, 284. John Calvin is a good example of one who maintains a non-termination understanding of Rom. 10:4 (he translates the word *complementum* [completion]), but contends that the two "righteousnesses" of Rom. 10:5–8 are antithetical (*Romans*, 383, 386).

92. For "termination," see Gerhard Delling, τέλος, in *Theological Dictionary of the New Testament* 10:49–87, esp. 59–60; for "fulfilment," see Badenas, *Christ the End of the Law*, esp. 81–151. For critical responses to Badenas's work, see Dunn, *Romans*, 589–90; Schreiner, "Paul's View of the Law," 117–20.

93. Brown (Edinburgh), *Romans*, 364.

94. Dunn, *Romans*, 589.

of Romans 10:4.[95] The interpretation of Romans 10:4, then, must be sensitive to these two horizons.

Paul does not affirm that Christ is τέλος νόμου in an absolute sense. He inserts two important qualifications. Christ is "the end of the law *unto righteousness for everyone who believes*" (τέλος νόμου <u>εἰς δικαιοσύνην παντὶ τῷ πιστεύοντι</u>, emphasis mine). The word δικαιοσύνην, of course, appears both in 10:3 (where Paul has contrasted the θεοῦ δικαιοσύνη with τὴν ἰδίαν [δικαιοσύνην]), and in 10:5–8 (where Paul will contrast "law righteousness" with "righteousness by faith"). The postpositive particles γὰρ at 10:4 and 10:5 only serve to reinforce this connection. The "righteousness" unto which Christ is τέλος νόμου, furthermore, is not for all human beings. It is only for a certain subset of persons—"everyone who believes" (παντὶ τῷ πιστεύοντι). Paul proceeds to take up the "righteousness which is by faith" (ἡ . . . ἐκ πίστεως δικαιοσύνη) at Romans 10:6. Undoubtedly, then, when Paul says that Christ is τέλος νόμου with a view "for righteousness to everyone who believes" (εἰς δικαιοσύνην παντὶ τῷ πιστεύοντι), he has in mind the imputed righteousness of Jesus Christ, received by faith alone.[96]

This context, moreover, defines the meaning of the word νόμου at Romans 10:4. Paul's concern for the law here is not as it establishes boundary markers between Jew and Gentile.[97] Nor is his concern for the law here as an economy or covenantal administration.[98] Paul's concern for the law, as Romans 10:5 indicates, is the commandments and precepts of the moral law.[99]

What does this mean for a definition of the word τέλος? While it is a thoroughly Pauline teaching that Christ is the goal of the law, or the one to whom the law points (whether considered as a covenantal administration or as commandments and precepts), that is not what Paul is claiming here. He is claiming that Christ is the "termination" of the law to the believer. Paul, however, is not affirming that the believer is thereby altogether free from the commandments and precepts of the law. Paul is no antinomian. The law as precept continues to bind believers. He is, however, claiming that the believer is free from the law's commandments *as they bring life to the one*

---

95. Moo, *Romans*, 636, 645. On the latter in particular, see Schreiner, "Paul's View of the Law," 123, and the literature cited at 123 n. 44.

96. For these two points, note the words of John Owen, *Works* 5:342: "The apostle sufficiently determineth his intention, in affirming not absolutely that he is the end of the law, but he is so εἰς δικαιοσύνην, 'for righteousness,' unto every one that believeth. The matter in question is a righteousness unto justification. And this is acknowledged to be the righteousness which the law requires. God looks for no righteousness from us but what is prescribed in the law."

97. *Pace* Dunn, *Romans*, 598.

98. As it is, for instance, in Gal. 3:15–29. For a proponent who sees this view taught at Rom. 10:4–8, see Westerholm, *Israel's Law and the Church's Faith*, 130.

99. Speaking on this verse, Owen, *Works* 5:342, says, "The law is nothing but the rule of righteousness, God's prescription of a righteousness, and all the duties of it, unto us."

who perfectly performs them and condemnation to the one who fails to meet this standard. He is, in other words, freed from the law as it functions within the covenant of works.[100] He no longer claims a righteousness that may be called "his own" (ἰδίαν, 10:3) or that is rooted in his own performance (ὁ ποιήσας αὐτὰ ἄνθρωπος, 10:5). He lays hold of a righteousness that is "of God" (τοῦ θεοῦ, 10:3) and "by faith" (ἐκ πίστεως, 10:6). He is freed from the law as a covenant of works because the righteousness of Jesus Christ has been imputed to him and received by faith alone.

Conclusion

This study of Romans 10:5 began with the observation that the Westminster divines cited this very text (among other texts) in support of its confessional statements concerning the covenant of works. This study has not only confirmed the wisdom of the Assembly in citing this text in reference to that doctrine, but it has also shown how defining "law" at Romans 10:5 as the decrees and commandments of the moral law operating within the covenant of works explains otherwise knotty questions in the passage. How is it that Paul can set one passage of Scripture (Leviticus) against another passage of Scripture (Deuteronomy)? How is it that Paul can find testimony to two methods of justification within the Pentateuch? What does Paul mean when he says that Christ is the "end of the law"? It is when one sees that Paul is engaging the moral law's precepts as they function within the covenant of works that he can understand that Paul affirms the whole Scripture to bear univocal witness to Jesus Christ and his "righteousness" for sinners.

What implications does this passage have for one's understanding of the relationship between the Mosaic covenant and the covenant of works? It is difficult to improve upon the comments of Patrick Fairbairn in relation to this very question.

> It is not difficult to understand how St. Paul should have singled out the brief passage under examination [i.e., Lev. 18:5] as being, when looked at merely by itself, descriptive of the righteousness which is won by obedience to precepts of law, while yet it was not meant that Israel were expected to attain to such righteousness, or were, in the strict and absolute sense, dependent on

---

100. Westminster Larger Catechism 97: "Q. What special use is there of the moral law to the regenerate? A. Although they that are regenerate, and believe in Christ, be delivered from the moral law as a covenant of works, so as thereby they are neither justified nor condemned . . ." "The law is abolished by Christ, not as a rule of life, but as a covenant prescribing the condition of life"— Hodge, *Romans*, 529.

the attainment of it for life and blessing. It set before them the ideal which they should earnestly endeavour to realize—which also to a certain extent they must realize as partakers, if only in an incipient state, of the Divine life; but not unless they were minded (as the unbelieving Jews of the apostle's day certainly were) to stand simply upon the ground of law, and be in no respect debtors of grace, was a complete and faultless doing to form the condition of receiving the promised heritage of life. In this case it assuredly was. The words must then be pressed in the full rigor and extent of their requirement; for life could only be ministered and maintained on a legal basis, if the condition of perfect conformity to law had been made good. That Moses, however, no more than the apostle, intended to assert for Israel such a strictly legal basis as the condition of life, is evident, not only from the connection in which that particular declaration stands, but also from other parts of his writings, in which the evangelical element comes into view, in his words to the covenant people. To one of these, the apostle now turns (vers. 6–9) for a proof of the righteousness of faith.[101]

Paul has, by the very fact of quoting both Leviticus 18:5 and Deuteronomy 30:12–14 in support of the two "righteousnesses" in justification, avoided the conclusion that the Mosaic covenant is not an administration of the covenant of grace. His fundamental point at Romans 10:5, however, must not be lost. The moral law is not unique to the Mosaic administration. It functioned within the covenant of works such that the "one who does these things shall live by them" (10:5).

Two matters have surfaced from this study of Paul's argument in Romans 10:5. First, Paul sustains his great concern for justification by faith alone in this epistle. E. Elizabeth Johnson correctly observes that postwar Pauline scholars have given concerted attention to the apostle's argument at Romans 9–11, not least to such questions as the place of Israel in God's redemptive plan and the place of Christianity in an increasingly pluralistic age.[102] Paul's claims at Romans 9:30–10:8, however, serve as a reminder that the apostle, far from dispatching with justification after Romans 5:21, sustains his interest in soteriology (generally) and justification (specifically) well through the letter.

Second, Paul articulates justification within a bicovenantal framework. Romans 10:4–8, then, does not only play a central role in the argument of the epistle to the Romans, but also offers a window into the very structure

---

101. Fairbairn, *The Revelation of Law in Scripture*, 492.
102. E. Elizabeth Johnson, "Romans 9–11: The Faithfulness and Impartiality of God," in *Pauline Theology*, vol. 3: *Romans*, ed. David M. Hay and E. Elizabeth Johnson (Minneapolis: Fortress, 1995), 211–12.

of redemptive history. Some within the Reformed churches are gravitating toward monocovenantalism (often not without grave consequences for their doctrine of justification).[103] To those interested in engaging that position biblically, the bicovenantalism of Romans 10:4–8 surely ought to play a central role in that engagement. At stake is the integrity of nothing less than the "word of faith which we preach" (10:8, τὸ ῥῆμα τῆς πίστεως ὃ κηρύσσομεν).

103. This is evident from the writings of individuals who have associated themselves with what is being called "the Federal Vision." For documentation and analysis of the monocovenantal sympathies of Federal Vision proponents, see Guy Prentiss Waters, *The Federal Vision and Covenant Theology: A Comparative Analysis* (Phillipsburg, NJ: P&R, 2006), 30–58. For the implications that this has had on their doctrine of justification, see the discussion at Waters, *Federal Vision*, 59–95.

8

ABRAHAM AND SINAI CONTRASTED IN GALATIANS 3:6–14

T. DAVID GORDON

In Galatians 3:6–14, Paul began a discussion of the differences between two covenant-administrations, one made with Abraham and another made with the Israelites at Sinai 430 years later.[1] Were the occasion of the letter different, he might very well have discussed their similarities, and it is no part of my thesis to deny that there are similarities between them, or to deny that Paul was aware of them. That is, one would not develop a full biblical theology of these two covenant-administrations merely by studying Galatians 3 and 4. Nonetheless, Galatians 3 (and 4) would make their own distinctive contribution to that discussion.

In substance, this essay has grown out of twenty years of teaching (and occasionally writing about) Galatians, at both the seminary and the college levels. Early in that study, I became aware of how utterly different my understanding of biblical covenants was from that of the late John Murray of Westminster Seminary, and this essay intends, in large measure, to function as a counterargument to Murray. I will argue that Paul enumerates

---

1. "This is what I mean: the law, which came 430 years afterward, does not annul a covenant previously ratified by God, so as to make the promise void" (Gal. 3:17).

five differences between the Abrahamic covenant and the Sinai covenant in Galatians 3. These five differences (some more than others) are fatal to Murray's thesis that:

> What needs to be emphasized now is that the Mosaic covenant in respect of the condition of obedience is not in a different category from the Abrahamic. It is too frequently assumed that the conditions prescribed in connection with the Mosaic covenant place the Mosaic dispensation in a totally different category as respects grace, on the one hand, and demand or obligation, on the other. In reality there is nothing that is principally different in the necessity of keeping the covenant and of obedience to God's voice, which proceeds from the Mosaic covenant, from that which is involved in the keeping required in the Abrahamic.[2]

Paul's Basic Argument in Galatians

Paul corrected the Galatians, who were requiring that members of the new covenant community identify themselves ceremonially as members of the Sinai covenant community. Paul effected this correction by placing the Sinai covenant in its own covenant-historical context, as a partial fulfilment of the Abrahamic covenant that would eventually yield to its entire fulfilment in the new covenant. To do so, he established the historical priority of the Abrahamic covenant over the Sinai, and he indicated several of the differences between those covenants, in which cases the new covenant is similar to the Abrahamic covenant and dissimilar to the Sinai covenant.

Paul understood the covenant with Abraham to include essentially three promises: that God would give Abraham numerous descendants ("seed"), that God would give Abraham (and his seed) the land of Canaan, and that God would bless all the nations of the world through Abraham and his seed. Plainly enough, the Israelites became numerous during their four hundred years in Egypt, and equally plainly, through Joshua and the judges, they inherited the land of Canaan. But they did not become the means by which all the nations/Gentiles were blessed until the calling of Paul. Arguably, as long as the Sinai covenant distinguished Jew from Gentile, the seed of Abraham could not become a blessing to all nations. That is, the terms of the Sinai administration itself, being made with one peculiar nation and excluding others through dietary, ceremonial, and other laws, prevented the entire fulfilment of the Abrahamic promise, even while it preserved memory

---

2. John Murray, *The Covenant of Grace: A Biblico-Theological Study* (London: Tyndale, 1954), 22.

of that promise and even while it preserved the integrity of Abraham's "seed" by prohibiting intermarriage with Gentiles.

Paul thus understood the Sinai covenant to be both subservient to the purpose of the earlier Abrahamic covenant (by preserving the integrity of Abraham's "seed" and the promises made thereto) and an obstacle to the fulfilment of that covenant. Ironically, Sinai was necessary (to preserve the "seed" and the promise) but Sinai was also a barrier (by excluding Gentiles, they could not be blessed). For Paul, this means that the Sinai administration must have been temporary, instituted as a vehicle to carry both the Abrahamic promise and the Abrahamic "seed" until that moment when the "Seed" would come through whom the promise would be fulfilled and the nations would be blessed (3:19).[3] Paul identified the "Seed" as Christ (3:16), and argued that the nations are indeed now being blessed by that Seed of Abraham, and that therefore the temporary covenant made only with Abraham's descendants must become obsolete and disappear, because its purpose to guard and protect the Abrahamic seed until the "Seed" would come (ἄχρις οὗ ἔλθῃ τὸ σπέρμα ᾧ ἐπήγγελται, 3:19) has been fulfilled.

Paul therefore discussed the entire matter in covenant-historical terms. He illuminated the realities of the new covenant by illuminating the realities of the Abrahamic and Sinai covenants respectively.[4] He perceived the Sinai covenant as guiding and guarding the people of God in the time of histori-

---

3. I intentionally distinguish "seed" from "Seed," because the original promise in the original Hebrew employed a collective noun, and might have been understood as a reference to Abraham's descendants collectively considered. The Septuagint, however, had no similar Greek collective noun, and therefore had to choose between translating the Hebrew as either dative plural (τοῖς σπέρμασιν) or dative singular (τῷ σπέρματι). They chose the latter, and Paul approves that decision in Galatians 3:16, expressly declaring there that the promise was not given to his collective seed but to his singular seed, which Paul there identifies as Christ. So, when I employ "seed" in the lower case, I am referring to the original, more ambiguous Hebrew, and when I employ "Seed" in the upper case, I am referring to Paul's understanding of the theologically correct interpretation of the Septuagint.

4. In some sense, then, my arguments here deliberately and self-consciously bypass all of the discussions over the last twenty-five years about the nature of Palestinian Judaism in the first century. Valid enough as a historical question in its own right, the question is irrelevant to interpreting Galatians, for two reasons. First, Paul is addressing the *Christian* assemblies at Galatia, not Jewish *synagogues* at Galatia. Second, and more importantly, Paul's reasoning in Galatians is covenant-historical. Paul distinguishes the Abrahamic covenant from the Sinai covenant as each was instituted by God, not as either covenant was or was not later perverted either by Jews or by Christians. When he says *nomos*, he most emphatically does not mean some first-century aberration of that covenant, whether Jewish or Christian. He means the Sinai covenant as it was instituted by God through the hand of Moses. The so-called New Perspective on Paul, whether as originally described by James D. G. Dunn in his article by that title, or as it is currently understood today, as a revision of Paul's understanding of justification in the works of scholars such as N. T. Wright, is irrelevant to my thesis. Paul's objections to *nomos*, throughout this letter, are not due to any misunderstanding of it. His objection is to the members of one covenant (the new covenant) implicitly or explicitly identifying themselves by the rites of another covenant (the Sinai covenant). Paul objects to Christians observing the Sinai covenant per se; he does not object to their *mis*-observing it.

cal minority, before and until the "fullness of time" came (Gal. 4:4, but cf. the other indications of the same reality at 3:23–26 and at 4:8–11). After that, he argued, its guardianship was not only no longer needed, but rather a positive hindrance to the realities of the fullness of times, including the reconciliation of all creation to its Creator, and therefore also the reconciliation of Jew and Gentile to one another through Abraham's Seed. If we could employ an anachronism in the history of doctrine, one might argue that Paul perceived the new covenant realities in Christ as bringing the final third of the Abrahamic promise to fruition; and he perceived the Sinai covenant as a "parenthesis" between the promise pledged to Abraham and the promise fulfilled in Christ. Part of how he achieved this was to indicate five ways in which the new covenant's realities are like the Abrahamic realities, but unlike the Sinai realities. To these five differences we now turn.

First Difference: The Abrahamic Covenant Includes the Nations/ Gentiles; the Sinai Covenant Excludes Them

The concern of the entire letter is, in many ways, the concern of Paul's entire ministry, since Paul was the apostle to the Gentiles (Gal. 1:16; 2:2, 7–9). Paul perceived his ministry as the initial means by which God was fulfilling the third part of his promise to Abraham. None in his day would have disputed the fact that the Sinai covenant was made exclusively with the descendants of Abraham, but perhaps some, if not many, in his day failed to perceive that such a one-nation covenant necessarily disrupted and prevented the promise to bless the nations through Abraham's seed. Paul therefore attempted to resurrect memory of the original Abrahamic promise: "And the Scripture, foreseeing that God would justify the Gentiles by faith, preached the gospel beforehand to Abraham, saying, 'In you shall all the nations be blessed'" (Gal. 3:8). But if the nations are still being treated as though they were *out* of covenant with God, then the pledge to Abraham has not been fulfilled. For Paul, the reason the church could not require circumcision (or the dietary laws or the Jewish calendar) was that they were part of a covenant-administration that excluded the nations.[5] And Paul focused on these three aspects of the Sinai administration not merely because they were parts of a nations-excluding covenant, but more so because they were those particular aspects of that covenant that marked the Jews as being distinct from the nations. But the original Abrahamic covenant comprehended the nations within its blessings, and envisioned

---

5. Although circumcision was originally given to Abraham as part of that covenant-administration, even there it was part of the "narrowing" of the covenant people to Abraham and his descendants, a distinction not made in the Edenic covenant or the postdiluvian covenant with Noah.

the various nations of the earth as one day finding blessedness through the
seed/Seed of Abraham.

Second Difference: The Abrahamic Covenant Blesses; the Sinai Covenant Curses

Some people cannot hear what Paul says in Galatians 3:6–14 because they
cannot imagine that he would say what he has said. They cannot imagine
that the Sinai covenant cursed, and some have difficulty imagining that the
Abrahamic did not in some senses curse. I am more than content to say that
Paul's treatment of each covenant is abbreviated here, and that he might
have said more about each of them. Nonetheless, the language he employs
to contrast them on this point must be permitted to speak.

Abrahamic	Sinai
[8]"In you shall all the nations be *blessed*."	[10]For all who rely on works of the law are under a *curse*; for it is written, "*Cursed* be everyone who does not abide by all things written in the Book of the Law, and do them."
[9]So then, those who are of faith are *blessed* along with Abraham, the man of faith.	
[14]so that in Christ Jesus the *blessing* of Abraham might come to the Gentiles.	[13]Christ redeemed us from the *curse* of the law by becoming a *curse* for us—for it is written, "*Cursed* is everyone who is hanged on a tree"—

A minor translation observation must be made at this point. Some English
translations are entirely gratuitous (and entirely wrong) to add the words
"rely on" here in verse 10.[6] The text says nothing about "relying on" the law
here, and note that the expression is semantically identical to that in verse 9,
where it is merely translated "who are *of faith*," not "who *rely on faith*."[7]
That is, the substantive use of the preposition *ek* to indicate characterization (those who are characterized by faith, or those who are characterized
by the works of the law) should either be translated by a simple ambiguous
English "of faith" and "of works of the law," or it should be translated by
a fuller, more periphrastic expression such as "characterized by faith" and
"characterized by works of the law." What is misleading and erroneous to
the point of irresponsibility is to translate *differently* in such a manifestly
parallel place. The hapless English reader does not perceive the Pauline parallel between the two expressions ("of faith" and "of works of the law"), and

6. Not all English translations commit this error. The Authorized Version competently translates: "For as many as are of the works of the law are under the curse," and the NKJV follows
this translation.
7. Though Paul does talk this way at Romans 2:17: "But if you call yourself a Jew and rely
on the law (ἐπαναπαύῃ νόμῳ) and boast in God."

worse, perceives the second in a pejorative manner because of the utterly gratuitous "rely on."[8]

This translation error, erroneous enough in its own right, also flies in the face of the text. Note that Paul does not condemn any alleged abuse of the Sinai covenant here. It is not those who abuse ("rely on") the law who are under a curse; it is those who are covenantally under the law that are under its threatening curse-sanction. Twice here Paul quotes the law's own words, indicating that the curse-sanction was an inherent part of the administration itself, long before anyone allegedly perverted or distorted it.[9] It was not, that is, some later false reliance on the law that cursed; it was disobedience to its statutes and ordinances in the first generation (and in all subsequent generations) that cursed.[10]

Again, one could (if one so desired) fault Paul for not mentioning other realities at Sinai, because in addition to the six tribes articulating the conditional curses from Mount Ebal there were six tribes articulating conditional blessings from Mount Gerizim (Deut. 27). But before faulting Paul we should first hear him; in some sense, he is saying that the Abrahamic covenant blessed and the Sinai covenant cursed. I have no interest in faulting Paul here, because I think his point is well taken: The Abrahamic covenant, taken as a whole, is largely promissory (though it does require circumcision): it pledges that an aging couple will have descendants more numerous than the sand of the sea; it promises that they will inherit a marvelous, arable land; and it promises that one day all the nations of the earth will be blessed by one of their descendants. When Sinai comes along, the point is not that there are not conditional blessings associated with it; the point is that what is new and distinctive is the threat of curse-sanctions, threats that are entirely absent from the Abrahamic administration. What is "new" or distinctive about Sinai is not the (conditional) blessing; what is new or distinctive is the conditional cursing. And Paul, knowing (as any first-century Jew would have known) Israel's actual history under those conditions, knew perfectly well that the prophets were right for pronouncing judgment on a people who rather con-

---

8. Indeed, such a gratuitous error is difficult to account for apart from sheer theological prejudice, a sheer unwillingness to grant that Paul is here speaking of the covenant-administration given at Sinai itself, not some later, alleged Jewish perversion thereof.

9. He cites Deut. 27:26 in 3:10, and Deut. 21:23 in 3:13.

10. In saying this, I am here rendering no opinion on the historical question of the nature of first-century Palestinian Judaism. I am merely saying that, in the rhetoric of Paul's argumentation, he is here in Galatians 3 discussing the nature of the Sinai covenant itself, as instituted through Moses. Paul is not addressing what may or may not have happened to that covenant in his generation. The "law" that Paul discusses in Galatians 3 is the one that was given "430 years after" the promise, and his citations of the Deuteronomy passages prove that what he is discussing is the curse-sanctions of the covenant itself.

sistently failed to remain obedient to their covenant duties. So, even though in theory Sinai proffered either blessing or cursing, in plain historical fact it rarely brought anything but cursing. The Israelites were constantly harassed by the indigenous nations during the period of conquest; their first monarch was removed from office in disobedience and shame; their second monarch was not permitted to build the house of God because he was a violent (and adulterous) man; their third could not even teach his own sons to heed the counsel of their elders (though his Proverbs constantly encouraged such); after which the Israelites were divided into two nations, weakened, and increasingly battered by (and once captured by) their enemies.

Third Difference: The Abrahamic Covenant Is Characterized by Faith; the Sinai Covenant Is Characterized by Works of the Law

Analogous to the previous difference, this difference is perfectly apparent in the text, if one is willing to allow Paul to speak for himself rather than for us. We might not have said this, we might not have put the matter this way, and we might be peeved with Paul for having put the matter as he did. But once all of this ill-will toward the apostle is vented, we still have his words to deal with, and we cannot safely deny what he said simply because we wish he had not said it.

Note how frequently in Galatians 3:6–14 Paul contrasts belief/faith on the one hand, with works/doing/law on the other hand. The contrasts are both frequent and sustained: There are five references to faith/belief on the Abrahamic side, and five references to doing, abiding, works, and "not faith" on the Sinai side.

Abrahamic

6. . . just as Abraham "*believed* God, and it was counted to him as righteousness"? 7Know then that it is those of *faith* who are the sons of Abraham. 8And the Scripture, foreseeing that God would justify the Gentiles by *faith*, preached the gospel beforehand to Abraham, saying, "In you shall all the nations be blessed." 9So then, those who are of *faith* are blessed along with Abraham, the man of *faith*.

Sinai

10For all who rely on *works* of the law are under a curse; for it is written, "Cursed be everyone who does not *abide by* all things written in the Book of the Law, and *do* them." 11Now it is evident that no one is justified before God by the law, for "The righteous shall live by faith." 12But the law is *not of faith*, rather "The one who *does* them shall live by them."

Again, if we were to write our own biblical theologies, we might do differently than Paul. We might, for instance, protest that Abraham's covenant had conditions also, such as circumcision, and we surely might wish to argue that Israel at Sinai was required not only to do but also to believe. This is all well and good, but it is all pettifogging. Yes, Abraham was required to circumcise Isaac, but had God not already fulfilled his promise to give Abraham descendants, there would have been no Isaac to circumcise. So Abraham's circumcision of Isaac was not a condition of getting Isaac; God had already fulfilled the pledge to give Abraham a seed before requiring that this seed be circumcised. At Sinai, however, the matter is entirely different: the conditional blessings depend upon Israel's obedience. If anyone doubts this, just ask the question: How many long years of blessedness did Moses and Aaron enjoy in the so-called "promised land"? Zero. And why was this so? Because the people disobeyed. While the land was eventually given to the Israelites, the terms of the Sinai covenant delayed their inheritance by forty years, and diminished the actual blessedness of the land during the generations of their tenure there. And even the inheritance of the land was due not to the stipulations of Sinai, but due to the promises made to the patriarchs, as Moses interceded for the Israelites in those terms: "Remember Abraham, Isaac, and Israel, your servants, to whom you swore by your own self, and said to them, 'I will multiply your offspring as the stars of heaven, and all this land that I have promised I will give to your offspring, and they shall inherit it forever.' And the LORD relented from the disaster that he had spoken of bringing on his people" (Ex. 32:13–14).

Some would have been much happier if Paul had not said "But the law is not of faith," but again, there must be some truth in his statement. Further, note that what follows this is a quotation from the Mosaic institution of the covenant itself, not some later abuse thereof: "But the law is *not of faith*, rather 'The one who *does* them shall live by them,'" citing Leviticus 18:5. Paul explains what he means by saying the law is not of faith by reference not to some first-century Jewish sect or misunderstanding, but by reference to the institution of that covenant-administration through the mediatorship of Moses. To understand Paul, we must recognize that he was speaking of these covenant-administrations in terms of their distinctives. In terms of its distinctives, contrasted with the Abrahamic administration, Paul could truthfully say that what was new and distinctive about Sinai is not faith, which was already taught in the Abrahamic administration. What was new and distinctive is a substantial body of legislation that required the obedience of the Israelites. If Abraham had one law (circumcise the males), Moses had hundreds of laws. What was therefore new and distinctive, compared to the earlier covenant, was this large body of legislation that required *doing*, not believing.[11]

---

11. Space does not permit me to reassert here what I have argued elsewhere regarding Romans 9:32. Paul does not, in Romans 9:32, say that Jews pursued the law the wrong way (by works). The only way for one to pursue the Sinai covenant is by works; the terms of that covenant do not

Fourth Difference: The Abrahamic Covenant Justifies; the Sinai Covenant Does Not

It should not be surprising by now to note this fourth contrast: The Abrahamic covenant is a justifying covenant; the Sinai covenant is not.

Abraham	Sinai
[6]. . . just as Abraham "believed God, and it was counted to him as *righteousness*"? [7]Know then that it is those of faith who are the sons of Abraham. [8]And the Scripture, foreseeing that God would *justify* the Gentiles by faith, preached the gospel beforehand to Abraham, saying, "In you shall all the nations be blessed."	[11]Now it is evident that *no one is justified* before God by the law, for "The righteous shall live by faith." [12]But the law is not of faith, rather "The one who does them shall live by them."

Paul argues here two things about the Sinai covenant: first, that no one is justified before God by the law,[12] and second, that the reason for this is that the law is not characterized by justifying faith, but rather by works. Since the Sinai covenant requires *doing*, and is not characterized by faith, it justifies no sinners. The Abrahamic covenant, by contrast, is promissory, requiring nothing of Abraham or Sarah as a condition of the promise being kept by God; its recipients merely believe in the trustworthiness of the promising God. In so believing they are justified.

Paul does not say here what many people fear he is saying. He does not say that none of the Israelites were justified. He says nothing about that matter, because it does not concern him in terms of the rhetorical needs of his situation. However, insofar as those Israelites were justified, it was because of the justification by faith that was already theirs through the Abrahamic covenant-administration; but the Sinai covenant, in terms of its own distinctive administration, did not justify anyone: "Now it is evident that no one is justified before God by the law." Surely, many Israelites, under the law, were justified by faith; but they were not justified before God "*by* the law"; rather, they were justified before God by Abrahamic faith.

Note also that Paul asserts this as an incontrovertible fact ("Now it is evident," δὲ ἐν), which would be utterly fatal, rhetorically, if he imagined any sect or party within Judaism or Christianity of the first century would have

---

say "*Believe* this and you will live," but "*Do* this and you will live." Many English translations supply the ellipsis in Romans 9:32 wrongly, asserting "Because they did not *pursue* it through faith" (RSV). "Pursue" is not in the original text, and the text is better understood if the copula supplies the ellipsis: "Because it (the Sinai covenant) *is* not of faith (not characterized by faith), but as by works." That is, Romans 9:32 says exactly what Galatians 3:12 says, except that the copula is expressed in Gal. 3:12, and only inferred at Romans 9:32. See T. David Gordon, "Why Israel Did Not Obtain Torah-Righteousness: A Translation Note on Romans 9:32," *Westminster Theological Journal* 54 (1992): 163–66.

12. Which he had already asserted at Galatians 2:16.

disputed it. Such rhetorical statements are employed to settle one dispute by appealing to an undisputed matter and building on it.[13] If the undisputed matter were, in fact, disputed, the entire rhetorical power of the statement would vanish. Thus, it is one thing for Paul to render his opinion that no one is justified before God by the law; but it is another entirely when he adds the rhetorical δὲ ἐν.

Fifth Difference: The Abrahamic Covenant Is Referred to as "Promise"; the Sinai Covenant Is Referred to as "Law"

Few contributions to Pauline studies in the last several decades are more important than the now widely recognized lexical reality that for Paul, ὁ νόμος means "the Sinai covenant" far more consistently than it means anything else. As Douglas Moo has said: "What is vital for any accurate understanding of Paul's doctrine of law is to realize that Paul uses *nomos* most often and most basically of the Mosaic law."[14] That is, Paul uses the term very differently than the term later came to be used in Christian theology, ordinarily to denote something like God's demand. Again, Moo is right to correct this notion: "As we have seen, the Reformers, as most theologians today, use 'law' to mean anything that demands something of us. In this sense, 'law' is a basic factor in all human history; and man is in every age, whether in the OT or NT, confronted with 'law.' What is crucial to recognize is that this is *not* the way in which Paul usually uses the term *nomos*."[15]

In no place is this distinctive use of *nomos* more obvious than in Galatians 3:17: "This is what I mean: the law, which came 430 years afterward, does not annul a covenant previously ratified by God, so as to make the promise void." Note here that what is distinguished are the two covenant-administrations spoken of throughout Galatians 3 and 4, covenant-administrations that are historically inaugurated 430 years apart from each other. But we may rightly ask: "Why does Paul use ὁ νόμος to designate the Sinai covenant?" The answer is by way of synecdoche: Since law-giving so characterizes that covenant-administration, it can be referred to by its dominating feature: law. Similarly, note that he can refer to the Abrahamic administration by a dif-

---

13. Ordinarily, Paul employs some form of γινώσκω or οἶδα. Cf., e.g., Galatians 2:16; 3:7; 4:13. Perhaps the most significant for my purposes is 2:16, where Paul asserts that "we ourselves are Jews by birth and not Gentile sinners; yet we know (εἰδότες) that a person is not justified by works of the law but through faith in Jesus Christ." Rhetorically, if some who were Jews denied this point, Paul lost all the power of his argument; but Paul considered it an incontrovertible reality that Jews (whatever the bewitched Gentiles at Galatia might have thought) knew perfectly well that no human was justified by observing the law.

14. Douglas J. Moo, "'Law,' 'Works of the Law,' and Legalism in Paul," *Westminster Theological Journal* 45 (1983): 80.

15. Moo, "Legalism in Paul," 88.

ferent synecdoche: promise (ἐπαγγελία). Note that Paul uses the "promise"
lexical stock 8 times between 3:14 and 3:22, because he conceives the Abrahamic covenant as distinctively (albeit perhaps not exclusively) promissory.
In the same way, he conceives the Sinai covenant as being distinctively (albeit
perhaps not exclusively) legal: "But the law is not of faith, rather 'The one
who does them shall live by them'" (3:12).

This consistent use of the synecdoche "promise" to refer to the Abrahamic
administration, and the equally consistent use of the synecdoche "law" to
refer to the Sinai administration, demonstrate convincingly that Paul did not
conceive these two covenants as similar in kind, but rather as dissimilar in
kind: one is characteristically promissory; the other is characteristically legal.
I prefer to say "characteristically," because I do not deny that each may have
other aspects to it. Insofar as the Sinai covenant reminds its recipients of the
gracious pledges made to Abraham, for instance, it has a "gracious" aspect
or dimension to it, one we do not wish to overlook. But even here, the gracious aspect is borrowed, as it were, from a previous covenant-administration,
and is therefore not its own distinguishing characteristic. I might even be
persuaded to go so far as Charles Hodge:

> Besides this evangelical character which unquestionably belongs to the Mo-
> saic covenant, it is presented in two other aspects in the Word of God. First,
> it was a national covenant with the Hebrew people. In this view the parties
> were God and the people of Israel; the promise was national security and
> prosperity; the condition was the obedience of the people as a nation to the
> Mosaic law; and the mediator was Moses. In this aspect it was a legal cov-
> enant. It said, "Do this and live."[16]

But Paul was not giving a thorough, comprehensive account of either covenant in Galatians 3. Here in Galatians 3 he was discussing their distinctives,
what distinguishes each from the other. And when the question is put that
way, he did not hesitate to call the one "promise" and the other "law."

Concluding Thoughts regarding the Five Differences
When one places portions of Galatians 3:6–14 in parallel columns side-
by-side, these five differences are very pronounced. The differences are less
pronounced if the text is left in a single column, without italicizing the differences. Once this typesetting voodoo is done, however, the differences are
stark. Many are uncomfortable with such contrasts, fearing that they are

16. Charles Hodge, *Systematic Theology*, 3 vols. (1886; Grand Rapids: Eerdmans, 1993),
2:375.

implicitly Lutheran (or worse, dispensationalist). In an effort to diminish these unwelcome contrasts, many in the Reformed tradition have dismissed the contrasts by suggesting that what Paul is contrasting is some first-century legalistic abuse of the Sinai covenant to the Abrahamic covenant, not the two covenant-administrations themselves. The evidence of the text will not permit such evasive action, however. Throughout the critical section of 3:10–14, Paul consistently cited Old Testament texts to prove his point. It was not some first-century rabbi who introduced the idea "Cursed be everyone who does not abide by all things written in the Book of the Law, and do them." Moses introduced this idea in Deuteronomy 27:26. Similarly, it was not some famous (or obscure) first-century Jewish sectarian who said, "The one who does them shall live by them"; it was Moses who said this in Leviticus 18:5. It was not the law as allegedly perverted a millennium after Moses that Paul discussed in Galatians 3, but the law which came 430 years after the Abrahamic covenant that Paul discusses (Gal. 3:17). When he illustrated the matter in chapter 4, for instance, citing Sarah and Hagar, he did not say that these two women were figuratively two ways of understanding the covenant, one right and one wrong. Rather, he said "these women are two *covenants* [αὗται γάρ εἰσιν δύο διαθῆκαι]. One is from Mount Sinai, bearing children for slavery; she is Hagar" (Gal. 4:24).

Some may not like Paul's opinion on the matter. What we must not do is evade the plain teaching of Paul that the Sinai covenant itself, as it was delivered by the hand of Moses 430 years after the Abrahamic covenant, was a different covenant, different in kind, characteristically legal, Gentile-excluding, non-justifying because it was characterized by works, and therefore cursing its recipients and bearing children for slavery. If this doesn't sound like any bargain, recall that the original Israelites did not consider it a bargain either, and they resisted Moses' efforts to engage them in it. All things considered, many of the first-generation Israelites, who received this covenant while trembling at the foot of a quaking mountain and then wandered in the wilderness, preferred to return to Egypt rather than to enter the covenant with a frightening deity who threatened curse-sanctions upon them if they disobeyed. I do not blame them; their assessment of the matter was judicious and well considered, albeit rebellious. The Sinai covenant-administration was no bargain for sinners, and I pity the poor Israelites who suffered under its administration, just as I understand perfectly well why seventy-three (nearly half) of their psalms were laments. I would have resisted this covenant also, had I been there, because such a legal covenant, whose conditions require strict obedience (and threaten severe curse-sanctions), is bound to fail if one of the parties to it is a sinful people.

But this administration, burdensome as it was for the hapless Israelites, was needed for a variety of reasons. In terms of Paul's concerns in Galatians, it was necessary for there to be a covenant that, at a minimum, preserved two things: memory of the gracious promises made to Abraham and his "seed," and the biological integrity of the "seed" itself. Sinai's dietary laws and prohibitions against intermarrying with the Gentiles, along with Sinai's calendar and its circumcision, set Abraham's descendants apart from the Gentiles, saving them (in some degree) from their desire to intermarry with the *am ha-aretz* until the time came to do away with such a designation forever. There were things necessary to teach, via the types and sacrifices of the Old Testament system, in order for the work of the coming Christ to make any sense when he appeared. During this season of preparing the world for the coming Christ, it was necessary to have a covenant administration that preserved both memory of the Abrahamic promises and the integrity of Abraham's seed until the "Seed" of Abraham came. Such a covenant-administration would need, by the harshest threats of curse-sanctions, to prevent intermarriage and idolatry among a people particularly attracted to both. Sinai's thunders did not prevent this perfectly, but they did so sufficiently that a people still existed on earth who recalled the promises to Abraham when Christ appeared, and the genealogy of Matthew's Gospel could be written.

How Did Murray Misunderstand the Matter So Badly?

It may be well now to reacquaint ourselves with Murray's assessment of these two covenant-administrations:

> What needs to be emphasized now is that the Mosaic covenant in respect of the condition of obedience is not in a different category from the Abrahamic. . . . In reality there is nothing that is principally different in the necessity of keeping the covenant and of obedience to God's voice, which proceeds from the Mosaic covenant, from that which is involved in the keeping required in the Abrahamic.[17]

Yet we have discovered five ways in which the Abrahamic covenant is different from the Mosaic, and at least four of them touch rather directly on precisely this question of the "condition of obedience." "Promise" does not differ from "law"? Is not promise, by definition, unconditional? "Blessing" is not different from "cursing"? "Those of faith" are not different from

17. Murray, *Covenant of Grace*, 22.

"those of works of the law"? A covenant that justifies is not different from a covenant that does not? I raise these questions gratefully, rhetorically, and instructively.

I raise these questions grateful that John Murray, to my knowledge, never wrote so much as a paragraph about the Galatian letter.[18] He could have made no sense of the letter, and anything he might have written about it would therefore have been obfuscatory in the highest degree. We can only speculate as to why such a prolific writer as he never wrote about it, and I like to think that he was, at some level, aware of his incapacity to make any sense of it (which explains why I, for instance, have never written about the Calculus). I like to think that he was aware that he was entirely flummoxed by Paul's reasoning, and that he therefore determined not to write anything about the matter until he could make some sense of it. Bravo for him, because many people go ahead and write about things that are entire mysteries to them.

I also raise these questions rhetorically, because I think all it takes to refute Murray's implicit monocovenantalism is to read Galatians (or the final chapters of Deuteronomy). If Paul says "these are *two* covenants" (Gal. 4:24), how can there be only one? And if Paul contrasts these two in as many ways as he does, how can we continue to resist the notion that some covenants have at least some substantial differences in kind? Indeed, one might even raise the question of why God would inaugurate a covenant at Sinai, unless it were in some important ways different from the already existing Abrahamic covenant.

But this rhetorical question raises also the instructive concern. How indeed? Since John Murray was very well read theologically, how can it be that he misunderstood significantly the differences between these two covenants, and perhaps the differences between others as well? At a minimum, I believe there are two answers to this, each of which is instructive.

First, as my friend and former colleague at Gordon-Conwell Theological Seminary David Wells has frequently said: To understand someone, you must understand his conversation partners. With whom is he speaking, and about what? And especially, with whom is he arguing, and about what? The

18. According to the bibliography published in volume 4 of *The Collected Writings of John Murray* (Carlisle: Banner of Truth, 1982), 361–74, from 1931 to 1973 Murray wrote 221 reviews, articles, essays, and books. Not one of these addresses Galatians generally, nor a particular passage within Galatians specifically. Considering that Murray was both a New Testament scholar and a professor of systematic theology, it seems odd that he would publish nothing about what many consider to be one of Paul's most important theological letters. Luther, for instance, was less squeamish than Professor Murray, and was quite willing to write a lengthy commentary on the letter. But then Luther was willing to recognize the covenantal contrasts in Galatians, and so was happy to write about it.

answer to this line of questioning, in John Murray's case, was dispensation-alism. Even the historic premillennialists once associated with Westminster Seminary felt such discomfort with Murray on this point that most left and affiliated with other institutions. And his nonscholarly literary output, for denominational and informal magazines, was dense with antidispensational argumentation. Knowing this helps us understand that Murray's reaction to dispensationalist thought pushed him away from the center of historic cov-enant theology, and moved him to believe that historic covenant theology needed what he called a "recasting," a recasting in a much more monocov-enantal direction.[19]

It was this desired recasting of covenant theology in a monocovenantalist way that was so attractive to Murray the opponent of dispensationalism. Murray the controversialist, facing the peculiar controversy of dispensa-tionalism in the mid-to-late twentieth century, sought to construe biblical covenants in such a manner as to place the construal in the sharpest distinc-tion from dispensationalism, which he did by saying: "From the beginning of God's disclosures to men in terms of covenant we find a unity of conception which is to the effect that a divine covenant is a sovereign administration of grace and of promise."[20] Now, if the administration is one of *sovereign* grace and promise, then it is not and cannot be conditioned upon the obedi-ence of the creature. Yet Sinai seems to be evidently conditioned thereupon; six tribes on Gerizim shout the blessings, while six tribes on Ebal shout the curses. In each case the blessing or curse is conditional:

And if you faithfully obey [אִם־שָׁמוֹעַ תִּשְׁמַע] the voice of the LORD your God, being careful to do all his commandments that I command you today, the LORD your God will set you high above all the nations of the earth. And all these blessings shall come upon you and overtake you, if you obey the voice of the LORD your God. . . . But if you will not obey [אִם־לֹא תִשְׁמַע] the voice of the LORD your God or be careful to do all his commandments and his statutes that I command you today, then all these curses shall come upon you and overtake you. (Deut. 28:1–2, 15)

This cannot be a sovereign administration of grace and/or promise by any meaningful and ordinary definitions of the terms. The condition by which either blessings or curses will come upon Israel is Israel's obedience or disobedience to God's commands. Murray's definition of covenant as

19. "It appears to me that the covenant theology, notwithstanding the finesse of analysis with which it was worked out and the grandeur of its articulated systematization, needs recasting" (Murray, *Covenant of Grace*, 5).
20. Murray, *Covenant of Grace*, 19.

being a "sovereign administration of grace and promise" simply does not accurately represent the closing chapters of Deuteronomy.[21] Nor does it accurately reflect the candid narratives of the Pentateuch. When the Israelites disobeyed, or even grumbled and murmured (Num. 16, 21), they were cursed by God. By contrast, Sarah and Abraham did some foolish, possibly even unbelieving things. Sarah laughingly disbelieved that God would keep his pledge to provide a descendant (Gen. 18, following her husband's similarly jocular response at Gen. 17:17), and she conspired to have Abraham have (adulterous) relations with Hagar in an effort to procure such a seed (Gen. 16). Yet God did not withdraw his pledge or his care from them, nor did he require forty years of wilderness wandering. Similarly, on two occasions Abraham told a prevaricating half-lie (Gen. 12, 20), in the process threatening the well-being of Sarah as seed-bearer, and in each case God delivered Sarah from the danger caused by Abraham, and placed no curse upon them. This is undoubtedly why Paul contrasted the two covenant-administrations as he did, mentioning "blessing" in association with the Abrahamic administration, and "curses" in association with the Sinai administration. The Abrahamic covenant was truly promissory; apart from Abraham and Sarah's obedience (and virtually no commandments were even given them to obey), God would give them descendants and land, and ultimately would bless the nations of the world through one of their descendants.[22] Whether Sarah laughed/scoffed at the notion of bearing children at her age was irrelevant to God's keeping his pledge. Whether Abraham's prevaricating endangered the promise itself (by endangering the bearer of the seed) was irrelevant; God would intervene and keep his unconditional pledge, because this particular covenant truly was one of sovereign grace and promise.

Perhaps even more fatal to Murray's thesis is that Paul used "promise" as a synecdoche for the Abrahamic covenant and that he used "law" as a

21. Nor, to my knowledge, does it have any lexical basis. I am entirely unaware of any parallels in other Semitic languages suggesting that *berith* or its cognates have anything at all to do with grace and/or promise. To the contrary, the ancient Hittite suzerainty treaties were routinely conditioned upon the vassal nation's satisfying the stipulations of the covenant. The land-grant covenants of the same period were indeed different in kind from the suzerain-vassal covenants; yet each was called "covenant" (*berith*), proving that neither the term itself, nor the concept thereby denoted, is necessarily one of sovereign grace and/or promise.

22. Nor does Abraham's willingness to sacrifice Isaac (Gen. 22) disprove this thesis. While it was an obedient act, it was not an act upon which the fulfilment of the promise was conditioned. Apart from the promise already being fulfilled, there would have been no Isaac to sacrifice. Similarly, at Genesis 26:5, it appears that the renewed pledge to Isaac is due to Abraham's obedience. But even here, the pious reference to Abraham (probably referring to his willingness to sacrifice Isaac) does not overshadow that the pledge is also grounded in God's own oath: "Sojourn in this land, and I will be with you and will bless you, for to you and to your offspring I will give all these lands, and I will establish the oath that I swore to Abraham your father. I will multiply your offspring as the stars of heaven and will give to your offspring all these lands" (Gen. 26:3–4).

synecdoche for the Sinai covenant. This is fatal to Murray's definition in two ways, partly because Paul did not (as Murray) perceive all covenants as being essentially alike, but also because Paul plainly did not consider "promise" to be an adequate way to speak of the covenant made at Sinai 430 years after the Abrahamic covenant. Paul actually contrasted the Sinai covenant ("law") and the Abrahamic covenant ("promise") by employing the very vocabulary that Murray assigned to *all* covenants.

There is a second instructive reason for speculating about how Murray so completely misunderstood Paul. We see in Murray nothing more than what we often see in ourselves: a tendency to seek systematic coherence at the expense of exegetical fidelity. That is, studying a book the size of the Bible is messy business, and sometimes the business is tidier if a few unruly texts (or even entire unruly books!) get swept under the rug. The existential challenge each of us faces, at least those of us who have the leisure to think about theology and exegesis, is whether we will live more easily with a less consistent system, on the one hand, that is exegetically faithful, or whether we will prefer a system that may appear (to our mind at least) more consistent, but with considerable exegetical problems. Put more simply, I think Murray's recasting of the covenant theology made it difficult for him to read Galatians and feel its actual weight. I think his monocovenantal system was so attractive to him, for whatever polemical reasons, that he simply did not feel the impress of the contrasts that appear in this letter.

In some senses, then, the most dangerous systematic conclusions are the ones that are the most comprehensive (and therefore the most abstract). Only a big thinker such as Murray can take on the bigger questions, such as the nature, definition, and/or conception of covenant itself.[23] Murray took it on, and decided this: "From the beginning of God's disclosures to men in terms of covenant we find a unity of conception which is to the effect that a divine covenant is a sovereign administration of grace and of promise."[24] Once this definition is admitted, every covenant is a sovereign administration of promise, and therefore the Abrahamic and the Sinai covenants cannot

---

23. I am not even sure there is a definition of covenant that I agree with or even need. To me it is an arrangement of *some* sort that binds *some* parties together in *some* ways, but I am hesitant to say much more than that for fear that the definition will exclude the content of some of the covenants that actually appear in Scripture. As much as I appreciate O. Palmer Robertson, for instance, I'm not sure *prima facie* that I want to say that a covenant is a bond "in blood," because there might very well be covenants that had no such bond. I tend to think that the less we say in our definition of "covenant" that would determine the content of various covenants, the better off we might be (see O. Palmer Robertson, *The Christ of the Covenants* [Phillipsburg, NJ: Presbyterian and Reformed, 1980], 3–15).

24. Murray, *Covenant of Grace*, 19.

be distinguished as Paul distinguished them (calling one "promise" and the other "law").

Implications for the Adamic Administration

While the purpose of this essay is to disclose the dissimilarities between the Abrahamic and Sinai covenants, and to disclose John Murray's incapacity to perceive those dissimilarities, there are broader biblical-theological implications as well. Murray's resistance to describing the Adamic administration in covenantal terms was more than lexical; it was more than the simple matter that the term "covenant" was not used to describe the Edenic administration.[25] If Murray's definition of "covenant" as a "sovereign administration of grace and promise" is permitted to stand, it would be impossible to describe the Adamic administration properly, since Adam's mortality is conditional. Murray therefore preferred to speak of it as the "Adamic administration."[26] Yet even here, his construal of the matter displayed the same implicit monocovenantalism revealed in his discussion of the Sinai covenant. Once the term "covenant" is defined in such a manner as to include grace and promise as part of the definition, then the historic two-covenant structure of covenant theology is no longer possible; and, as Murray desired, it would be necessary to construct a "recasting" of the covenant theology, one that removes from any covenant any true sense of conditionality on the part of the human party thereto. Once this conditionality is removed, faith inevitably blends with works, since each is merely the human response to grace.

And so, Murray's disciples inevitably move in a monocovenantal direction; all covenants become essentially the same: Norman Shepherd cannot easily distinguish Abrahamic faith from Sinaitic works; Greg Bahnsen could not distinguish Israel's laws from the laws of nontheocratic nations; the paedo-communionists cannot distinguish a house meal (Passover) from a corporate meal (the Lord's Supper); the so-called Federal Vision cannot easily distinguish the visible (the "outward Jew" of Rom. 2) from the invisible

---

25. With the possible exception of Hosea 6:7: "But like Adam they transgressed the covenant; there they dealt faithlessly with me." It is worth noting here that Hosea is referring to members of the Sinai covenant: "Ephraim," "Judah," the "house of Israel," and that they transgressed the covenant as Adam did. Does this not at least suggest that the Sinai covenant had a works dimension analogous to the original covenant of works? How could one transgress a promissory covenant "like Adam"? See chapter 6 in this present volume.

26. John Murray, "The Adamic Administration," in *Collected Writings of John Murray*, 2:47–59. See also his article "Covenant," in J. D. Douglas, ed., *The New Bible Dictionary* (Grand Rapids: Eerdmans, 1977), 264–68; and his "Covenant Theology," in *Collected Writings*, 4:216–40, in which he argues that the expression "covenant of works" to refer to the Adamic administration did not appear until the end of the sixteenth century.

(the "inward Jew" of Rom. 2) church. Though Murray himself committed none of these errors, his monocovenantal tendency would inevitably have the effects it has had in each of these areas.

Conclusion

In Galatians, Paul addressed only three of the biblical covenants: the Abrahamic covenant, the Sinai covenant, and the new covenant.[27] He said nothing about pre- or post-diluvian covenants, nothing about a covenant with Phinehas regarding priests, nothing about David building God's house, and nothing overt about the Adamic administration (which he addressed overtly in Rom. 5). Paul attempted to make sense of the new covenant by pointing out its similarities to the Abrahamic administration and its dissimilarities to the Sinai administration.[28] Like the Abrahamic administration (and unlike the Sinai administration), the new covenant is characterized by faith-not-works, and therefore truly blesses and justifies both Jew and Gentile who receive what was promised to Abraham, the man of faith who appeared 430 years before the mediator of the law-covenant.

27. It need hardly be said that Paul did not address here the later distinction between "covenant of works" and "covenant of grace" of Reformed dogmatics. That is, the later dogmatic designation of those various covenants by which God accomplishes the redemption of sinners as "covenant of grace" is many years post-Pauline. In this later designation, the Abrahamic and Sinai covenants would both be parts of the "covenant of grace," though "differently administered" (Westminster Confession of Faith 7:5) "under various administrations" (7.6).

28. And he does not mention all of the dissimilarities. He says nothing about theocracy vs. nontheocracy; he does not mention that one of the primary Sinai sacraments (Passover) was a house-meal vs. a community meal; he stunningly says nothing about the temple, and says nothing about whether the land of Canaan is still holy or not.

9

---≈---

GALATIANS 5:1–6 AND PERSONAL OBLIGATION
Reflections on Paul and the Law

S. M. BAUGH

I n his comments on 2 Corinthians 3, the old Princeton biblical scholar and systematic theologian Charles Hodge observed the following on Paul and the law:

> Every reader of the New Testament must be struck with the fact that the apostle often speaks of the Mosaic law as he does of the moral law considered as a covenant of works; that is, presenting the promise of life on the condition of perfect obedience. He represents it as saying, Do this and live; as requiring works, and not faith, as the condition of acceptance.[1]

Remarkably, what struck Hodge and "every reader" as obvious back then is lost on most people today even among Hodge's Reformed descendants.

The background of Hodge's statement above is that the precise character of a covenant of works resides in the imposition of an obligation to personal

---

1. Charles Hodge, *An Exposition of the Second Epistle to the Corinthians* (1862; Grand Rapids: Eerdmans, 1973), 57.

and perfect (or entire) obedience to its specified stipulations.[2] The Mosaic law imposes such an obligation; therefore—at the very least—it embodies a works principle within its broader covenantal administration. The key point here as I will discuss further is *personal* over against *mediated* or *substitutionary* performance of the covenantal stipulations.[3] Granted, the Mosaic covenant in its typological priestly embodiment of mediation (the ceremonial law) must be viewed as an administration of the covenant of grace.[4] Nevertheless, the Mosaic law more narrowly considered embodies what can only be described best as a works principle.[5] This is what others and I mean by "republication" of the covenant of works in Moses.[6]

The question, then, is whether there is biblical teaching that describes the Mosaic law as imposing: (1) an obligation, (2) to personal obedience, and (3) to perfect obedience to its stipulated requirements. I believe there are actually quite a number of places in the Scriptures where this is taught, but there is no clearer place than Galatians 5:1–6 where all these essential ideas of the works principle are stated as required in the Mosaic law. Furthermore, Paul's clear and repeated statements in Galatians 5:1–6 that the one who takes on circumcision will not have Christ as his mediator confirm this line of thought. That is what I hope to establish.

My plan in this chapter is simply to examine Galatians 5:1–6 in some detail after a few introductory remarks. We will see that in this passage Paul presents two mutually exclusive principles of meeting the demands of God's covenant stipulations and thereby attaining eschatological righteousness: one either adheres to Christ the covenant mediator by grace through faith

2. This is articulated most clearly and concisely in the Westminster Confession of Faith in regard to the Adamic covenant: "The first covenant made with man was a covenant of works, wherein life was promised to Adam; and in him to his posterity, *upon condition of perfect and personal obedience*" (7.2; all emphasis added).
3. The concept of a biblical covenant entails a solemnly bound commitment between two or more parties where the solemnity of the engagement is normally expressed through a self-maledictory oath.
4. Paul can be seen to make this sort of distinction. For example, he clearly includes the Mosaic covenant as one of the "covenants of promise" and therefore a covenant of grace (Eph. 2:12; cf. Rom. 9:3–5), yet he sets the Mosaic *law* (not "covenant") over against the Abrahamic promissory *covenant* which Moses cannot annul or mediate (Gal. 3:15–22). The latter is discussed in S. M. Baugh, "Galatians 3:20 and the Covenant of Redemption," *Westminster Theological Journal* 66 (2004): 49–70.
5. The typological character of this works principle is primarily concentrated on the national level of Israel and her tenure in the land (Lev. 26 and Deut. 28). This was discussed among the Reformed early on as illustrated by Herman Witsius (*De oeconomia foederum Dei cum hominibus* [1677] now available as *The Economy of the Covenants between God and Man: Comprehending a Complete Body of Divinity*, vol. 2 [1822; Phillipsburg, NJ: Presbyterian and Reformed, 1990], 186). Further reflection on these ideas is certainly desirable.
6. Granted that other Reformed theologians certainly have other ways of expressing these ideas and that some demur from the idea of republication altogether.

alone, or one must vainly attempt to meet the law's demands for personal and entire performance of its commands on one's own, divorced from Christ and from divine grace. The quest for eschatological righteousness through law-keeping must be vain since no law can "make alive"; hence, our righteousness is not from law but from faith in Christ as a gift to those who believe (Gal. 3:21–22; cf. Rom. 5:17). One must therefore choose either the freedom of divine grace or the exacting slavery of the law. The apostle conceives of no third option.

In current scholarly debates touching on whether Paul viewed the Mosaic law as requiring perfect obedience or not, Galatians 3:10 invariably receives far more attention than Galatians 5:1–6. And even when Galatians 5 is mentioned in this connection, often only verse 3 is cited while the vital contribution of the whole pericope is neglected. However, the whole of Galatians 5:1–6 should be given significant weight, because in this passage Paul summarizes and recaps his teachings on the law that he had been developing earlier in the epistle.

We will not survey all of the secondary opinions on Galatians 5:1–6 or on Paul and the law of Moses in general—for that would be unnecessarily tedious and distracting. Instead we will consider a few key interpretations that are currently popular in the English-speaking world including some of the so-called New Perspective interpreters of Paul.[7] As Charles Hodge believed, a nuanced Reformed perspective that the Mosaic covenant contained in the law itself a "re-enactment" or "republication" of the covenant of works principle is the best way to resolve the tensions raised by Galatians 5:1–6 and other passages where Paul pits the law over against divine grace.[8]

Covenant of Works or of Grace?

Before getting on with the task, let me mention that some people object when we apply the terms "covenant of works" or a "works principle" to the Mosaic law, particularly if they are not intimately familiar with the qualifications and precise meaning of the terms used in classic Reformed theol-

---

7. For Paul and the law and bibliography see, for example: A. Andrew Das, *Paul, the Law, and the Covenant* (Peabody, MA: Hendrickson, 2001); Thomas R. Schreiner, *The Law and Its Fulfillment: A Pauline Theology of Law* (Grand Rapids: Baker, 1993); and Frank Thielman, *Paul and the Law: A Contextual Approach* (Downers Grove, IL: InterVarsity, 1994).

8. Note that the Westminster Confession of Faith 7.2 cites Gal. 3:10 and 3:12—which refer to the demand for personal obedience and the curse of the *Mosaic law*—as part of the biblical evidence for this covenant of works with Adam.

ogy.[9] In particular, they insist that the Mosaic law was wholly "gracious."[10] I certainly agree that the Mosaic covenant more broadly considered than its typological stipulations was an administration of the covenant of grace, particularly in its priestly and sacrificial statutes—what I prefer to describe succinctly as operating on a principle of substitutionary mediation.[11] But when we talk about a republication of the covenant of works in the Mosaic law (as did Hodge and other Reformed luminaries), we are speaking more narrowly about the Mosaic covenant as it also administered *law*, which Paul opposes to grace in places (e.g., Rom. 6:14–15).[12]

The issue of the opposition between the covenants of works and of grace and the resolution of the common confusion surrounding these terms is that "grace" in the term "covenant of grace" and "works" in the "covenant of works" point to something very specific, namely, to whether there is *substitutionary mediation* in the covenant arrangement or not. The antithesis of these covenantal commitments does not revolve around issues of God's beneficence, whether there are conditions in the covenant or not, or even the benefits of the covenant relationship, but rather their difference focuses on the very narrow issue of who comes under obligation in the covenant to fulfil its stipulations: the human covenant partner himself (covenant of works) or a mediator on his behalf (covenant of grace).[13] This idea is expressed admirably by the seventeenth-century Dutch theologian Herman Witsius (1636–1708), who says:

> In the covenant of works there was no mediator: in that of grace, there is the mediator Christ Jesus. . . . In the covenant of works, the condition of perfect obedience was required, to be performed by man himself, who had consented

9. For example, Tom Schreiner in an appendix to *The Law and Its Fulfillment*, 247–51.

10. So Schreiner: "Old Testament scholarship today generally agrees that the Mosaic covenant was gracious" (*Law and Its Fulfillment*, 250).

11. That is, substitutionary mediation is the principle by which one evaluates the nature of the so-called ceremonial law over against the moral and civil law. Ephesians 2:12 ("covenants of promise") in its context is a particularly important place where Paul himself interprets the Mosaic covenant as an administration of the covenant of grace, not just of law or works.

12. We see the same distinction in Gal. 3:17 when Paul contrasts the Abrahamic *covenant* with the Mosaic *law*. For this passage see again Baugh, "Galatians 3:20," 49–70.

13. This distinction is clearly embodied in Reformed confessions that stress the covenant of works or the requirements of the moral law as requiring *personal* obedience and present Christ as covenant Mediator or Surety (Latin, *Sponsor* derived from ἔγγυος in Heb. 7:22) whose obedience and sacrifice on our behalf are imputed to us. For example, the distinction is clearly articulated in Q/A 71 of the Westminster Larger Catechism: "Q71: How is justification an act of God's free grace? A71: Although Christ, by his obedience and death, did make a proper, real, and full satisfaction to God's justice in the behalf of them that are justified; yet inasmuch as God accepteth the satisfaction from a surety, which he might have demanded of them, and did provide this surety, his own only Son, imputing his righteousness to them, and requiring nothing of them for their justification but faith, which also is his gift, their justification is to them of free grace." See also 20 and 93; Westminster Confession of Faith 7.2; 8.3; 19.1; the Canons of Dort 2.2, etc.

to it. In that of grace, the same condition is proposed, as to be, or as already performed, by a mediator. *And in this substitution of the person, consists the principal and essential difference of the covenants.*[14]

When the Mosaic law was enacted with the blood of the covenant in Exodus 24 (cf. Heb. 9:18–21), the covenant people twice recognized that they must personally fulfil the obligation imposed in this covenant: "All the terms that the LORD has spoken *we will do*" (Ex. 24:3) and "All that the LORD has spoken *we will do, and we will be obedient*" (Ex. 24:7).[15] In consequence, the term "covenant of works" should be thought of as a covenant of *personal obligation* whereas the "covenant of grace" is best seen as a covenant of *mediation* or even a covenant of *substitutionary performance*. This is what we see in our target passage, Galatians 5:1–6.

Importance of the Passage

Frank Matera has observed that scholars tend to treat the material in Galatians 5–6 as exhortational material and therefore as having less value for understanding Paul's theology than earlier passages in the epistle.[16] Their assumption is built on the familiar "indicative-imperative" structure in Paul's letters. Yet Matera persuasively argues that though Galatians 5–6 does have paranaetic sections, on the whole it is Paul's summary and conclusion to his previous chapters and therefore has some of the most important doctrinal passages built directly upon his prior arguments. While scholars recognize that Paul's conclusions in his own hand have similar importance as summaries of the epistle's contents (e.g., Gal. 6:11–18), they have not generally recognized this function as early as the beginning of chapter 5 in Galatians.[17] Perhaps this explains

14. Witsius, *Economy*, 1:49 (emphasis added). Cf. Augustine's comments on Psalm 89:28, "On His account, the Testament is faithful: in Him the Testament is mediated: He is the Sealer, the Mediator of the Testament, the Surety of the Testament, the Witness of the Testament, the Heritage of the Testament, the Coheir of the Testament" (Nicene and Post-Nicene Fathers, 1:8). (Note that *testamentum* rendered "Testament" is the Latin word Augustine [following the Vulgate] consistently uses for "covenant" in place of later *foedus* or *pactum*. Hence, "covenant" is actually a better rendering here.)

15. "Words" here should be understood as covenant stipulations as is found elsewhere in connection with "confirming the words" of a covenant in the Old Testament; e.g., "And the men who transgressed my covenant and did not keep the *terms* of the covenant that they made before me, I will make them like the calf that they cut in two and passed between its parts" (Jer. 34:18; cf. Deut. 27:26; 1 Kings 2:4; 6:12).

16. Frank J. Matera, "The Culmination of Paul's Argument to the Galatians: Gal. 5:1–6:17," *Journal for the Study of the New Testament* 32 (1988): 79–91.

17. For the letter's close, see especially Jeffrey A. D. Weima, *Neglected Endings: The Significance of the Pauline Letter Closings*, Journal for the Study of the New Testament Supplement 101 (Sheffield:

why Galatians 3:10 is often given precedence or exclusive place in the discussions of Paul and the law.[18]

Let me illustrate the relative neglect of Galatians 5:1–6 in favor of Galatians 3:10 with a prominent example. Initially E. P. Sanders in his well-known book *Paul and Palestinian Judaism* said that Paul taught "that one must achieve legal perfection" in Galatians and other places. He saw Paul as opposed to contemporary Judaism concerning which Sanders wrote, "The Amoraic literature always emphasizes that one should confirm the law, not keep it without error. . . . Human perfection was not considered realistically achievable by the Rabbis, nor was it required."[19] A few years later, however, Sanders reversed himself to assert that Paul, like his contemporaries in Judaism, did not believe that the law required perfect obedience.[20]

To validate his change of opinion, Sanders had to reckon with both Galatians 3:10 and 5:1–6, but, curiously, his discussion in a section headed "Galatians 5:3" mentions the verse only in passing with no thought to its context.[21] Furthermore, he appears to have Galatians 3:10 more in mind as can be seen when he speaks at length on the premises required to come to the conclusion that the one who accepts circumcision is under a curse. Interestingly, in a later journal article proposing to examine both Galatians 3:10 and 5:3, Michael Cranford follows Sanders's method and conclusions by giving only a cursory glance at Galatians 5:3 in a little more than one (unsatisfying) page.[22] We will return to these treatments briefly below, but this illustrates the relative neglect of Galatians 5:3 and especially of the whole pericope of verses 1–6 in important discussions on Paul and the law.

The importance of Galatians 5:1–6 as a clear and forceful statement of Paul's convictions on the issue of justification is made obvious in the passage itself. Paul's solemn tone ("I, Paul declare"), the repetition in verses 2 and 3, and his transparent attitude that the Galatian church was on a theological precipice all combine to show that Galatians 5:1–6 should be recognized as considerably important. Rather than focus on these and other important issues in further preliminary remarks, we will now simply examine Gala-

---

Sheffield Academic, 1994); and E. Randolph Richards, *The Secretary in the Letters of Paul*, Wissenschaftliche Untersuchungen zum Neuen Testament 2.42 (Tübingen: Mohr Siebeck, 1991).

18. Note Jan Lambrecht's article where he shows similarities between Gal. 5:1 and 3:13: "Abraham and His Offspring: A Comparison of Galatians 5, 1 with 3, 13," *Biblica* 80 (1999): 525–36.

19. E. P. Sanders, *Paul and Palestinian Judaism: A Comparison of Patterns of Religion* (Philadelphia: Fortress, 1977), 137. Not all experts on ancient Judaism agreed with Sanders on this point as will be noted below.

20. See E. P. Sanders, *Paul, the Law, and the Jewish People* (Philadelphia: Fortress, 1983), 23.

21. Sanders, *Paul, the Law, and the Jewish People*, 27–29.

22. Michael Cranford, "The Possibility of Perfect Obedience: Paul and an Implied Premise in Galatians 3:10 and 5:3," *Novum Testamentum* 36 (1994): 242–58 and only pp. 254–55 for Gal. 5:3.

tians 5:1–6 itself in some detail. Afterward, we will return to the theological implications related to the interests of this volume.

Structure and Style

The dreadful consequences of the Galatians' actions are the repeated issue in Galatians 5:1–6. The passage can be outlined as follows:

> (v. 1) Statement and exhortation to freedom
>> (v. 2) Testimony and warning of dire consequences
>> (v. 3) Repeated testimony and restatement of consequences
>>> (v. 4) Consequences developed
>>>> (v. 5) Rationale for validity of consequences
>>>> (v. 6) Further rationale for validity of consequences

The repetition here of Paul's appeal and testimony (vv. 2–3) and rationale (vv. 5–6) develops his argument but also serves to reinforce the seriousness of the issues involved.[23] Paul wants no confusion; he is stating things very clearly as one does in a crisis situation. These factors alone show that we must give this pericope very serious attention.

The staccato style of the Greek and of the thoughts in Galatians 5:1–6 is notably abrupt and direct.[24] There is here no luxurious, unfolding periodic style.[25] Nor are there any rhapsodic, semipoetic flights that we find elsewhere in Paul as in Romans 8:31–39. Instead, Galatians 5:1–6 is unvarnished, direct, heartfelt appeal, warning, and testimony, because the audience's actions carry the gravest of consequences.

Look, for example, at the construction of verse 4: "You are severed from Christ, you who would be justified by the law; you have fallen away from grace." The two vivid indicative verbs (κατηργήθητε and ἐξεπέσατε) are placed in emphatic positions as both the first and last words in the sentence

23. The whole epistle obviously displays the gravity of the issues involved which comes across most forcefully in Gal. 5:12, "I wish those who unsettle you would emasculate themselves!"
24. Hans Dieter Betz, *Galatians* (Philadelphia: Fortress, 1979), 255, says that this section "is marked by an abrupt new start." The variety of textual variants in v. 1 undoubtedly arose from this abruptness and from the unusual cognate dative τῇ ἐλυεθερίᾳ; see Bruce M. Metzger, *A Textual Commentary on the Greek New Testament*, 2nd ed. (New York: UBS, 1994), 528; Ernest de Witt Burton, *The Epistle to the Galatians*, International Critical Commentary (1921; Edinburgh: T&T Clark, 1988), 270–71; and Richard N. Longenecker, *Galatians*, Word Biblical Commentary (Dallas: Word, 1990), 220, 223.
25. As, for example, in Ephesians or Philippians; see Charles J. Robbins, "Rhetorical Structure of Philippians 2:6–11," *Catholic Biblical Quarterly* 42 (1980): 73–82 and "The Composition of Eph 1:3–14," *Journal of Biblical Literature* 105 (1986): 677–87.

with no conjunction connecting them ("asyndeton").[26] The sentence flow
is interrupted in the middle by the relative clause (οἵτινες) which would
more naturally have been expressed as a substantive participle phrase.[27] Paul
expresses himself in Galatians 5:1–6 in high voltage language and style.[28]

Freedom in Christ

Our passage opens in verse 1 with a strong statement of our freedom in
Christ and Paul's urging us to stand and to resist the allure of going back
under "a yoke of slavery." The topic of freedom connects Galatians 5 to
Galatians 4. Chapter 5 develops the foregoing illustration of freedom and
slavery from Hagar and Sarah, the Jerusalem above and Mount Sinai. This
is a natural development of thought and explains why some versions (e.g.,
NEB), Greek editions (UBS), and commentators see Galatians 5:1 as concluding chapter 4 rather than as part of 5:2–6. Perhaps it is best to see
verse 1 as a transitional bridge between chapters 4 and 5, especially since
the idea of freedom in verse 1 belongs equally to both Galatians 4 and 5
and, indeed, may be seen as "the basic concept underlying Paul's argument
throughout the letter" according to H. D. Betz.[29]

So Paul strongly urges the Galatians in verse 1 to stand in their freedom
won by Christ. But freedom from what? The answer takes us immediately to
the heart of the issue of the law as embodying a principle of personal obligation and a matter for some debate in scholarly literature. This leads to two
interrelated subquestions that must be settled for us to understand accurately
the nature of the freedom and the slavery which Paul expresses: (1) How does
taking on circumcision represent a type of slavery? (2) How will Gentiles who
become circumcised go under a yoke of slavery *again* (πάλιν in v. 1)?

It is obvious from Galatians 4:21–31 that the law delivered on Mount
Sinai was a covenant of law which bound Israel under "a yoke . . . that nei-

---

26. The same sentence structure can be found also in Gal. 4:21.

27. As, for example: Gal. 2:8; 3:5; 5:21; 6:6, 8, 13. The Greek of Gal. 5:4 with a participle phrase
and conjunctions would have less abruptly read something like this: οἱ γὰρ ἐν νόμῳ δικαιούμενοι
κατηργήθητε ἀπὸ Χριστοῦ τῆς δὲ χάριτος ἐξεπέσατε. The English translation might be the same,
but this would be smoother Pauline Greek style.

28. The passive of the verb καταργέω found here with ἀπό is not what one expects for the
meaning "to be severed from" rather than ἀποκόπτω, ἐκκόπτω or even the ἀνάθεμα . . . ἀπό phrase
with similar meaning in Rom. 9:3. The only other biblical examples of καταργέω (normally, "annul,"
"abolish," "destroy") with ἀπό are in Rom. 7:2 and 6 where the relation to the law is rent; see
"καταργέω," in W. Bauer et al., *Greek-English Lexicon of the New Testament*, 526.

29. Betz, *Galatians*, 255; see also Don Garlington, *An Exposition of Galatians: A New Perspec-
tive/Reformational Reading*, 2nd ed. (Eugene, OR: Wipf and Stock, 2004), 233–35. For discussion
of the ways v. 1 has been treated see Longenecker, *Galatians*, 223–24, who interestingly sees 5:1–12
as an inclusio recapping the strong statements of 1:6–10 (221–22).

ther our fathers nor we have been able to bear" (Acts 15:10), for circumcision was not viewed as a simple cleansing ceremony, but it brought with it the obligation to keep the law as we read clearly in Acts 15:5: "But some believers who belonged to the party of the Pharisees rose up and said, 'It is necessary to circumcise them and *to order them to keep* [τηρεῖν] *the law of Moses.*'"[30] Hence, this slavery is the obligation which the law imposed for *personal* performance of the covenant obligations: "All the words that the LORD has spoken *we will do*" (Ex. 24:3).[31]

How then can Gentiles who come under obligation to the Sinai covenant through circumcision *again* come under a yoke of slavery (Gal. 5:1)? There is no mistaking that this is what Paul intends to say, since he has already said it emphatically in Galatians 4:9: "But now that you have come to know God, or rather to be known by God, how can you turn back again [πάλιν] to the weak and worthless elementary principles of the world [στοιχεῖα], whose slaves you want to be all over again [πάλιν ἄνωθεν]?"[32]

The link between a "return" to paganism and submitting to the slave-yoke of the law is a fascinating one, since infant Israel was enslaved under the στοιχεῖα of the world until the appearance of the Son at the fullness of time (Gal. 4:3–4). Whatever else these verses mean, this much seems clear: the law imposed a burden that Paul compares with slavery analogous to the bondage of paganism. F. F. Bruce says, "This is an astonishing statement for a former Pharisee to make; yet Paul makes it—not as an exaggeration in the heat of argument but as the deliberate expression of a carefully thought out position."[33] Bruce says that what Jews under the Mosaic law and Gentiles—though technically ἄνομοι (1 Cor. 9:21)—have in common is that both are "under legalism as a principle of life."[34]

The term "legalism" to describe the Jews under the law and the pagan Gentiles is perhaps not the happiest because it suggests either an unhealthy

---

30. Paul expresses this imposition of the law's obligation as "living Jewishly" (Ἰουδαϊκῶς ζῆς and Ἰουδαΐζειν) in Gal. 2:14 and, quite subtly, with a present participle of περιτέμνεσθαι ("to be circumcised") in Gal. 5:2–3; see Moisés Silva, *Explorations in Exegetical Method: Galatians as a Test Case* (Grand Rapids: Baker, 1996), 79.

31. Hence, Charles Cosgrove's statement that this freedom in Gal. 5:1 is "freedom as ethical obligation" seems to typify the theological muddle in contemporary interpretations on these issues; Cosgrove as cited by Garlington, *Galatians*, 233.

32. This is the only NT occurrence of πάλιν ἄνωθεν together, though the Septuagint has one in the Wisdom of Solomon 19:6. Bauer, *Greek-English Lexicon*, under ἄνωθεν (4) says that this adverb is "often strengthened by πάλιν," but gives only Wis. 19:6 and a passage in the *Corpus Inscriptionum Graecarum*. The Liddell-Scott-Jones lexicon lists only Gal. 4:9 for the two adverbs together. This suggests that πάλιν ἄνωθεν is emphatic in Gal. 4:9.

33. F. F. Bruce, *Epistle to the Galatians* (Grand Rapids: Eerdmans, 1981), 202–3.

34. Bruce, *Galatians*, 203; see also A. J. Bandstra, *The Law and the Elements of the World: An Exegetical Study in Aspects of Paul's Teaching* (Kampen: J. H. Kok, 1964) for both groups under "religiosity."

attitude or an empty performance of external regulations.[35] Paul says that both Jew and Gentile were under τὰ στοιχεῖα τοῦ κόσμου, which suggests that this is a prime state common to all human beings.[36] Two discussions of related issues in Galatians and Romans have made suggestive lines of thought in answer to this particular issue.

The first is by T. L. Donaldson in a journal essay on Galatians 3:13–14.[37] In the course of his discussion of how Israel's experience and redemption can extend to the Gentiles, Donaldson writes:

> Israel serves as a "representative sample" for the whole of humankind. Within Israel's experience, the nature of the universal human plight—bondage to sin and to the powers of this age—is thrown into sharp relief through the functioning of the law. The law, therefore, cannot accomplish the promise; but by creating a representative sample in which the human plight is clarified and concentrated, it sets the stage for redemption. Christ identifies not only with the human situation in general (γενόμενον ἐκ γυναικός, 4. 4), but also with Israel in particular (γενόμενον ὑπὸ νόμον), thereby becoming the representative individual (ὑπὲρ ἡμῶν, 3. 13) of the representative people.[38]

Donaldson's comments are intriguing in that if the Jews who are under the στοιχεῖα of the law cannot be redeemed from the curse of that law through their law-keeping—for no law can make alive (Gal. 3:21)—then how much less can Gentiles under the στοιχεῖα of idolatry. You will recognize the similarity of this argument to Romans 1–3 which culminates in Romans 3:19 with the whole world, both Jew and Greek, being liable to God for judgment (ὑπόδικος). God dealt with Israel in a definitive, world-convincing demonstration of human failure through law-keeping, so that no return to Israel's state under the law may be contemplated now that Christ has appeared as the one mediator for all peoples, both Jew and Greek (1 Tim. 2:3–7).

The second suggestive comment comes from Sigfred Pedersen in an essay working primarily in Romans where he concludes with regard to Romans 5:

35. Note Paul's testimony to his contemporary Jews' zeal in Rom. 10:1–3; their problem was an attempt to establish their own righteousness (v. 3), not rote or empty performance of the law's demands.

36. For survey of literature and positions on the issue of στοιχεῖα in Galatians 4 see Clinton E. Arnold, "Returning to the Domain of the Powers: *STOICHEIA* as Evil Spirits in Galatians 4:3, 9," *Novum Testamentum* 38.1 (1996): 55–76; see also Philipp Vielhauer, "Gesetzesdienst und Stoicheiadienst im Galaterbrief," in *Rechtfertigung: Festschrift für Ernst Käsemann zum 70. Geburtstag*, ed. Johannes Friedrich, Wolfgang Pöhlmann, and Peter Stuhlmacher (Tübingen and Gottingen: Mohr Siebeck and Vandenhoeck & Ruprecht, 1976), 543–55.

37. T. L. Donaldson, "The 'Curse of the Law' and the Inclusion of the Gentiles: Galatians 3.13–14," *New Testament Studies* 32 (1986): 94–112.

38. Ibid., 105–6.

"In other words there exists a hitherto unexplored philological background for the assumption that the 'Law' whose appearance is referred to in [Rom.] 5:13–14 and 5:20 . . . is the biblical creation commandment with its inherent link between violation and sin and death."[39] I may demur from some details in Pedersen's essay, but here he comes close to articulating what the Reformed have identified as the covenant of creation (or natural law), which is discussed elsewhere in this volume.

Going back to the beginning of our pericope, when Paul says in Galatians 5:1 that the Gentile Galatians must not submit again to slavery by coming under the yoke of the Mosaic law, the link between the two—Gentile slavery and Jewish slavery—is God's demand to both groups for *personal* obedience by virtue of being either "sons of Adam" under the covenant of creation or "sons of Abraham" under the Mosaic covenant. This "works principle" is embodied in the covenants dealing with both groups, which must drive both to the covenant of substitutionary mediation offered in the gospel. This principle demanding personal performance of God's stipulations is the essential significance of στοιχεῖα in Galatians.[40]

Solemn Testimony

Going further into our passage now, it is obvious from a casual reading of Galatians 5:2–3 that Paul is most solemnly forewarning the Galatians that their faith is about to wreck on the shoals of circumcision. Ἴδε ἐγὼ Παῦλος λέγω ὑμῖν, "Look here! I Paul declare to you . . ." (v. 2). The initial words of verse 2 alert the hearer to the solemn and binding character of his affirmation. The arresting ἴδε, "Look here!" (used only here in Paul's writings) accentuates the grave nature of the statement as also does the redundant use of the personal pronoun ἐγώ joined to a performative λέγω.[41] Paul is speaking out of his apostolic authority of an assured truth from which there is no appeal to higher authority since the apostle speaks in the name of God (cf. 1 Cor. 5:4–5; Gal. 1:4; 1 Thess. 2:13; 1 Tim. 2:6–8; Heb. 2:3–4).[42] The parallel opening in verse 3—μαρτύρομαι δὲ πάλιν, "I testify again"—confirms the interpretation of verse 2 as solemn declaration.[43]

39. Sigfred Pedersen, "Paul's Understanding of the Biblical Law," *Novum Testamentum* 44.1 (2002): 1–34, esp. 19.
40. See the essay by David VanDrunen in this volume.
41. Many versions have milder "say to you" (e.g., KJV, NIV, ESV), which lacks the formal tone for λέγω as it is often found in orders, solemn declarations, and imperial edicts: "I (hereby) declare to you"; see Bauer, *Greek-English Lexicon*, meanings 2c–d.
42. Bruce, *Galatians*, 228–29; Longenecker, *Galatians*, 225.
43. Bruce (*Galatians*, 229) writes: "This solemn asseveration repeats and reinforces the warning of v 2" (see also Longenecker, *Galatians*, 226). Burton, *Galatians*, 274–75, takes πάλιν as referring

The heart of Galatians 5:1–6, as shown in the outline above, is Paul's expression in verses 2–4 of the severe consequences—both negative and positive—for those who attempt to use circumcision and its intrinsic obligation to the Mosaic law to satisfy God's justice. Negatively, Christ will be of no benefit to them (v. 2), for they have been severed from Christ and have fallen from grace (v. 4).[44] Notice especially that the statement in verse 4 is not hypothetical but a declaration that some of them are already apostate. Positively, Paul states that the obligation to the law is personal and entire. Let us look further at these points in reverse order.

Consequence of Obligation

Paul tells us in Galatians 5:3 the nature of the law's obligation: absolute for all of its commandments. In itself the law can only condemn sinful acts as transgressions (Gal. 3:19; Rom. 7:7–24; etc.). No law can make us alive as can the Spirit (Gal. 3:21; 5:5; Rom. 8:3–4; 2 Cor. 3:6); hence our righteousness cannot come from a law of personal obligation and performance which therefore cannot mediate the promise because the law can only be a "ministry of death" in a postlapsarian world (Gal. 2:21; 2 Cor. 3:7).[45] This is Paul's solemn testimony in verse 3: "I testify again to every man who accepts circumcision that he is obligated to keep the whole law" (ὀφειλέτης ἐστὶν ὅλον τὸν νόμον ποιῆσαι).

Prior discussion of the threat of verse 3 has focused on the adjective ὅλος in the expression ὅλον τὸν νόμον, especially in light of Paul's similar expression ὁ . . . πᾶς νόμος in verse 14. F. F. Bruce writes: "Whereas ὅλος ὁ νόμος in v 3 is the sum-total of the precepts of the law, ὁ πᾶς νόμος here [v. 14] is the law as a whole—the spirit and intention of the law."[46] This is helpful and needs no further elaboration. The law is "holy and righteous and good" (Rom. 7:12), but obedience to its commandments can never be the basis for eschatological righteousness "which we eagerly await" (Gal. 5:5).

While ὅλος is interesting, there are other elements in verse 3 that deserve more extensive attention. The first is that Paul uses the rather rare predicate noun ὀφειλέτης here where equivalent ὀφείλει ποιῆσαι ("he is obligated to

---

back to some statement elsewhere in Galatians or to something Paul said to them earlier in person rather than to v. 2, but this is not at all likely.

44. See Bauer, *Greek-English Lexicon*, on ὠφελέω for other examples of the expression οὐδὲν ὠφελήσει, "will be of no benefit," "will profit nothing" in v. 2. As with many commentators and translations, I read present tense δικαιοῦσθε in v. 4 as conative (tendential) expressing an attempt of what is not possible; see also Burton, *Galatians*, 275–76.

45. For mediation and the Mosaic law see discussion and citations in Baugh, "Galatians 3:20," 61–66.

46. Bruce, *Galatians*, 241.

perform") or δεῖ ποιῆσαι ("he must perform") might be expected.[47] The way Paul does express himself here with the noun stresses that the individual who takes on circumcision is himself liable for complete performance of the law. "It is *he* who is obligated" may be a suitable paraphrase.

The aorist tense form of the infinitive ποιῆσαι is especially noteworthy. Paul says that the Galatian who takes on circumcision comes under liability "to perform [ποιῆσαι] (or complete) the whole law." Of course, the meaning of Greek tense forms has been the subject of considerable research and discussion in recent years among both New Testament scholars and classicists.[48] There are also commendable warnings against misinterpretation or overinterpretation of the aorist tense in Greek.[49] My evaluation of the aorist tense form of ποιῆσαι in Galatians 5:3 fits within a larger framework of research which I relay here only as it relates to this infinitive. The conclusion I will defend is that the aorist infinitive ποιῆσαι has a "resultative" meaning here, whereby Paul expresses the obligation to *complete* performance of the law for the person cut off from Christ and divine grace.

The infinitive ποιῆσαι in Galatians 5:3 acts as a virtual complement with the noun expression ὀφειλέτης ἐστίν and specifies the content of the obligation.[50] The choice of tense form for a complementary infinitive may some-

47. For ὀφειλέτης here Bauer, *Greek-English Lexicon*, gives "one who is under obligation in a moral or social sense, *one under obligation, one liable for*." See Rom. 15:27 where both the noun (ὀφειλέτης) and cognate verb (ὀφείλω + infinitive) are found together with related meanings: εὐδόκησαν γὰρ καὶ ὀφειλέται εἰσὶν αὐτῶν· εἰ γὰρ τοῖς πνευματικοῖς αὐτῶν ἐκοινώνησαν τὰ ἔθνη, ὀφείλουσιν καὶ ἐν τοῖς σαρκικοῖς λειτουργῆσαι αὐτοῖς, "They were pleased to do it, and indeed they owe it to them. For if the Gentiles have come to share in their spiritual blessings, they ought also to be of service to them in material blessings." The other uses of the noun in Paul are in Rom. 1:14 and 8:12; it appears seven times in the NT and is not used in the Septuagint. See Bruce, *Galatians*, 229.

48. Chrys C. Caragounis, *The Development of Greek and the New Testament*, Wissenschaftliche Untersuchungen zum Neuen Testament 167 (Tübingen: Mohr Siebeck, 2004); Buist M. Fanning, *Verbal Aspect in New Testament Greek* (Oxford: Clarendon, 1990); Stanley Porter, *Verbal Aspect in the Greek of the New Testament*, Studies in Biblical Greek 1 (New York: Peter Lang, 1989); idem, *Idioms of the Greek New Testament* (Sheffield: JSOT, 1992); K. L. McKay, *A New Syntax of the Verb in New Testament Greek: An Aspectual Approach*, Studies in Biblical Greek 5 (New York: Peter Lang, 1994); idem, "Time and Aspect in New Testament Greek," *Novum Testamentum* 34 (1992): 209–28; Stanley E. Porter and D. A. Carson, eds., *Biblical Greek Language and Linguistics: Open Questions in Current Research*, Journal for the Study of the New Testament Supplement 80 (Sheffield: Sheffield Academic Press, 1993). For classics see Albert Rijksbaron, *The Syntax and Semantics of the Verb in Classical Greek: An Introduction*, 2nd ed. (Amsterdam: J. C. Gieben, 1994); Peter Stork, *The Aspectual Usage of the Dynamic Infinitive in Herodotus* (Groningen: Bouma's Boekhuis, 1982). See also B. Comrie, *Aspect: An Introduction to the Study of Verbal Aspect and Related Problems*, Cambridge Textbooks in Linguistics 2 (Cambridge: Cambridge University Press, 1976).

49. See Charles R. Smith, "Errant Aorist Interpreters," *Grace Theological Journal* 2 (1981): 205–26; Randy Maddox, "The Use of the Aorist Tense in Holiness Exegesis," *Wesleyan Theological Journal* 16 (1981): 106–18; Frank Stagg, "The Abused Aorist," *Journal of Biblical Literature* 91 (1972): 222–31; D. A. Carson, *Exegetical Fallacies* (Grand Rapids: Baker, 1984), 69–77.

50. I am taking the expression we have in Gal. 5:3 as the equivalent of ὀφείλει . . . ποιῆσαι.

times be set by Greek usage and require the user to employ either the present or aorist tense form in most contexts where the complement is used. This expected form is called the "unmarked" or "default" form and carries no aspectual information.[51] However, ὀφειλέτης occurs only one other time in the New Testament with an infinitive (below), and so the sample is too small to see the construction as requiring this aorist of ποιῆσαι in Galatians 5:3.[52]

The other factor that contributes to an author's choice of tense form for an infinitive is the inherent meaning of the lexeme in the context. This is a very complex subject, but put very simply, infinitives that convey meanings of "atelic" states, relationships, processes, activities, and such tend to the present tense forms when other contextual factors allow. Infinitives where "telic" meanings are conveyed tend to the aorist; these meanings are actions that are completed with little or no extension in time like "die," "give," "fall," "glance," and "seize."[53] The other New Testament use of an infinitive complement with ὀφειλέτης illustrates the tendency to use the present tense form with atelic meanings: "So then, brothers, *we are debtors* [ὀφειλέται ἐσμὲν], not to the flesh, *to live* [τοῦ . . . ζῆν] according to the flesh" (Rom. 8:12). The infinitive of stative ζῆν appears some forty-six times in the New Testament and Septuagint in its present tense form but only four times in its aorist form.[54] The atelic (stative) meaning of ζάω in the context of Romans 8:12 influenced Paul's choice of the present tense form rather than the aorist for ζῆν with ὀφειλέτης.[55] But can the same be said for aorist ποιῆσαι in Galatians 5:3?

The meaning of ποιῆσαι in Galatians 5:3 cannot be evaluated in a vacuum, in part because this lexeme in general has a wide variety of meanings some of which cross over the simplified boundary between "atelic" and "telic" meanings.[56] Our analysis must narrowly focus upon the meaning of "*doing*

---

51. For example, after ἄρχομαι and μέλλω one normally finds present tense infinitive complements; see Mark 2:23; John 6:6; Acts 1:1; and 22:26 for ποιεῖν (but not ποιῆσαι) with these verbs. After δύναμαι or θέλω there is a decided preference for the aorist; see, for example, Matt. 9:28; 20:15; Eph. 3:20; and Philem. 14 for ποιῆσαι after these verbs (though ποιεῖν also occurs). This is a Greek language phenomenon, not something restricted to the NT.

52. Interestingly, ὀφείλω occurs more often with a present tense complementary infinitive in both the NT and Septuagint, though the frequency of this form is low enough that such results cannot be conclusive. As noted above, the noun ὀφειλέτης does not appear in the Septuagint.

53. The classification of "states of affairs" into "atelic" and "telic" meanings is a simplification of the more complex analysis of Fanning, Rijksbaron, and others, but has been validated by my independent research into biblical and nonbiblical Greek texts.

54. The aorist is in the Septuagint only at 2 Kings 15:34; Ezek. 3:18; 13:19, 22.

55. When the present and aorist forms alternate in the same context and same construction, this lexical influence is usually what determines tense form choice; e.g., Phil. 1:21, Ἐμοὶ γὰρ τὸ ζῆν ("to live"; present, atelic) Χριστὸς καὶ τὸ ἀποθανεῖν ("to die"; aorist, telic) κέρδος.

56. For example, the aorist infinitive ποιῆσαι is found quite often with a variety of meanings normally indicated by a singular direct object: *make* a hair white or black (Matt. 5:36), *make* a

law" in Galatians 5:3 or equivalent statements like "doing the things written in the law." The precise question is: With all other factors being neutral, did this meaning of "doing law" lead Paul to use the aorist tense form in the context of Galatians 5:3? If the aorist is the expected or unmarked form, then the aorist form itself has little or no semantic value. If it is not the default form, then the aorist was a specific choice that carries an aspectual nuance because it is marked.

What makes answering this question difficult is that "to do law" was not a commonly used expression throughout the Greek world but was picked up by Paul from the equivalent Hebrew expression,

לעשות את-התורה

which is found as an infinitive in several OT passages.[57] The equivalent Greek phrase ποιῆσαι τὸν νόμον ("to do the law") is found only twice in the New Testament: our passage and at Galatians 3:10 which we will discuss in a moment. This means that we must look to the Septuagint to see if there is a preference for ποιεῖν τὸν νόμον (present tense form) or ποιῆσαι τὸν νόμον (aorist as in Galatians 5:3).

To shorten a rather lengthy possible discussion, interestingly, where the Septuagint uses an infinitive for "to do law" and equivalent expressions, the present tense form of the infinitive (ποιεῖν) predominates by far in various constructions rather than the aorist (ποιῆσαι).[58] And when the aorist expression ποιῆσαι τὸν νόμον was used in the Septuagint, the infinitive was not used as a complement as in Galatians 5:3 but was part of different constructions where the aorist was the unmarked, expected form.[59] The following are just two examples. "For Ezra had set his heart

---

disciple (Matt. 23:15; cf. Acts 26:28), *make* a tent (Acts 7:44) or a clay pot (Rom. 9:21) or a donation (Rom. 15:26 middle), *perform* a miracle (Matt. 9:28; Mark 6:5), *produce* a piece of fruit or a kind of water (James 3:12), *render* judgment (Jude 15), *wage* war or a battle (Rev. 12:17; 13:7; 19:19), *to do* something for someone (Mark 7:12) or *to do* anything (Luke 12:4; and with neuter relative pronoun as, e.g., Gal. 2:10), *to do* wrong (2 Cor. 13:7), or *to perform* someone's will (Heb. 10:7, 9; 13:21).

57. I am including "doing the words of this law" and similar phrases as equivalent expressions. See, for example: Deut. 27:26; 28:58; 29:28; 31:12; 32:46; Josh. 1:7–8; 22:5; 23:6; 2 Chron. 14:3; Ezra 7:10; and Neh. 9:34. One also "keeps" or "guards" ("observes") the law and its "words" (i.e., stipulations), commandments, regulations, testimonies, etc. The Hebrew infinitive in these passages has various functions such as explanatory or purpose. For "observing" (φυλάσσω) the law" see Gal. 6:13 and Rom. 2:26 in Paul.

58. Some key passages in Deuteronomy, for example, are: Deut. 4:13–14; 5:1; 11:32; 17:19; 27:26 (aorist); 28:58; 29:29; 31:12; and 32:46.

59. For example: εἶπεν τῷ Ἰούδα . . . ποιῆσαι τὸν νόμον καὶ τὰς ἐντολάς, "he told Judah . . . to perform the law and the commandments" (2 Chron. 14:4; 14:3 in Masoretic text/Septuagint), where indirect discourse led to use of the aorist; there is no aspectual nuance of the aorist here.

to study (ζητῆσαι) the Law of the LORD, and to do it (ποιεῖν) and to teach (διδάσκειν) his statutes and rules in Israel" (Ezra 7:10). Notice that two present tense infinitives are parallel with aorist ζητῆσαι, showing that the present forms of those two verbs were the unmarked forms. The second example is: "Only be very careful to observe (ποιεῖν) the commandment[s] and the law" (Josh. 22:5).

The conclusion I draw from this Septuagint evidence for the phrase "to do the law" is that the present tense form ποιεῖν τὸν νόμον and its equivalents are probably the unmarked, expected forms. The lexeme ποιέω in these Septuagint phrases seems best taken as pointing to an activity one engages in over time: "to observe the law." I identify this kind of verb meaning as atelic where the present infinitive form is unmarked. This leads to the conclusion that Paul's aorist ποιῆσαι τὸν νόμον in Galatians 5:3 is marked and therefore carries one of the aspectual meanings of the aorist. Now we have to see what aorist meaning for ποιῆσαι best fits its context in Galatians 5:3.

The first step in aspectual analysis is to determine whether a tense form is marked at all, which we have just been at pains to do. Then the tense form itself should be conceived as presenting a range of meanings much the same as a lexeme's range of meanings. And, like a lexeme, the range of meanings of a tense form is determined entirely by its context—which includes the lexical meaning in this context, particularly if the meaning is atelic or telic.

For example, one of the range of meanings of the aorist with an atelic verb meaning is the *inceptive* nuance. In Galatians 5:3, the inception of the activity is abstractly possible: "He is debtor *to begin observing* (ποιῆσαι) the whole law." But this meaning does not fit our context because the one who takes on circumcision *has already begun* observing the law by being circumcised. Therefore the inceptive meaning of aorist ποιῆσαι is eliminated.

Not to belabor the issue, when one looks carefully at the context of Galatians 5:3, the best meaning of the aorist form with an atelic verb is the *resultative* (or "consummative") meaning, which points to the completion of the extended activity.[60] Paul indicates this meaning by specifying that it is the whole law that must be completed. Hence, we could alternately communicate this resultative force of the aorist of ποιῆσαι in Greek with πληρῶσαι, "*to fulfil* the whole law," which, most notably, is found as a minor

---

60. Cf. Ernest De Witt Burton, *Syntax of the Moods and Tenses in New Testament Greek* (1990; Grand Rapids: Kregel, 1994), §§35 and 98; and Daniel Wallace, *Greek Grammar beyond the Basics* (Grand Rapids: Zondervan, 1989), 559–61.

variant for ποιῆσαι in Galatians 5:3.[61] This variant should be appreciated as representing the resultative interpretation of ποιῆσαι—whether unwitting or deliberate—of an ancient native Greek speaker.

My analysis, then, has shown that Paul says that the law imposes an exacting obligation to fulfil all of its commandments and statutes personally. One must *finish off* performance of the whole law as the only alternative to Christ's mediation and divine grace. If Paul were presenting the law's obligation merely as an effort or lifestyle here—that is, Ἰουδαϊκῶς ζᾶν or Ἰουδαΐζειν "to live as a Jew" (Gal. 2:14)—he would have chosen the present infinitive ποιεῖν in Galatians 5:3.[62]

Therefore, the view of some scholars that Paul is merely saying in Galatians 5:3 that the circumcised Galatians must merely be law-observant in a sincere but imperfect way is not correct. Paul, by using ποιῆσαι in Galatians 5:3, says that the circumcised Galatian must "fulfil" the obligation of the whole law through actual complete performance of its commandments, not merely through a general pattern of behavior with understandable exceptions or with the mere intention to obey, as found in later rabbis.[63]

Before moving to the next point, let me mention that the only prime Septuagint example of aorist ποιῆσαι τὸν νόμον (as is found in Gal. 5:3) is at Deuteronomy 27:26. Interestingly, Paul quotes this text in Galatians 3:10: "For all who rely on works of the law are under a curse; for it is written, 'Cursed be everyone who does not abide by all things written in the Book of the Law, and *do* [τοῦ ποιῆσαι] them.'" Although absolute proof is impossible, it certainly appears that this infinitive also has a resultative meaning in the Septuagint and may have influenced or confirmed Paul's own view of complete performance of the law. It is striking that the resultative meaning of ποιῆσαι fits the context of Deuteronomy 27:26 (and Gal. 3 and 5) very well.

Paul presents the positive consequences of the Galatians' attempt to be justified by law as bringing them under the obligation to perfect personal performance of the entire Mosaic law. The other, negative consequence of their attempt at personal justifying righteousness is the most dreadful: being cut off from Christ.

61. The Nestle-Aland[27] gives πληρῶσαι in 436, 1505, sy[h], Mcion[E], and *pc*. Longenecker (*Galatians*, 220, note d) says that this variant was to harmonize Gal. 5:3 with 5:14 and perhaps Matt. 5:17. See also Warren Carter, "Jesus' 'I have come' Statements in Matthew's Gospel," *Catholic Biblical Quarterly* 60 (1998): 44–62.

62. Cf. equivalent present infinitive τηρεῖν the law or commandments in Acts 15:5 and Matt. 28:20; and φυλάσσειν the commandments in Acts 16:4; Josh. 1:7 in the Septuagint.

63. For the role of intention and fulfilment of commandments in the Talmud, see Robert Goldenberg, "Commandment and Consciousness in Talmudic Thought," *Harvard Theological Review* 68 (1975): 261–71; interesting examples may be found in *Berakoth* 12a and 13a–b.

Consequence of No Mediation

As already intimated, Paul presents the alternative to this demand for personal fulfilment of the law for the circumcised as a mediatorial arrangement in Christ Jesus. If rejection of Christ "profits you nothing" (οὐδὲν ὠφελήσει), acceptance will profit us everything. This is expressed in Galatians 5:6 when Paul says that only "faith working through love" is of any validity (ἰσχύει).

Evangelicals are used to speaking about Christ's "substitutionary atonement" reinforced especially during controversies throughout the twentieth century.[64] But Christ's work on our behalf also has a positive side. Christ, by being "born under the law" (Gal. 4:4), personally fulfilled all of the law's demands as our covenant Mediator or Surety. This is how Christ is "our righteousness": his righteous, perfect keeping of the law in every particular is imputed to me as a free gift (Rom. 5:17). Paul does not develop this point in our Galatians 5:1–6 passage, but he does express it when he says: "For through the Spirit, by faith, we ourselves eagerly wait for *the hope of righteousness*" (Gal. 5:5). I believe this principle of substitutionary mediation is expressed even more strongly—if succinctly—when Paul shows our complete identity with Christ in his death and in his life earlier in Galatians:

> For through the law I died to the law, so that I might live to God. I have been crucified with Christ. It is no longer I who live, but Christ who lives in me. And the life I now live in the flesh I live by faith in the Son of God, who loved me and gave himself for me. I do not nullify the grace of God, for if justification [δικαιοσύνη] were through the law, then Christ died for no purpose. (Gal. 2:19–21)

Paul makes absolutely clear in the Galatians 5 passage that the two ways of righteousness are mutually exclusive: one either appropriates the gift of our Mediator's righteousness for which we hope and eagerly await through the Holy Spirit by faith (v. 5; cf. Rom. 5:17; 2 Cor. 5:21) or one attempts to acquire that standing derived from the "works done by us in righteousness" (Titus 3:5). The latter is what the law of Moses commands: perfect performance by the individual, and there can be no admixture of circumcision and Christ (Gal. 3:3). Ironically, Paul says in Romans 7:6 that we in Christ have been severed from the law (κατηργήθημεν ἀπὸ τοῦ νόμου), but he says in

---

64. See esp. Gal. 3:13: "Christ redeemed us from the curse of the law by becoming a curse for us."

Galatians 5:4 that those who come under the law have been "severed from Christ" (κατηργήθητε ἀπὸ Χριστοῦ).

Furthermore, verse 4 unequivocally shows that there is no "gracious" fulfilment of the law which God accepts as a substitute for perfect and entire performance of its commands by the obligated person (ὀφειλέτης, v. 3). Paul says that all who would attempt to be justified by law have necessarily fallen from grace, since "grace" in this use is tied to the appropriation of the benefits of Christ's substitutionary mediation through faith and received as a gift (e.g., Eph. 2:8). The law here is tied to personal obligation without mediation; hence it is not "gracious" in this sense.[65] This is what Paul had already communicated in brief in Galatians 2:21 where he links divine grace only to Christ's substitutionary death whereas justification through personal law-keeping is antithetical to and a vitiation of grace.[66]

Alternative Interpretations

Before concluding, let me briefly contrast the interpretation of Galatians 5:1–6 offered above with one prominent and influential view. I already indicated above that E. P. Sanders and other New Perspective scholars tend to focus on Galatians 3 and to give our passage in chapter 5 too little attention. In the end of the day, my interpretation of the passage undermines Sanders's unwarranted filtration of Paul's theology through the alleged grid of Second Temple Judaism.

Sanders's interpretation of "the pattern of religion" of ancient Judaism as "covenant nomism" is well known and may simply be illustrated with one quote. Note in particular the last line:

> The pattern is this: God has chosen Israel and Israel has accepted the election. In his role as King, God gave Israel commandments which they are to obey as best they can. Obedience is rewarded and disobedience punished. In case of failure to obey, however, man has recourse to divinely ordained means of atonement, in all of which repentance is required. As long as he maintains his desire to stay in the covenant, he has a share in God's covenantal promises, including life in the world to come. The intention and effort to be obedient constitute the *condition for remaining in the covenant*, but they do not *earn* it.[67]

---

65. Mediation in the Mosaic law is present through the Levitical priesthood and temple sacrifices which Christ has fulfilled and supplanted.

66. "I do not nullify the grace of God, for if justification [δικαιοσύνη] were through the law, then Christ died for no purpose" (Gal. 2:21).

67. E. P. Sanders, *Paul and Palestinian Judaism: A Comparison of Patterns of Religion* (Philadelphia: Fortress, 1977), 180 (original emphasis).

Although Sanders does not apply the term "covenant nomism" to Paul, the curious fact remains that his Paul looks remarkably like Paul's "covenant nomist" opponents.[68] "In Paul, as in Jewish literature," Sanders writes, "good deeds are the *condition* of remaining 'in', but they do not *earn* salvation."[69] If ancient Judaism taught that one "gets into" covenant fellowship and salvation through a gracious, corporate divine election, Paul too, we are told, teaches that one retains title to these blessings only through a sort of nonmeritorious obedience to the law.[70]

Sanders's own interpretation of Galatians 5:1–6 centers on the key verse 3 in only a very brief treatment and is given in connection with Galatians 3:10.[71] Initially in his book *Paul and Palestinian Judaism*, Sanders saw Paul as teaching in these passages "that one must achieve legal perfection." In contrast, "The Amoraic literature always emphasizes that one should confirm the law, not keep it without error. . . . Human perfection was not considered realistically achievable by the Rabbis, nor was it required."[72] Later on, however, Sanders changed his view to assert that Paul, like his contemporaries in Judaism, did not believe that the law required perfect obedience.[73]

But what about the apparently dire threat in Galatians 5:3? For Sanders, Paul is merely "reminding his converts that, if they accept circumcision, the consequence would be that they would have to begin living their lives according to a new set of rules for daily living."[74] He summarizes his interpretation as follows:

> It would, in short, be extraordinarily un-Pharisaic and even un-Jewish of Paul to insist that obedience of the law, once undertaken, must be perfect. Such a position would directly imply that the means of atonement specified in Scripture itself were of no avail. Appeal to Paul's pre-Christian views lends no support to the position that the weight of Paul's argument in Galatians 3 rests on the word "all" in [Galatians] 3:10, or to the position that Paul came to his

68. Assuming for the sake of argument that Sanders's description of ancient Judaism is accurate, compare critiques such as D. A. Carson, Peter T. O'Brien, and Mark A. Seifrid, eds., *Justification and Variegated Nomism*, vol. 1 (Grand Rapids: Baker, 2001), or Mark A. Elliott, *The Survivors of Israel: A Reconsideration of the Theology of Pre-Christian Judaism* (Grand Rapids: Eerdmans, 2000).

69. Sanders, *Paul and Palestinian Judaism*, 517.

70. Francis Watson remarks that, according to New Perspective advocates, "What Paul is propounding is, in effect, an inclusive, universal, liberal form of Jewish covenant theology" (Watson, "Not the New Perspective" [paper delivered to the British New Testament Conference in 2001], 14).

71. "For all who rely on works of the law are under a curse; for it is written, 'Cursed be everyone who does not abide by all things written in the Book of the Law, and do them.'" See Cranford, "The Possibility of Perfect Obedience" for recent discussion.

72. Sanders, *Paul and Palestinian Judaism*, 137.

73. Sanders notes that he changed his view in *Paul, the Law, and the Jewish People*, 23.

74. Ibid., 29.

negative stance on righteousness by the law because it cannot be adequately fulfilled. Paul's Pharisaic past counts heavily against both positions.[75]

Hence, Galatians 5:1–6 becomes for Sanders Paul's mild advice about a change of lifestyle, because his understanding of Paul's Pharisaic past and of Second Temple Judaism so dictates.[76]

I would submit over against Sanders that Paul is aware of the Jewish notion that "the intention" and "effort" to obey the law are required for *eschatological righteousness* and that this is *precisely* what he refutes in Galatians 5:1–6. Rather than conforming to contemporary Judaism, Paul stands in sharp contrast in that he presents two modes of justification: one through perfect, personal, and perpetual obedience to the law, and another through Christ our Surety and Mediator and divine grace. The two positions are not compatible.

What is particularly problematic about Sanders's position on Galatians 5:3 is that it ignores verse 4: "You are severed from Christ, you who would be justified by the law; you have fallen away from grace" (Gal. 5:4). Note in particular that Paul pronounces this truth about the Galatians who take on circumcision for justification. It is not that they will be severed from Christ or will fall from grace, but that they already have! This is a most awful situation that makes our passage as a whole one that we cannot ignore.

Conclusion

In conclusion, this examination of Galatians 5:1–6 has shown that Paul presents here two mutually exclusive ways of eschatological righteousness and justification. The one comes by faith in Christ's substitutionary mediation as our Surety, which is bestowed on us by divine grace apart from personal fulfilment of the law's demands. The other that the Galatians were seeking through their circumcision moved them into a closed system of obligation to personal, perfect obedience to the law as it embodied a principle of the republished covenant of works.

The Mosaic law itself did not originate the notion of personal obedience *de novo*, since it recapitulated a more fundamental creational principle

75. Ibid., 28. Although he adds some nuances of his own, this is also essentially the position taken by James D. G. Dunn in *The Epistle to the Galatians*, Black's New Testament Commentaries (Peabody, MA: Hendrickson, 1993), 260–69, esp. 266.

76. See also Cranford, "The Possibility of Perfect Obedience," 243. Compare S. M. Baugh, "The New Perspective, Mediation, and Justification," in *Covenant, Justification, and Pastoral Ministry: Essays by the Faculty of Westminster Seminary California*, ed. R. Scott Clark (Phillipsburg, NJ: P&R, 2007), 137–63 (esp. 145–47); Watson, "Not the New Perspective," 14; cf. Thomas R. Schreiner in "Paul and Perfect Obedience to the Law: An Evaluation of the View of E. P. Sanders," *Westminster Theological Journal* 47 (1985): 245–78.

of righteousness through obedience to the Creator's covenant stipulations. Further, the Mosaic law did not introduce a new way of salvation through a covenant of works, but it did embody this principle for pedagogical and typological functions in the history of redemption. But Paul does not elaborate on these sorts of essential qualifications in Galatians 5:1–6. Rather this passage is his urgent testimony to avoid even placing one foot on the path to a righteousness based on personal law-keeping whether mixed with supposed divine grace or Christ's mediation or not. The two are not compatible, as Paul makes abundantly clear.

PART THREE

THEOLOGICAL STUDIES

10

~∞~

NATURAL LAW AND THE WORKS PRINCIPLE UNDER ADAM AND MOSES

DAVID VANDRUNEN

No study of the Mosaic law in the Reformed tradition can hope to attain any degree of completeness without attention to the idea of natural law. The ideas of natural law and of the works principle in the Mosaic covenant in fact share an intriguingly similar history. While both concepts were standard features of early Reformed theology—natural law unambiguously and the works principle in the Mosaic covenant with some variation—both have fallen upon hard times in Reformed thought in the last century. Could it be that the disuse of the doctrine of natural law among so many contemporary Reformed theologians and their disuse of the idea of the works principle in the Mosaic covenant are theologically related? To put the question differently: could it be that there is a systematic relation between natural law and the works principle such that the loss of one concept among Reformed theologians will tend to hasten the loss of the other? While the present essay cannot address the historical development of Reformed thought on these two issues, it does explore the question of a systematic relation between them.[1]

Before beginning this exploration, a few initial points of clarification may be in order. First, by "natural law" I refer to the idea as it was commonly received through the first several centuries of the development of Reformed theology. According to the Reformed tradition, the content of God's moral law is made known to every human being through natural revelation. It is "written on the heart" and perceived through the judgments of conscience. Though fallen sinners have a continual propensity to repress and pervert this law, it is known to all people and, through the mystery of providence, serves to constrain all people against the full outbreak of lawlessness in this world. It has the negative function of reminding all people of their sin and just condemnation before God (and of their need for a Savior) and the positive (though nonsaving) function of serving as the standard for the development of civil law. The evidence that this basic perspective is the overwhelming consensus of the early centuries of Reformed theology is itself overwhelming. To associate the idea of natural law merely with a philosophical ethical theory of Roman Catholicism that fails to account for the devastating impact of sin upon human knowing and willing is quite simply erroneous historically.

Second, by the "works principle" I refer to the idea as it is discussed in many other essays in this collection. I take the works principle to describe the law's demand for perfect, personal obedience, with sanctions of blessing and curse to follow obedience and disobedience respectively to this demand. The Reformed tradition held that the works principle was proclaimed in the original covenant of works, that with Adam at creation. As explored throughout this volume, much of the Reformed tradition has also seen a works principle operative in the Mosaic covenant within God's broader, gracious dealings with Israel, not as a way of attaining everlasting life (impossible for sinners) but for redemptive-historical, typological purposes such as reminding sinners of their fall and judgment under Adam, their inability to provide perfect obedience to God themselves, and their hope of a coming

1. The loss of the doctrine of natural law in Reformed theology in the past century is a major issue that demands historical analysis. A significant step forward has recently occurred with the publication of Stephen J. Grabill, *Rediscovering the Natural Law in Reformed Theological Ethics* (Grand Rapids: Eerdmans, 2006). I hope to present additional work on this subject in the near future in David VanDrunen, *Natural Law and the Two Kingdoms: A Study in the Development of Reformed Social Thought* (Grand Rapids: Eerdmans, forthcoming). Several previous essays in the present volume offer historical studies of the fate of the works principle in the Mosaic covenant in the history of Reformed theology, though much work remains to be done.

Messiah who would himself be born under this works principle and satisfy its requirements on behalf of his people.[2]

The thesis of this essay is perhaps somewhat complex, though I hope that the argument as it unfolds will be sufficiently clear. I argue first of all that the Reformed tradition has been correct to teach that the natural law proclaims the works principle, both in the original Adamic covenant of works and in the lingering testimony of every human heart. Second, I argue that the Reformed tradition has been correct to see the natural law (and hence the works principle) as underlying the Mosaic law—specifically, in its seeing the Mosaic law as an application of the natural law to the specific, unique situation of Old Testament Israel. Finally, and climactically, I argue that the common foundation of the Adamic and Mosaic covenants in the works principle–proclaiming natural law helps to explain systematically the purpose of the works principle under Moses in God's larger plan of redemption. Specifically, in this last part of the argument, particularly through reflection upon Galatians 4:3, 9, I propose that God, by giving to Israel a law grounded in the works principle–proclaiming natural law, made manifest *in Israel* the basic predicament of the *whole human race*, that is, that all human beings stand condemned under the covenant of works, from which no person can extricate himself by his own efforts. Space constraints mean that I cannot pursue any of the topics addressed in this essay with the desirable thoroughness. My hope is that the discussions in this essay will be helpfully suggestive and stimulate future, and more thorough, exploration of its themes.

Natural Law, the Works Principle, and the Adamic Covenant

In this first section, I explore the connection of natural law and the works principle. Initially, I reflect upon this subject as handled in the Reformed tradition. Though I certainly cannot offer a comprehensive study, I present a considerable amount of evidence that Reformed theologians—particularly in the sixteenth and seventeenth centuries, but also more recently—have commonly seen the works principle as revealed in the natural law and, correspondingly, have commonly seen the natural law as a crucial part of that moral obligation placed upon Adam in the covenant of works (and also as a lingering moral standard brewing in the hearts of sinners to the present day). Then, I consider several strands of biblical evidence that suggest that Reformed theology was correct in these insights.

---

2. See n. 30 below for some important comments on the relation of the requirement of perfect obedience to God's administration of the Mosaic covenant.

Natural Law and the Works Principle in the Reformed Tradition

The Reformed tradition sports a strong history of seeing the works principle generally as known by nature both as a constitutive aspect of the Adamic covenant of works and as a lingering reminder to fallen humanity of God's just demands. For historic Reformed theology, the natural law reveals the works principle. This entails, then, that the law of nature not only imparts knowledge of and obligation to God's basic moral will but also makes known the *sanctions* that attach to this obligation: life and blessing for obedience and death and curse for disobedience. Thus, to put the point more precisely: historic Reformed theology has held that the natural law makes known humanity's basic moral obligation to God as well as the fact that God will richly reward obedience and fiercely punish disobedience.

A number of examples from eminent sixteenth- and seventeenth-century Reformed theologians provide evidence for this claim. At an early date, the Larger Catechism of Zacharias Ursinus (1534–83) provides a succinct and representative example in its explanation of the difference between the law and the gospel: "The law contains the natural covenant, established by God with humanity in creation, that is, it is known by humanity by nature, it requires our perfect obedience to God, and it promises eternal life to those who keep it and threatens eternal punishment to those who do not" (Q&A 36).[3]

In the mature orthodoxy of the middle and later seventeenth century, John Owen (1616–83), Francis Turretin (1623–87), Wilhelmus à Brakel (1635–1711), and Herman Witsius (1636–1709) provide prominent examples. Owen speaks broadly at some points of the natural knowledge possessed by all people not only of basic moral obligation but also of the fact that God is a just judge who will call sin to account.[4] Elsewhere he clearly ties this continuing natural knowledge of the works principle to the original covenant of works.[5]

3. For English translation, see Lyle D. Bierma, with Charles D. Gunnoe Jr., Karin Y. Maag, and Paul W. Fields, *An Introduction to the Heidelberg Catechism: Sources, History, and Theology* (Grand Rapids: Baker, 2005), 168–69.

4. E.g., see John Owen, "A Dissertation on Divine Justice," in *The Works of John Owen*, vol. 10, ed. William H. Goold (Edinburgh: Banner of Truth, 1967), where, after writing of "an innate conception . . . implanted by God in the minds of men" and citing Rom. 1:32 in support, Owen comments: "Here they [the barbarians] argue from the effect to the cause; which, in matters relating to moral good or evil, they could not, unless convinced in their consciences that there is an inviolable connection between sin and punishment, which they here ascribe to Justice" (517–18). Shortly thereafter, he adds: "The consciences of all mankind concur to corroborate this truth; but the cause which has numberless witnesses to support it cannot fail. . . . Conscious to themselves of their wickedness, and convinced of the divine dominion over them, this idea above all dwells in their minds, that he with whom they have to do is supremely just, and the avenger of all sin" (519).

5. E.g., see John Owen, *The Works of John Owen*, vol. 11, *An Exposition of the Epistle to the Hebrews*, ed. William H. Goold (London/Edinburgh, 1850; Philadelphia: Leighton, 1869), 388: "There were and are, indeed, general notions of good and evil indelibly planted on the faculties of

Turretin makes relevant comments in a number of places. In speaking of the different characteristics of the "covenant of nature" (the Adamic covenant of works), for example, Turretin grounds this covenant in human nature generally and in the natural law specifically.[6] Strikingly, Turretin explains shortly thereafter that Adam's natural obligation was more fundamental in the covenant of works than was the obligation that God placed upon him by special revelation.[7] Wilhelmus à Brakel, in the midst of a larger discussion of Adam's obligations under the covenant of works, refers to "the law which is embedded in the nature of the heathen and is a remnant of that law which Adam had embedded in his nature" (which, he says, "is identical to the law of the ten commandments").[8] Witsius dealt with similar matters when addressing the Socinian claim that God did not hold out any promises to the human race at creation but wanted to show that he owed nothing to anybody. He responded to this attack on an important aspect of the Reformed doctrine of the covenant of works by appealing first of all to the reality of natural law, which teaches both moral obligation and that sanctions attach to it.[9]

---

our souls, with a power of judging concerning our actions and moral practices, whether they are conformable unto those notions with respect unto the superior judgment of God. . . . And that this might now be permanent, he reduced the substance of the whole law unto 'ten words,' or commands, writing them in tables of stone, which he appointed to be sacredly kept amongst them. The law thus declared and written by him was the same, I say, materially, and for the substance of it, with the law of our creation, or the original rule of our covenant obedience unto God."

6. Francis Turretin, *Institutes of Elenctic Theology*, trans. George Musgrave Giger, ed. James T. Dennison Jr., 3 vols. (Phillipsburg, NJ: P&R, 1992–97), 1:575: "It is called 'natural,' not from natural obligation (which God does not have towards man), but because it is founded on the nature of man (as it was at first created by God) and on his integrity or powers. It is also called 'legal' because the condition on man's part was the observation of the law of nature engraved within him."

7. Ibid., 1:577: "The whole duty was partly general, partly special (according to the twofold law given to him: the moral or natural and the symbolic). The general was the knowledge and worship of God, justice towards his neighbor and every kind of holiness; the special was abstinence from the forbidden fruit. . . . The former was founded on the law of nature not written in a book, but engraven and stamped upon the heart. . . . The latter was founded upon the symbolic and positive law. The former was principal and primary; the latter, however, only secondary. For although he was bound to obey each special precept or that symbolic law given to him, still most especially was obedience to the natural law required of him (for exploring of which this symbolic precept only served, as will be shown hereafter)." Turretin also comments on the natural law as impressed by God on human conscience from creation in *Institutes*, 2:2.

8. Wilhelmus à Brakel, *The Christian's Reasonable Service*, trans. Bartel Elshout, 4 vols. (Ligonier, PA: Soli Deo Gloria, 1992–95), 1:359 (see 357–60 generally).

9. Herman Witsius, *The Economy of the Covenants between God and Man*, trans. William Crookshank (1822; Phillipsburg, NJ: Presbyterian and Reformed, 1990), 1:71: "1st. Man's natural conscience teaches him, that God desires not to be served in vain, nor that obedience to his commands will go unrewarded and for nought. The very Heathens were also apprized of this." Shortly thereafter he writes in the same vein: "In like manner, we find it among the articles of the Jewish faith, as a thing naturally known, that *there are rewards as well as punishments with God*; according to that common saying, *God defrauds no creature of its reward*. The worship of God presupposes the belief of this: *For he that cometh to God must believe that he is, and that he is a rewarder of them that diligently seek him*, Heb. xi. 6" (1:72).

Moving ahead a couple of centuries, one sees the idea still alive in a more recent Reformed theologian such as Herman Bavinck (1854–1921), who also associated the Adamic covenant of works with the common human consciousness of the moral law and its corresponding sanctions.[10]

Surely it is interesting and relevant to note at this point that Karl Barth's (1886–1968) massively influential reworking of Reformed theology entailed rejection of both the covenant of works and natural law. Barth himself argued that historic Reformed views of natural law and the covenant of works (and of the *logos insarkos*, the preincarnate Son of God) were so intertwined that rejecting one demands rejection of the other.[11]

The idea that the natural law proclaims the works principle—the obligation to obey the moral law, with sanctions to follow upon obedience or disobedience—therefore has an impressive pedigree in the Reformed tradition. Among many of these same theologians, it may be noted how they closely associated the works principle–proclaiming natural law with human creation in the image of God. They teach that it is precisely the image-bearing nature with which God created human beings that makes his imposition of the works principle upon them appropriate and even that the image-bearing nature itself impresses this natural knowledge of the law and its consequences upon human consciousness.[12] This idea also found

10. See Herman Bavinck, *Reformed Dogmatics*, vol. 2, *God and Creation*, trans. John Vriend, ed. John Bolt (Grand Rapids: Baker, 2004), 564–65: He comments that Adam's "condition was provisional and temporary and could not remain as it was. It either had to pass on to higher glory or to sin and death. The penalty for transgressing the command was death; the reward for keeping it, by contrast, was life, eternal life. Our common conscience already testifies that in keeping God's commands there is great reward, and that the violation of these commands brings punishment, and Holy Scripture also expresses this truth over and over." In further discussion of the Adamic covenant he also writes: "In distinction from the covenant of grace this was then called the covenant of nature or of works. . . . It was called 'covenant of nature,' not because it was deemed to flow automatically and naturally from the nature of God or the nature of man, but because the foundation on which the covenant rested, that is, the moral law, was known to man by nature, and because it was made with man in his original state and could be kept by man with the powers bestowed on him in the creation, without the assistance of supernatural grace" (567).

11. E.g., see Karl Barth, *Church Dogmatics*, IV/1, *The Doctrine of Reconciliation*, trans. G. W. Bromiley, ed. G. W. Bromiley and T. F. Torrance (New York: T&T Clark, 1956), 54–66.

12. E.g., see Ursinus's Larger Catechism in *An Introduction to the Heidelberg Catechism*, 164–65: In a relevant progression of thought from Q&A 10 through Q&A 12, it first asks what the divine law teaches and then provides a threefold response. Particularly pertinent here is the first ("It teaches the kind of covenant that God established with mankind in creation") and its explanation ("that is, what kind of person God created, for what purpose"). Then it proceeds to ask what kind of person was created and answers: "Someone who is in the image of God." The next question asks what this image is and responds: "A true knowledge of God and the divine will, and the inclination and desire of the whole person to live according to this knowledge alone."

Also see Turretin, who raises this issue in his defense of the existence of a covenant of nature and its appropriateness, in *Institutes*, 1:575–76: "Also since he was created after the image of divine holiness, he ought to have been led to a communion of that happiness also which is the inseparable attendant of holiness." Later in his argument he adds: "Such a covenant was demanded not only by the goodness

expression in the Westminster Standards and other Reformed confessional documents.[13]

Pursuing these issues in the early Reformed tradition more deeply would reveal a number of interesting and related matters that might be explored.[14] Perhaps most pertinent for present purposes is whether the

---

and philanthropy . . . of God . . . , but also by the state of man and the desire of happiness impressed upon his heart by God. Since it cannot be doubted that it was right and lawful, it could not be empty and frustrated, but ought to be fulfilled on the ground of man's obedience (unless we hold that God wished to feed man with a vain desire and thus deceive him—which even to think is blasphemous)."

Whereas Turretin in these passages points to the reality of the image as a way of highlighting the appropriateness of God's promise of blessing to the obedient, Owen also stresses the epistemological dimension, that through the reality of the image of God human beings know the obligation and sanctions of the natural law. For example, in the appendix to his Hebrews commentary cited above (*The Works of John Owen*, vol. 11), Owen writes: "The old creation comprised in it the *law of the obedience* of all creatures unto God. This was therein and thereby implanted on their natures, with inclinations natural or moral unto the observation of it. . . . The law of the old creation unto man consisted principally in the image of God in him and concreated with him; for hereby did he both know his duty and was enabled to perform it. . . . But this law in the state of creation fell under a double consideration, or had a double use,—first as a *rule*, and then as a *principle*. As a rule, the light that was in the mind of man, which was a principal part of the image of God in him, acquainted him with his whole duty, and directed him in the right performance of it" (405). "First, he was made a rational creature, and thereby necessarily in a moral dependence on God: for being endowed with *intellectual faculties*, in an immortal soul, capable of eternal blessedness or misery. . . . And this the order of his nature, called 'the image of God,' inclined and enabled him unto. For it was not possible that such a creature should be produced, and not lie under an obligation unto all those duties which the nature of God and his own, and the relation of the one to the other, made necessary. Under this consideration alone, it was required, by the *law of man's creation*, that some time should be separated unto the solemn expression of his obedience" (336–37). "And although, it may be, we cannot now discern how in particular his natural light might conduct and guide him to the observance of all these things, yet ought we not therefore to deny that so it did, seeing there is evidence in the things themselves, and we know not well what that light was which was in him; for although we may have some due apprehensions of the substance of it, from its remaining ruins and materials in our lapsed condition, yet we have no acquaintance with that light and glorious lustre, that extent of its directive beams, which it was accompanied withal, when it was in him as he came immediately from the hand of God, created in his image" (347).

Anybody still reading this footnote may be interested and capable of pursuing further research on this subject, and one fascinating angle may be the thought of the controversial Reformed theologian Johannes Cocceius (1603–69) on such matters. For a taste of Cocceius's approach, see the collected quotations from his writings in Heinrich Heppe, *Reformed Dogmatics*, rev. and ed. Ernst Bizer, trans. G. T. Thomson (1950; London: Wakeman, n.d.), 283–89. One of the few published studies of Cocceius's covenant theology discusses these matters briefly; see Willem J. van Asselt, *The Federal Theology of Johannes Cocceius (1603–1669)*, trans. Raymond A. Blacketer (Leiden: Brill, 2001), 254–55, 259–60.

13. E.g., see Westminster Confession of Faith 4.2; Westminster Larger Catechism 17. For another example, consider the Irish Articles (1615), article 21: "Man being at the beginning created according to the image of God (which consisted especially in the Wisdom of his mind and the true Holiness of his free will) had the covenant of the law ingrafted in his heart: whereby God did promise unto him everlasting life, upon condition that he performed entire and perfect obedience unto his Commandments, according to that measure of strength wherewith he was endued in his creation, and threatened death unto him if he did not perform the same."

14. For example, is it in fact natural (and thus necessary) for God himself to give reward to human beings for their obedience and punishment for their disobedience, a question that Witsius takes up at considerable length in *Economy of the Covenants*, 1:76–82. In this remarkable section,

Adamic covenant, in light of its association with natural law, was itself part of (created) nature or something above and additional to nature. À Brakel represents one line of thought in the earlier Reformed tradition in stating explicitly that Adam "was created in this covenant from the very first moment of his existence."[15] Yet among other Reformed theologians there has been some ambiguity, in my judgment. Turretin and Bavinck, for example, both claim that God made man in his image with a natural knowledge of the moral law and the awareness that a judgment of reward or punishment must follow obedience or disobedience. At the same time, both also fear to assert that God had any sort of natural obligation to grant eschatological life to Adam upon his obedience and therefore speak of the covenant, with its unexacted promise to reward obedience with life, as something added on to creation in the divine image.[16]

Witsius concludes strongly that "God cannot, consistent with his goodness, refuse to grant to his holy creature the communion of himself." Yet he is not able to offer a conclusive judgment on the question of whether it was necessary for God to grant *eschatological* communion with himself to his obedient creature.

15. À Brakel, *The Christian's Reasonable Service*, 1:384.

16. An example of this ambiguity in the earlier Reformed tradition appears in Turretin's discussion of the covenant with Adam. As observed above, Turretin on the one hand says not only that the obligation of the law is known by nature but also that the image of God with which human beings were created demands that a holy creature enjoy blessed communion with God. See *Institutes*, 1:575; and also *Institutes*, 1:576. Yet on the other hand he also claims that God could have prescribed obedience for his human creatures without promise of a reward, but that he "added" a covenant which in fact offered such a promise. See *Institutes*, 1:574; and also *Institutes*, 1:577. Turretin, therefore, seems to end up somewhat incoherent in claiming both that God was obliged to give an obedient Adam blessedness by virtue of his nature as image-bearer and that God had no obligation to reward obedience apart from the covenant relation that he freely established. These dual claims could make sense were the act of creation and the act of establishing the covenant of works the same act, but Turretin writes as though the two acts are distinguishable, the latter being subsequent.

A similar ambiguity appears in Bavinck's treatment of the Adamic covenant of works. Again, as noted above, Bavinck asserts that the moral law is evident by nature and that the "common consciousness" of humanity offers testimony that obedience brings reward and disobedience brings punishment. See Bavinck, *Reformed Dogmatics*, 2:564–65, 567. In other words, the works principle (both obligation and sanctions) is known by nature. But he goes on to insist, in no uncertain terms, that though the law itself (the obligation) is known by nature, human beings could not know, apart from a positive covenantal revelation and relationship, that a reward of eternal life (the sanction) would follow their obedience. The covenant, then, is something added on to the original creation in the divine image. He writes: "After creating men and women after his own image, God showed them their destiny and the only way in which they could reach it. Human beings could know the moral law without special revelation since it was written in their hearts. But the probationary command is positive; it is not a given of human nature as such but could be made known to human beings if God communicated it to them. Nor was it self-evident that keeping that command would yield eternal life. In that sense the 'covenant of works' is not a 'covenant of nature.' Initially, the church did not yet clearly understand this, but gradually it became obvious—and was taught as such— that God was in no way obligated to grant heavenly blessedness and eternal life to those who kept his law and thereby did not do anything other than what they were obligated to do. There *is* no natural connection here between work and reward." See *Reformed Dogmatics*, 2:571. For Bavinck, then, "Adam knew the moral law by nature," yet the covenant of works itself "is added to the creation in God's image." See *Reformed Dogmatics*, 2:572, 574. Could human beings, and Adam

To be clear, the question here is not whether God, in some abstract sense, has an obligation to reward obedient rational creatures with eternal life. The question is whether the very way in which God made human beings—as image-bearers with the natural law inscribed on their hearts—entailed a natural human knowledge of both their obligation to obey God's moral will and the consequences that would follow upon their obedience or disobedience, and hence an obligation on God's part to impart this reward or punishment. To put it somewhat differently, did the very way in which God created human beings entail the sort of relationship that Reformed theology has described in terms of the covenant of works? Even eminent Reformed theologians have answered ambiguously, suggesting both affirmative and negative responses in different places.

A Reformed theologian of recent days has cut through this ambiguity—however unwittingly, given that he does not interact with his predecessors or use the terminology of natural law on this point. Meredith G. Kline (1922–2007) follows his Reformed predecessors closely in affirming the works principle operative in the covenant with Adam and in associating this works principle with the reality of the image of God. He resolves the ambiguity patent in many of his predecessors, however, by refusing to separate the act of creation in the image of God from the establishment of the covenant with Adam. For Kline, the very act of creation in God's image entails the establishment of the covenant, with its requirement of obedience and its prospect of eschatological reward or punishment. By separating these two acts, older theologians seemed to be caught on the horns of a dilemma, namely, being compelled to speak of a natural knowledge of the works principle while feeling constrained to defend the meaningfulness of a covenant relationship that is not simply superfluous. By identifying these two acts, Kline has no such dilemma. God's creating Adam in his image and the establishment of the covenant are aspects of the same act, and thus Adam's image-derived natural human knowledge that obedience brings eschatological life was at the very same time covenantal knowledge of the special relationship that he enjoyed with God.[17]

---

in particular, then, know that obedience brings reward? Bavinck seems to give different answers at different places. Though they may add further nuance to a description of Bavinck's view, I can only conclude that the following sentences do not resolve the tension: "The probationary command relates to the moral law as the covenant of works relates to man's creation in God's image. The moral law stands or falls in its entirety with the probationary command, and the image of God in mankind in its entirety stands or falls with the covenant of works. The covenant of works is the road to heavenly blessedness for the [first] human beings, who were created in God's image and had not yet fallen." See *Reformed Dogmatics*, 2:572.

17. These considerations suggest that when God gave the probationary command in Gen. 2:17, threatening death for disobedience and (implicitly) life for obedience, he was not conveying any fundamentally new information to our first parents, but bringing their basic moral situation, which they knew by nature, into focus through a concrete probationary test. For Kline's treatment of

A Constructive Account of Natural Law and the Works Principle

In the previous subsection, I have offered a number of pieces of evidence that the Reformed tradition historically has understood the natural law to proclaim the works principle (obligation and sanctions), both in the Adamic covenant of works and in the continuing testimony within every fallen human being. Despite some ambiguity concerning the relationship between the creation of this inward testimony of natural law through the image of God and the establishment of the Adamic covenant of works, the basic idea that the natural law proclaims the works principle itself is well attested. In this subsection I offer a brief theological defense of this historic Reformed teaching.

First, I believe that this association of the natural law with the works principle is indeed well supported by biblical teaching on the image of God, especially as drawn from the opening chapters of Genesis. The Reformed tradition was correct in this insight. At an initial level, the image of God clearly entails an inherent righteousness and holiness, along with awareness of it. In other words, the originally created image-bearer possessed knowledge of the obligation of the law of God and a concrete orientation toward keeping it. This is evident in Paul's statements about the image as restored in Christ in Ephesians 4:23–24 and Colossians 3:9–10. In the former, Paul exhorts his readers to be renewed in the spirit of their mind (τῷ πνεύματι τοῦ νοὸς ὑμῶν) and to put on the new man which has been created according to God (ἐνδύσασθαι τὸν καινὸν ἄνθρωπον τὸν κατὰ θεὸν κτισθέντα) in the righ-

---

this issue, see, e.g., Meredith G. Kline, *Kingdom Prologue: Genesis Foundations for a Covenantal Worldview* (Overland Park, KS: Two Age, 2000), 92: "Man's creation as image of God meant, as we have seen, that the creating of the world was a covenant-making process. There was no original non-covenantal order of mere nature on which the covenant was superimposed. Covenantal commitments were given by the Creator in the very act of endowing the man-creature with the mantle of the divine likeness. And those commitments were eschatological. The situation never existed in which man's future was contemplated or presented in terms of a static continuation of the original level of blessedness. For the God in whose likeness man was made is the consummating God of the Sabbath. This sabbatical aspect of the divine image was present in the image as imparted to man and it came to expression in the promise of consummation contained in the creational ordinance of the Sabbath. Blessing sanction promising a consummation of man's original glory as image of God was thus built into man's very nature as image of God. This eschatological prospect was in-created. It was an aspiration implanted in man's heart with his existence as God's image. That being so, to restrict man to the mere continuation of his original state of beatitude would be no blessing at all, but a curse. For it would frustrate man's longing to realize his in-created potential as image of God by disappointing his hope of entering into the Creator's Sabbath rest and thereby experiencing the perfecting of his likeness to the divine paradigm of the Glory-Spirit. The blessing sanction of the covenant of creation was, therefore, no artificial addition to the covenant but was already involved in man's God-like eschatological-sabbatical nature and was essentially nothing other than the perfecting of that nature." Taking a different view is Guy Prentiss Waters, *The Federal Vision and Covenant Theology: A Comparative Analysis* (Phillipsburg, NJ: P&R, 2006), 25–26, 42. Ironically, Waters calls the idea of a covenantal creation "a dubious doctrine" as part of a critique of bitter opponents of Kline on the covenant of works.

teousness and holiness of the truth (ἐν δικαιοσύνῃ καὶ ὁσιότητι τῆς ἀληθείας). The apostle's use of the concept of renewal, as well as the way that his language echoes that of Genesis 1:26 (κατ᾽ εἰκόνα), indicates that the reality of the image possessed by Christians hearkens back to the image as originally created in Adam. Central to this image, then, were righteousness and holiness. Paul speaks in similar terms in Colossians 3:9–10, reminding believers that they have taken off the old man (τὸν παλαιὸν ἄνθρωπον) and put on the new man (ἐνδυσάμενοι τὸν νέον) which is being renewed unto knowledge according to the image of the one who created him (τὸν ἀνακαινούμενον εἰς ἐπίγνωσιν κατ᾽ εἰκόνα τοῦ κτίσαντος αὐτόν). Here again, the language of renewal and the similar language to Genesis 1:26 point the redeemed Christian back to the image as originally bestowed. Considered narrowly, Paul's point is intellectual rather than moral: renewal unto knowledge. Yet this is clearly a knowledge that includes—perhaps especially—moral knowledge. As in Ephesians 4:23–25, Paul appeals to the reality of the restored image in Colossians 3:9–10 in order to ground a moral exhortation (in fact, the same moral exhortation: telling the truth). Furthermore, putting on the restored image in 3:10 contrasts with the old man of 3:9 which Paul describes in terms of "its deeds" (ταῖς πράξεσιν αὐτοῦ). The restoration of the image unto knowledge in Colossians 3:10 refers to a knowledge that understands moral truth and undergirds its practical execution.

At a richer level, I would argue that the image of God entails not only a knowledge of the righteous and holy requirements of God's law but also an awareness that sanctions attach to these requirements: life and blessing for obedience and death and curse for disobedience. In other words, those who bear the image of God carry within their bosom knowledge of the works principle and even some sort of orientation toward seeing it implemented for themselves. Though this claim could be explored at great length, I point here briefly to two considerations in support of it: the association of image-bearing with judgment and the association of image-bearing with a work-rest, sabbatical pattern.

First, then, being an image-bearer involves rendering judgment. By nature, an image-bearer knows that action demands a verdict and is oriented toward rendering one. The relevance of this idea for the present argument is this: a naturally judgment-oriented creature is one who displays the works principle, in both its demand for sanctions and its imposition of obligation. One who, by nature, knows the right and is programed to render a verdict upon human action is one who knows that action demands judgment and its consequences.

Seeing the biblical testimony about human beings as image-bearing judgment-renderers is aided by recognition of its teaching about God, whom human beings image, as the archetypal judgment-renderer. The opening stories in Genesis present him in precisely this way. Following his creative acts, he issues verdicts on his own actions: he sees that his creation is good (Gen. 1:4, 10, 12, 18, 21, 25), even very good (Gen. 1:31). When his creatures begin to act, God then issues a verdict on their actions: condemnation and curse (Gen. 3:14–19). This evidence seems sufficient to establish God as archetypal judgment-renderer, but a significant piece of additional evidence is forthcoming if one adopts the divine council/heavenly court view of Genesis 1:26, which has a very ancient pedigree, is the consensus position of mainstream biblical scholarship, and has been defended in recent years in Reformed and other conservative circles.[18] This position takes God's exhortation "Let *us* make" not as intratrinitarian speech but as God's address to his heavenly council.[19] Others have defended this view competently, and there is no space to repeat the arguments here, though it is entirely convincing to me. If it is not correct, the evidence outlined above concerning God as archetypal judgment-renderer still stands. If it is correct, however, then Genesis 1:26 adds further evidence in this direction by portraying God on his royal seat of judgment, surrounded by his court of glory. Here, as in other descriptions of the heavenly court in Scripture, God is a royal judge.[20] This is particularly pertinent for present purposes (and, incidentally, becomes all the more exegetically compelling) in light of the fact that this proclamation of God from the midst of his council is precisely the word that creates man as his image-bearer. God's proclamation as royal judge establishes man in his image. Would we not then expect the image to entail some sort of royal-judicial office that entails judgment-rendering?

This indeed seems to be the case. The first human beings, upon their creation, are immediately given a mandate to exercise dominion over the earth, a royal task (Gen. 1:26, 28). The language of Genesis 1:26, reinforced by the context, suggests that God made man for the very purpose of his task of dominion.[21] Psalm 8:5–8 offers inspired commentary on this point. In

18. That this is the consensus view in mainstream biblical scholarship is maintained by W. Randall Garr, *In His Own Image and Likeness: Humanity, Divinity, and Monotheism* (Leiden: Brill, 2003), 20–21, who defends a version of this view at great length in this work. Among conservative scholars, see, e.g., Meredith G. Kline, *Images of the Spirit* (Grand Rapids: Baker, 1980), ch. 1; and Gordon J. Wenham, *Genesis 1–15*, Word Biblical Commentary (Waco: Word, 1987), 27–28. Wenham also includes comments on the ancient and modern support for this view.

19. In *In His Own Image and Likeness*, Garr takes this council to be composed of gods, though I would reject a polytheistic view of this text and follow those such as Kline who see the council as composed of the angelic host.

20. E.g., see Pss. 89:5–7; 99:1–4; 1 Kings 22:19–22; and often throughout Revelation.

21. The indirect volative נעשׂה, likely, though not necessarily, indicates purpose; see Paul Joüon, S.J., *A Grammar of Biblical Hebrew*, trans. and rev. T. Muraoka (Rome: Editrice Pontificio Instituto Biblico, 1991), 2:381. The context seems to support this reading in that the God that man is created

Genesis 2:19–20, God gives Adam the task of naming the animals, a job
that presumes a discerning, judicial authority and mimics the name-granting
authority exercised by God in the previous chapter (Gen. 1:5, 8, 10). After
the fall, the often puzzling statement that the man had become "like one
of us" (Gen. 3:22)—the language of image—is much more comprehensible
when the thing that makes the man like God, his "knowing good and evil,"
is taken as a knowledge of judgment. Adam has sinned, but he has sinned
as only an image-bearer can sin: he has made a judgment between good
and evil. Finally, Genesis 9:6 likely provides additional evidence. Though
the appeal to the image that occurs in this covenant with Noah is ordinarily
taken as an explanation for why murder is such a terrible crime, another
viable interpretation (which is again entirely convincing to me, though I
have no space to defend it) is that the appeal to the image is in fact an
explanation for why one human being is given the awesome task of inflict-
ing capital punishment upon another human being: image-bearing man has
a royal-judicial office that entails the authority to deal out just punishments
for crime.[22] In all of these lines of evidence, image-bearing human beings are
ectypal judgment-renderers.

A second line of evidence in support of historic Reformed teaching that
image-bearing involves knowing and being orienting toward the works principle by nature is the association of the image of God with a work-rest,
sabbatical pattern. Again, Scripture portrays God himself as the archetypal
worker-rester, Sabbath-keeper. After working through the six days of Genesis
1, he rests on the seventh day, having finished his work (Gen. 2:1–3). In Genesis 1:26–28, God clearly creates human beings for the purpose of *working*
as he has. They are to exercise dominion over the earth as God has done
and be fruitful as God has been. If man is to image God in his work, does
not good and necessary consequence suggest that man is made also to image
God in his rest? Whatever doubt the opening chapters of Genesis might
leave about such a conclusion, the account of the fourth commandment in
Exodus 20:8–11 (and Ex. 31:14–17) explicitly supports it. There the work-
rest, sabbatical pattern that God called Israel to follow is grounded in the
work-rest, sabbatical pattern established by God in the creation week. The
pertinence of this point for present purposes should again be clear: human

---

to image has himself been exercising supreme dominion over his world through Gen. 1:1–25. This
reading then would yield the translation: "And God said, 'Let us make man in our image, according to our likeness, *so that* he might rule.'" A different view is presented by Bruce K. Waltke and
M. O'Connor, *An Introduction to Biblical Hebrew Syntax* (Winona Lake, IN: Eisenbrauns, 1990),
653–54, who see here not an indirect volative but a conjunctive *waw*, joining two clauses "not
otherwise logically related."

22. Kline supports and discusses this view in *Kingdom Prologue*, 252–53.

beings are not only made to work (that is, to fulfil the dominion mandate given by God) but also to reach a *telos* and just consequence of that work, a rest. Here again, therefore, the works principle seems inscribed into nature itself. A sanction and just consequence must follow the performance of the work (or lack thereof).

Before leaving this point, however, one might note that biblical teaching about creation and the sabbatical pattern suggests not only that the works principle in general (sanctions to follow dis/obedience) is inscribed upon human nature, but even that an eschatological sanction must follow upon human obedience or disobedience. If true, this gives credence to Kline's disambiguating of the Reformed tradition on the relation of creation and covenant-establishment. Once again there is no space to defend this point, but Hebrews 2:5–10 and 4:1–14 provide significant biblical evidence for the idea that the sabbatical pattern inscribed into human nature entails the knowledge of and even longing for an eschatological destiny to follow the moral response to God's law. In these passages, the inspired author teaches that God made human beings from the outset with an eschatological goal (2:5–8), the eschatological Sabbath rest (σαββατισμὸς) held out for human beings now in the gospel (4:9) being a share in God's own seventh-day Sabbath rest which he offered to Adam from the beginning (4:1–11), a Sabbath rest already attained by Christ (2:9–10; 4:14).[23]

The biblical teaching on the image of God, then, suggests that by nature human beings know the way of moral righteousness and understand that (eschatological) sanctions must follow moral conduct. This gives initial support to the historic Reformed idea that the natural law proclaims the works principle. Another line of support for this idea emerges from the first two chapters of Romans, particularly in 1:32 and 2:14–15. Though 1:32 and 2:14–15 are part of a larger argument by Paul, it is worth looking at them consecutively. The opening verses of the pericope of which 1:32 is the conclusion, 1:18–20, are a classic proof-text for the doctrine of natural revelation, speaking as they do of the invisible attributes of God (ἀόρατα αὐτοῦ) being understood in the things that have been created (τοῖς ποιήμασιν), resulting in the inexcusability of all people before the divine bar, whether or not they had access to special revelation. Paul's larger point, of course, is precisely that every person is inexcusable (εἰς τὸ εἶναι αὐτοὺς ἀναπολογήτους). Though all people have this knowledge of God, they fall into a morass of rebellion, which Paul chronicles in 1:21–31. It is not to be overlooked that the

---

23. On this point also note Geerhardus Vos, *Biblical Theology* (Grand Rapids: Eerdmans, 1948), 140: "The eschatological is an older strand in revelation than the soteric. The so-called 'Covenant of Works' was nothing but an embodiment of the Sabbatical principle."

wide variety of sins listed here (nearly all of the precepts of the Decalogue are implicated directly or indirectly) are indulged as a result of suppressing *natural knowledge* of God. All of the transgressions recounted in these verses, and not just the sexual perversion mentioned in 1:26, are evidently παρὰ φύσιν, against nature. One does not need Scripture in order to know that such conduct is wrong, for the natural law makes it plain to all. As an initial matter, then, Romans 1:18–31 adds important evidence to the doctrine that natural law reveals the basic moral obligation of the human race. But what about the richer thesis of the present section, namely, that natural law proclaims the works principle: not just moral obligation but the fact that sanctions must follow obedience or disobedience? Romans 1:32, as it brings this immediate section to a conclusion, addresses just this point. All people know the righteous decree of God (τὸ δικαίωμα τοῦ θεοῦ ἐπιγνόντες) that those who do such things are worthy of death (ἄξιοι θανάτου εἰσίν). In other words, what is known by nature is not just the moral way of life, but also that failure to follow this way has consequences, that disobedience demands death at the hands of a just God. Here, in concise form, Paul teaches that the natural law proclaims the works principle, with its obligation and sanctions.

Consideration of Romans 2:14–15 is somewhat more difficult, given the recent exegetical dispute about these verses and their surrounding context. A common interpretation among Reformed theologians, exemplified by Charles Hodge and defended rigorously of late by Douglas Moo, and sometimes called (rather unfelicitously) the "hypothetical" view, is that Paul's descriptions of God rendering judgment according to works in 2:6–13 are statements of a general principle of justice, of the law rather than the gospel. Thus, they constitute a literal portrayal of what will transpire for the wicked who are condemned on the last day but present a standard of justification that in fact none can satisfy by their own efforts (except Christ).[24] According to this line of exegesis, 2:14–15 follows primarily as an explanation for how it is possible that judgment can take place according to one's obedience to the law (2:13) when many people do not have the law (of Moses) and hence cannot be judged according to it (2:12). The answer of 2:14–15 is that even those who do not have the written law of Moses are in fact under a law,

---

24. Among older Reformed theologians, see, e.g., Charles Hodge, *A Commentary on Romans* (1864; Edinburgh: Banner of Truth, 1972), 49–57; and Geerhardus Vos, "The Alleged Legalism in Paul's Doctrine of Justification," in *Redemptive History and Biblical Interpretation: The Shorter Writings of Geerhardus Vos*, ed. Richard B. Gaffin Jr. (Phillipsburg, NJ: Presbyterian and Reformed, 1980), 393–94. Among more recent exegetes, see, e.g., Douglas J. Moo, *The Epistle to the Romans* (Grand Rapids: Eerdmans, 1996), 125–77; and Guy Prentiss Waters, *Justification and the New Perspective on Paul: A Review and Response* (Phillipsburg, NJ: P&R, 2004), 175–77.

namely, the natural law written on their hearts, by which their consciences render judgments of accusation or excuse upon their works, a self-judgment that anticipates God's final judgment on the last day (2:16).

In the broader context of Romans, 2:1–16 thus serves to bolster Paul's goal in 1:18–3:20 to demonstrate both the sinfulness of the entire human race and its consequent accountability to divine judgment, climaxing with the conclusion that no person can be justified by works of the law (3:20), but that God has made manifest his own righteousness, and hence a way of salvation from this predicament, in Jesus Christ (3:21 and following). If this interpretation is correct, then the thesis of this section of the chapter is further supported. The natural law proclaims the works principle, guaranteeing the justice of God's judgment according to works even over those who have not heard the law through special revelation. In fact, the natural law causes the works principle to be reenacted day by day in the breast of each person, as conscience, on the basis of this law, renders judgment according to works. Natural law teaches not only obligation but also that judgment must follow.

Many commentators have challenged either aspects or the whole of this exegesis of Romans 2:1–16 in recent years. The most thorough challenge has come from those, such as C. E. B. Cranfield and N. T. Wright, who regard the entirety of 2:6–13 as speaking of what will actually take place on the day of judgment, not only in regard to the wicked but also the righteous. In other words, 2:7, 10, 13 in particular speak of a judgment according to works on the last day in which the sanctified, if imperfect, works of Christians will receive a favorable verdict from God. Romans 2:14–15, then, refers not to the natural law at work among unbelieving Gentiles but to a law written on the heart of Gentile Christians in redemption, along the lines of Jeremiah 31:33. Thus, "by nature" (φύσει) in 2:14 refers not to externally good works that unbelieving Gentiles do (i.e., to what immediately follows τὰ τοῦ νόμου ποιῶσιν in 2:14) but to the state of these Gentiles as being born outside of the Mosaic covenant (i.e., to what immediately precedes ὅταν γὰρ ἔθνη τὰ μὴ νόμον ἔχοντα in 2:14).[25] From a wide variety of theological perspectives, other commentators (such as John Murray, Thomas Schreiner, James Dunn, and Joseph Fitzmyer) have agreed that 2:6–13 (or at least 2:6–11) refers to a positive verdict to be rendered upon the imperfect yet sanctified works of

---

25. For various distinctive examples of this line of interpretation, see C. E. B. Cranfield, *A Critical and Exegetical Commentary on the Epistle to the Romans*, vol. 1, International Critical Commentary (Edinburgh: T&T Clark, 1975), 146–63; N. T. Wright, *The Letter to the Romans*, New Interpreter's Bible 10 (Nashville: Abingdon, 2002), 437–43. Though his treatment of 2:14–15 is rather different, see also Ernst Käsemann, *Commentary on Romans*, trans. and ed. Geoffrey W. Bromiley (Grand Rapids: Eerdmans, 1980), 52–68.

Christians on the last day, but have held to some sort of natural law interpretation of 2:14–15.[26]

Once again, there is no space here to examine these exegetical issues in any kind of detail, but a few comments are in order. I would suggest distinguishing the popular interpretations into three major categories (leaving aside various nuances that could further distinguish them): the Hodge-Moo trajectory that Paul throughout 2:1–16 is driving his readers to understand how things operate under the law; the Cranfield-Wright trajectory that Paul throughout 2:1–16 is explaining to his readers the favorable verdict that God will render upon Christians for their imperfect sanctified works on the last day; and the Murray-Schreiner trajectory, a hybrid of the first two in following the Cranfield-Wright trajectory in regard to 2:6–11 (and maybe 2:12–13) and in following the Hodge-Moo trajectory in regard to 2:14–15.

Looking first at the first two of these interpretations, I would observe that they both see a works principle consistently operative all the way throughout 2:6–16. The first sees a *strict* works principle (obedience brings justification, disobedience brings condemnation) while the latter sees a *soft* works principle (a relatively good obedience, even though imperfect, brings justification). Despite the many criticisms leveled against it of late, I take the former interpretation to be by far the strongest in terms of both internal and contextual considerations, and I believe that the popular arguments advanced in support of the latter interpretation, despite some initial plausibility, are all beset by crucial difficulties.[27] The Cranfield-Wright trajectory at least has

26. John Murray, *The Epistle to the Romans*, vol. 1 (Grand Rapids: Eerdmans, 1959), 60–79; Thomas R. Schreiner, *Romans*, Baker Exegetical Commentary on the New Testament (Grand Rapids: Baker, 1998), 111–26 (and also 137–45, where he exegetes 2:25–29 in a way formative for his earlier interpretation of 2:6–16); James D. G. Dunn, *Romans 1–8*, Word Biblical Commentary (Dallas: Word, 1988), 77–107; and Joseph A. Fitzmyer, S.J., *Romans: A New Translation with Introduction and Commentary*, Anchor Bible 33 (New York: Doubleday, 1993), 296–312. Also see Richard B. Gaffin Jr. *"By Faith, Not by Sight": Paul and the Order of Salvation* (Waynesboro, GA: Paternoster, 2006), 94–99; Gaffin rejects the "hypothetical" view of 2:6–11, explicitly refrains from taking a position on 2:12–13, and does not discuss 2:14–15.

27. Perhaps the most thorough recent defense of the general view that I adopt here is advanced by Moo, *The Epistle to the Romans*, 125–77. In my judgment, the context of Paul's larger argument from Rom. 1:18 through 3:20 demands a strong presumption in favor of this position. Paul's point through these chapters is to consign all people—Jews and Gentiles alike—under the condemnation of God for sin. Paul, in fact, tells us explicitly in 3:9 that this has been his point. This culminates in the litany of OT verses establishing the utter lack of righteousness of any human being before God (3:10–18) and the necessary conclusion that "by works of the law will no flesh be justified before him" (3:20). Paul's goal to demonstrate that no one can be justified by works of the law is very difficult to reconcile with the idea that as part of his argument in getting to this goal he teaches that God in fact will justify people because of their doing of the law (2:13; and see also 2:6–7). Many of those who contest this interpretation point to many other Pauline (and other NT) texts that refer to Christians facing a judgment of works on the last day. Many other passages certainly do speak of this, and other proponents of my view freely affirm it, but this does not establish that this is Paul's concern here in the context of Rom. 1–3. Those who contest the interpretation

the virtue of internal consistency, however, recognizing that if Paul is not speaking about a strict works principle in 2:6–13, then he is not appealing to the natural law in 2:14–15. In my judgment, the various hybrid views that hover in the netherworld between Hodge-Moo and Cranfield-Wright suffer from a fatal flaw in their (perhaps unwitting) attempt to combine a strict and a soft works principle in the same Pauline argument. If we assume for the moment that the natural law interpretation of 2:14–15 is correct, which not only Hodge, Moo, Murray, Schreiner, and Fitzmyer do, but which also a consensus of medieval, Reformation, and post-Reformation theologians did, and that 2:14–15 is in some way advancing the argument being made in 2:6–13, then I suggest that seeing an actual judgment of Christians by (relatively good) works anywhere in 2:6–13 is problematic.[28]

My reason for this conclusion is simple: the natural law proclaims the strict, not a soft, works principle. The natural law is the law of the original Adamic covenant of works, the law known through endowment with the image of God, in which even one sin would, and in fact did, bring the judgment of death. The natural law proclaims no soft works principle by which an imperfect obedience will bring a favorable divine verdict. Thus it is incorrect to say that "nothing in Romans 2 indicates that Paul is envision-

---

offered here also commonly appeal to 2:25–29 to demonstrate that Paul has redemptive and not just legal concerns in mind in 1:18–3:20 (thus strengthening the claim that 2:6–13 envisions the actual experience of redeemed Christians rather than simply explains how things work under the law). This is perhaps the strongest argument offered by proponents of this view. But though it may be true that 2:29 alludes to the gracious work of the Spirit in circumcising the heart, Paul seems to raise this matter only for the purpose of breaking down Jewish confidence in outward circumcision (as he had previously broken down their confidence in their external possession of the law), and the previous verses, 2:25–28, give no indication that Paul has ceased explaining how things work under the law and has adopted a new perspective (and God in fact commanded Israel to circumcise their hearts as part of the requirements of the Mosaic law; see Deut. 10:16). Another argument sometimes utilized by those rejecting a natural law reading of Rom. 2:14–15 is that Paul seems to use language similar to Jer. 31:33, where the prophet speaks about the law written on the heart as a redemptive blessing of the new covenant. I believe that there is good reason to reject the proposal that Jeremiah and Paul are speaking of the same phenomenon; see discussion below for a brief argument why.

28. E.g., see Thomas Aquinas, *Summa Theologiae*, 1a2ae 91.2; Martin Luther, "Lectures on Romans," in *Luther's Works*, vol. 25, ed. Hilton C. Oswald (St. Louis: Concordia, 1972), 186–87; Luther, "Against the Heavenly Prophets in the Matter of Images and Sacraments," in Luther's Works, vol. 40, ed. Conrad Bergendoff (Philadelphia: Fortress, 1958), 97; John Calvin, *Commentary on Romans*, 2:14–15; Jerome Zanchi, "On the Law in General," trans. Jeffrey J. Veenstra, in *Journal of Markets and Morality* 6 (2003): 330 (this is a translation of D. Hieronymus Zanchius, *Operum theologicorum*, vol. 4, *De primi hominis lapsu, de peccato, and [sic] de legi Dei* [Geneva: Samuel Crispin, 1617], ch. 10, "De lege in genere," fols. 185–221); Turretin, *Institutes*, 1:577; 2:4; and Johannes Althusius, *Politica* (*Politics Methodically Set Forth and Illustrated with Sacred and Profane Examples*), trans. and ed. Frederick S. Carney (Indianapolis: Liberty Fund, 1995), 140 (originally published in 1603 as *Politica methodice digesta*). Romans 2:14–15 was also an original proof-text for the statement about the law of God written in the heart in the Westminster Confession of Faith 4.2 and Westminster Larger Catechism 17. Augustine, however, is not so sure; see "The Spirit and the Letter," in *Augustine: Later Works* (Philadelphia: Westminster, 1980), 226–32.

ing perfect (= flawless) obedience."[29] That Christians' sanctified good works will in fact be acknowledged by God on the last day, as taught elsewhere in Scripture, *is not a truth known by natural revelation*. If one, with the weight of the Christian tradition, takes 2:14–15 to refer to the natural law, then seeing a strict works principle in 2:6–13 is the interpretation that seems to ensure the coherence of Paul's argument.

In this section I have presented evidence that the Reformed tradition has held that the natural law proclaims the works principle, and I have suggested, through appeal to biblical teaching on the image of God and Paul's argument in Romans 1–2, that this idea is theologically correct. Next we turn to consideration of what this has to do with God's dealings with Israel in the Mosaic covenant.

Natural Law and the Mosaic Covenant

This next section begins to take up the question of natural law and the works principle in the Mosaic covenant. Here I address first the way in which the Reformed tradition has associated the natural law and the Mosaic law and then offer some brief arguments in support of the traditional Reformed doctrine. Though I do not take up here explicitly the idea of a republication of the covenant of works as an aspect of the Mosaic covenant, the implications of the conclusions of this section, in connection with the conclusions of the previous section, should be evident: if the Reformed tradition is correct in seeing the Mosaic law as a particular application of the natural law for theocratic Israel, and if the natural law proclaims the works principle, then there is at least an initial presumption for recognizing the works principle as *one of* the constitutive aspects of the Mosaic covenant.[30]

29. These are the words of Kent L. Yinger, *Paul, Judaism, and Judgment according to Deeds* (Cambridge: Cambridge University Press, 1999), 166. Also compare his words later on page 177, regarding Romans 2:6–11: "Apart from the concern over contradiction [with 3:20], nothing would incline us normally to view these statements as hypothetical or in any way unpauline."

30. As other essays in this collection also explore, the presence of the works principle in the Mosaic covenant does not make it the *only* thing present in it. As the Westminster Standards teach, the Mosaic covenant is an administration of the covenant of grace, and thus God administered redemption to his OT people through it. As I discuss below, the Mosaic works principle itself served redemptive-historical, typological purposes. In light of what I argued about Romans 2 at the immediate end of the previous section, I would note that the Mosaic law (reflecting the natural law) clearly demanded perfect obedience: the love of God with *all* of one's heart, soul, and might (Deut. 6:5), the keeping of the *whole* commandment given by God (Deut. 11:8), the keeping of all of the commandments *always* (Deut. 11:1). This accords with Paul's explicit interpretation in Gal. 3:10: a curse comes upon all who do not do *all* of the things written in the law. Because both the works principle and redemptive grace were administered in the Mosaic covenant, God did not enforce the works principle strictly and in fact taught his OT people something about the connection of obedience and blessing by giving them, at times, temporal reward for relative (imperfect) obedience.

Natural Law and Mosaic Law in the Reformed Tradition

In this section I first consider the perspective of the Reformed tradition on the relationship of natural law and Mosaic law. As with so much else covered in this essay, much more could be said if space permitted. To put it briefly, a strong consensus seems to exist, in the earlier Reformed tradition as well as in the preceding medieval traditions, that the Mosaic law is in some sense founded upon the natural law, such that the Mosaic law expresses and applies the natural law. More specifically, the Mosaic moral law expressed identical moral content to that of the natural law, and the Mosaic civil law applied the natural law to the particular social situation of God's Old Testament covenant people (I must set aside consideration of the ceremonial law).

According to the common threefold classification of the Mosaic law, which dates back at least to the high Middle Ages and was utilized throughout the early centuries of the Reformed tradition,[31] the moral law represents the enduring moral obligation binding upon all people by virtue of their common humanity and accountability to God. Though given to Israel, then, its content was not unique to Israel. The Reformed and other Christian traditions routinely viewed the Decalogue as a basic summary of the moral law.[32] Furthermore, these traditions identified the moral content of the moral law with that of the natural law. In Turretin's succinct formulation, the moral law and natural law differ not as to substance but as to "mode of delivery," the one being written and the other unwritten.[33] Thus, one important connection between natural law and Mosaic law for the Reformed tradition was its conception of the moral law as a written expression for Israel of the fundamental natural law obligation binding upon all humanity.

A second way in which the Reformed tradition associated the natural and Mosaic laws was through seeing the Mosaic civil law as an application of the natural law to the theocratic social life of the Old Testament covenant people. A number of pieces of evidence in the writings of earlier Reformed theologians could illustrate this point, but one in particular may be worth highlighting here. When Reformed writers addressed the perennial question concerning the contemporary applicability of the Old Testament civil law, they regularly adopted the approach already taken before them by figures

31. E.g., see Bonaventure, *Breviloquium*, 5.9.1; Thomas Aquinas, *Summa Theologiae*, 1a2ae 91; John Calvin, *Institutes of the Christian Religion*, 4.20.14; Turretin, *Institutes*, 2:145; Westminster Confession of Faith 19.2–4.

32. E.g., see Westminster Shorter Catechism 41; Westminster Larger Catechism 98.

33. See Turretin, *Institutes*, 2:6–7. On these issues, also see Calvin, *Institutes*, 2.8.1; 4.20.15–16; Althusius, *Politica*, 139–40, 144; Samuel Rutherford, *The Divine Right of Church-Government and Excommunication* (London, 1646), 75, 79; and Owen, *Works*, 11:366–69, 395.

as diverse as Thomas Aquinas and Martin Luther: they rejected the idea that the Mosaic civil law as such should be incorporated into contemporary civil law, but permitted the application of those parts of the Mosaic civil law that applied the natural law in a way still appropriate in their contemporary social setting. Where more appropriate contemporary applications of the natural law were viable, these should be preferred to the Mosaic civil law.[34] The perspective underlying this doctrine was that the Mosaic civil law was in fact founded upon the natural law, but also that the natural law always needs to be applied to concrete circumstances, and given the unique theocratic and typological circumstances pertaining to Old Testament Israel, the civil applications of natural law would not always be the same in other civil societies.

A Constructive Account of Natural Law and Mosaic Law

Is this historically Reformed way of associating natural law and Mosaic law theologically compelling? Though a thorough investigation of this question could fill a volume of its own, I briefly offer here a few reasons to conclude that it is.

First, a recollection of the previous discussion of Romans 1–2 provides strong evidence at least for the insight that the Mosaic law contains a "moral law" that is substantively identical to the natural law. In the larger argument in Romans 1:18–3:20, Paul displays to his readers that all people, whether Jews under the Mosaic law or Gentiles under the natural law, stand equally condemned before God, being judged and condemned according to the law appropriate to each. This very point depends upon the substantive identity of the Mosaic and natural laws. If these two laws promulgated fundamentally different moral standards, then the same judgment could not fall justly upon all. Thus, in Romans 1:21–32, Paul is able to consign Gentiles to the same death as Jews because the natural law that he describes as being suppressed is one whose violations sound just like the violations of the Mosaic law. With the exception of the fourth commandment, all of the precepts of the Decalogue are associated with the natural law in 1:21–31. In 2:14–15, Paul appeals to the reality of the natural law in order to explain how, in the light of 2:12–13, all people can be judged according to the law when clearly not all people have the law of Moses. The answer is that the works of the

---

34. E.g., see Turretin, *Institutes*, 2:167. Also see relevant material in Thomas Aquinas, *Summa Theologiae*, 1a2ae 104.3; Martin Luther, "How Christians Should Regard Moses," in *Luther's Works*, vol. 35, ed. E. Theodore Bachmann (Philadelphia: Fortress, 1960), 165; Luther, "Lectures on Romans," 180; Calvin, *Institutes*, 4.20.14–16; and Zanchi, "On the Law," 323, 338–40, 379–80, 394.

(Mosaic!) law are written on the heart. For Paul's point to stand, the natural law must be substantively identical to the Mosaic law.

A second line of evidence for the historic Reformed understanding of the association of natural law and Mosaic law is internal to the Mosaic law, though very much related to the first line of evidence drawn from Romans 1–2. Several places in the Mosaic law itself speak as though Israel and the neighboring nations were under the same law and subject to the same sanctions. Given that the Mosaic law, with its commands and sanctions, was imposed upon Israel and was mostly or entirely unknown to these other nations, the fact that these other nations would be accountable to the same basic moral standard and liable to the same judgment indicates that the law under which the Gentile nations did exist, the natural law, is substantively identical to the Mosaic law. One example is Leviticus 18:24–28.[35] Here God states that the very sexual sins that he has just prohibited in 18:1–23 are the basis upon which he is driving out the previous residents of the land of Palestine. They made the land unclean, and Israel is not to do the same things and make the land unclean in their own turn. In judgment, God made the land vomit out the previous Gentile inhabitants, and in judgment God will make the land vomit out Israel if it acts similarly. These Gentile nations obviously had no knowledge of the as yet nonexistent law of Moses. How could they then be responsible under pain of judgment for the sins of Leviticus 18:1–23? Their knowledge of and accountability to the natural law is the only plausible explanation. (I mention only in passing, though hope the reader will be more than casually provoked by it, the fact that Scripture's first statement of its most concise formulation of the works principle occurs earlier in this pericope, Leviticus 18:5: the one who does these things will live by them.)[36]

A second example is Deuteronomy 30:7.[37] Whereas in Leviticus 18:24–28 Israel is to look in retrospect at the Gentiles who had suffered the same judgment as threatened them for the same sins, so here Israel is to look prospectively to the time in which they will have been restored from punishment and exile and will see God place all these curses on the nations that had

35. "Do not make yourselves unclean by any of these things, for by all these the nations I am driving out before you have become unclean, and the land became unclean, so that I punished its iniquity, and the land vomited out its inhabitants. But you shall keep my statutes and my rules and do none of these abominations, either the native or the stranger who sojourns among you (for the people of the land, who were before you, did all of these abominations, so that the land became unclean), lest the land vomit you out when you make it unclean, as it vomited out the nation that was before you." (ESV)
36. See Bryan Estelle's essay elsewhere in this volume for further discussion of these issues in Lev. 18.
37. "And the LORD your God will put all these curses on your foes and enemies who persecuted you." (ESV)

persecuted them. The same curses will fall on the nations as fell on Israel. Identical judgment can justly befall only identical sin. If the Gentile nations receive the same judgment as Israel received, then they must be under the same fundamental law. If they were not under the Mosaic law—which was in fact the case—then here is one more piece of evidence for the substantive identity of the natural and Mosaic laws.[38]

A third line of evidence for the historic Reformed understanding of the association of the natural and Mosaic laws is drawn from the perhaps initially troubling, yet factually undeniable, similarity of certain parts of the Mosaic civil law to more ancient legal codes of the ancient Near East. The Old Testament civil law, revealed by God on Mount Sinai, looked strikingly similar to some of the laws of the nations around Israel. This reality need not be theologically troubling if the Mosaic law is in fact grounded in and an application of the natural law. One might even say that such a similarity of legal codes is precisely what we might expect if the traditional Reformed doctrine of the relationship of natural and Mosaic laws is correct. Two related lines of evidence are useful for exploring this issue.

A first example is the striking similarity in both substance and structure between the laws of Hammurabi and the so-called covenant collection of Exodus 20:23–23:19. This ancient Babylonian code predates the Mosaic law by several centuries even on a traditional, conservative early dating of the latter. As David P. Wright recounts in his recent article on their relationship, the similarity was great enough that, shortly after the Hammurabi material was discovered about a century ago, some scholars proposed that the biblical author must have depended directly upon it. More moderate views, suggesting an indirect oral relationship between these two sets of legal material (and other ancient Near Eastern legal material) but not a direct literary relationship, became more common. Wright himself, however, has attempted to reopen a case for a direct relationship in his detailed analysis of the Hammurabi and biblical texts, claiming that the correlations between them are even more extensive than previously recognized.[39] I do not have the competence to referee this debate, nor is its resolution particularly crucial for present purposes. Whatever exposure Moses may have had to extant

38. A sermon on Deut. 30:1–10 by Zach Keele at Escondido Orthodox Presbyterian Church in 2006 initially called my attention to the significance of this passage for the present essay.

39. David P. Wright, "The Laws of Hammurabi as Source for the Covenant Collection (Exodus 20:23–23:19)," *Maarav* 10 (2003): 11–87. A respectful though critical response to Wright's article has been offered by Bruce Wells, "The Covenant Code and Near Eastern Legal Traditions: A Response to David P. Wright," *Maarav* 13.1 (2006): 85–118. Wells argues that direct dependence is unlikely. Wright has continued this dialogue in "The Laws of Hammurabi and the Covenant Code: A Response to Bruce Wells," *Maarav* 13.2 (2006): 211–60.

Mesopotamian legal codes, the Mosaic civil law bears much more than passing resemblance to its neighbors' civil law. God's Old Testament people Israel and its pagan neighbors resolved judicial disputes among its citizens in all sorts of similar ways.

A second and related line of evidence concerns the *lex talionis*, the law of retribution. Variations of the talionic principle appear three times in the Mosaic law, in Exodus 21:23–25, Leviticus 24:18–21, and Deuteronomy 19:21. According to the first of these, harm shall be retributed "life for life, eye for eye, tooth for tooth, hand for hand, foot for foot, burn for burn, wound for wound, stripe for stripe" (ESV). This principle was hardly unique to the Mosaic law, as it appeared in preexisting Mesopotamian law such as the Code of Hammurabi, as well as in legal cultures far removed from Israel.[40] Though the talionic principle is easy to dismiss as primitive and even grotesque (as it has often been dismissed), it is interesting to note that many scholars of ancient law with no particular theological stake in defending the moral integrity of the Old Testament have enumerated many ways in which the *lex talionis* promoted an equitable system of justice, especially in Israel.[41]

It is tempting to conclude that the talionic principle is in fact a succinct expression of the natural law, and with it the works principle, applied to concrete circumstances of civil life. As several authors have argued, in different ways, the talionic principle was not designed to be (at least ordinarily) applied literally, but was a way of driving at the goal of establishing a perfectly just, exact punishment for harm done.[42] In the original

40. See especially the recent study by William Ian Miller, *Eye for an Eye* (Cambridge: Cambridge University Press, 2006), in which he examines not only the biblical texts but also the legal codes and sagas of other ancient honor cultures such as the Hammurabian, Anglo-Saxon, Old Norse, and Icelandic. Miller also discusses the ways in which the principle survives in many ways in our own modern liberal culture. The talionic principle also appears in the Twelve Tables of early Roman law. J. Gwyn Griffiths comments in *The Divine Verdict: A Study of Divine Judgment in the Ancient Religions* (Leiden: Brill, 1991), 348: "For the most part, the doctrine of punishment is squarely based on the principle of retribution. If it is spelled out most clearly in the Hebrew *lex talionis*, it is stated or implied in all the ancient religions." For additional discussion by older, respected Old Testament scholars about the relationship of the talionic principle in Israel and its neighbors, see also Gerhard von Rad, *Old Testament Theology*, vol. 1, *The Theology of Israel's Historical Traditions*, trans. D. M. G. Stalker (New York: Harper & Row, 1962), 30–33; and Shalom M. Paul, *Studies in the Book of the Covenant in the Light of Cuneiform and Biblical Law* (Leiden: Brill, 1970), 77.

41. See Miller, *Eye for an Eye*; and Paul, *Studies in the Book of the Covenant*, 75–76.

42. Miller, *Eye for an Eye*, discusses throughout how compensation payments in talionic cultures were often (even ordinarily) substituted for literal plucking of an eye or pulling of a tooth, but how the threat of literal execution of the penalty could subtly serve to make compensation payments more equitable. And he also suggests: "Let's just say that the eye/tooth statement perfectly captures the rule of equivalence, balance, and precision in a stunning way. It holds before us the possibility of getting the measure of value right." See *Eye for an Eye*, 30. From a Reformed perspective, Meredith G. Kline comments in "*Lex Talionis* and the Human Fetus," *Journal of the Evangelical Theological Society* 20 (Sept 1977): 197: "The consensus that has prevailed through the centuries

covenant of works, God demanded of Adam his whole self and whole devotion, and upon his failure to render this the *lex talionis* demanded of him his whole self as an exact and just punishment. In the civil setting, where the relationship is not per se between God and a human person but between two human people, and therefore in which one party does not owe her entire self and devotion to any other, the same absolute execution of the *lex talionis* is not appropriate. But insofar as obligations are owed to one another, an analogous talionic principle applies: life for life and eye for eye. Might one make the argument, therefore, that the *lex talionis* appears to be a fundamental principle of Mosaic jurisprudence as well as of many other legal systems because it is, in a nutshell, the works principle–proclaiming natural law striving to find expression in the civil law of a fallen world?[43]

There is much work left to be done on these issues, both in regard to the actual relationship of the Mosaic and contemporaneous foreign legal codes and in regard to a theological interpretation of this phenomenon. For present purposes, I suggest for now only this: because Moses, under divine inspiration, could incorporate concepts and even concrete regulations from the legal systems of surrounding cultures, there must have been, for all of their imperfections, considerable justice and equity in these neighboring legal systems. This points to the conclusion that these pagan legal cultures accurately derived many of their laws from the natural law and therefore

---

that the talion principle in the Bible was never intended to be applied in the form of such literal mutilations appears to be sound. . . . [In Deut. 19:15–21] Clearly we have to do with a fossilized formula whose graphic terms are meant to express only the general principle that the offense must receive a just punishment, neither more nor less." Among older commentators, Roland de Vaux somewhat similarly, though underwhelmingly, comments in *Ancient Israel: Its Life and Institutions*, trans. John McHugh (New York: McGraw-Hill, 1961), 149–50, that though the Mosaic law states the *lex talionis* sharply, "this formula seems to have lost its force, merely asserting the principle of proportionate compensation."

43. Miller, *Eye for an Eye*, 147, makes the perhaps disturbing observation that reciprocity and revenge lie at the core of our moral sensibility. Though we ought to recognize how sin perverts our seemingly natural desires for vengeance, might our theological doctrine of the image of God suggest that Miller has a point—and a positive, and not merely negative, point? Is desiring revenge/reciprocity part of our nature per se not because we are sinners but because we are image-bearers, which means that (a) we take injuries to ourselves as something that needs to be accounted for and (b) we have a judicial office and desire to punish wrongs? Also relevant here perhaps is the fact that the talionic principle has tended to be expressed most explicitly in honor cultures. Bearing the image of God means that we have a certain dignity, and hence does it also mean that offenses to ourselves rightly require redress of the damage to this dignity and not merely to our economic loss or the like? In *Eye for an Eye*, 202, Miller also makes the intriguing observation that we have feebler understanding of human motivation in contemporary Western society in comparison with the understanding of older honor cultures, in our attending to our pleasure much more than to our honor. Do the comments above in regard to honor and the image of God suggest that when we have lost the sense of honor we have also put ourselves out of touch with who we are by nature?

also adds more evidence to the Reformed idea that the Mosaic law, even in its civil aspect, is itself an application of the natural law designed for the particular situation of Old Testament Israel.[44]

Parenthetically, one might note the irony of the conclusions I am drawing in this section in light of the claims of the so-called theonomy school of thought popular in some circles of contemporary Reformed Christianity. Ironically, my conclusions suggest that there is a very important insight that theonomy contributes to theological discussion of the Mosaic law, but that in this very insight theonomy gets things backwards. Their insight is that there is a universal relevance to the civil law of Moses. But whereas theonomy understands this universal relevance to prescribe that the Mosaic civil law should be a *model for the civil law of other nations*, my conclusions suggest that the civil law of other nations was, in a certain sense, a *model for the Mosaic civil law*. The Mosaic civil law is universally relevant in its being like the laws of other nations, not in other nations' laws being like Moses'. This claim may provoke the objection that this is somehow demeaning to God in making him a copycat of the pagan nations. But this would be, I suggest, an overly hasty and simplistic objection that fails to account for the larger purposes of God in redemptive history. It was God himself who wrote the natural law on human hearts and preserved its testimony among the pagan peoples. Furthermore, as explored in the next section, God had beautiful and wise redemptive purposes in mind when he established Israel as his Old Testament covenant people in such a way that preserved their significant resemblances to and commonality with the sea of humanity around them.

In this section I have set forth and suggested some pieces of evidence in support of the traditional Reformed understanding of the relationship between the natural and Mosaic laws. In short, the Mosaic law expressed and applied the natural law to the unique situation of Old Testament Israel. Though I have not explored the doctrine of republication specifically here, a simple syllogism is lurking in the background: if natural law proclaims the works principle (section one), and if the Mosaic law expresses and applies

44. Note the similar conclusion drawn by Peter Enns in *Inspiration and Incarnation: Evangelicals and the Problem of the Old Testament* (Grand Rapids: Baker, 2005), 58, where he suggests that their similarities indicate "a way of behaving that may precede any written codes of conduct" and later adds that this "reflects a deeper reality, that God has set up the world in a certain way and that way is imprinted on all people." Further evidence for this sort of conclusion may be provided by F. A. Hayek's claim that Hammurabi and many other ancient legislators were codifying existing customs more than making new law, since this would suggest a widespread social acceptance of the equity of such practices rather than something handed down from the wisdom of a few; see *Law, Legislation and Liberty*, vol. 1, *Rules and Order* (Chicago: University of Chicago Press, 1973), 81. See also my discussion of these matters in David VanDrunen, *A Biblical Case for Natural Law* (Grand Rapids: Acton Institute, 2006), 63–65.

the natural law (section two), then we would expect to find the works principle operative in the Mosaic covenant. We turn now to explore what God's purposes might be in all of this.

Natural Law, the Works Principle, and Systematic Reflections on the Doctrine of Republication

As I begin this final section I ask readers to assume with me a few things. Assume that the natural law does indeed proclaim the works principle, both in the Adamic covenant of works and as a lingering reminder to all of fallen humanity of the basic requirement of God's law and justice. Assume also that the Mosaic law is an expression and application of the natural law to the unique situation of Old Testament Israel, and hence that the Mosaic law itself must proclaim the works principle. Finally, assume that the Mosaic covenant must therefore contain some sort of republication of the covenant of works (what else would a proclamation of the works principle be?). What larger, redemptive-historical purposes would such a proclamation of the works principle, such a republication of the covenant of works, serve? It could not be as a way of salvation, for there is no salvation by obedience to the law. As a general matter, the law was given to Israel for the historical purpose of serving as a pedagogue unto Christ (Gal. 3:24), who alone brings salvation.

I suggest here, particularly through reflection on Paul's subsequent discussion in Galatians, that one of God's purposes in establishing the Mosaic law as an expression and application of the natural law, and thereby proclaiming the works principle to his people, was to show forth in Israel, in bright clarity, the basic predicament of the whole of humanity. In Adam, the whole human race was created under the works principle. In Adam, the whole human race has fallen under the judgment of the works principle, the fact of which the natural law reminds every person every day through its gnawing, relentless testimony. In the Mosaic law, God has made perfectly lucid by special revelation what is more obscurely known by natural revelation. Moral obligations bind the human race, and sanctions attach to them. Judgment must follow works. As the Mosaic law constantly reminded Israel of this basic fact, Israel served as a microcosm of the nations. Through the Mosaic law's expression and application of the universal natural law, Israel is linked to the world in a common human predicament and brings into sharp focus what all must know, namely, that all lie under the judgment of the works principle. In the special revelation given to Israel, of course, there is also made known what the natural law could not make known: God is providing a way out of this seemingly hopeless predicament.

Once again, I raise an issue worthy of detailed exploration but to which I can devote only a little attention. The idea that Israel's experience under the Mosaic law encompasses the situation of the whole human race is not an obscure one in contemporary biblical and theological reflection. N. T. Wright, for example, has advocated this idea at some length in the exposition of his allegedly new and fresh perspective on Paul.[45] Despite my own serious misgivings about crucial aspects of the various permutations of the New Perspective on Paul, Wright is certainly not wrong to seek theological integration of the ideas of Gentile inclusion and individual salvation, nor in his seeing Old Testament Israel as a recapitulation of Adam and representative of the nations, nor in pointing to the importance of the concepts of creation and covenant. If what I suggest in this section is correct, however, one hardly needs a new and fresh perspective to account for these themes and their integration. Traditional Reformed covenant theology, which includes its conception of natural law and the works principle, accounts for them all. Significantly, though, since Wright seeks to account for them through a theological system (apologies to NTW for noting that he does not escape doing systematic theology) unfriendly to the idea of an operative works principle, he does present a distinctly different accounting.

Despite Wright's claim to have deciphered what Saint Paul really said, I suggest now that the apostle's argument early in Galatians 4 gives credence to the way that the earlier Reformed tradition accounted for these various themes and, especially for present purposes, gives some insight into the relationship of the natural and Mosaic laws and how this relationship enabled Israel to serve as a microcosm of the nations in showing forth the basic human predicament under the works principle.

The context in which Galatians 4 appears is obviously significant. Paul has taught in the second half of Galatians 3 that God gave the law to Israel not as an alternative way of salvation to the covenant promised to Abraham, but as something added on (3:19), in order to lock them up under sin and thus to function as a pedagogue unto Christ, to serve the purposes of justification by faith (3:23–24). Early in Galatians 5, Paul warns his readers about going back under the law through reembracing circumcision, which would be submission to a yoke of slavery and tantamount to a rejection of Christ (5:1–2). Such a move entails an obligation to perform the entire law, to execute perfect obedience (5:3), as S. M. Baugh helpfully discusses elsewhere

---

45. E.g., see N. T. Wright, *Paul: In Fresh Perspective* (Minneapolis: Fortress, 2005), 31, 37, 109, 120.

in this volume. Paul has already explained that the law teaches this works principle: the law brings curse upon those who do not do everything that it prescribes (3:10) and life to those who do (3:12). It is crucial to note here that the law teaches this (in Romans 10:5, where Paul quotes Leviticus 18:5 as he does in Galatians 3:12, he asserts that Moses writes about it); finding the works principle in the Mosaic law is not a legalistic Jewish perversion of the law.[46] This is why returning to the law brings one right back under the works principle. The question is not whether the Mosaic law proclaims the works principle—Galatians 3:10, 12 and 5:3 state clearly that it does—but whether one sees the works principle in the Mosaic law as God intended it to be seen according to Galatians 3:15–29, namely, as a means for showing the hopelessness of sin and thus for leading people to Christ. Where the law is chosen over against Christ after his coming (the scenario described in Galatians 5:1–4), then only the naked works principle remains, shorn of its typological (and thus ultimately redemptive) purpose.

In the midst of this larger argument falls the material of particular interest in this final section, Galatians 4:3, 9. In both of these verses Paul speaks of being enslaved to the στοιχεῖα, which I will refer to in simple transliteration as the *stoicheia*, in order to avoid offering a translation that would be prematurely prejudicial. The remarkable, even shocking, thing about this dual appeal to the *stoicheia* is that in 4:3 Paul refers to slavery under the *stoicheia* as Israel's situation under the Mosaic law,[47] and in 4:9 he refers to slavery under the *stoicheia* as the consequence of Gentiles returning to their life under the bondage of false gods (see 4:8). Paul therefore identifies slavery under the *stoicheia* as something that life under the Mosaic law and life under paganism had in common. That Paul the Pharisee could say such a thing is indeed remarkable. But perhaps it should not be shocking to those nurtured by the ideas of Reformed theology discussed in the previous sections of this chapter. Given the vast differences between the Old Testament religion revealed by God himself and the pagan idolatry of the Gentiles, in

---

46. This point is argued in more detail in the essays by Bryan Estelle and Guy Waters elsewhere in this volume.

47. That Paul is referring specifically to OT Israel ("we") in 4:3 is perhaps a minority position in the recent literature. Among those believing that Paul intended to include all Christians, Jew and Gentile, in this reference, see David R. Bundrick, "*TA STOICHEIA TOU KOSMOU* (Gal. 4:3)," *Journal of the Evangelical Theological Society* 34 (Sept. 1991): 355; and Ronald Y. K. Fung, *The Epistle to the Galatians* (Grand Rapids: Eerdmans, 1988), 181. The view that I adopt, which sees "we" as a reference to OT Israel, is defended, e.g., by Linda J. Belleville, "'Under Law': Structural Analysis and the Pauline Concept of Law in Galatians 3:21–4:11," *Journal for the Study of the New Testament* 26 (1986): 68; Richard N. Longenecker, *Galatians* (Dallas: Word, 1990), 164; and Frank J. Matera, *Galatians* (Collegeville, MN: Liturgical, 1992), 149.

what could possibly lie their similarity? The answer that I suggest is their common relation to the natural law, and hence to the works principle.

The plausibility of this claim in part depends upon what exactly the *stoicheia* are. Many recent writers have interpreted the *stoicheia* as a cosmological reference to the astral bodies or as a reference to demonic forces.[48] A number of dissenters from this view have argued instead for a translation along the lines of "elementary principles" or "basic teachings." Several considerations make the latter position the more plausible, including the weighty difficulty of seeing the divinely bestowed Mosaic law as an imprisonment under astrological or demonic powers.[49] When God put Israel under the Mosaic law, he did not place them under the sway of the stars or of the devil, but he did place them under the dominion of the works principle insofar as the law expressed and applied the law of nature. And since even pagans under their own false systems of religion abide by necessity under the unyielding demands of the natural law (which their religions corrupt but cannot entirely suppress), here indeed is a point of commonality between Israel and the nations. Old Testament Israelites and pagans lived under the same *stoicheia* of the world, the same elementary principles or basic teachings, because both lived with the constant reminder of the works principle ringing in their hearts through the natural law and (in the case of Israel) in their ears through the Mosaic law's expression and application of the natural law.

This interpretation not only identifies a point of commonality between Israel and the pagan nations without denigrating the Mosaic covenant but also fits perfectly in the context of Galatians 3 and 5 discussed above. The Mosaic law taught the works principle (3:10, 12), for the purpose of leading Israel unto Christ and justification by faith (3:21–24), and a return to the law after knowing Christ puts one under the works principle stripped of its typological purpose (5:1–3). Such a move is no different from a return to paganism after knowing Christ, for that too constitutes a rejection of the one way of justification by grace through faith and a consignment under the

48. Clinton E. Arnold has offered a recent, robust defense of this line of interpretation in "Returning to the Domain of the Powers: STOICHEIA as Evil Spirits in Galatians 4:3,9," *Novum Testamentum* 38.1 (Jan. 1996): 55–76; and in *The Colossian Syncretism: The Interface between Christianity and Folk Belief at Colossae* (Grand Rapids: Baker, 1996), 183–84.

49. For arguments in support of this line of interpretation, see, e.g., Wesley Carr, *Angels and Principalities: The Background, Meaning and Development of the Pauline Phrase* hai archai kai hai exousiai (Cambridge: Cambridge University Press, 1981), 72–76; Belleville, "'Under Law,'" 53–78; Longenecker, *Galatians*, 165–66, 181; Bundrick, "TA STOICHEIA," 353–64; and Matera, *Galatians*, 149–50, 154–56 (it may be noted that he takes the reference to the *stoicheia* in 4:9 somewhat differently from the reference in 4:3, though still concluding that the *stoicheia* held both the OT Jews and Gentiles under their sway).

natural law–proclaiming works principle. Through the natural law and its works principle, Israel indeed served as a microcosm of the nations.[50]

A Consideration of One Objection

The claims in this chapter may well evoke many questions and objections, and before concluding this chapter I wish to address one in particular that I would regard as serious and substantive. If the natural law written on the heart proclaims the works principle, and if in Christ we are no longer under the works principle (either ultimately, as God's redeemed people have never been, or typologically, as God's Old Testament people were), then are New Testament Christians in fact not under the natural law, though it seems to be constitutive of the very image of God in which we are being re-created? To add additional weight to this objection, Jeremiah 31:33 says explicitly that one of the primary benefits of the new covenant is God's placing his law within his people and writing it on their hearts. How are my claims in this chapter reconcilable with these considerations?

I hope to explore this and related issues in some detail in another forum soon, but the following is an indication of how I believe this objection should be answered. First, in regard to the question whether New Testament Christians are under the natural law the answer is yes and no, and this answer depends upon the historic Reformed "two kingdoms" doctrine. Insofar as they are called to live in common with the world in the civil kingdom, Christians still exist under the authority of the natural law. The state, for example, remains grounded in the creation order, and its function is to render judgment according to works (Rom. 13:1–7). But insofar as they are called out of the world into the kingdom of Christ, Christians do not operate according to the natural law (though their basic moral obligations remain the same), for they are not under the works principle, either in regard to their justification before God or in regard to their conduct toward one another. The kingdom of Christ knows no law of retaliation; the Lord Jesus banished the *lex talionis* from his kingdom (Matt. 5:38–42). How this twofold dynamic works out in practice is a good question, but one for another forum.

What then of Jeremiah 31:33? The answer that I propose is quite simply that it does not refer to the natural law. Jeremiah 31:33 and Romans

50. Compare here also the argument in William N. Wilder, *Echoes of the Exodus Narrative in the Context and Background of Galatians 5:18* (New York: Peter Lang, 2001), 84–86. Wilder's interpretation of the opening of Gal. 4 seems to me generally to reinforce my claims here, though he is at pains to emphasize that "it is the Gentiles who must be related to the Jewish covenantal experience, not the other way around."

2:14–15 speak of different things. Romans 2:14–15 describes a law written on the heart by nature that operates according to the works principle, accusing and excusing in anticipation of future judgment (see 2:12–13, 16). Jeremiah 31:33 describes not a law written on the heart by nature but by a redemptive covenant. It says nothing about this law accusing and excusing, nothing about rendering judgment. The only judgment that this law of the heart knows is that of judgment past, judgment already accomplished: "I will forgive their iniquity and I will remember their sins no more" (31:34). Where the works principle is operative, there is no forgiveness of sins; where there is forgiveness of sins, the works principle has been satisfied and holds sway no longer. Romans 2:14–15 has to do with the protological image: working in the pursuit of rest. Jeremiah 31:33 has to do with the redeemed, eschatological image: working in gratitude for the gift of rest definitively bestowed in Christ.

Conclusion

In this chapter I have argued, in defense of ideas prominent in much of the Reformed tradition, that the natural law proclaims the works principle and that the natural law undergirds both the Adamic and Mosaic covenants. These basic doctrines, if true, add another piece of evidence to the case for seeing a republication of the covenant of works as an aspect of the Mosaic covenant, as explored from various angles in the present volume, for where the natural law is expressed and applied, there the works principle must be found. Finally, I suggested a way in which this connection of natural law and the works principle provides a systematic coherence to the doctrine of republication that it might otherwise lack. Through its foundation in the works principle–proclaiming natural law, the Mosaic law governed Israel as a microcosm, showing forth the basic predicament of the whole world under the demand for perfect obedience and the inevitable judgment of death that sin brings. In Israel, therefore, the whole world, under the sway of natural law, was pointed to Christ, the one who fulfilled the natural law through his obedience to the Mosaic law and thereby earned life and blessing for his chosen ones from every nation under heaven that they may face the judgment of the works principle no longer.

11

OBEDIENCE IS BETTER THAN SACRIFICE

MICHAEL HORTON

As other essays in this volume have argued, there has been a strong strain in Reformed orthodoxy which understands the original relationship of humanity-in-Adam as a covenant of works and the Sinai covenant as in some sense a republication of that covenant. With respect to the latter, there has always been a spectrum of opinion regarding continuities and discontinuities. Nevertheless, the broad support for some version of republication is well established.

It has also been evident in many of the previous essays that the doctrine of republication is closely tied to convictions about justification and the active obedience of Christ. Insofar as the Mosaic covenant taught a principle of works, it served as a pedagogue unto Christ and showed the Savior who alone could fulfil the terms of the law. An understanding of the active obedience of Christ and an appreciation for its Old Testament background, therefore, are crucial matters for exploration in this present study of the doctrine of republication.

The idea of the imputation of the active obedience of Christ has come under attack by some in contemporary Reformed circles. At the heart of these misgivings seems to be the notion of merit as a legitimate category in the Creator-creature relationship. How can any creature claim God's blessing as a reward? How could Adam—even in his state of integrity—have attained the consummation apart from grace? More crucially still, does not such a scheme represent a legalistic rather than personal relationship? After all, God's giving of the law was understood as Israel's unique gift, a treasure that distinguished her from the nations as God's own people. Furthermore, repeated instances of God's patience in the face of Israel's transgressions seem to contradict the view that this covenant required "punctilious obedience" (a common description in federal theology) as a condition of this relationship.

Although the antithesis between legal and personal relationships is a modern (Gentile!) presupposition that would not have occurred to the prophets and the apostles, it should be conceded that a one-sided emphasis on "bookkeeping" can lend support to the caricature that federal theology abstracts the legal from the personal. In other words, the impression can be given that God's expectation in establishing the covenants with Adam and Israel was simply to get a perfect score from his covenant partner rather than to receive an appropriate response in a personal relationship.

Among the many advantages of the doctrine of Christ's active obedience is the fact that here, more than anywhere else, we recognize the integral connection between law and love (in fact, law as the stipulations of genuine love)—the legal and relational aspects of the covenant of works. Moral perfection cannot be abstracted from the personal relationship between Yahweh and his human partners. What God's heart has been longing for is not only a perfect score, or even an innocent covenant partner, but human life wholly devoted to him: an image-bearer who truly mirrors, in a fully human and responsive manner, his righteousness, holiness, love, goodness, and justice. Only this life—which humanity in Adam was capable of fully realizing before the fall—is well pleasing to the Lord. Transgression is not simply a matter of accounting, but also of "fall[ing] short of the glory of God" (Rom. 3:23).[1]

So conceived, merit cannot be reduced to an arbitrary set of hoops through which humanity must jump in order to attain eternal blessedness. Rather, it refers to that perfect human response for which we were created: a life unfailingly devoted to love of God and each other, as defined by his law.

Therefore, my focus is on the active obedience of Christ as the Last Adam and True Israel. This essay focuses narrowly on the meaning of the statement "obedience is better than sacrifice." The theme is picked up in various passages, including in Psalm 40:

1. All Scripture quotations are taken from the NRSV unless otherwise noted.

Sacrifice and offering you have not desired,
    but you have given me an open ear.
Burnt offering and sin offering
    you have not required.
Then I said, "Behold, I have come;
    in the scroll of the book it is written of me:
I desire to do your will, O my God;
    your law is within my heart."
        (Ps. 40:6–8 ESV; cf. Prov. 21:3; Matt. 9:11–13)

Similar passages can be found in the prayer of confession in Psalm 51:17, and the prophets especially indict the people for bringing sacrifices while they profane God's name and oppress their neighbor. Isaiah 1:11 is typical of this charge: "What to me is the multitude of your sacrifices? says the LORD; I have had enough of burnt offerings of rams and the fat of well-fed beasts; I do not delight in the blood of bulls, or of lambs, or of goats" (ESV; cf. Isa. 66:2–4; Jer. 6:20; Dan. 8:11; Hos. 8:13; Zeph. 1:7). So much for the caricature of Yahweh as a bloodthirsty deity who delights in bloody altars! The only reason that the law prescribed the sacrificial cult was in order to direct God's people to the need for forgiveness and the coming Lamb.

With these Old Testament passages in mind, this essay will explore New Testament interpretations of this remarkable phrase, "obedience rather than sacrifice," focusing especially on Hebrews 10.

In my book *Lord and Servant* I refused the false choice between anthropology or Christology as a starting point, or theologies from above versus theologies from below, arguing that the covenantal context requires a dialectical relationship with both rooted in an understanding of the narrative plot leading from Adam to Israel to Christ.[2] I also highlighted there the significance of the communicative and liturgical dimension of that vocation entrusted to humanity as *imago dei*: summoned into being and answering back in faithful trust and obedience, until the whole earth is full of God's glory and enjoying the consummation of God's everlasting "seventh day."[3] I do not have the space here to summarize those arguments, except simply to say that the *imago dei*, corresponding to the proper response of the covenant servant, "Here I am," is the presupposition for the view of Christ's active obedience that I will be advocating in this essay.

---

2. Michael S. Horton, *Lord and Servant: A Covenant Christology* (Louisville: Westminster John Knox, 2004), 120–55.
3. Ibid., 91–119.

From Sinai to Zion, or From Christ's Active and Passive Obedience to His Ascension

The Psalter, of course, is the hymnal for this liturgical-covenantal ontology. As the Israelites made their way up Mount Zion for annual pilgrimages, various songs were composed for antiphonal chant. The Israelites knew that they were engaged in high drama, a play not only *about* but a play *for* the triumph of God over the principalities and powers that would undo his plan. In this covenant dialogue, their actions in the script were not only descriptive of that contest, but belonged to the trial itself. How they answered back made all the difference.

Among those songs of ascent was Psalm 24, the first half of which reads as follows:

> The earth is the LORD's and all that is in it,
>   the world, and those who live in it;
> for he has founded it on the seas,
>   and established it on the rivers.
> Who shall ascend the hill of the LORD?
>   And who shall stand in his holy place?
> Those who have clean hands and pure hearts,
>   who do not lift up their souls to what is false,
>   and do not swear deceitfully.
> They will receive blessing from the LORD,
>   and vindication from the God of their salvation.
> Such is the company of those who seek him,
>   who seek the face of the God of Jacob. (vv. 1–6)

Clearly, Israel is cast as the faithful nation, the Adamic office-bearer and therefore image of God that refuses to participate in the cultus of the nations and orders even the minutest aspects of its personal and social life according to the commands of its Suzerain.

However, if we see only this, we not only fail to see beyond the failure of Israel to fulfil these conditions for entrance into God's typological sanctuary; we miss the import of the second half of the psalm:

> Lift up your heads, O gates!
>   and be lifted up, O ancient doors!
>   that the King of glory may come in.
> Who is the King of glory?
>   The LORD, strong and mighty,
>   the LORD, mighty in battle.

Lift up your heads, O gates!
  and be lifted up, O ancient doors!
  that the King of glory may come in.
Who is this King of glory?
  The LORD of hosts,
  he is the King of glory. (vv. 7–10)

In this psalm of ascent, the focus of the liturgical action shifts from the people to the King of glory whose procession to the sacred gates demands entry. The scene conjured here is of a military victory parade in which the conquering general would process to the capital with captives in tow. Thus, rather than a simple indication of the arrival of the worshipers to the earthly temple, where they appear before the King of glory, they are here part of a victory procession led by the King of glory personally.

Psalm 24 is still a significant part of the Jewish liturgy and, as Jon Levenson notes, "is chanted by Jews today on Sunday mornings."[4] In his marvelous survey of the march from Sinai to Zion, Levenson marks the transition from the conditional nature of the covenantal relationship to the eternal and inviolable security above and beyond the exigencies of human agency and history. "There is, however, one area in which the relationship is reversed, the Temple," says Levenson.[5] In Psalm 24, "The Temple represents the victory of God and the ethical ascent of man. The cosmic center is also the moral center."[6]

Drawing on rabbinical tradition, Levenson shows how Judaism understood the temple on Mount Zion as a new Eden, with the high priest (representing the whole people of Israel) as the new Adam. Like Adam, Israel had a covenant to fulfil, a greater destiny than simply occupying a piece of real estate in Palestine. Along with space, time is given eschatological and covenantal coordinates, with its cycles of work followed by Sabbath, again analogical of God's act of creation-and-conquest.[7] "The Sabbatical experience and the Temple experience are one," corresponding to "time" and "space," says Levenson.[8] "'The seventh day is,' in Abraham Joshua Heschel's splendid phrase, 'like a palace in time with a kingdom for all. It is not a date but an atmosphere.'"[9]

4. Jon D. Levenson, *Sinai and Zion: An Entry into the Jewish Bible* (San Francisco: Harper San Francisco, 1985), 170.
  5. Ibid., 148.
  6. Ibid., 172.
  7. See ibid., 143–44.
  8. Ibid., 145.
  9. Ibid., 183, citing Abraham Heschel's *The Sabbath: Its Meaning for Modern Man* (New York: Farrar, Straus, and Young, 1951), 21.

Psalm 92, according to the Talmud, "is a psalm and a song of the era to come, for the day which will be entirely Sabbath, for eternal life," Levenson concludes.[10] Levenson explains the relationship between the Sabbath and the temple:

> If the Temple is both a protological and an eschatological reality, and if the creation of the world and the construction of the Temple are parallel events, then the completion of the eschatological Temple coincides with the eschatological Sabbath, of which the present Sabbath is a prefigurement. . . . The destruction of the Temple did not close the gates of heaven to those who walk the path of Sinai up to the world of which Zion is the symbol.[11]

Throughout Levenson's study we learn that, according to traditional Jewish interpretation, Sinai represents the conditional and earthly aspects of the covenant, while Zion represents its unconditional and heavenly inviolability, beyond the exigencies of human obedience or disobedience.

The brilliance of Levenson's exegesis reveals a problem that can be solved only by either the descent of Christ or the ascent of humans—precisely the "two ways" of attaining righteousness that the apostle Paul contrasts in Romans 10:1–10. While Levenson finally assimilates Zion to Sinai (in a single covenant), the New Testament distinguishes these as two covenants.

According to Paul, this grueling ethical test is not only an ideal, but the righteousness of God that we must meet. Although we have not met it, and in our condition cannot meet it, Christ has fulfilled the law for us and won the right to enter the Promised Land. Neither collectively nor through any of its distinguished leaders was Israel able to fulfil the assignment: "Like Adam [Israel] transgressed the covenant" (Hos. 6:7). Israel too has broken ranks with the thanksgiving parade, going its own way like sheep without a shepherd. Yet Yahweh himself will descend, providing in his own flesh a sacrifice of atonement so that we can be not only forgiven but be transformed ourselves into a sacrifice of thanksgiving. The prophets anticipate a feast that transcends the economy of debt and scarcity altogether. The table has been set at the host's expense. The summons goes out to Jew and Gentile alike to come without money, and simply to enjoy the lavish food and wine in joyful company (see Isa. 55).

Fulfilling the original mandate—the covenant of creation—by his faithful obedience, Jesus recapitulates the history of Adam and Israel, picking up the fallen baton and leading creation in his train to the Promised Land. As G. K.

10. Ibid., 145.
11. Ibid., 184.

Beale notes, Luke's genealogy works backward from Jesus to Adam, ending in 3:38: "the son of Adam, the son of God." Beale explains the relationship between Adam, Israel, and Jesus:

> Jesus, as true Israel, is the micro-Israel who has replaced the macro-national Israel. Hence, years are reduced figuratively down to days. Each response by Jesus to Satan is taken from a response by Moses to Israel's failure in the wilderness (Deut. 8:3 in Matt. 4:4; Deut. 6:16 in Matt. 4:7; Deut. 6:13 in Matt. 4:10). Jesus succeeds in facing the same temptations to which Israel succumbed. . . .That Eden's temptations are in mind is apparent from Mark's comments that after Jesus successfully endured the temptations in the wilderness, "he was with the wild beasts, and the angels were ministering to him" (which shows that he, in fact, was the promised one of Ps. 91:11–12, and compare 91:13).[12]

Even before Golgotha, then, Jesus Christ was winning our redemption and restoring the eucharistic liturgy on behalf of his ungrateful people. His active obedience is therefore as crucial soteriologically as his passive obedience.

In addition to Psalm 24, Levenson points to Psalm 15 as underscoring the importance of fulfilling a probationary test in order to ascend the hill of the Lord. "In other words, between him and the shrine above lies the grueling ethical test, but if he has passed the test, it is as if he already dwells atop the sacred mountain."[13] However, since he thinks that these psalms refer to our own ethical ascent, he is eager to add that this is not a demand for legalistic perfection; rather, it is an ideal toward which the people should strive. Levenson writes:

> Now, just as the cosmic mountain was an idealization of Zion, so was the worshipper fit for admittance there an idealization. . . . His own life may have veered from the moral prerequisites of the Temple as much as the earthly Jerusalem fell short of the heavenly. . . . The point is that the ascent into the Temple and participation in the liturgy that took place there were thought to endow the worshipper with a higher self, as it were.[14]

The point, Levinson says, is obvious: "Zion is a catalyst for moral improvement."[15]

---

12. G. K. Beale, *The Temple and the Church's Mission*, New Studies in Biblical Theology (Downers Grove, IL: InterVarsity, 2004), 172.
13. Levenson, *Sinai and Zion*, 173; cf. Ps. 125:1–2.
14. Ibid., 175.
15. Ibid., 176.

Whatever the point may have been or may be in rabbinical Judaism, however, this psalm has been differently interpreted in Christian teaching. In fact, in Galatians 4 Paul interprets the two mountains surveyed by Levenson in what appears to be at first similar terms. Sinai stands for conditionality—an ethical test to be fulfilled personally by each Israelite, while Zion represents the unconditionality and inviolability of God's everlasting promise. Yet where Levenson says that in Judaism Zion is finally absorbed into Sinai, Paul says that, after Christ has come, Sinai represents bondage (Hagar) and corresponds to the earthly Jerusalem, while Zion represents freedom (Sarah) and corresponds to the heavenly Jerusalem. Christ has passed the "grueling ethical test," leading the true children of Abraham in his train, into the heavenly sanctuary and the everlasting inheritance, beyond the law's condemnation.

The most direct account of Christ's ascension, of course, comes from Luke 24 and Acts 1, which reprises this episode in its opening verses. The promise of the Holy Spirit is reiterated, followed by the ascension report in verses 6–11. Thus the ascension became part of the evangelical announcement itself. As Peter preaches, not only was Jesus crucified and raised according to the prophets, but the Messiah will be sent again, "that is, Jesus, who must remain in heaven until the time of universal restoration that God announced long ago through his holy prophets" (Acts 3:20–21).

In the epistles, the ascension marks the present heavenly work of Jesus Christ on behalf of his church. "Who is to condemn? It is Christ Jesus, who died, yes, who was raised, who is at the right hand of God, who indeed intercedes for us" (Rom. 8:34). Paul's language in 1 Corinthians 15 (the relationship of the firstfruits to the full harvest, everything being placed under subjection to Christ, who is the "man of heaven" whose image rather than Adam's we now are) assumes the ascension, as does his expectation of Christ's return from heaven (1 Thess. 4:13–5:11), a day of both salvation and judgment—as the "day of the LORD" announced by the prophets (Rom. 2:5; 1 Thess. 5:2; cf. Heb. 10:25; James 5:3; 2 Peter 3:10).

Uniting believers to Christ, God "raised us up with him and seated us with him in the heavenly places in Christ Jesus, so that in the ages to come he might show the immeasurable riches of his grace in kindness toward us in Christ Jesus" (Eph. 2:6–7). A little later we read,

> But each of us was given grace according to the measure of Christ's gift. Therefore it is said, "When he ascended on high he made captivity itself a captive; he gave gifts to his people" [Ps. 68:18; cf. Col. 2:15]. (When it says, "He ascended," what does it mean but that he had also descended into the

lower parts of the earth? He who descended is the same one who ascended far above all the heavens, so that he might fill all things). (Eph. 4:7–10)

The writer to the Hebrews appeals to the ascension as part of the contrast between old and new covenant worship. The old covenant priests were always standing, performing their service, and eventually died; Christ is now seated, having finished his redeeming work, and never dies. He is now "exalted above the heavens" (Heb. 7:23–26). "For Christ did not enter a sanctuary made by human hands, a mere copy of the true one, but he entered into heaven itself, now to appear in the presence of God on our behalf" (Heb. 9:24).

Similarly, for John, Christ is now the believer's *parakletos* or defense attorney in heaven, interceding for them when they sin (1 John 2:1). He does not simply show the way to Zion; he is the way. Having passed the grueling ethical test, he has secured our way to the Father's throne (John 14:1–10). This prepares the ground for Jesus' promise of the Holy Spirit. In chapter 17, Jesus' prayer includes the petition, "Father, I desire that those also, whom you have given me, may be with me where I am, to see my glory, which you have given me because you loved me before the foundation of the world" (John 17:24).

Thus, even where it is not directly asserted, the ascension is assumed as a link in the redemptive-historical chain leading from the incarnation of Christ in humiliation to the return of Christ in glory.[16] So Levenson is not entirely wrong when he interprets Psalms 15 and 24 in terms of humanity's ethical ascent, a trial that must be passed, in order to enter successfully the gates of Zion. Where Judaism and Christianity part ways, of course, is in their interpretation of the proper agent of this ascent. And where Christian interpretation veers toward the Jewish reading, it turns the victory of the "King of glory" into a general pattern for human striving.

Why start at the ascension? Is not the active obedience of Christ concerned with his thirty-three years of loving submission to the Father's will? The reason for beginning here is that it is the denouement for everything that led up to it. On the basis of his life as well as his sacrificial death, Jesus is raised from the dead and glorified at the right hand of the Father with captives in his train. It is he alone who had the right to demand entrance through the ancient doors of the heavenly Zion. So now, in an effort to understand what is intended by "obedience more than sacrifice," we will turn to the institution of the sacrificial system.

16. The Heidelberg Catechism nicely summarizes this catholic article in Q & A 46.

Two Classes of Sacrifice

In the old covenant, however, we already encounter various kinds of sacrifice. The first five chapters of Leviticus describe each. First, there are the
atonement offerings, imputing one's guilt to the victim (Lev. 1:4–9; all of
chapter 4). Yet there are also sacrifices of thanksgiving (for example, the
grain offering of chapter 2). All of these sacrifices can therefore be grouped
into two categories: sacrifices of atonement and sacrifices of thanksgiving.
I would suggest that the thank-offering was a prelapsarian ritual representing the joyful obedience that is the goal of all divine covenants and that the
bloody guilt offering was instituted after the fall (recall that Cain's rejection
by God resulted from his refusal to bring this offering before the Lord, in
contrast to Abel's sacrifice).

It seems clear enough that in his institution of the Supper, Christ draws
together both types of sacrifices. On one hand, lifting the cup, he gave thanks
(Matt. 26:27), just as we give thanks for God's bounty (1 Cor. 10:30). On
the other hand, it is a meal of the "last will and testament," the proclamation of Christ's death until he comes again (1 Cor. 11:26). The one who
offers up thanks to God is also about to offer himself up to God as no other
worshiper in redemptive history has done: as an atoning sacrifice. The cup
raised in the Supper is "the cup of blessing" for us because it was the cup
of wrath that Christ drank for us. Therefore, this cup is "a participation in
the blood of Christ," as the bread is "a participation in the body of Christ"
(1 Cor. 10:16–17 ESV), because through them we receive the inheritance that
his death secured. The new covenant went into effect with his death.

As the writer to the Hebrews reminds us, "Where a will is involved, the
death of the one who made it must be established. For a will takes effect
only at death, since it is not in force as long as the one who made it is alive.
Hence not even the first covenant was inaugurated without blood" (Heb.
9:16–18). Yet Christ "has appeared once for all at the end of the age to
remove sin by the sacrifice of himself" (v. 26). The thanksgiving that Christ
offers for the meal is but a token of the entire life of thanksgiving that he
lived before the Father. Christ is both the thank-offering par excellence
(active obedience) and the only satisfactory offering for sin (passive obedience). Believers are also called into this festal economy both to receive the
unique guilt offering (Christ) and to offer up their bodies as thank-offerings
in union with Christ.

The animal sacrifices for human fault could never replace the eucharistic
life of covenantal obedience and love for which God created humanity. It
is not the offering of representative sacrifices, but the offering of oneself

in thanksgiving that is God's delight: "Let us come into his presence with thanksgiving" (Ps. 95:2); "Enter his gates with thanksgiving, and his courts with praise. Give thanks to him, bless his name" (Ps. 100:4). Referring to those whom God has redeemed, the psalmist exhorts, "Let them thank the LORD for his steadfast love, for his wonderful works to humankind. And let them offer thanksgiving sacrifices, and tell of his deeds with songs of joy" (Ps. 107:21–22). The animal sacrifices, both of atonement and thanksgiving, were never ends in themselves. In fact, the psalmist could declare, "Sacrifice and offering you do not desire, but you have given me an open ear. Burnt offering and sin offering you have not required. Then I said, 'Here I am; in the scroll of the book it is written of me. I delight to do your will, O my God; your law is within my heart'" (Ps. 40:6–8; cf. Ps. 51:16). Mediating God's dispute with his people, the prophets repeat the psalmist's refrain against those who dare to bring their sacrifices while violating his covenant (Hos. 6:6; Amos 4:4; Mal. 1:8). Jesus takes up the theme as well (Matt. 9:13).

So we can already begin to see that Psalm 40 and its parallels are not evidence of an antipriestly polemic. Rather, as Peter Craigie observes,

> The context of the royal liturgy provides the appropriate setting for interpretation. The king is now engaged in a liturgy of supplication; he can only participate in such a liturgy (which may well have included sacrifices) after having faithfully performed all his royal tasks as king, which included the offering of appropriate sacrifices. But the offering of the sacrifices alone was not enough; more was required of him. The general background, then, to these verses is to be found in the "law (or Torah) of kings" (Deut. 17:14–20).[17]

When Jesus takes up the theme, he is the royal liturgist who is David's greater Son. This, I suggest, is precisely the interpretation of Psalm 40 that we find in Hebrews 10.

The Interpretation of Psalm 40 in Hebrews 10

Far from being a work of Christian Platonism, Hebrews, as Douglas Farrow reminds us, is thoroughly eschatological. It is not Plato's two worlds, but the two ages of Jewish and Christian apocalyptic that dominate the writer's horizon. "Hebrews is the classic Christian restatement (in the context of, and over against, an educated *diaspora* Judaism) of the Old Testament journey motif. The journey in question is the exodus, viewed here

17. Peter Craigie, *Psalms 1–50*, Word Biblical Commentary (Nashville: Thomas Nelson, 1983), 315.

as a pilgrimage into 'the world to come.'"[18] Psalms 8 and 110, along with Daniel 7, are echoed in the language about Jesus: "Namely, that 'he sat down' in the presence of God as the Melchizedekian priest-king. This bit of ascension theology, repeated at key intervals, is the focal point which holds Hebrews together."[19] Thus, "His whole life is seen as an act of self-offering that culminates in the cross. In the ascension this offering is received on high. . . . The reference therefore is not to an ideal or supra-sensual realm but to the divine Rest from which the present creation has been barred, but which Jesus has entered."[20]

Hebrews 10 is an interpretation on Psalm 40, beginning with the following thesis statement of sorts:

> For since the law has but a shadow of the good things to come, instead of the true form of these realities, it can never, by the same sacrifices that are continually offered every year, make perfect those who draw near. Otherwise, would they not have ceased to be offered, since the worshipers, having once been cleansed, would no longer have any consciousness of sin? But in these sacrifices there is a reminder of sin every year. For it is impossible for the blood of bulls and goats to take away sins. (vv. 1–4 ESV)

The point is not that the sacrifices of the old covenant were worthless; after all, they were commanded in the law. Far from failing to do their job, these sacrifices pointed out Israel's sin and their need for forgiveness in Christ. So the sacrifices fulfilled their *telos*. However, that *telos* itself was limited. Furthermore, the prophetic critique was not directed at the sacrificial system per se, but at the parody that Israel had made of it. Without faith or repentance, worshipers nevertheless went on going through the typological motions.

The sacrificial cult was never intended to take away sins, but to cover them over until Christ came. It was a shadow, where Christ's priesthood is the reality. So the sacrifices could "never . . . make perfect those who draw near." And again in verse 4: The sacrifices could not "take away [*aphaire*] sins." The problem is not the type itself, but the fact that sin is so serious that the type itself cannot solve the dilemma. How could an animal sacrifice possibly satisfy the demands of God's justice and righteousness? This point

18. Douglas Farrow, *Ascension and Ecclesia: On the Significance of the Doctrine of the Ascension for Ecclesiology and Christian Cosmology* (Grand Rapids: Eerdmans, 1999), 33; See also L. D. Hurst, *The Epistle to the Hebrews: Its Background of Thought*, Society for New Testament Studies Monograph Series 65 (Cambridge: Cambridge University Press, 1990); Barnabas Lindars, *The Theology of the Letter to the Hebrews* (Cambridge: Cambridge University Press, 1991).
19. Farrow, *Ascension and Ecclesia*, 33, referring to Heb. 1:3; 8:2; 10:12; 12:3.
20. Ibid., 34–35.

was reiterated in the annual ritual of Yom Kippur. Instead of being an annual reminder of sins forgiven, it is an annual reminder of sins that need to be forgiven. The conscience is never freed from a sense of a debt that cannot be paid by the worshiper. The old covenant has gone as far as it can go, having accomplished all that it was ever designed to achieve, namely, the consciousness of guilt, the need for forgiveness, and the faith that the Lord himself will provide this sacrifice that finally and forever takes away sins.

This is the dilemma in which we find ourselves when we meet the great transition in verse 5:

Consequently, when Christ came into the world, he said,

> "Sacrifices and offerings you have not desired,
>   but a body have you prepared for me;
> in burnt offerings and sin offerings
>   you have taken no pleasure.
> Then I said, 'Behold, I have come to do your will, O God,
>   as it is written of me in the scroll of the book.'" (vv. 5–7 ESV)

The Septuagint here reads "a body you prepared for me," while the Masoretic text has "ears you have dug out for me." My own view is that whereas the Hebrew idiom is a synecdoche (the part standing for the whole), the Septuagint quite literally fleshes out the reference. In a covenantal context, the ear is the most important organ. Giving ear to God's word is the same as the whole body giving itself to obedience.[21]

The contrast is between the sacrifices and offerings on one hand and the body prepared for Christ on the other. Notice that here at least the contrast is not simply between animal sacrifices and Christ's self-offering, but between guilt offerings and a living body. This is in no way to downplay the significance of Christ's sacrifice on the cross, which is also highlighted here and especially in chapters 7–9, but to say that something more than sacrificial offering is in view.

Even Christ's sacrificial offering could achieve no more than forgiveness. As great as forgiveness surely is, however, God has something far greater in mind by sending Christ. For once, there is a worshiper whose own life of obedience corresponds to the sacrifice that he offers. He is not a hypocrite, deaf to God's commands while active in pious exercises and public rituals. His sacrifice of atonement was that of one who had already rendered per-

---

21. For a similar interpretation, see also F. F. Bruce, *The Epistle to the Hebrews*, New International Commentary on the New Testament (Grand Rapids: Eerdmans, 1964), 232–34.

fectly a sacrifice of thanksgiving—a "living sacrifice" of praise. And he is not only bringing a sacrifice, but he himself is the sacrifice; it is not for himself, but for his sinful coheirs.

In verses 8–9 the writer himself interprets the meaning of Psalm 40 on Christ's lips: "When he said above, 'You have neither desired nor taken pleasure in sacrifices and offerings and burnt offerings and sin offerings' (these are offered according to the law), then he added, 'Behold I have come to *do* your will'" (ESV). Guilt offerings remind both God and the worshiper of the breach, whereas what God delights in is his *imago dei* actually reflecting its Creator. Even in our familiar relationships, we understand this desire. As spouses and parents, we know how forgiveness restores communication, but we delight in the positive attitudes and actions that are appropriate to the relationship. Better than tearful apologies is actually doing what we should have done. Of course, Christ's self-offering is far greater than any sacrifice that we might bring for fault. In fact, the latter is an insult to God. Nevertheless, the comparison holds: our heavenly Father loves to forgive, but his heart swells with joy when his righteousness is satisfied.

Instead of completing the work that God gave him to do, Adam went his own way—and took us all with him as his willing accomplices. Since then, there has never been a faithful servant who perfectly rendered the obedience in which God delights. Moses was barred from entering Canaan. David and his royal seed, whose unfaithfulness stretches across the pages of the history of Israel and Judah, fell short of the glory of God. In covenantal terms, righteousness (*tsedaqah*) is not simply a matter of legal bookkeeping, but of *hesed*, loyalty to the Great King in a personal relationship. Justice is not simply a matter of punishing and absolving, but of righting wrongs and establishing God's will in all the earth. God not only wants to forgive, but to restore; not only to bring us back to Adam's prefallen state of rectitude, but to have a people that appear before him who delight in him and his will. God not only wants to do away with our sin; he wants to delight in us. The goal is to have a humanity that glorifies God and enjoys him forever.

To get to that goal, however, the debt economy that dominates the sacrificial system must be set aside. "He abolishes the first [i.e., the sacrificial system] in order to establish the second [i.e., the living sacrifice of praise]" (Heb. 10:9b). "Abolishes" (*anairei*) means to set aside, wipe away, or get rid of something. He renders the sacrificial economy obsolete not by circumventing his own self-offering, but precisely in that final sacrifice. John Calvin comments, "There is no small importance in this, that when he professes that he would do the will of God, he assigns no place to sacrifices; for we hence conclude that without them there may be a perfect obedience to God, which could not be true were not the Law annulled."[22]

Once again, I am not saying that the writer is excluding the sacrificial character of Christ's work. On the contrary, he is saying that it fulfils the law both in terms of his rendering the perfect life-offering (active obedience) and perfect guilt-offering (passive obedience), so that we can enter into God's courts not only with Good Friday sorrow, but with Easter praise, forever beyond the debt economy altogether. Christ's active obedience serves as the basis for his transcending the debt economy in his resurrection and ascension.

I think Hebrews 10:10 pushes us in that direction: "And by that will we have been sanctified through the offering of the body of Jesus Christ once and for all." Sanctification here is not to be understood in its usual Pauline sense, as progressive conformity to Christ's image here and now, but as a definitive act of setting apart that occurred at the cross. However, it is not only at the cross that this sanctification occurs. In his high priestly prayer, Jesus petitions the Father as the successful covenant-keeper claiming his just reward (John 17:17–19). Our sanctification in this sense occurs not in our act of consecration, but in Christ's. Throughout John's Gospel we meet this emphasis: "For I have come down from heaven, not to do my own will, but the will of him who sent me" (John 6:38). His teaching is not his own, but has the Father for its author (John 7:16–18), and the only thing that matters is glorifying God by doing his will. "Has not Moses given you the law? Yet none of you keeps the law. Why do you seek to kill me?" (v. 19 ESV). On we could go with similar references. Jesus appeals to his own obedience as the ground on which he claims title to the reward of everlasting life, for him and for "all whom you have given me."

As we turn back to Hebrews 10, then, the argument continues to unfold. There is the grand *ephapax* ("once and for all"). Unlike the world's religions, in Christianity the whole notion of an expiatory sacrifice is wholly past, with continuing effects. There are no further sacrifices of this type. There is nothing left to be done for the forgiveness of sins now that Christ has offered himself once and for all (vv. 11–13). Both the typological priest on earth and the true high priest in heaven were liturgists ("service" here being *leitourgōn*). Both liturgies in a certain sense recapitulate the pattern of six days of creation followed by the Sabbath enthronement, with the creature-kings (led by the vassal-king) paraded before the Great King as they are welcomed into the

---

22. John Calvin, *Commentaries on the Epistle of Paul the Apostle to the Hebrews*, trans. John Owen (Grand Rapids: Baker, 1996), 227.

consummation.[23] However, where the one priest is always working, the other has entered his rest, seated in Sabbath glory at the Father's right hand. The Aaronic-Levitical priesthood looked backward to Adam's and forward to Christ's. Having accomplished everything—both the obedient life and the obedient self-oblation—he is the head of a new humanity, the True Israel of God that joyfully ascends the hill of the Lord and stands in his holy place. So what is he doing now? We are told in verse 13: waiting, not working—but this is a productive waiting, as the Spirit brings about the "amen" to the work accomplished "once and for all." The conquest is over; the victory lies in the past. Now he is waiting to see the fruits of his labors mature until the final harvest.

And what is this that he beholds even now as he sits at the Father's right hand? Verses 15–25 tell us. Picking up where he left off in his citation of Jeremiah 31 in chapter 8, the writer reminds us that the new covenant promises two things: "I will put my laws in their hearts, and I will write them on their minds," and "I will remember their sins and their lawless deeds no more." He summarizes, "Where there is forgiveness of these, there is no longer any offering for sin" (vv. 16–18). In other words, the debt economy is over. All that is left is for us to join the procession to Zion as liberated captives in Christ's train (Heb. 10:19–25).

Our obedience is not the basis or condition of this justification, but precisely for this reason the law's true purpose can begin even now to be realized in us: perfectly in our representative head, and in us in principle by the new birth as a result of his life, death, and resurrection. The law no longer stands over us as tablets of stone demanding our condemnation, but is written on our hearts. When we are glorified, on the basis of Christ's meritorious obedience as our federal head, the whole body will be not only forgiven but will everlastingly render the obedience due to the triune God. It is this future glory of which our imperfect progress in sanctification is now a prolepsis.

This, I maintain, is what the psalmist had in mind when he recognized the weakness of the old covenant sacrificial system. *Forgiveness is good, but obedience is better.* God loves to cancel debts, but delights in a life of praise. Christ not only fulfils this goal for us representatively as our head, but on that basis legally justifies and progressively renews us. Justification is not merely forgiveness (as the common slogan "just-as-if-I'd-never sinned" implies), but a standing in perfect righteousness before God. On this basis, God can begin now and complete in the future the restoration of the whole

23. On the significance of this interpretation of Genesis 1 and 2, see, e.g., M. G. Kline, *Kingdom Prologue: Genesis Foundations for a Covenantal Worldview* (Overland Park, KS: Two Age, 2000), 34–38.

body that is united to its Living Head. By itself, the cross is retributive justice, but the whole complex of Christ's redeeming work yields restorative justice as well.

If this is the psalmist's understanding, then it is even more explicit in the prophets. Prosecuting the covenant lawsuit (*riv*), they point up the hypocrisy of going through the motions of offering their tithes, bulls, lambs, and goats in atonement for their sins while they nevertheless oppress their neighbor and serve idols. Like a professing Christian today who goes to confession seeking the priest's absolution or "walks an aisle" in rededication without any care for actually keeping God's commands, the Israelites had separated forgiveness and obedience. Robert Godfrey has aptly captured this attitude: "God likes to forgive; I like to sin—what a great relationship!" It is easy to bring a vicarious sacrifice for atonement and to bring a thank-offering in place of one's own grateful obedience.

In Christ, however, both types of sacrifices converge: not only is he the only qualified substitute for the guilt of sinners; he is the only one capable of rendering the life of thankful obedience in which God truly delights. In this regard, the author of Hebrews writes:

Consequently, when Christ came into the world, he said,

"Sacrifices and offerings you have not desired,
    but a body you have prepared for me;
in burnt offerings and sin offerings
    you have taken no pleasure.
Then I said, 'See, God, I have come to do your will, O God'
    (in the scroll of the book it is written of me)."

When he said above, "You have neither desired nor taken pleasure in sacrifices and offerings and burnt offerings and sin offerings" (these are offered according to the law), then he added, "See, I have come to do your will." He abolishes the first in order to establish the second. And it is by God's will that we have been sanctified through the offering of the body of Jesus Christ once for all. (Heb. 10:5–10)

Therefore, it is not simply that Jesus has transcended the temporary sacrifices of the old covenant; he has transcended the sacrificial economy altogether—not by abolishing it, but by fulfilling it.

Paul especially picks up on these themes so clearly enunciated by the writer to the Hebrews. Together, this total life of the Servant, living before the Father in the Spirit and giving himself up for the guilty, becomes "a fragrant offering and sacrifice to God" (Eph. 5:2). The New Adam leads his covenant people in a triumphant procession into the promised *shalōm*. As a result of our union with Christ, therefore, we too can be designated a fragrant sacrifice—and our lives, though still full of corruption, can nevertheless become eucharistically oriented.

> But thanks be to God, who in Christ always leads us in triumphal procession, and through us spreads in every place the fragrance that comes from knowing him. For we are the aroma of Christ to God among those who are being saved and among those who are perishing; to the one a fragrance from death to death, to the other a fragrance from life to life. Who is sufficient for these things? (2 Cor. 2:14–16)

The language of being led by Christ in "triumphal procession" underscores the covenantal, representative character of this economy of grace. While we ourselves cannot render an adequate sacrifice of thanksgiving any more than an offering for guilt, the perfume of Christ's living and dying runs down his face to every part of his ecclesial body. Even the stench of sin clinging to our best works is overpowered by this scent. This removes our fear of the imperfections of our love and good works.

No longer paralyzed by anxiety in a debt economy, we are free to live imperfectly yet joyfully in the eucharistic economy, between Christ's finished work and our final glorification. We are no longer debtors to God in any respect—not even to his grace, but are grateful heirs. For this first time, we can render obedience that comes from the heart of sons rather than slaves. In Christ, the Great King finally has received the *human* service in which his fatherly heart delights. And the whole creation will enter with thanksgiving behind its new Adam (Rom. 8:18–24).

That is why Paul can say, "I appeal to you therefore, brothers and sisters, by the mercies of God, to present your bodies as a living sacrifice, holy and acceptable to God, which is your spiritual worship" (Rom. 12:1). It is in view of the triumphant indicatives—"God's mercies"—which Paul has enumerated throughout the epistle, that the imperative is issued. No longer offering dead sacrifices (of atonement), believers offer their own bodies as living sacrifices (of thanksgiving), in a "spiritual worship" that goes far beyond the bloody altars of the old covenant. Jesus Christ alone offered a sufficient sacrifice for sin (Heb. 5:1; 9:26; 10:12), and this brings to an end any notion of debt in our relation to God. "Through him, then, let us continually offer a sacrifice of praise to God, that is, the fruit of lips that confess his name" (Heb. 13:15). Or, as we find it in 1 Peter 2:5, "Like living stones, let yourselves be built into a spiritual house, to be a holy priesthood, to offer spiritual sacrifices acceptable to God through Jesus Christ." Since we cannot give God any gift as a recompense (i.e., guilt offering), all that is left is the thank-offering that he has wanted all along.

Resuming the Thanksgiving Parade: Serving Our Neighbor

Christ Jesus did not simply pick up where the first Adam left off; he undid Adam's transgression by his sacrificial death and successfully fulfilled Adam's vocation by his obedient life. If there is no debt to God, but only thanksgiving, where do our good works go? There is only one direction: outward to our neighbor. We look up in faith toward God and out to our neighbor in loving service.

Gustav Wingren nicely summarizes Luther's concern with the neighbor as the recipient of the believer's good works. Instead of living in monasteries, committing their lives in service to themselves and their own salvation, Luther argues, believers should love and serve their neighbors through their vocations in the world, where their neighbors need them.[24] "God does not need our good works, but our neighbor does."[25] Elsewhere, Wingren writes:

> When one presents works before God in the kingdom of heaven, God's order is disrupted in both realms. Since the reign of Christ is in giving, and in grace and the gospel, to proffer gifts here is an attempt to depose Christ from his throne. A human being lets his works compete with the King of heaven. At the same time, his neighbor on earth is neglected since his good works have clearly been done, not for the sake of his neighbor, but to parade before God. . . . The human being who in his vocation serves his fellow-men fulfills his task out of love for Christ. . . . Christ is excluded whenever the ordinary neighbor is excluded.[26]

God descends to serve humanity through our vocations, so instead of seeing good works as our good works for God, they are now seen to be God's works for our neighbor, which God performs through us.

That is why both orders are upset when we seek to present good works to God as if he needed them. Wingren writes:

24. Gustav Wingren, *Luther on Vocation*, trans. Carl C. Rasmussen (Evansville, IN: Ballast, 1994), 2.
25. Ibid., 10.
26. Ibid., 13, 31.

Through vocation God's presence is really with man. As the God of the law, he places himself above man's self-will and drives man to prayer, which is answered by God's love and care. In vocation works are constrained to move toward one's neighbor, toward the earth; and faith alone, trust, prayer, all without works, ascends heavenward. In all this one is incorporated into Christ; the cross in the vocation is his cross, and the faith which breaks forth from that cross in the vocation is his resurrection.[27]

Interpreting this strange freedom displayed in Luther's *Treatise on Christian Liberty*, Wingren adds,

In faith, which accepts the gift, man finds that it is not only "heaven that is pure with its stars, where Christ reigns in his work," but the earth too is clean "with its trees and its grass, where we are at home with all that is ours." There is nothing more delightful and lovable on earth than one's neighbor. Love does not think about doing works, it finds joy in people; and when something good is done for others, that does not appear to love as works but simply as gifts which flow naturally from love.[28]

The commandment to love, Luther insists, is *lex naturae*.[29] Thus, the same law that was inscribed in the human conscience in the covenant of creation and on tablets in the covenant at Sinai is now written on our hearts in the new covenant.

Under the law, in Adam, one is trapped in the cycle of sin and death, resentment and despair, self-righteousness and self-condemnation. Yet under grace, in Christ, one is not only justified apart from the law but is able for the first time to respond to that law of love that calls from the deepest recesses of our being as covenantally constituted creatures. It is not the law itself that changes, but our relation to it, and that makes all the difference.

A new day has dawned on this side of the resurrection, and that is why the law no longer takes on an awful specter, exciting sin and leading to judgment. As we read in 1 John 2:7–14, this new relationship to the law is eschatologically defined, in terms of our being in Christ and Christ's being in us:

Beloved, I am writing you no new commandment, but an old commandment that you have had from the beginning; the old commandment is the word that you have heard. Yet I am writing you a new commandment that is true *in him and in you*, because *the darkness is passing away and the true light is already shining*. Whoever says, "I am in the light," while hating a brother

27. Ibid., 33.
28. Ibid., 42–43.
29. Ibid., 44.

or sister, is still in the darkness. Whoever loves a brother or sister lives in the light, and in such a person there is no cause for stumbling. . . . I am writing to you, little children, because *your sins are forgiven* on account of his name. I am writing to you, fathers, because *you know him* who is from the beginning. I am writing to you, young people, because you have *conquered the evil one.* I write to you, children, because you know the Father. . . . I write to you, young people, because you are strong and *the word of God abides in you,* and you have overcome the evil one.

In the debt economy of this fading age, my neighbor is a burden, but in the gift economy of Christ's kingdom, my neighbor is a gift. Freedom, in the economy of this fading age, means self-possession and self-determination: the ability to choose for oneself apart from any external constraints. The gospel, by contrast, exposes this autonomous freedom as the original bondage of humanity as, in Augustine's phrase, "curved in on itself."

"But what is this strange gift of evangelical freedom?" asks John Webster:

> It is a *strange* gift because it can only be known and exercised as we are converted from a lie—the lie that liberty is unformed and unconstrained self-actualization. It is *evangelical* because it is grounded in the joyful reversal and reconstitution of the human situation of which the gospel speaks. We may define it thus: In evangelical freedom I am so bound to God's grace and God's call that I am liberated from all other bonds and set free to live in the truth. "The law of the Spirit of life in Christ Jesus has set me free from the law of sin and death" (Rom. 8.2).[30]

We cannot give anything to God that would obligate a return on his part (Rom. 11:35), but part of the wonder of God's condescension is that he delights in receiving the prayers and praises of his creation. In one sense, these are gifts, but they are qualitatively and not merely quantitatively different from God's gift.

In this view, God is not a member in the economy of gift exchange, but the unobliged donor of all good gifts, whether of saving or common grace. "Every good gift and every perfect gift is from above, coming down from the Father of lights with whom there is no variation or shadow due to change. Of his own will he brought us forth by the word of truth, that we should be a kind of firstfruits of his creation" (James 1:17–18 ESV). On the basis of this indicative (the vertical line pointing downward from God), James

30. John Webster, *Holiness* (Birmingham: SCM, 2003), 92–93.

follows with the imperative (horizontal line) to be doers as well as hearers of the word, caring for our neighbors (vv. 21–27).

Conclusion

This account draws together the active and passive obedience of Jesus Christ. As important as it is that Christ bore the penalty of our sins on the cross, it is just as important that he triumphed over the powers of evil and recapitulated the history of fallen humanity in Adam and Israel. Adam was commanded to obey God's law and failed, Israel was commanded to obey God's law and failed, but Christ came into this world and completed a life of perfect obedience to the law of his Father. Christ the Righteous One was indeed the Last Adam, the True Israel.

Because we have not only been forgiven on the basis of Christ's curse-bearing death but justified on the basis of his probation-fulfilling life, we have a new heart and the law is written on our mind. In Jeremiah 33:10–11, we find the renewed pledge that Yahweh will be our God and we will be his people, and

> there shall be heard again the voice of mirth and the voice of gladness, the voice of the bridegroom and the voice of the bride, the voices of those who sing, as they bring thank offerings to the house of the LORD:
>
> > "Give thanks to the LORD of hosts,
> >   for the LORD is good,
> >   for his steadfast love endures forever!" (ESV)

Later in the same passage we read the fitting conclusion for this essay:

> Behold, the days are coming, declares the LORD, when I will fulfill the promise I made to the house of Israel and the house of Judah. In those days and at that time I will cause a righteous Branch to spring up for David, and he shall execute justice and righteousness in the land. In those days Judah will be saved and Jerusalem will dwell securely. And this is the name by which it will be called: "The LORD is our righteousness." (vv. 14–16 ESV)

CONTRIBUTORS

S. M. Baugh (Ph.D., University of California, Irvine) is professor of New Testament at Westminster Seminary California.

Richard P. Belcher Jr. (Ph.D., Westminster Theological Seminary) is professor of Old Testament at Reformed Theological Seminary, Charlotte.

Byron G. Curtis (Ph.D., Westminster Theological Seminary) is associate professor of biblical studies at Geneva College.

Bryan D. Estelle (Ph.D., The Catholic University of America) is associate professor of Old Testament at Westminster Seminary California.

Brenton C. Ferry (M.A.R., Westminster Theological Seminary) is pastor of Covenant Reformed Presbyterian Church in Mount Airy, North Carolina.

J. V. Fesko (Ph.D., University of Aberdeen) is pastor of Geneva Orthodox Presbyterian Church in Woodstock, Georgia, and adjunct professor of theology at Reformed Theological Seminary, Atlanta.

T. David Gordon (Ph.D., Union Theological Seminary in Virginia) is professor of Greek and religion at Grove City College.

D. G. Hart (Ph.D., Johns Hopkins University) is the director of Partnered Projects at the Intercollegiate Studies Institute.

Michael S. Horton (Ph.D., University of Coventry and Wycliffe Hall, Oxford) is J. Gresham Machen Professor of Systematic Theology and Apologetics at Westminster Seminary California.

David VanDrunen (J.D., Northwestern University School of Law; Ph.D., Loyola University Chicago) is Robert B. Strimple Professor of Systematic Theology and Christian Ethics at Westminster Seminary California.

Guy P. Waters (Ph.D., Duke University) is associate professor of New Testament at Reformed Theological Seminary, Jackson.

Index of Scripture

Index of Subjects and Names

Maccabeans, 120
Machen, J. Gresham, 15, 126n76, 134, 146, 169
Mandeville, Bernard, 53
Mari, 172n5
Masoretic text, 127n79, 176, 182, 184, 187, 188, 189, 327
Matera, Frank, 263
McConville, J. G., 126n77
McCosh, James, 55
McGowan, Andrew, 97
mediated or substitutionary performance, 260
merit, 315–16
messianic psalms, 148
Metzger, Bruce M., 140n132
Meyer, D. H., 53–54
Milgrom, Jacob, 114n19, 115, 116n33, 117
Miller, J. Maxwell, 196n83, 208
Miller, Patrick D., 128n88
Miller, Samuel, 49
Miller, William Ian, 306nn40,42
"mixed" covenant, Mosaic covenant as, 100–101, 211n3
Mohrmann, Doug C., 116n35
monocovenantalism, 16, 26, 239, 253–58
Moo, Douglas, 249, 297, 298–300
moral agency, 52, 54
moral government theory of atonement, 48, 68–69
moral law, 225, 302
    and covenant of works, 231, 238
    Hodge on, 61–63
    material republication of, 91–92
    and Mosaic covenant, 212, 225–26
    universality of, 229n74
moral philosophy, 49–55, 59, 60
Morland, Kjell Arne, 134
Mosaic covenant
    and Adam's state in garden, 10
    as administrative covenant, 98–99
    as "bastard" covenant, 102
    Calvin on, 26–33, 39–43
    as covenant of grace, 14, 78, 98–102, 132n100, 262

as covenant of works, 90–98, 301n30
differences from Abrahamic covenant, 241–58
as distinct covenant, 99–100
Hodge on, 56–58
as mixed covenant, 100–101, 211n3
Murray on, 15–17, 240–41, 252–58
as national covenant, 37–38, 39, 101
and natural law, 301–9
Old Princeton on, 45
Paul on, 221–23
as pedagogue unto Christ, 315
planned obsolescence of, 18, 130, 137
in psalms, 160
in Reformed tradition, 11–13, 20
relation to new covenant, 77, 80–90
as republication, 77, 92
as subservient covenant, 101
and temptation of Jesus, 9
Turretin on, 12
Westminster Confession on, 25, 42–43
Witsius on, 33–43
Mosaic law
    as covenant of works, 259
    as gracious, 262
    and moral law, 225–26
    three-fold classification of, 302
    works principle in, 312
Muller, Richard, 39n43, 41
Murray, John, 13, 81n16, 88–89, 136n114, 221, 231n79, 298–300
    on Mosaic covenant, 15–17, 240–41, 252–58

national covenant, Mosaic covenant as, 13, 37–38, 85–87, 97, 101
nations, blessing of, 241–44
natural covenant, 34, 286–87. *See also* covenant of works
natural law, 39n43, 269, 283–84, 334
    and covenant of works, 63
    in Hodge, 45
    and Mosaic covenant, 285, 301–9
    in Old Princeton, 48, 69
    and Reformed theology, 60